PSYCHOLOGICAL TRAUMA AND THE ADULT SURVIVOR

Theory, Therapy, and Transformation

Brunner/Mazel Psychosocial Stress Series
Charles R. Figley, Ph.D., Series Editor

BRUNNER/MAZEL PSYCHOSOCIAL STRESS SERIES NO. 21

PSYCHOLOGICAL TRAUMA AND THE ADULT SURVIVOR

Theory, Therapy, and Transformation

by I. LISA McCANN, Ph.D.
and LAURIE ANNE PEARLMAN, Ph.D.

Brunner-Routledge
New York & London

Published by
Brunner-Routledge
711 Third Avenue,
New York, NY 10017

Published in Great Britain
Brunner-Routledge
2 Park Square, Milton Park,
Abingdon, Oxfordshire OX14 4RN
First issued in paperback 2014

*Routledge is an imprint of the Taylor and Francis Group,
an informa business*

Library of Congress Cataloging-in-Publication Data

McCann, I. Lisa.
   Psychological trauma and the adult survivor : theory, therapy, and
transformation / by I. Lisa McCann and Laurie Anne Pearlman.
      p.   cm.—(Brunner/Mazel psychosocial stress series ; no. 21)
   Includes bibliographical references.
   Includes indexes.

   ISBN 978-0-87630-594-2 (hbk)
   ISBN 978-1-138-00479-5 (pbk)

   1. Post-traumatic stress disorder. 2. Post-traumatic stress
disorder—Treatment. I. Title. II. Series.
   [DNLM: 1. Ego. 2. Psychological Theory. 3. Psychotherapy—methods.
4. Stress, Disorders, Post-Traumatic—therapy. W1
BR917TB no. 21 / WM 170 M478p]
   RC552.P67M38   1990
   616.85′21—dc20
   DNLM/DLC
   for Library of Congress   90-2336
                                                                  CIP

Series Note

The growth of the field of traumatic stress in the last ten years has been extraordinary. A half-dozen journals and hundreds of books have focused attention on the immediate and long-term psychosocial consequences of intensely traumatic events. *Psychological Trauma and the Adult Survivor: Theory, Therapy, and Transformation,* by Lisa McCann and Laurie Pearlman, is an important contribution to this burgeoning literature.

Moreover, this book is a welcome addition to the Brunner/Mazel Psychosocial Stress Book Series. It is the 21st book in a distinguished group that has focused on a variety of psychosocial stressors, including the stressors of war, normative transitions, family relationships, crime victimization, substance abuse, incest, and unemployment. Several books have addressed a large group of stressors and have presented conceptual models useful for the study, diagnosis, prevention, and treatment of one or more types of psychosocial stress. *Psychological Trauma and the Adult Survivor* is such a book.

The foundation from which this book draws is a collaborative process involving the authors themselves, their colleagues and their clients at the Traumatic Stress Institute. The TSI is a private mental health organization that specializes in clinical intervention, research, and training in the area of traumatic stress. The staff of the TSI have worked together on numerous journal articles, workshops, and presentations at national scientific meetings. Lisa McCann is founder and clinical director of TSI. She received her Ph.D. in clinical psychology from the University of Kansas and her M.S.W. from Columbia University. Laurie Pearlman is director of research at TSI. She received her Ph.D. in clinical psychology from the University of Connecticut.

Among other features, authors McCann and Pearlman provide here a careful review of the scientific literature related to psychological trauma survivors, introduce a new personality theory especially useful with this population, and offer an impassioned plea for sensitivity toward traumatized people. Of particular significance is their new theoretical model emerging from constructivist theory and their description of its application to clinical assessment and treatment. They call their model a constructivist self development theory (CSDT). The focus of CSDT is on the interaction between the person and the situation. CSDT pays special attention to self in development and asserts that complex cognitive representations of self and others underlie much of an individual's interpersonal behavior.

McCann and Pearlman's theoretical and treatment approach is based on the assumption that individuals construct their personal realities as they interact with their environment. Thus, people actively create, although not always consciously, their representational models of the world. Traumatic experiences shape or disrupt these models in dysfunctional ways.

This comprehensive personality theory represents an integration of several theoretical and empirical contributions. It draws upon the contributions in the traumatic stress literature, constructivist theory, developmental theory, self psychology, social learning theory, and other cognitive theories. CSDT is useful to both clinicians and researchers as it provides frameworks for understanding and treating adult trauma survivors.

The authors extend the work of memory processing, particularly the processes of experiencing, denial, and approach-avoidance, by emphasizing the important role of schemas. Traumatized people find that reexposure to the traumatic imagery is extremely painful. This is because it challenges the ego resources and self capacities, and disrupts the psychological needs and cognitive schemas about self and world. Survivors must assimilate meanings of the trauma into existing schemas or change schemas to integrate a new reality. They may avoid the process of accommodation because the transformation of inner models of self and world is extremely disruptive psychologically.

Besides helping clinicians understand the process by which survivors experience traumatic life events, McCann and Pearlman attempt to sensitize clinicians to the uniqueness of every survivor's experience. The key for clinicians is to balance efforts to identify the common features among survivors with attempts to delineate the unique features among various survivors and survivor groups. They point to the danger of depriving trauma survivors of their individuality and uniqueness by focusing exclusively on their commonalities in response patterns.

The authors hope, as I do, that you will gain important insight from this book, and that it will further your understanding of the myriad struggles of adult trauma survivors—the unique and common features among them. Please let us know what you think of this book and your experiences in attempting to apply its principles.

Charles R. Figley, Ph.D.
Series Editor

Contents

Acknowledgments

As anyone who has written a book can attest, the process is challenging, stimulating, and at times arduous. In addition to being close colleagues, the two authors are close friends. The process of collaborating on this book has been one of personal and professional growth for both of us, and has stretched and nurtured our relationship as well. Throughout the planning and execution of this major project, we have worked closely—stimulating, questioning, inspiring, and helping one another. In developing this theory and creating this book, we have also contributed to the continuing growth of a deep and meaningful friendship. The theory and book reflect a synthesis of our individual understandings of personality and trauma.

We would like to express our appreciation to a number of individuals who provided collegial and emotional support, as well as inspiration, for this work. First, we would like to express thanks to our clients at The Traumatic Stress Institute who have taught us so much about the human capacity for growth and recovery in the face of unimaginable traumas and adversity. Sharing in our clients' journeys has been a privilege which has deepened our respect and admiration for all survivors.

We would also like to thank our colleagues at the Institute for the tremendous support they have given throughout the years, including the many hours spent in meetings discussing and critiquing the evolution of the theory. Specifically, we would like to thank Mark Hall, Ph.D., Betty Rich, Ph.D., Naomi Himmelfarb, Ph.D., Charles Field, Ph.D., and David Sakheim, Ph.D. for their many helpful comments as well as the intellectual and collegial support and stimulation they provided throughout this process. Other colleagues who have provided valuable support and input are Lake McClenney, Ph.D., Rob Neiss, Ph.D., and Irving Kirsch, Ph.D.

We are particularly indebted to Daniel Abrahamson, Ph.D., our business partner and Administrative Director at the Institute. Without his collegial, emotional, and administrative support throughout this process, this book would not have been written. Grace Johnson, M.A., our hardworking research assistant, has also provided essential support for the process. The same is true of our office staff members, Judy Jaekle and Sharna Gordon. Finally, we are indebted to Charles Figley, Ph.D., editor and founder of the Psychosocial Stress Series, for initially encouraging us to write this book.

I, Lisa McCann, would like to personally acknowledge certain special people in my life who have provided the emotional base which nurtured my creativity. With love and gratitude, I thank my husband, James O'Neil, and son, Peter McCann, for their patience and understanding for the many hours I devoted to this project, always knowing that both of them would be there to encourage and support me. Special thanks to my father, John McCann, my mother, Rosalie McCann, my aunt, Paula Geluso, and to all the other members of my wonderful extended family, for providing a family environment which has always nurtured and supported my creativity and intellectual development. To my mentor, Franklin Shontz, Ph.D., from the University of Kansas, I acknowledge his continuing influence on my thinking and particularly my interest in understanding whole persons. Finally, I would like to thank the circle of friends and colleagues, too numerous to name here, who have been a source of emotional support and intellectual inspiration.

I, Laurie Pearlman, would like to express my love and thanks to those who extended their patience, love, and warm support to me throughout the process of writing this book. This includes my many close friends, my parents, May and Bill Pearlman, and other family members. In addition, I thank my mentor, Jules Rotter, for challenging me to think critically.

Part 1
THEORY

1. Introduction and Overview

> When I was a child, I spoke as a child, I understood as a child,
> I thought as a child: but when I became (an adult) I put away
> childish things.
>
> For now we see through a glass darkly; but then face to face:
> now I know in part; but then shall I know even as also I am
> known.
>
> *The Bible:* I Corinthians 13:9–13.

The biblical passage quoted above, reflects one of the major premises of our work: that trauma survivors often view themselves and the world as if through a glass darkly, a psychological experience in which inner representations of self and world are disrupted, coloring all future perceptions. An understanding of the unique inner experience of survivors is essential as helpers guide the survivor gradually to transform these disrupted representations of self and world into a new reality that is both adaptive and positive.

In this book, we present a new conceptualization of the unique experience of trauma survivors. We offer both a new theoretical model which we call constructivist self development theory (CSDT) and a description of its application to clinical assessment of and intervention with adult trauma survivors. Constructivist self development theory focuses on the interaction between the person and the situation, with particular focus on the self in development. Our work integrates a number of theoretical and empirical contributions by many who have studied both trauma and self development and is based in a constructivist perspective (Mahoney, 1981).

Initially, theorists attempted to understand responses to trauma by focusing on the individual's preexisting pathology, suggesting that those who were more psychologically vulnerable were most deeply affected. This view was widely held by psychodynamic theorists who studied war trauma among World War II veterans (e.g., Brill, 1967; Lidz, 1946). Other theorists at the time recognized that under certain conditions, all individuals were vulnerable to breakdown, and that post-trauma reactions were related to the unique stressors of war (e.g., Grinker &

3

Spiegel, 1945; Kardiner, 1959). Since the mid-1970s, the characteristics of the stressor have become more focal as researchers empirically validated that certain events such as the Vietnam combat experience, rape, and incest produced psychological difficulties in most individuals who were exposed to them (e.g., Courtois, 1979; Foy, Sipprelle, Rueger, & Carroll, 1984; Kilpatrick, Veronen, & Best, 1985; Laufer, Brett, & Gallops, 1985). Since the mid-1970s, numerous research reports have confirmed Freud's (1920/1953) original assertion that a traumatic event of a certain magnitude will affect almost all who are exposed to it (see Scurfield, 1985, for a review of these issues).

The next step in the evolution of theorizing about trauma was a consideration of the person-situation interaction, a perspective that is gaining more prominence in theories of trauma (e.g., Epstein, 1985, in press a; Green, Lindy, & Wilson, 1985; Hendin & Haas, 1984; Scurfield, 1985; Wilson, Smith, & Johnson, 1985). This perspective takes into account both the individual's unique psychological development and the role of the traumatic experience itself in post-trauma adaptation. Although more complex, the interactive approach allows for a more complete understanding of unique adaptation to trauma because it can consider both the empirically demonstrated important characteristics of the event and the full complement of person characteristics beyond simply "preexisting pathology." Constructivist self development theory extends the interactionist tradition and, in addition, emphasizes the importance of the individual as an active agent in creating and construing his or her reality, a view that is basic to any constructivist theory (Mahoney, 1981; Mahoney & Lyddon, 1988).

In relation to this evolving paradigm shift, we believe that a current challenge in the field of traumatic stress studies is to avoid the danger of depriving trauma survivors of their individuality and uniqueness by focusing exclusively on the commonalities in response patterns among survivors. We must remember that trauma is experienced by persons, not by dehumanized "victims," and that their differences, as well as their commonalities, must be respected and understood. A number of theorists have supported this basic position through theoretical and research paradigms that focus on unique persons and their psychological development (e.g., Danieli, 1985; Green, Lindy, & Wilson, 1985; Lifton, 1988; Lindy, 1988; Roth, 1989). Our hope is to extend this position to enable clinicians and researchers to develop a greater understanding of the variations and differences in human adaptation to trauma.

THE DEVELOPMENT OF CONSTRUCTIVIST SELF DEVELOPMENT THEORY

This theory has been developed within the context of our professional commitment to studying and treating survivors of a variety of traumatic events. These include rape, childhood sexual and physical abuse, war, domestic violence, other crimes, chronic illness, accidents, and other serious stressors. Within the field of traumatic stress, we view ourselves as generalists who are interested in understanding the individual variations in adaptation to trauma. Our work has been a collaborative effort with our colleagues and clients at The Traumatic Stress Institute. The Institute is a private mental health organization which specializes in understanding and treating trauma survivors. Our ideas have evolved through intensive, ongoing study of the existing literature as it applies to our clinical work. We are currently involved in empirically validating our ideas with a wide variety of adult survivors. We hope these ideas will stimulate further research and the expansion of theory by other colleagues working in the field.

Early in our work at the Institute, we began to see the need for a heuristic model that would integrate the literature on trauma and individual psychological development. The theory we have developed brings together many lines of thinking about trauma and provides a map that can help researchers and clinicians understand both common and unique responses to trauma. As we apply the theory to our clinical work, we continue to learn about the richness and complexity of individuals' experiences of trauma. This in turn leads to revisions in the theory which lead us to a deeper understanding of our clients and their healing processes.

THE IMPORTANCE OF THEORY

A theory, like a map, provides a framework for exploration. Theory provides a way of understanding pieces of an individual's experience which otherwise might seem unrelated (see Rotter, 1954, on the importance of theory in clinical psychology). It allows the therapist to make connections, to know what else to look for, and to help the client develop ways of understanding his or her experience. Such a map allows the therapist to put the individual trauma survivor's experience in context and to guide him or her in exploring and resolving all aspects of it. Even without a map, the explorer may be fortunate enough to take the necessary turns that will lead through the healing process. However, there are many pitfalls that may be encountered along the way, posing risks to both client and therapist. We believe that a map, or a comprehensive framework, enables the clinician to navigate the journey in a way that is most beneficial for the trauma survivor. While no map can be an exact guide to any individual's experience, the theory we present here has enabled us to lead our clients gently through rocky terrain toward healing and it has contributed to our own growth as clinicians.

CONSTRUCTIVIST SELF DEVELOPMENT THEORY: AN OVERVIEW

Here we provide a brief overview of the theory that will be elaborated in subsequent chapters in this book. We propose that adaptation to trauma is a result of a complex interplay between life experiences (including personal history, specific traumatic events, and the social and cultural context) and the developing self (including self capacities, ego resources, psychological needs, and cognitive schemas about self and world). The experience of trauma begins with exposure to a non-normative or highly distressing event or series of events that potentially disrupts the self. The individual's unique response to trauma is a complex process that includes the personal meanings and images of the event, extends to the deepest parts of a person's inner experience of self and world, and results in an individual adaptation.

The major underlying premise of constructivist self development theory is that individuals possess an inherent capacity to construct their own personal realities as they interact with their environment. This constructivist position asserts that human beings actively create their representational models of the world (Epstein & Erskine, 1983; Mahoney, 1981; Mahoney & Lyddon, 1988).

Continuing psychological development depends upon the evolution of increasingly complex and differentiated psychological systems. We are interested here in three major psychological systems: (1) the self (or the individual's sense of himself or herself as a knowing, sensing entity, complete with capacities to regulate self-esteem and ego resources to negotiate relationships with others); (2) psychological needs (which motivate behavior); and (3) cognitive schemas (or conceptual frameworks for organizing and interpreting experience). This aspect of the theory draws upon and is consistent with a number of theoretical perspectives, including developmental object relations theory (Mahler, Pine, & Bergman, 1975), Kohut's (1971) self psychology, and Epstein's (1985, in press b) cognitive-experiential self-theory.

These systems evolve over the course of the life span. As persons grow and develop, they assimilate or incorporate more and more of the surrounding environment into their existing schemas for experience or conceptual frameworks. In object relations terms, these schemas are equivalent to mental representations of self and others. The processes whereby such changes take place are accommodation and assimilation, first described in Piaget's cognitive developmental theory (Piaget, 1971). When the environment presents new information that cannot be assimilated into existing schemas, cognitive schemas are modified, a process called accommodation. The complex interplay and balance between accommodation and assimilation results in the increasing differentiation and maturation of the psychological systems. We refer to this growth as progressive self development.

Trauma, by definition, requires accommodation, or a modification in schemas. Because the trauma-induced disruptions are, again by definition, in psychologically central areas, the accommodation process is difficult. Thus, trauma disrupts, at least temporarily, the individual's psychological growth.

All experience is encoded in the memory system, with the imagery system of memory (Paivio, 1986) associated with strong emotions and other vivid sensory impressions. The return of these traumatic images is one of the hallmarks of the post-trauma experience (Brett & Ostroff, 1985). The reexperiencing of traumatic imagery is very painful and disruptive, creating a defensive tendency to avoid this material. The processes of reexperiencing and denial were first described by Freud (1939/1964), later elaborated by Horowitz (1979, 1986), and most recently described within an approach-avoidance paradigm by Roth and Cohen (1986).

We extend this thinking to include the notion that the return of traumatic imagery is so painful because it challenges the self resources and capacities and disrupts the psychological needs and cognitive schemas about self and world. The individual is faced with the task of assimilating the meanings of the trauma into existing schemas, and/or accommodating or changing schemas to integrate a new reality. Individuals often attempt to avoid the process of accommodation because the transformation of inner models of self and world is extremely disruptive psychologically. The previous developmental history of the individual, including the evolving self, needs, and schemas, will shape what is remembered about the trauma and how the event is experienced and interpreted. The process of healing and transformation must ultimately result in renewed developmental progression, a process in which the self-capacities and resources are strengthened, psychological needs are balanced, and schemas are adjusted to incorporate new information in a way that enables the individual to experience pleasure and satisfaction in his or her life.

THE BOOK: AN OVERVIEW

The theory we have sketched above will be described in detail in the chapters that follow. Chapter 2 presents our model of individual psychological development; here we describe our understanding of the self, psychological needs, and schemas. We also describe the experience of trauma, focusing particularly on the imagery system of memory, corresponding emotional experiences, and the way in which schemas color what is remembered about the trauma.

Chapter 3 presents data regarding the prevalence and incidence of victimization, a synthesis of current theories of trauma, and a review of research findings regarding the commonalities in response patterns across traumatic events. While we cannot fully review the many useful theories of trauma that have emerged over the past 15 years, Chapter 3 provides a context for understanding how our own theory integrates and extends insights from many others.

We elaborate upon disruptions in cognitive schemas in Chapter 4. This chapter provides a theoretical context for understanding the powerful impact of schemas on the individual's interpretation of and unique adaptation to trauma. The following six chapters relate to clinical assessment and intervention. In Chapter 5, we provide an overview of adaptation to trauma and a general framework for clinical assessment and intervention with survivors.

Chapter 6 begins by providing a framework for assessing and understanding the important impact of life experiences as they are perceived by the survivor, including personal history, characteristics of the trauma, and the social and cultural context within which trauma occurs. Chapter 7 describes the reparative self work that is essential for many trauma survivors in order to enable them to regulate self-esteem and tolerate the painful work involved in memory integration. Although we draw upon thinking from self psychology theory (Kohut, 1971, 1977), our intent is to present our distillation of these concepts in a way that is understandable for clinicians without a specific background in self psychology.

Chapter 8 presents a paradigm for systematically assessing schemas that have been seriously disrupted, resulting in problems in self-world relations and other aspects of adaptation. Chapter 9 describes therapeutic interventions focused on restoring positive schemas and resolving disturbed schemas. Chapter 10 integrates existing knowledge about the experience of traumatic memories, with a focus on assessing verbal and imagery systems of memory as a prelude to memory integration. In Chapter 10 we also discuss resistances to recovering repressed or avoided memories and their resolution, as well as techniques for managing the emergence of distressing, intrusive imagery.

The next section covers special issues. Chapter 11 focuses on understanding transference reactions and resistances in constructivist self development theory terms. In Chapter 12 we discuss the application of the theory to such special issues as self-destructive behaviors, affective disturbances, and interpersonal difficulties. Next, we review findings related to different treatment modalities, including crisis management, group, family, and couples therapy, and finally, pharmacological interventions. In Chapter 13 we focus on special populations, including survivors of childhood trauma, victims of violence and other traumas in adulthood, survivors of historical or cultural traumas, and persons exposed to life-threatening illness. In this chapter, we synthesize important insights from previous research and interpret these findings in constructivist self development theory terms in the hope of shedding new light on these populations.

Finally, in Chapter 14, we describe four cases in depth by systematically applying the theory to assessment and treatment of survivors with unique styles of adaptation.

Because it attempts to be comprehensive, this theory is complex. Our hope is that we have presented it in enough detail that it can serve as a map for others.

2. Constructivist Self Development Theory

This chapter presents our thinking about self development, including the interconnected aspects of the self (self capacities, ego resources, psychological needs, and cognitive schemas) and the encoding of traumatic experiences in memory. The theory is interactive—that is, it focuses on the complex interaction between person and environment, an increasingly common view in the trauma literature. Figure 1 depicts the psychological experience of trauma as understood through this complex person-situation interaction. While constructivist self development theory acknowledges the great importance of the psychological situation (described by Rotter [1954] as the individual and his or her meaningful environment), like other interactive theories, it has yet to articulate the way in which specific aspects of situations elicit particular schemas, feelings, needs, and so forth, from individuals. This is part of the future work of developing the theory and testing its hypotheses empirically. We first provide a working definition of trauma, based upon our theory. We then present the basic tenets of the theory.

DEFINITION OF TRAUMA

We define psychological trauma as follows: An experience is traumatic if it (1) is sudden, unexpected, or non-normative, (2) exceeds the individual's perceived ability to meet its demands, and (3) disrupts the individual's frame of reference and other central psychological needs and related schemas. The first part of the definition serves to exclude the chronic difficulties of life, which, although themselves important and at times severe, must be distinguished from trauma if the construct is to serve any heuristic purpose, as Anna Freud (1967) and Henry

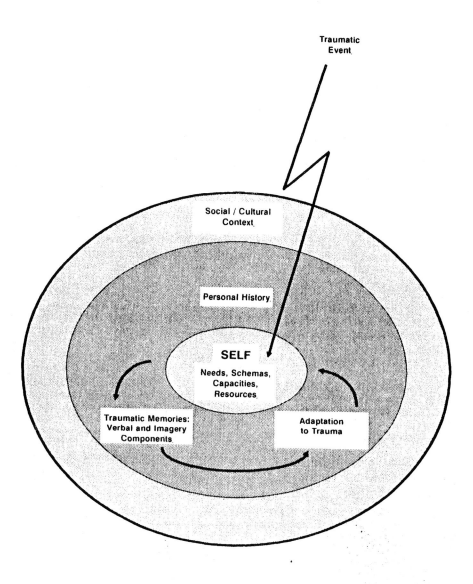

Figure 1. The Psychological Experience of Trauma (© 1989 by The Traumatic Stress Institute, South Windsor, CT).

Krystal (1978) have pointed out. Our definition includes experiences which may not be unexpected for the individual, such as ongoing incest, but which, from the perspective of the larger society, are non-normative.

The second part of our definition is consistent with Richard Lazarus's (1966) transactional model of stress. He defines stress as the discrepancy between the demands of the situation and the individual's perceived ability to meet those demands. He thus squarely places "stress" into the realm of the psychological; it is our intention to do so with "trauma." A recent article by Koss and Burkhart (1989) cites a statement by Lazarus and Folkman (1984) that is particularly relevant to our point of view. Koss and Burkhart state,

> Appraisals are influenced by both situation factors (e.g., predictability, duration, and ambiguity of the stressor) and person factors: that is, "commitments—what is important to the person; beliefs—personally formed or culturally shared preexisting notions about reality which serve as a perceptual lens . . . and existential beliefs—faith in God, fate, or some natural order . . . that enables people to create meaning out of life, even out of damaging experiences, and to maintain hope." (Lazarus & Folkman, 1984, pp. 58–77) (Koss & Burkhart, 1989, p. 30)

In constructivist self development theory terms, to be defined later in this chapter, Lazarus and Folkman's "commitments" are equivalent to psychological needs; "beliefs" are equivalent to schemas; and "existential beliefs" would be equivalent to the broadest schemas for experience, those related to frame of reference. In this regard, the Lazarus and Folkman (1984) view of trauma is most similar to our own.

This second portion of our trauma definition highlights our quintessentially constructivist view of personality. Thus, an essential part of what determines whether an experience is traumatic is the individual's sense that it is so. As will become evident in subsequent chapters, this appraisal is related to the individual's self capacities and ego resources, constructs which we define below.

Finally, we emphasize the importance of individual differences in the third part of the definition. An experience is traumatic in part because it in some way threatens the psychological core of an individual. Thus, one person's trauma may be another person's difficult experience. This final part of the definition is similar to the definition of "Gross Stress Reactions," a diagnosis in DSM-I (American Psychiatric Association, 1952), proposed by Weiss and Payson (1967) who write,

Gross stress is any unusual influence or force perceived as threatening a vital goal or need of an individual or group. In its severest form, it brings about an insoluble conflict of vital goals or needs. (p. 1027)

Note that Weiss and Payson define "gross stress" as the external force. Here we differ, defining trauma not as the stressor but as the individual's psychological response. In this we are consistent with Krystal (1978) who describes trauma as "a paralyzed, overwhelmed state, with immobilization, withdrawal, possible depersonalization, evidence of disorganization" (p. 90). Figley also conceptualizes trauma as the response rather than the stressor; in his excellent edited volume, *Trauma and Its Wake* (1985), he "use(s) the concept of trauma to represent *an emotional state of discomfort and stress resulting from memories of an extraordinary, catastrophic experience which shattered the survivor's sense of invulnerability to harm*" (p. xviii) (original italics).

CONSTRUCTIVIST SELF DEVELOPMENT THEORY: AN OVERVIEW

Constructivist self development theory is a synthesis of developmental theory (Mahler, Pine, & Bergman, 1975), self psychology (Kohut, 1977), social learning theory (Rotter, 1954), and other cognitive theories (e.g., Mahoney, 1981; Piaget, 1971). Within the trauma literature, we have also integrated concepts derived from the theories of Parson (1984), Epstein (in press a), Janoff-Bulman (1985, 1989a, 1989b), Horowitz (1986), and Roth (1989). We have taken notions from these theories and attempted to integrate them into a comprehensive personality theory which is useful to both clinicians and researchers; here we apply it specifically to understanding and treating the adult trauma survivor. The theory is, of course, open to empirical investigation and will undoubtedly continue to evolve as research data accumulate.

The major features of constructivist self development theory are listed in Table 2.1. In the following sections, we attempt to discuss these notions in enough detail to provide the reader with a working understanding of the theory. We describe these major concepts in more detail in later chapters.

CONSTRUCTIVISM

The theory is based in a constructivist perspective. This is described in detail by Mahoney (1981) and Mahoney and Lyddon (1988). The

TABLE 2.1
Major Assumptions of Constructivist Self Development Theory

Constructivism
  Individuals construct their own realities
The Self
  The self is the seat of the individual's identity and inner life
  The self develops over the life span through internalization and assimilation
    and accommodation
  The self comprises four interrelated aspects:
    Self capacities allow for the development and maintenance of positive self-
      esteem
    Ego resources regulate interaction with others and the environment
    Psychological needs motivate behavior
    Cognitive schemas are the cognitive manifestation of psychological needs
Traumatic memories
  Traumatic experiences are encoded in the verbal and imagery systems of memory
Adaptation to trauma
  Trauma can disrupt any or all parts of the self, including capacities, resources,
    needs, and schemas
  Adaptation to trauma reflects an interaction between life experiences and the
    self

---

constructivist perspective is based upon the philosophical thinking of
Immanuel Kant. Its roots in psychology grow from the work of Wilhelm
Wundt, Alfred Adler, George Kelly, and Jean Piaget. It underlies the
work of other psychological theories, such as Seymour Epstein's (1985)
cognitive-experiential self-theory. Mahoney and Lyddon (1988) write,

> The constructivist perspective is founded on the idea that humans
> actively create and construe their personal realities. The basic
> assertion of constructivism is that each individual creates his or
> her own representational model of the world. This experiential
> scaffolding of structural relations in turn becomes a framework
> from which the individual orders and assigns meaning to new
> experience. Central to the constructivist formulations is the idea
> that, rather than being a sort of template through which ongoing
> experience is filtered, the representational model actively creates
> and constrains new experience and thus determines what the
> individual will perceive as "reality." (p. 200)

THE SELF

Previous Conceptualizations

Westen (1989) states, "Few terms in either psychology or psychoanalysis are endowed with as many and ambiguous meanings as 'self' "

(p. 47). We quite agree. We review here some of the relevant previous conceptualizations which form the background for our own. Our thinking about the self is based in the self psychology literature (Kohut, 1977; White & Weiner, 1986), although we neither use all of Kohut's constructs nor do we claim to be orthodox Kohutian thinkers. Baker and Baker (1987) and White and Weiner (1986) do an excellent job of distilling and clarifying the main concepts of self psychology; Parson (1984, 1988) applies these to the Vietnam combat veteran. Because these latter writers are somewhat more accessible, we refer to their work here rather than relying exclusively on Kohut's original writings.

From a self psychology perspective, as opposed to a traditional analytic view, a focus on the integrity of the self does not presume the existence of pathology. Rather, self psychology supports the notion that extreme failures of empathy in an unresponsive environment, which often occur in severe trauma, can produce fragmentation or regression in a previously well-developed self (e.g., Brende, 1983; Brende & McCann, 1984; Parson, 1984, 1988; Ulman & Brothers, 1988; Westen, 1989).

Kohut (1977) described the self as occupying the central position in the personality, serving as "the basis for our sense of being an independent center of initiative and perception, integrated with our central ambition and ideals and with our experience that our body and mind form a unit in space and a continuum in time" (p. 177). More simply put, the self is "the center of the individual's psychological universe" (p. 311). For many self psychology thinkers, the notion of the self is so compelling as to transcend the need for definition. Others have grappled with defining this very complex construct. Parson (1984) presents one of the most useful discussions of the concept of the self. He states that the self " . . . is the central, all-encompassing supraordinate-agent-of-the-personality" (p. 22), of which the ego functions are all aspects.

Parson (1984) also states that " . . . the self contains experiencing, as well as observing capabilities" (p. 23). This parallels Stolorow's (1984) formulation of the self as both organizing one's experience of oneself, and initiating and undertaking activity. Constructivist theorists also include in their conception of the self the notion that it is self-organizing (Epstein, 1985, in press b; Mahoney & Lyddon, 1988). Parson (1984) adds that self is " . . . a phenomenological term" (p. 21).

Jung (1960) wrote that before a self can emerge, individuation must occur. He defined the individuation process as one in which every system in the personality reaches the fullest degree of differentiation, development, and expression. Thus, according to Jung, all human beings strive for individuation and self-development. This is similar to Adler's

(1935) notion of the creative self. He called it the active principle of human life. Werner (1948) introduced the term orthogenesis to refer to development that proceeds from a state of lack of differentiation to one of increased differentiation and integration. According to Mahoney and Lyddon (1988),

> the construction of self-knowledge or "learning to be a self" is the fundamental orthogenetic process by which the human organism progressively scaffolds knowledge about itself into a coherent, integrated whole—or self-identity. (p. 209)

Jordan (1984) presents a slightly different view of the self. Her conceptualization of the self rests upon the notion that the self is fluid, dynamic, and made up of a variety of self-representations or "schemas which form through the processes of accommodation and assimilation" (p. 6). She states that lasting changes in the self representations can come about through "self-empathy," a process of observing and tolerating one's previously unintegrated affect.

Traditionally, a well-developed self is characterized by autonomy; as Varela (1979) writes,

> [autonomy] represents generation, internal regulation, assertion of one's own identity: definition from the inside. [External law] represents consumption, input and output, assertion of identity of other: definition from the outside. (p. xii)

Jordan (1984), however, emphasizes the equal importance of relatedness. She suggests that autonomy and relatedness are not mutually exclusive, and that the well-developed self can move appropriately between these two states. Young-Eisendrath and Wiedemann (1987) also view a well-developed self as one in which empathy and a healthy dependency (as distinguished from passivity) are evident. We agree with the view of these feminist authors who see both independence and intimacy (in CSDT terms) as important needs that can be expressed and met in mature, appropriate ways.

CSD Theory's Conceptualization of "Self"

The self is a hypothetical construct we use to describe the psychological foundation of the individual. We view the self as the seat of the individual's identity and inner life. The self comprises: (1) basic capacities whose function is to maintain an inner sense of identity and positive self-esteem; (2) ego resources, which serve to regulate and enhance one's interactions with the world outside oneself; (3) psychological needs, which motivate behavior; and (4) cognitive schemas,

TABLE 2.2
Aspects of the Self and Their Functions

Self capacities (Regulate self-esteem)
    Ability to tolerate strong affect
    Ability to be alone without being lonely
    Ability to calm oneself
    Ability to regulate self-loathing
Ego resources (Regulate interactions with others)
    Intelligence
    Ability to introspect
    Willpower
    Initiative
    Ability to strive for personal growth
    Awareness of psychological needs
    Ability to take perspective
    Empathy
    Ability to foresee consequences
    Ability to establish mature relations with others
    Ability to establish boundaries
    Ability to make self-protective judgments
Psychological needs (Motivate behavior)
    Frame of reference
    Safety
    Trust/dependency
    Esteem
    Independence
    Power
    Intimacy
Cognitive schemas (Organize experience of self and world)
    Beliefs, assumptions, and expectations related to psychological needs

which are the beliefs, assumptions, and expectations, both conscious and unconscious, through which individuals interpret their experience (see Table 2.2). The self develops as a result of reflection, interactions with others, and reflection upon those interactions. Although all four aspects of the self (to be described in more detail below) are equally important and interdependent, we use the term "self" in the remainder of this book to include only self capacities and ego resources, referring to needs and schemas separately. We do this in order to highlight the importance of needs and schemas which are central to an understanding of the experience of trauma.

SELF DEVELOPMENT

Because our theory is developmental, it is important to explicate our understanding of personality development. Both trauma and psychotherapy are processes of change, so our way of understanding how individuals grow and change over the life span must also be explained. Our understanding of individual development draws heavily on the object relations (Mahler, Pine, & Bergman, 1975) and self psychology (Kohut, 1971, 1977) literature. Other developmental frameworks for understanding trauma have been elaborated by Eth and Pynoos (1985), Krystal (1978), Parson (1984, 1988), and Wilson (1980), among others.

As an infant interacts with significant people in his or her environment, he or she develops an increasingly differentiated sense of self and style of relating to others. Over time, s/he develops a unique constellation of self capacities, ego resources, psychological needs, and cognitive schemas. This development can continue over the life span, resulting in continuing differentiation and psychological growth.

From a developmental perspective, the assimilation of information about the self and others takes place through the process of internalization. According to object relations theory and self psychology, a child's mental representations of self and others develop through interactions with others. The development of a stable and cohesive self and the internalization of positive self and other representations depend upon empathy (Jordan, 1984), a "good enough" holding environment (Winnicott, 1958), positive mirroring, the ability to idealize important others, and the acceptance of early needs to feel "a degree of alikeness with other people" (Baker & Baker, 1987), which self psychologists refer to as twinning.

In addition to these positive experiences with others, the "minor empathic misinterpretations" of the caregiver contribute to the development of the individual's separate identity (Philipson, 1985). Philipson points out that it is through the mother's inability to comprehend perfectly what the child wants that the child comes to realize s/he is a separate person and to take over some of the mother's need-fulfilling activities.

Initially, others are needed to provide emotional stability for and definition of the emerging self. Over time, given appropriate validation and encouragement, the individual internalizes these "self-objects" (or others whom the infant experiences as existing primarily to meet his or her needs) and becomes increasingly able to meet his or her own physical and psychological needs with less external support.

From a social learning theory perspective (Rotter, 1954), the development of a unique self takes place through the process of reinforcement. The infant gradually learns how to get important needs, such as the need for food, met, by pleasing the caretaker or engaging in whatever behaviors will elicit the appropriate response. Over time, this generalizes so that the child learns to elicit responses to other, socially learned, needs, such as the need for love and affection. Again, in a positive early environment, the child will continue to develop the ability to get needs met and will grow increasingly independent, while also developing the ability to sustain intimate and interdependent relationships with others.

Constructivist self development theory views these two ways of understanding early learning as compatible. While each has its own research implications, they are not inconsistent from a clinical perspective. We rely upon social learning theory for a description of the mechanism (reinforcement) that underlies the process which object relations theory terms internalization. Westen (1989) provides an excellent integration of cognitive and object relations theories. According to his view, "object representations" might equally well be thought of as "person schemas" (p. 15) (or what we would call self schemas).

The Social Context of Self Development

Naturally, individual development takes place in a social and cultural context which shapes the individual's experience. Westen (1989) has noted the dearth of theorizing that accounts for the role of culture in individual development. Over time, through interactions with others, the child assimilates available information about the family, the subculture, and the society. If the family lives in poverty or otherwise deprived circumstances, the infant may develop an overall sense of deprivation. In part as a result of the family's attitudes toward its life situation, whatever it may be, the child develops certain expectations and beliefs about himself or herself, others, and the world. This is the context for the individual's appraisal and subsequent experience of life events. These expectations and beliefs will influence the child's interactions with peers and others as s/he moves out into the world. The meanings to the society of the child's social class, race, gender, and so forth will affect people's behaviors toward the child, further shaping his or her way of understanding the world and relating to self and others.

Stewart and Healy (1989) present a model for understanding the impact of social-historical events upon individuals. Their model and the data they present suggest that an individual's developmental stage in part determines the impact of social events upon the individual. They write, social experiences, in interaction with individual development, have consequences for individuals' worldviews when they are experienced in childhood, for their identities when they are experienced in late adolescence and the transition to adulthood, and for their behavior when they are experienced in mature adulthood. (pp. 39–40)

This perspective has particular relevance to the experience of child victims whose entire psychological development is impacted by trauma, as well as the experience of Vietnam veterans, most of whom were in late adolescence at the time of their participation in the war (Wikler, 1980; Wilson, 1980). It can also be helpful as one part of understanding the effects of other historical events, such as the Holocaust and the Cambodian genocide, upon survivors of different age cohorts. With regard to this issue, Laufer (1988) writes:

The relationship between the self and the environment, and especially the issue of continuity in the developmental process that allows the self-system to master the environment, is central to the idea of unity of personality or coherent and healthy ego identity . . . Indeed, we would argue that a plausible explanation of self and post-traumatic stress theories is that it is the exposure of the self-system to a hostile environment that fundamentally undermines the ability of the organism to unfold its potentialities, which shatters the self-system. (p. 38)

In a recent article on culture and PTSD, Young and Erickson (1989) write, "a sense of continuity in a cultural context provides the individual with the foundation for arriving at a definition of the self" (p. 434). They describe how trauma can disrupt an individual's experience of continuity, resulting in a sense of alienation and isolation. Furthermore, they state, "an individual who experiences a traumatic event during historical transition may experience a greater sense of alienation than if the culture were more stable" (p. 437). Thus, understanding the social and cultural context in which trauma occurs is fundamental to recovery.

We discuss the importance of the cultural, social, and historical context in understanding adult trauma survivors in Chapter 6.

SELF CAPACITIES

The self capacities allow the individual to maintain a consistent sense of identity and positive self-esteem. We consider four self capacities, drawn from the self psychology literature (Kohut, 1977), important to trauma survivors (see Table 2.2).

The first is the ability to tolerate and regulate strong affects without self-fragmentation or acting out. This means that the individual can experience deep feelings, whether of pain or joy, without a major or permanent disruption in his or her sense of psychological stability.

The second self capacity is the ability to be alone without being lonely (Winnicott, 1958). This means that the individual is capable of enjoying time alone and does not experience feelings of emptiness or anomie when alone.

The third self capacity is the ability to calm oneself through processes of self-soothing. This means that the individual can usually recover from emotional distress without overreliance upon other people or other external supports.

The fourth self capacity is the ability to moderate self-loathing in the face of criticism or guilt. This refers to the individual's ability to accept and integrate criticism without major or permanent damage to his or her sense of self-worth.

We focus on these capacities because they are central to understanding the internal experience of trauma and enabling the client to tolerate the painful work of therapy and integrate the affects and meanings associated with the trauma.

EGO RESOURCES

A second important aspect of the self is the ego resources (see Table 2.2). These are conscious abilities which are used to relate to the world outside oneself, including other people and tasks, in a constructive way. One could name many resources as important to the individual. The resources we describe here, many of which we take from Murray and Kluckhohn (1953), are important to the trauma survivor primarily in one of two ways.

The first group of ego resources will be very helpful to the therapy process. They include intelligence, the ability to introspect, willpower, initiative, the ability to strive for personal growth, an awareness of one's psychological needs, the ability to view oneself and others from more than one perspective, and empathy.

The second group includes ego resources that enable the trauma survivor to protect herself or himself from future harm. These include the ability to foresee consequences, the ability to establish mature relations with others, the ability to be aware of and to establish personal boundaries between self and others, and the ability to make self-protective judgments. Obviously these resources will serve the individual well in a variety of situations; the division into two groups is for heuristic purposes only.

If these ego resources and self capacities are reasonably well developed, psychotherapy will be much easier than if they are undeveloped or have been seriously impacted by trauma. We discuss in Chapter 7 ways of strengthening the self in cases in which the ego resources and self capacities require development.

PSYCHOLOGICAL NEEDS

Another important psychological characteristic that differentiates one individual from another is psychological needs, which are a central aspect of the self (see Table 2.2). Psychological needs motivate behavior and shape the individual's interactions with others. Needs are often not within an individual's awareness (Murray & Kluckhohn, 1953). Needs develop from infancy, on the basis of both inborn and environmental factors. Here we describe how needs develop and their importance to the trauma survivor's experience. Our understanding of the development of psychological needs is based in social learning theory (Rotter, 1954, p. 115ff).

Some of what shapes personality is genetic, having a physiological basis. These factors include some aspects of temperament, intellectual capacity, physical health, stamina, resilience, and physical appearance (Vale, 1973). Recent research with twins suggests that other aspects of personality may have a genetic basis (Pedersen, Plomin, McClearn, & Friberg, 1988; Tellegen, Lykken, Bouchard, Wilcox, Segal, & Rich, 1988). From birth, these factors influence people's responses to the infant. These in turn shape the infant's style of relating, the manner in which s/he learns to elicit what s/he needs. For example, learning how to get food (e.g., by crying, smiling, etc.) generalizes to learning how to get other things (i.e., attention, affection, etc.). The positive reinforcements (i.e., caregiver love and affection) originally associated with food generalize to other situations and reinforcements (e.g., smiling brings adult smiles). Through this process, the individual develops more differentiated needs, which underlie and motivate his or her behavior throughout life. The effect of early experience is to create particular patterns of salient needs within each individual. It is beyond the scope of this book to explore the various paths that lead to such individual differences.

While many other interesting and useful explications of needs exist, we have chosen to use a short list of central psychological needs, drawn largely from Rotter's (1954) social learning theory. (See Rotter, 1954, pp. 74–77 for a summary of the history of such lists of needs.) Although they are universal human needs, we have chosen these needs because they are especially important to an understanding of trauma survivors. None of these needs is in itself more or less adaptive, nor does having a particular need reflect a problem. Each is subject to more and less mature expression. The following needs are the focus of constructivist self development theory:

> *Frame of reference:* the need to develop a stable and coherent framework for understanding one's experience
>
> *Safety:* the need to feel safe and reasonably invulnerable to harm
>
> *Trust/Dependency:* the need to believe in the word or promise of another and to depend upon others to meet one's needs, to a greater or lesser extent
>
> *Esteem:* the need to be valued by others, to have one's worth validated, and to value others
>
> *Independence:* the need to control one's own behavior and rewards
>
> *Power:* the need to direct or exert control over others
>
> *Intimacy:* the need to feel connected to others, through individual relationships; the need to belong to a larger community

The individual's genetic endowment and developmental experience (including self capacities and ego resources) will determine which needs are more or less salient or conflictual. Here we have an opportunity to note the complex interaction among psychological needs, cognitive schemas, self capacities, and ego resources. These aspects of the self develop and are affected by trauma interdependently. For example, an individual with well-developed self capacities may evidence more balanced psychological needs, with a greater ability to restore his or her frame of reference and self-esteem after a trauma. More specifically, an individual whose needs for independence are thwarted by trauma may be better able to restore this need and the associated disrupted schemas to an adaptive balance if resources such as willpower and ability to strive for personal growth are well-developed. While endless combinations and examples could be developed (and must eventually be drawn from clinical material and tested empirically), the point here is only to demonstrate the highly interlinked nature of these four aspects of the self which we have separated only for heuristic purposes.

A need may become salient when it is disrupted by trauma, as described in the vignettes below. Such disruptions can result in generalized negative schemas related to that need. Under such circumstances, one can come to believe that need cannot, will not, or should not be met. These assumptions, beliefs, and expectations are represented by cognitive schemas related to frame of reference and other needs.

While psychological needs may change over time through the accretion of new experiences, needs become more stable as the person matures, requiring more dramatic experiences to effect major changes. The following example demonstrates the regression to a less mature expression of trust/dependency needs.

> Clarissa, a woman in her 30s, had a family and a career as a fashion magazine writer. She had strong relationships with friends, coworkers, and family, which she found important and satisfying. One day on her way to her office, she was cornered by two men and raped. Although she seemed to be managing reasonably well immediately after the event, after a few weeks she began to crave contact with others, phoning friends and family members hourly to talk about the event. She wanted her husband to accompany her everywhere, refused to be alone in her home, and insisted on having coworkers around her at all times during working hours.

An adult's need structure is fairly consistent across situations. One hallmark of healthy psychological adjustment, however, is the ability to move among needs according to the situation, seeking to meet those that are appropriate in the situation. For example, an individual may have strong dependency needs, but will function better socially if s/he can identify situations (such as loving, trusting relationships) in which such needs are appropriate and likely to be met, and discriminate these from situations (such as the workplace) where such needs are less likely to be met.

Better post-trauma psychological functioning is also characterized by an ability to meet one's needs in socially and personally acceptable ways. An example of healthy post-trauma adjustment would be an individual with a strong need for recognition who, after a rape, becomes an activist working for better rape crisis services in her community. A less adaptive adjustment for an individual with a strong need for recognition would be for a traumatized war veteran to attempt to take hostages while demanding a news conference about the nation's ineffective policies concerning veterans' needs.

We have discussed ways in which trauma can affect psychological needs. Conversely, the individual's dominant needs are a major determinant of the psychological response to events. One component of our definition of a traumatic experience is that it disrupts the individual's salient needs. An individual who, for example, has strong, unmet safety needs may experience a minor automobile accident as traumatic, whereas someone for whom safety is a lesser concern might experience the same accident as an unfortunate occurrence, but one without extensive psychological ramifications.

In addition, the need structure in part determines the person's specific response to the traumatic event. One person who is mugged while on vacation may respond by feeling his safety is threatened; another may feel his independence threatened. This stems from individual differences in psychological needs.

COGNITIVE SCHEMAS

The cognitive manifestations of psychological needs are schemas, or beliefs, expectations, and assumptions about self and others. Cognitive schemas have been variously described as personal constructs for organizing reality (Epstein, 1985, in press b), "mental structures that represent our general knowledge of objects, situations, and events" (Paivio, 1986, p. 27), and "characteristic and repetitive ways of interpreting events" (Rotter, 1989). Paivio (1986) notes that "the term schema came into modern psychology through the writings of Head (1920), Piaget (1926), and Bartlett (1932)" (p. 27). Constructivist self development's "schemas" correspond to Epstein's (1985) "postulates" and Janoff-Bulman's (1985) "assumptions." Westen's (1989) conceptualization is consistent with our own; he writes, "The concept of 'schema' in social cognition is similar to the concept of 'object representation' in psychoanalysis" (p. 28).

In mature, psychologically healthy individuals, schemas comprise a fairly realistic set of expectations which are fluid and responsive to the environment (Jordan, 1984). Schemas change in the face of discrepant information through the process of accommodation, although more specific schemas may be more open to change than are more generalized schemas (Rotter, 1954; Westen, 1989). Schemas of particular importance to trauma survivors are those that derive from the seven needs described above. As we describe further below, schemas are impacted or disrupted by traumatic experiences and they determine the way the traumatic experience is encoded in memory.

THE RELATION BETWEEN THE SELF AND SCHEMAS

It should be clear at this point that the self capacities, ego resources, psychological needs, and cognitive schemas develop in connection with and impact upon one another. For example, when psychological needs are balanced and are being met in mature ways, cognitive schemas and self-esteem are likely to be largely positive. Alternatively, if self capacities are undeveloped so the individual is in a constant state of internal chaos and low self-esteem, it is more likely that affectively charged negative schemas will be activated (Westen, 1989). While constructivist self development theory does not focus heavily on affect, except as it accompanies traumatic imagery and disrupted schemas, implicit in our definition of the self capacities is the understanding that undeveloped or severely disrupted self capacities are accompanied by a state of affective disturbance. In other words, if an individual has little affect tolerance or ability to soothe himself, it is obvious that that person will often be in a state of emotional turmoil. Conversely, an individual with impaired affect tolerance may experience a complete state of affective paralysis and feel nothing, as is actually the case for some trauma survivors at some times.

The self schemas, those beliefs and expectations that relate directly to the self capacities and ego resources, are part of the individual's way of understanding and experiencing himself or herself. If, for example, one of the self schemas is, "I can't handle emotion," this will result in either serious anxiety or emotional numbing from time to time, at the very least. Westen (1989) discusses the relation between self schemas and affect with specific reference to borderline personality disorder. He presents another illustration of the connection between parts of the self (here between needs and schemas) in stating, ". . . a person who has difficulty investing in other people in mature ways [*which in CSDT terms would translate as the need for intimacy*] is likely to have pathological representations of self and others [*or, in CSDT terms, self schemas*]" (Westen, 1989, p. 53). In addition, whether one views affect or cognition as primary, few would dispute the premise that there is indeed a direct relation between the two.

Following is a case example demonstrating the disruption of psychological needs and schemas.

Ernie is a working-class man in his 40s who grew up in a family with a harsh, punitive father and a mother who was too overwhelmed by her own needs to respond to any of her son's needs for care or support. When Ernie went to Vietnam, he experienced a profound disillusionment in both his military leaders and the American government for failing to fulfill the promises they had made to him. Furthermore, his need for esteem and recognition was thwarted by the hostility and lack of validation he experienced during the homecoming. As a result of these frustrations of his needs for support (trust/dependency) and esteem, he developed generalized beliefs that a man would be a fool to trust anyone and that he himself was an unworthy failure. Finally, these disrupted schemas affected his overall frame of reference, resulting in a cynical view of the world as malevolent and meaningless. The affects associated with these disrupted schemas were anger, depression, and loneliness.

Having provided an overview of the self, we now turn to a description of memory and trauma. We refer the reader back to Table 2.1 for an outline of these topics as they fit together within constructivist self development theory.

TRAUMA AND MEMORY

In this section, we present our conceptualization of the experience of trauma and synthesize existing knowledge about the psychological experience of trauma as represented through memories.

Here we present the major conceptualizations of human memory that inform our work. While we are aware that the cognitive theorists whose work we cite view their theories as not entirely compatible, we have taken from each those concepts that appear relevant to trauma survivors, blending them into our own theory in a way that is consistent with our clinical experience, just as we have borrowed from clinical theories as disparate as object relations and social learning theory. Over time, as constructivist self development theory is tested empirically, these borrowed concepts may be integrated or discarded, as appropriate.

We find Bower's (1981) definition and model of memory useful in understanding the experience of trauma survivors. Bower defines memory as "an associative network of semantic concepts and schemata that are used to describe events" (1981, p. 134). He reports a synthesis of research concerning the relation between mood and memory. He found evidence that mood impacts upon free associations, upon one's expectations, predictions, and interpretations in interpersonal situations, and upon imaginative constructions (in his research, these were projective stories), all of which fall under the rubric of cognitive schemas in constructivist self development theory. Bower's work suggests that certain emotional states may become associated with memories of events that occurred while the individual was in that state. That is, a mood can both shape and elicit a particular memory, and a memory or memory fragment can elicit a related mood state. This is consistent with Eich's (1980) notion of state-dependent learning, as well as with Greenberg and van der Kolk's (1987) description of the organization of traumatic experience through sensorimotor or iconic rather than linguistic/symbolic forms.

The other important theory of memory we draw upon is that of Paivio (1986). In Paivio's model, memories are stored in two distinct, although coordinated, representational systems: verbal and imagery. Traumatic memories may be experienced as repeated imaginal representations of the trauma that are emotionally painful and disruptive. These disturbances in imagery represent a fundamental aspect of the post-trauma experience (Brett & Ostroff, 1985). The verbal system of memory is less emotionally evocative and includes the factual reporting of the sequence of events. When trauma survivors are asked to describe what happened to them, they may either give a verbal report about what they experienced or describe the imagery associated with the event. The descriptions based in the imagery system of memory might include sounds, tactile sensations, odors, and visual images, the visual being the most accessible, or perhaps the most readily describable, of the imagery traces.

Whole Memories

The therapist must be aware of the independent importance of both the verbal and imagery systems of memory. Taken together, the material in these systems, the complex connections among this material, and the evocative stimulus cues (Paivio, 1986; Tulving, 1983) represent a whole memory. Working through a traumatic memory requires exploring the verbal memory traces as well as the corresponding imagery and affect.

Some individuals may have access to whole memories, while for others, a traumatic memory may be entirely repressed. While this may in part relate to the recency of the event, it also represents one aspect of the individual's adaptation. Often, a memory of a traumatic experience is fragmented. The individual may have access only to a bit of an image, a repetitive phrase, or a feeling that is inexplicable in the current situation. The fragments can be very unsettling to the individual who cannot understand what a particular recurring image or thought means (especially if strong, disturbing emotion accompanies it) or to the individual who feels consumed by terror or rage for no reason he or she can understand. Fragments of a traumatic memory may become intrusive or disruptive to the individual's psychological or interpersonal functioning. These fragments may come back to haunt the individual, stimulated by something outside (e.g., a seemingly minor interaction with a man in authority, a TV special on incest, a smell, a sound), or inside (a fleeting thought or feeling, an image fragment which is often followed by a flood of emotion, most often fear or rage). Any image, affect, or verbal fragment related to the traumatic memory may elicit other fragments.

In her account of her own childhood sexual abuse, Sylvia Fraser (1988) describes her emotions that were disconnected from any event she could recall consciously. In describing the experience of going to kiss her grandmother's cheek, she wrote:

> Why this revulsion for an old woman's kiss? I do not know. I cannot say. The truth belongs to my other self, and it is a harsh one: Other Grandmother's caved-in cheek is the same squishy texture as daddy's scrotum. (p. 19)

This is an example of an often-relived association whose deeper meaning had remained hidden for years, only to be revealed by extensive therapeutic work in adulthood.

Although the various models of memory have important differences, each has a way of accounting for this triggering, including Anderson and Bower's (1980) model of human associative memory, Bower's (1981) model of mood and memory, Paivio's (1986) dual coding model of memory, and Tulving's (1983) model of episodic memory. It is beyond the scope of this work to address the differences among these models. For our purposes, it is sufficient to note that the process of one portion of a memory in some way evoking another is widely recognized.

Braun (1979) draws a distinction between knowledge and memory. While knowledge is a series of facts, as represented in verbal memory, memory includes imagery and associated affects. Thus, a client may claim s/he "remembers" what happened because s/he has conscious access to the sequence of events. Yet in reporting these traumatic events, the client may experience little emotion and have limited access to imagery. Until the imagery portions of the memory are reunited with the verbal portions, survivors cannot integrate the memories and put them to rest.

Imagery

The most important portion of a traumatic memory is imagery, most often in the form of disturbing visual imagery. The underestimated personal and clinical importance of imagery has been described for both general therapy clients (Singer & Pope, 1978) and PTSD sufferers (Brett & Ostroff, 1985), with Horowitz's (1976) theory standing as an exception. Individuals often experience disturbing images as fragments, without context or meaning (Horowitz, 1976). These may take the form of flashbacks, nightmares, or intrusive thoughts, often accompanied by overwhelming affect. The image fragment may be inexplicable, foreboding, highly symbolic in nature, or it may be a composite memory which is difficult to comprehend.

> Estelle, a woman in her 30s, suffered chronic low self-esteem, sexual dysfunction, and intimacy problems. She initially had no awareness of early sexual abuse. She reported a dream image of a man with a hawk's face who was taunting her and saying, "You'll never know who I am." The therapist was first alerted to the possibility of sexual abuse when Estelle reported a recurrent dream in which she called out to her mother, "Mommy, why did you abandon me?"

The traumatic images are usually visual, vivid, recurring, and unbidden (Horowitz, 1976). The disturbing images often come into awareness when the individual is experiencing feelings similar to those that accompanied the original event, as Bower (1981) suggests. The content of these images varies, and seems to be closely tied to the external characteristics of the traumatic event (see Green, Wilson, & Lindy, 1985).

Flashbacks are a common and frightening part of the trauma survivor's experience. A flashback is the experience of reliving a moment or part of the past. The images and feelings experienced in a flashback are vivid and often terrifying. During a flashback, the individual feels as if the experience were happening now, and is entirely immersed in it without any awareness that it is a past event. Parson (1984) points out that the individual is retraumatized by reexperiencing, through a flashback, the original helplessness associated with the event. Flashbacks and other reexperiencing phenomena (such as nightmares and hallucinations) are also frequently accompanied by physiological responses such as sweating and autonomic nervous system arousal (e.g., Kolb, 1984; van der Kolk & Greenberg, 1987). Below, we describe a clinical example of a vivid and frightening flashback:

Martha was in her early 30s when she came to therapy because of intense, inexplicable experiences that began shortly after the birth of her first child. She had no conscious awareness of childhood victimization, although she would eventually discover that she had been abused by both her biological father and the priest at the orphanage where she had lived temporarily. She reported distressing flashbacks connected with going in to check on her infant son during the night. Upon entering his room, she would experience "something big swooping toward me." Then, when she reached into the crib to cover the baby, her perception shifted so that she felt as though she were the infant in the crib, and two big hands, dissociated from a body, were reaching for her. These experiences felt real and extremely distressing to her.

In the above case, the flashback did not replicate a specific traumatic experience, but rather was a symbolic manifestation of a traumatic memory. Other individuals may experience a flashback which more directly represents a specific traumatic event. There are a variety of other perceptual disturbances that can follow from victimization. These include hallucinations, and hypnagogic hallucinations (Ellenson, 1985; Gelinas, 1983; Horowitz, 1979). These can be distinguished from psychotic symptoms by the direct relation of their content to the traumatic experience, although this may not be evident if the client does not have conscious access to the traumatic material.

Emotion

The reexperiencing of imagery is associated with powerful emotional states, whether these images are conscious or repressed. While many traumatized individuals may be unaware of their feelings at times, strong emotions may be evoked by an internal stimulus, such as a memory fragment in the form of an image, a thought, or another feeling. As mentioned above, these emotional states may also elicit memory fragments (Bower, 1981). Often the trauma victim comes to treatment because s/he is experiencing inexplicable sadness, anxiety, or rage.

Belinda is a woman in her 40s who presented in therapy with chronic depression and anxiety. She had no awareness of any history of abuse. She often experienced feelings of choking when drinking certain beverages, nausea when she smelled her husband's semen, and panic when anyone touched her around her neck. Over time, her therapist began to help her connect these emotional memories with abusive events in her distant past.

In the event that distressing emotions are connected to repressed traumas, an essential goal of therapy is to make a connection between these affective states and the whole memories of the trauma.

Approach-Avoidance

Clinicians who work with victims will readily recognize that individuals appear to move back and forth between approaching or being intruded upon by traumatic memories and avoiding or having no access to them. This process was originally described by Freud in 1939 (Freud, 1964), when he talked about the tendency to repeat or reexperience a trauma as an attempt to master it. He also described the use of denial as a defense against the painful affect that accompanies repetition.

Horowitz (1976) later described the processes of intrusion and denial within the context of an information-processing model. Roth and Cohen (1986) focus on the concepts of approach and avoidance in their review of the related formulations and provide a synthesis of the literature with a view toward understanding individual differences in this dimension of response to trauma. They view approach-avoidance as a metaphor for emotional and cognitive activity moving the individual either toward or away from threat. Their conceptualization of this process allows for an understanding of individuals moving back and forth between the two modes, according to their needs at the time, rather than suggesting that people are "approachers" or "avoiders," or that all victims manage traumatic material similarly.

These conceptualizations suggest that people avoid traumatic material because it is potentially painful. The return of traumatic memories may indeed result in overwhelming affect. Krystal (1978), in fact, defines trauma in terms of overwhelming affect and the fear of disintegration. "The fear of affects frequently represents the dread of the return of the infantile type trauma. Under certain circumstances . . . the affective responses may become overwhelming and initiate the traumatic state" (Krystal, 1978, p. 92). However, avoidance or denial may serve a self-protective function beyond affect regulation. Confronting traumatic memories may pose a seemingly unresolvable discrepancy with the individual's existing schemas about self and the world. Thus, it is important to recognize that the return of traumatic memories is potentially disruptive not only because of the fear of overwhelming affects it may produce, but because the disruption to the individual's frame of reference is perhaps the most central experience of trauma against which individuals defend.

In addition, traumatic memories may pose an intolerable threat to other psychological needs and related schemas. A rape victim with high needs for independence may find it extremely difficult to recall and acknowledge her helplessness in the rape situation. Avoidance may be essential until her self capacities are strong enough to allow approach. The client's avoidance of difficult material is a signal to the therapist that important groundwork must be done, and provides the time to do it. As Roth (1989) points out, although the ideal therapeutic situation moves toward approach and integration, approach can potentially produce painful affects that are psychologically disruptive unless the individual is able to "dose" himself or herself with tolerable levels of affect. Thus, avoidance should not be challenged until the client has established resources within the self for confronting the painful affects and meanings in therapy, capacities for tolerating the painful affects associated with challenges to existing schemas, and alternative ways of meeting psychological needs. According to Roth and Cohen (1986), ". . . in the long run, the positive consequences of avoidance are largely effects that work to facilitate approach" (p. 817). These notions represent some of the underlying premises of our understanding of trauma integration and resolution.

The Connection Between Imagery and Central Schemas

As we discussed above, traumatic imagery is potentially disruptive to individuals' schemas about self and world. Furthermore, we propose that the images that are most salient for individuals are shaped or colored by schemas about self and world. In other words, a rape victim for whom schemas related to safety are central will be preoccupied with different aspects and images of the traumatic experience than would a victim for whom schemas related to trust are more salient. The specific meanings of the traumatic memories, including other people's reactions to the experience, are embedded in trauma-related themes. These themes reflect both characteristics of the stressor and deep emotional meanings for the individual. They constitute much of the content that clients present in therapy and provide clues for the therapist to specific areas of psychological disturbance. For example, a client who talks about themes of abandonment, betrayal, and broken promises is struggling with issues of trust, while one who is talking about themes of degradation and defilement is expressing conflicts concerning esteem. This will be discussed in more depth in Chapter 9.

THE POST-TRAUMA ENVIRONMENT

The events that surround a trauma, the meanings of these events to the victim, and the responses of others all contribute to the victim's response. Symonds (1980) originally wrote about the "second injury" which results from unsupportive or blaming reactions from others. Lifton (1973) described the disillusionment experienced by Vietnam veterans when they returned home to a hostile, unwelcoming nation. Parson (1984) wrote about the empathic failure of others that resulted in a narcissistic injury for the returning Vietnam veteran. In an elaboration of this work, Ulman and Brothers (1988) present the returning Vietnam veteran as a wounded warrior, like Achilles, who is betrayed by those who contributed to his vulnerability. The role of others' reactions is central to many conceptualizations of victim responses (e.g., Green, Wilson, & Lindy, 1985; Sgroi & Bunk, 1988). Furthermore, responses of those who are called upon for assistance, including the police, legal system, therapists, friends, and family, will also shape the victim's memories of what happened. All of this becomes part of the memory of the trauma. We describe the role of the recovery environment in more depth in Chapter 6.

While we do not focus on the characteristics of the stressor as in themselves determining individuals' responses, the meanings the specific stressor has both to the individual and to those in his or her subculture and recovery environment will shape responses. For example, domestic abuse has meanings to each person who is the victim of it, and these meanings may in part come from those around him/her. To the extent that others blame the woman for allowing herself to be battered, she too may come to experience this with guilt and shame. The cultural/social meanings of specific events are explored in Chapter 6.

SUMMARY

In this chapter, we have presented the basic outline of constructivist self development theory as well as our ideas about memory as it relates to the experience of adult trauma survivors. The theory is complex and multifaceted. We discuss in later chapters the application of the theory to assessment of and interventions with adult trauma survivors.

3. Trauma and Victimization: A Review of the Literature

In this chapter, we provide a context for understanding the historical developments in the field of traumatic stress studies as well as a synthesis of research and theoretical perspectives related to the psychological consequences of victimization. First we review the data on the incidence and prevalence of various types of victimizing events. Then, we review the historical evolution of views of post-trauma reactions, as well as current definitions of post-traumatic stress disorder. Next, we describe data on other trauma-related disturbances in psychological functioning reported in the clinical and empirical literature. Finally, we review current theories of post-trauma adaptation and their relevance to constructivist self development theory.

THE INCIDENCE AND PREVALENCE OF VICTIMIZATION

The converging evidence regarding the incidence and prevalence of violence or other traumas experienced by human beings suggests that victimization is a pressing concern for mental health professionals. The data indicate that a significant proportion of human beings has experienced an event or series of events that can be considered to be traumatic at some point in their lives. Here we present a summary of these data as a way of providing a societal context for this topic area.

Child Abuse

The data on child sexual and physical abuse suggest that an alarming number of children are subjected to trauma by adults entrusted with their care. With regard to child physical abuse, available evidence suggests that approximately 1.4 million American children from the ages of 3 to 17 experience acts of violence perpetrated against them by family members each year (Gelles & Cornell, 1985). The most methodologically sound research in this area has been conducted by one group of researchers (Gelles, 1978; Gelles & Cornell, 1985; Straus, Gelles, & Steinmetz, 1980). In their study of family violence in a nationally representative sample of 2,146 individual family members, Straus et al. (1980) found that 3% of parents admitted to kicking, biting, or punching their children, and 1% reported beating their children at least one time over the previous year. In a replication study conducted with 3,520 families, Straus and Gelles (1986) found a 47% lower incidence of child abuse. The authors speculate that this might be due to differences in method, increased reluctance to report, or actual decreases in child abuse. Despite these perplexing and somewhat puzzling findings, the authors point out that even such a reduction would mean that at least a million children each year are victims of physical abuse. The complexities inherent in obtaining accurate data regarding the incidence of child abuse continue to pose a challenge for researchers.

With regard to childhood sexual abuse, Herman (1981) analyzed data from five surveys reported since the 1940s and found that 20% to 30% of adult women reported an unwanted sexual encounter with an adult male in childhood. In more recent years, Russell (1984) conducted an interview study of sexual victimization in a random sample of 930 women in San Francisco. These data revealed that 16% of women reported at least one incident of sexual abuse by a blood relative, while 31% reported at least one incident of sexual abuse by a nonrelative in childhood. Combining these two categories, she found that 38% of adult women reported at least one incident of incestuous or extrafamilial sexual abuse in childhood. Russell defined extrafamilial child sexual abuse as . . .

> One or more unwanted sexual experiences with persons unrelated by blood or marriage, ranging from attempted petting (touching of breasts or genitals or attempts at touching) to rape, before the victim turned 14 years, and completed or attempted forcible rape experiences from the ages of 14 to 17 years (inclusive). (Russell, 1984, p. 180)

She defined incestuous child abuse as . . .

> Any kind of exploitative sexual contact or attempted sexual contact, that occurred between relatives, no matter how distant the relationship, before the victim turned 18. (Russell, 1984, p. 181)

Young women with stepfathers are particularly vulnerable to being abused (17% rate for women with stepfathers versus 2% with biological fathers) (Russell, 1984). Russell's findings are consistent with the Herman (1981) data as well as with another national random sample in which 27% of women reported that they had experienced at least one incident of childhood sexual abuse (San Francisco Chronicle, 1985). These latter figures are somewhat lower than in the Russell sample, perhaps because the interviews were conducted on the phone in contrast to the in-depth face-to-face interviews conducted by Russell.

Other Crime

The findings on criminal victimization suggest that crime has been epidemic in America since the mid-1970s. In 1984, approximately 37 million Americans experienced a criminal victimization (Herrington, 1985). Of these, 6 million were victims of a violent crime. The family violence research conducted by Straus, Gelles, and Steinmetz (1980) revealed that 16% of spouses reported violence between them in the year of the survey, while 28% reported acts of violence at some point in their marriage. While these acts of violence included "milder" varieties such as slapping, an analysis of violence that had a higher risk of serious physical injury revealed that 3.8% of women were victims of severe violence during the year of the survey. A projection of these rates to all women would suggest that approximately 1.8 million women are victims of family violence each year.

These data support the view of Straus and his colleagues that the marriage license is a hitting license (Straus et al., 1980). However, these researchers replicated this study more recently and found a 27% decrease in spouse abuse (Straus & Gelles, 1986), a finding which is also difficult to interpret due to the complexities of reporting. Again, these researchers point out that domestic violence is still a pressing social problem, with estimates of nearly a million and a half women battered by their partners each year.

Another serious criminal victimization is rape. In a random sample of 930 women, Russell (1984) found that 24% reported at least one rape over their lifetime, while 31% reported being a victim of an attempted rape. With regard to marital rape, 14% of married women reported a sexual assault by their husbands. In another national sample of 3,187 college women, Koss, Gidycz, and Wisniewski (1987) found that 27.5% reported being a victim of a rape or attempted rape. With regard to male rape, 7.7% of college men reported a rape or attempted rape. Virtually none of these victims had been involved in the criminal justice system. This finding was confirmed in the Russell (1984) sample in which only one in 12 attempted or completed rapes was ever reported. The above findings underscore the significant problem in underreporting of rape and other types of sexual victimization.

Natural Catastrophes

In a study that analyzed data regarding natural disasters, Gleser, Green, and Winget (1981) found that 836 major disasters involving over 100 deaths or injuries had occurred worldwide from 1947 through 1973. The Armenian earthquake in the Soviet Union is but one recent example of a widespread disaster that is likely to impact the lives of millions for years to come.

War and Genocide

The largest scale victimizations and atrocities have clearly resulted from war, with genocide being the most horrifying outcome of war. The Vietnam war is perhaps the most recent event in U.S. history that continues to affect the lives of 500,000 to 800,000 Vietnam era veterans and their families (Center for Policy Research, 1979). With regard to the Nazi Holocaust, Danieli (1985) summarizes data that suggest that among the 8,861,000 Jews living in pre-World War II Europe, only 400,000 to 500,000 escaped through the underground and only about 75,000 escaped the death camps. Among the victims of war in Southeast Asia, the genocide of the Cambodians during the Pol Pot regime was responsible for two million deaths. Since 1975, more than 700,000 refugees from Southeast Asia have settled in the United States, many with histories of extreme trauma including torture (Mollica, Wyshak, & Lavelle, 1987).

Overall, these data suggest that the field of traumatic stress should be a focal one for mental health professionals working in a variety of settings. Even those professionals who do not specialize in this field but work in settings where there is a high concentration of survivors (e.g., the Veterans' Administration) should become knowledgeable about the area of traumatic stress because of the strong likelihood that they will be working with clients who have been victimized.

THE PSYCHOLOGICAL CONSEQUENCES OF VICTIMIZATION

The literature on psychological responses to victimization reveals a variety of response patterns that are common among victimized populations. The official categorization of post-trauma reactions is represented in the diagnostic criteria for post-traumatic stress disorder (PTSD).

This diagnosis was first defined in DSM-III (American Psychiatric Association, 1980) and later revised in DSM-III-R (American Psychiatric Association, 1987). The revised criteria for PTSD reflect changes arising from the criticism that DSM-III criteria were biased toward reexperiencing rather than denial symptoms (see Brett, Spitzer, & Williams, 1988, for a discussion of these changes).

The criteria for PTSD continue to be controversial, with some authors arguing that the only unique features of PTSD are the presence of a severe stressor and reexperiencing phenomena (Breslau & Davis, 1989). These authors discuss the considerable overlap between the symptoms of this disorder and other disorders such as depression, anxiety, and substance abuse. This issue has been addressed in the literature and is one of the reasons these latter symptoms are not included in the DSM criteria (Lyons, Gerardi, Wolfe, & Keane, 1988). With regard to the reexperiencing symptoms, Breslau and Davis (1989) point out that in depression, intrusive memories, and ruminations are also common and are therefore not restricted to post-trauma reactions. They conclude that trauma does not cause a specific psychiatric disorder, an opinion that is supported by the vast number of response patterns associated with trauma. Despite this continuing debate, the diagnosis appears to be fairly reliable, and validated PTSD scales (e.g., The Mississippi Scale of the MMPI [Keane, Caddell, & Taylor, 1988]) have been found to differentiate between PTSD and non-PTSD comparison groups among Vietnam veterans. We agree with others that the PTSD diagnosis is merely a "slice of the pie" that is not meant to incorporate the complex psychological phenomena associated with trauma but rather represents the most parsimonious view of post-trauma sequelae that differentiates it from other disorders (e.g., Brett, 1988; Lyons et al., 1988).

A number of other post-trauma reactions have been noted in the literature, in addition to those described in the DSM criteria. Our review of the empirical literature on psychological responses to victimization (McCann, Sakheim, & Abrahamson, 1988) revealed disturbances in five areas of psychological functioning across survivors of rape, childhood sexual or physical abuse, domestic violence, crime, disasters, and the Vietnam war. Some of these symptom patterns overlap with those described in DSM while some overlap with other psychological problems. Here, we will condense the findings reported in McCann et al. (1988). This review does not represent all the literature that reports these response patterns but rather a selected sample of the research reports that generally fulfill criteria for empirical research.

EMOTIONAL RESPONSE PATTERNS

Fear and Anxiety

Fear and anxiety are common reactions to traumatization among survivors of rape (Calhoun, Atkeson, & Resick, 1982; Ellis, Atkeson, & Calhoun, 1981); child (Burgess, Hartman, McCausland, & Powers, 1984; Mannarino & Cohen, 1986) and adult (Briere, 1984; Sedney & Brooks, 1984) victims of childhood sexual abuse; battered women (Hilberman & Munson, 1977-1978; Stewart & de Blois, 1981); other crime (Bard & Sangrey, 1986; Frederick, 1980; Maguire, 1980); environmental disasters involving children (Terr, 1981) and adults (Wilkinson, 1983); and Vietnam veterans (De Fazio, Rustin, & Diamond, 1975).

Depression

Depression is also a common reaction among victims of rape (Atkeson, Calhoun, Resick, & Ellis, 1982; Frank, Turner, & Duffy, 1979); child victims of sexual (Mannarino & Cohen, 1986) and physical (Kazdin, Moser, Colbus, & Bell, 1985) abuse; adult survivors of childhood sexual abuse (Bagley & Ramsey, 1985; Briere & Runtz, 1985; Bryer, Miller, Nelson, & Krol, 1986; Gold, 1986; Peters, 1984); domestic violence (Stark, 1984; Walker, 1985); other crime (Ochberg & Spates, 1981); environmental disasters (Jones, 1985; Murphy, 1984; Wilkinson, 1983); and Vietnam combat (Foy, Sipprelle, Rueger, & Carroll, 1984; Helzer, Robins, Wish, & Hesselbrock, 1979).

Decreased Self-esteem or Identity Problems

Disruptions in self-esteem or identity have been noted in victims of rape (Kilpatrick, Veronen, & Best, 1985; Veronen & Kilpatrick, 1980); child victims of physical abuse (Kazdin et al., 1985); adult survivors of childhood sexual abuse (Bagley & Ramsey, 1985; Courtois, 1979; Gold, 1986); female victims of domestic violence (Mills, 1984) and marital rape (Shields & Hanneke, 1985); other crime (Bard & Sangrey, 1986; Krupnick, 1980) and Vietnam combat (Wilson, 1980; Wilson & Krauss, 1982).

Anger

Anger, rage, and fear of one's own rage have been noted among victims of rape and incest (Kilpatrick, Resick, & Veronen, 1981; Roth & Lebowitz, 1988), injuries or personal loss (Krupnick & Horowitz, 1981), crime (Smale & Spickenheurer, 1979), domestic violence (Hil-

berman, 1980), and Vietnam combat (Egendorf, Kadushin, Laufer, Rothbart, & Sloan, 1981).

Guilt and Shame

This set of symptoms has been deleted from the DSM-III-R criteria
due to lack of empirical validation. However, within the clinical literature, these reactions have been cited among victims of rape (Burgess
& Holmstrom, 1974), childhood sexual abuse (Gelinas, 1983; Herman,
1981), other crime (Bard & Sangrey, 1986), and Vietnam combat (Glover,
1984, 1988; Shatan, 1973). For a more thorough clinical description of
issues surrounding death guilt or survivor guilt, the reader is directed
to Lifton (1988) and Glover (1988).

COGNITIVE RESPONSE PATTERNS

Perceptual disturbances and intrusive mental activity are not uncommon among trauma survivors. Reexperiencing phenomena include flashbacks, nightmares of the event, and other intrusive recollections which
leave the victim feeling as if he or she were reliving the events or
experiencing some portion of the traumatic memories. They continue
to be viewed as the hallmark of post-trauma reactions (Brett & Ostroff,
1985; Horowitz, 1986) and have been documented in the literature
among victims of all severely stressful life events. Dissociation, an
alteration of consciousness in which experiences and affects are not
integrated into memory and awareness (Putnam, 1985), is another type
of cognitive disturbance that can occur in some cases. Dissociative
symptoms, including depersonalization and derealization, have been
described most often in victims of severe child physical or sexual abuse
(Ellenson, 1985; Gelinas, 1983). Dissociation is a defense most often
associated with the development of Multiple Personality Disorder (MPD)
among survivors of extreme childhood traumas (Braun & Sachs, 1985).
A useful framework for conceptualizing the cognitive distortions among
child sexual abuse victims with MPD has recently been elaborated by
Fine (1989).

The question of whether other, more generalized, cognitive disturbances are associated with trauma has been a difficult one to answer.
Within the area of child abuse, physically abused delinquent adolescents
evidence greater cognitive deficits relative to nonabused delinquents
(Tarter, Hegedus, Winsten, & Alterman, 1984). Most recently, empirical
findings indicate that PTSD is associated with cognitive deficits, such
as impaired verbal fluency, memory, and attention, and a general decline

in intellectual functioning as compared to non-patients (Gil, Calev, Greenberg, Kugelmass, & Lerer, 1990). These deficits, however, were very similar to those found in a psychiatric comparison group. Clearly, more research is needed to understand the specific cognitive sequelae associated with specific types of trauma.

BIOLOGICAL RESPONSE PATTERNS

Physiological Hyperarousal

It is now well documented that the chronic anxiety symptoms associated with post-trauma reactions are correlated with increased autonomic nervous system arousal in a subset of Vietnam combat veterans (Blanchard, Kolb, Pellmeyer, & Gerardi, 1982; Giller, 1990; Kolb, 1984), victims of severe child abuse who develop MPD (Braun, 1983), and persons who are exposed to chronic threat, as are the residents of Three Mile Island (Davidson & Baum, 1986). The theory underlying these findings will be discussed subsequently.

Somatic Disturbances

Children who are physically abused may show evidence of injury to the central nervous system, a phenomenon that can be associated with a wide variety of neurobehavioral dysfunctions (e.g., Monane, Leichter, & Lewis, 1984). Likewise, increased generalized somatic complaints relative to non-victim controls have been noted among adult victims of child sexual abuse (Briere, 1984; Sedney & Brooks, 1984) and those who develop MPD (Bliss, 1980; Braun, 1983), female victims of domestic violence (Stark & Flitcraft, 1981), and children who live in violent homes (Hilberman & Munson, 1977-1978). Furthermore, increased health problems have been noted after exposure to some natural disasters (Melick, Logue, & Frederick, 1982) and exposure to the chemical defoliant agent orange in Vietnam (New York Times, 1987).

BEHAVIORAL RESPONSE PATTERNS

Aggressive and Antisocial Behaviors

There is evidence that some victims develop aggressive or antisocial behavior patterns, including child victims of sexual or physical abuse (Kazdin et al., 1985; Tufts New England Medical Center, 1984) and children who live in violent homes (Jaffe, Wolfe, Wilson, & Zak, 1986). In adult survivors, these patterns have been observed among some male psychiatric patients with childhood abuse histories (Carmen, Rieker, & Mills, 1984) and some Vietnam veterans who were exposed to heavy combat (Yager, Laufer, & Gallops, 1984). Finally, although the group differences did not reach statistical significance, Calvert and Hutchinson (1989) found that Vietnam vets who had engaged in heavy war combat reported higher levels of postwar violent behavior than did noncombat Vietnam veterans.

Suicidal Behaviors

Suicidal behaviors, often associated with serious depression, have been noted among a number of survivor groups. In a random community sample of over 2,000 adult women, it was found that suicide attempts were significantly more frequent among crime victims than among non-victims, and more frequent among rape victims than among victims of other crimes (Kilpatrick, Best, Veronen, Amick, Villeponteaux, & Ruff, 1985). Furthermore, victims of childhood sexual abuse (Briere, 1984; Bryer et al., 1986; Sedney & Brooks, 1984) and female victims of domestic violence (Stark & Flitcraft, 1981; Stark, 1984) frequently report histories of suicidal ideation or attempts. Finally, recent evidence suggests that Vietnam veterans were more likely to commit suicide after the war than their non-veteran cohorts (Hearst, Newman, & Hulley, 1986).

Substance Abuse

The survivor groups in which substance abuse has been found to be a significant problem are primarily those that have been exposed to prolonged trauma, including childhood sexual abuse (Briere, 1984; Peters, 1984), domestic violence (Stark & Flitcraft, 1981), and Vietnam veterans exposed to heavy combat or atrocities (Yager et al., 1984).

Impaired Social Functioning

Impaired social functioning may become manifest in a variety of ways, including social withdrawal and isolation among victims of rape (Scheppele & Bart, 1983), domestic violence (Hilberman, 1980) and other crime (Bard & Sangrey, 1986), decreased school performance and poor peer relations among child victims of physical abuse (Kazdin et al., 1985) and those living in violent homes (Jaffe et al., 1986), poor social adjustment among college women with a history of sexual abuse (Harter, Alexander, & Neimeyer, 1988), and decreased occupational achievement among Vietnam veterans (Egendorf et al., 1981).

Personality Disorders

One controversial issue in the literature is the degree to which post-trauma reactions can "mimic" or produce severe personality disturbance.

There is some suggestion that the symptoms of undisclosed incest can resemble patterns associated with borderline personality disorder (Briere, 1984), with MMPI profiles of some survivors suggesting "core personality disturbance" (Scott & Stone, 1986). Others have noted an overlap between borderline personality and MPD (Horevitz & Braun, 1984). Furthermore, an overlapping of symptoms of borderline personality disorder is also apparent in some Vietnam veterans with chronic PTSD (Scurfield, 1985).

Most recently, Herman, Perry, and van der Kolk (1989) found that significantly more subjects with borderline personality disorder reported histories of severe trauma relative to other psychiatric samples: 81% gave histories of major childhood trauma, including physical abuse (71%), sexual abuse (68%), and witnessing serious domestic violence (62%). Another important finding they report is that the borderline subjects did not report current symptoms of PTSD, suggesting that the traumatic memories had been incorporated into the entire personality. Thus, these individuals were more likely to present with disguised forms of the disorder (e.g., symbolic reenactments, disturbed affective states) and thus did not perceive a connection between early traumas and their current distress. The clinical implications of this finding are significant and will be addressed further in Chapter 7.

Most recently, Westen and his colleagues (Westen, Ludolph, Misle, Ruffins, & Block, 1990) compared 27 inpatient adolescent girls meeting criteria for borderline personality disorder with 23 inpatient controls. They found significantly higher rates of sexual abuse (52% vs. 19% of controls) and physical abuse (52% vs. 26% of controls) among those diagnosed as borderline.

INTERPERSONAL RESPONSE PATTERNS

Sexual Problems

Problems in sexual functioning have been noted among victims of sexual trauma, such as rape (Becker, Skinner, Abel, & Cichon, 1986) and adult survivors of childhood sexual abuse (Courtois, 1979; Meiselman, 1978). Precocious sexuality has been observed in child victims of sexual abuse (Mannarino & Cohen, 1986). Finally, battered women (Stark & Flitcraft, 1981) and Vietnam veterans with PTSD (Garte, 1986) have been found to evidence sexual adjustment problems.

Intimate Relationship Problems

Intimate relationship problems may be manifest in a number of ways, including decreased trust in men among female rape victims (Ellis et al., 1981) and greater marital and family problems among survivors of childhood sexual abuse (Courtois, 1979; Meiselman, 1978), battered women (Stark & Flitcraft, 1981), and Vietnam combat veterans (Carroll, Rueger, Foy, & Donahoe, 1985; Penk, Robinowitz, Roberts, Patterson, Dolan, & Atkins, 1981).

Revictimization

The issue of revictimization is an important one, particularly as clinicians often report seeing a large number of victim clients with multiple victimizations throughout the life span. There is evidence that survivors of childhood sexual abuse are more likely to be victims of a later crime or accidents (Sedney & Brooks, 1984), rape (Russell, 1986), and domestic violence (Walker, 1985).

With regard to the effects of revictimization, there is evidence that victims of rape are likely to show a higher degree of anxiety and depression if they have been victimized previously (Santiago, McCall-Perez, Gorcey, & Beigel, 1985). With regard to Vietnam veterans, there is some suggestion in the clinical literature that a history of parental neglect or abuse may be associated with increased vulnerability to PTSD in adulthood (e.g., Sudak, Martin, Corradi, & Gold, 1984). Further evidence in this area is the association between childhood sexual abuse histories and later victimization as child prostitutes (James & Meyerding, 1977).

Victim Becomes Victimizer

The question of whether victimization in early childhood is correlated with later victimizing patterns is a complex one that will not be fully addressed here. The evidence that a high percentage of rapists and child abusers report childhood abuse histories is correlational in nature and should not be viewed as a causal relation. The complex issues involved in this area of research are addressed more fully by Araji and Finkelhor (1986), Finkelhor (1986), and Gelles and Cornell (1985).

In addition to the victim groups described in this review, serious and prolonged post-trauma reactions have been described in the literature regarding prisoners of war (Tennant, Goulston, & Dent, 1986; Ursano, 1981; Ursano, Boystun, & Wheatley, 1981); Israeli combat veterans (Lerer, Bleich, Kotler, Garb, Hertzberg, & Levin, 1987); Cambodian refugees (Mollica, Wyshak, & Lavelle, 1987); Holocaust survivors (Krystal, 1968; Niederland, 1968) and their children (Danieli, 1985, 1988); Army nurse corps Vietnam veterans (Stretch, Vail, & Maloney, 1985); parents whose child was murdered (Rinear, 1988); persons exposed to the AIDS virus (Martin, 1988); accident victims (Modline, 1967); and emergency workers (Mitchell, 1985).

CURRENT THEORIES OF POST-TRAUMA REACTIONS

Psychoanalytic Schools of Thought

Freud's Three Theories of Trauma. Breuer and Freud (1895/1955) simultaneously described two distinct trauma theories in *Theories of Hysteria*. These theories have been described and critiqued by Krystal (1978). The first was the "unbearable affect theory," which focused on emotions that overwhelm the psyche and produce psychological after-effects. The second theory is described by Krystal as the "unacceptable impulse theory," which postulated that traumatic events produce a conflict between the ego and some idea presented to it. Freud (1920/1955) subsequently described psychic trauma as a process whereby the ego is overwhelmed by stimuli, resulting in a breach in the stimulus barrier. Freud (1926/1959) later reconciled these two theories of trauma by suggesting that anxiety functioned as a signal of danger and that "automatic anxiety" occurred when repression failed to protect the psyche from overwhelming affects.

In *Moses and Monotheism* (1939/1964), Freud distinguished between two major effects of trauma by focusing on the repetition compulsion. As mentioned previously, this formulation originally emerged as an attempt to explain the traumatic dreams of World War I veterans. The first effect was described as a repetition phenomena, in which the individual reexperiences or remembers the traumatic event in an attempt to master it. The second effect was described as the defensive process of avoidance, denial, or inhibition. These ideas were later incorporated into the information processing model of Horowitz (1976) and have been viewed as the hallmark of post-trauma reactions (DSM-III, American Psychiatric Association, 1980). More recently, Roth and Cohen (1986) described an approach-avoidance model of coping that focuses on the costs and benefits of each of these coping orientations. These various psychoanalytic theories are reviewed and critiqued in a paper by Brett (in press).

Krystal's Theory of Catastrophic Trauma. Henry Krystal (1978, 1984) has developed the most comprehensive psychoanalytic model of trauma and has written extensively about survivors of extreme catastrophes, such as the Nazi holocaust, from this perspective. In this model, Krystal posits a distinction between adult and childhood experiences of trauma. The crux of this distinction lies in crucial differences in emotional development, with particular focus on how individuals tolerate strong emotions. In infantile trauma, the child becomes overwhelmed or flooded with intolerable and excessive emotions. In early stages of development, emotions are primarily somatized, undifferentiated, and nonverbal. Therefore, when affect is intense and unmodulated, the child is unable to defend against this danger, resulting in a state of utter helplessness.

For most adults (Krystal, 1978), emotions become increasingly desomatized, differentiated from bodily states, and associated with language. As a result, adults can better anticipate and defend themselves in situations where they are threatened by intense emotions. In adults, traumatic experiences may initially result in uncomfortable feelings of anxiety and helplessness. However, unlike the child, they are able to anticipate the danger and respond by blocking the emotions before they become overwhelming. Thus, Krystal suggests trauma is believed to be experienced differently by adults. Krystal postulated a surrender pattern in adults, which may include behavioral paralysis, emotional blocking, and progressive cognitive constriction. This view, which focuses on adaptive failure in the face of overwhelming threat, may have particular relevance when conceptualizing post-trauma reactions to extreme and prolonged threat, such as concentration camp confinement or war combat (Brett, in press).

Lifton's Symbolization Theory of Trauma. Psychiatrist and psychohistorian R.J. Lifton has made a number of significant contributions to the understanding of traumatic stress. On the basis of studies of survivors of Hiroshima (1968), natural disasters (1976), and the Vietnam war (1973), Lifton has developed a theory of trauma based upon the person's symbolization of life experiences. This theory proposes that individuals develop images and symbolic forms of their life experience that contribute to a sense of continuity or discontinuity (Lifton, 1976). Lifton suggests that trauma disrupts these primary symbols.

In a number of works (e.g., Lifton & Olson, 1976; Lifton, 1979; Lifton, 1988) Lifton described five major manifestations of this disruption. The first of these includes the "death imprint" or vivid memories of death or destruction that are associated with death anxiety. Persons who are immersed in the death experience may feel increasingly vulnerable to further traumatization and may experience the world as unpredictable.

The second manifestation is death guilt or survival guilt in which the individual experiences guilt over surviving where others did not, resulting in a feeling that one does not deserve to be alive. Lifton (1988) suggests that the self-condemnation associated with survivor guilt is associated with the extreme helplessness during the trauma and what he calls a "failed enactment" in which one's actual survivor behaviors are discrepant with one's ideal survivor behaviors (e.g., preventing the trauma or heroically saving other victims).

The third manifestation is psychic numbing or the loss of ability to feel. Psychic numbing is believed to be a defense against the immediate trauma but may continue as a defense against death anxiety and death guilt.

The fourth manifestation of this disruption is impaired human relationships resulting from a sense of disconnectedness from other human beings. In *The Broken Connection*, Lifton (1979) describes the profound effects of this disruption in human relatedness.

Finally, the fifth category includes the need for transformation and reanimation of these symbols as individuals find new meaning and significance in their lives. Lifton views the ability to derive meaning from the traumatic experience as the ultimate transformation of these disrupted life symbols. With regard to this process he writes:

> And here we come to the survivor's overall task, that of formulation, evolving new inner forms that include the traumatic event, which in turn requires that one find meaning or significance. Formulation requires establishing a lifeline on a new basis. That basis includes proximate and ultimate involvements. The survivor seeks vitality both in immediate relationships and ultimate meaning, the one impossible without the other. (Lifton, 1988, p. 26)

Self Psychological Theories. Within the psychoanalytic tradition, a self psychology perspective of PTSD has emerged, reflecting some of the ideas of Kohut (1971, 1977). Kohut originally asserted that repeated empathetic failures by self-objects (persons who are an extension of the self, such as early parental figures) are at the root of all severe psychopathology. Self psychologists believe that a cohesive and stable self concept results from positive "mirroring," in which the self-object reflects or mirrors back to the child a sense of self worth. As the self structures become increasingly mature and differentiated, the person becomes less dependent upon self-objects to supply these basic needs.

Although Kohut, like many psychoanalytic thinkers, focused primarily on the assaults to the self that occur in childhood, some theorists within the field of traumatic stress have suggested that a self psychology perspective is relevant to understanding the self pathology that is sometimes associated with extreme trauma. This view was originally described in relation to Vietnam veterans (Brende, 1983; Brende & McCann, 1984; Brende & Parson, 1985; Fox, 1974; Parson, 1984; 1988) and more recently with regard to survivors of other trauma, including rape and incest (Ulman & Brothers, 1988). Brende and Parson, in their collaborative and separate works, suggest that extreme trauma produces self-fragmentation and severe self pathology, which is at the core of chronic PTSD. For example, the trauma of combat and the homecoming is believed to have produced a narcissistic wound in some Vietnam veterans, who are subsequently vulnerable to further narcissistic injury and narcissistic rage (Brende & Parson, 1985; Parson, 1984; Ulman & Brothers, 1988). Likewise, the loss of combat buddies during the war has been conceptualized as a loss of a mirror relationship, resulting in narcissistic injury and narcissistic rage (Fox, 1974).

Self-psychology theory holds that narcissistic rage is a disintegration byproduct of a severe disruption in self-object relations. Furthermore, this injury to the self is believed to result in splits in the self-concept or basic identity, as represented by an omnipotent, grandiose self split which defends against a hidden victim self introject (Brende, 1983). In a similar vein, Hymer (1984) writes about self splits among crime victims in which the unconscious, vulnerable self is split off from the conscious, invulnerable self. This self fragmentation is associated with such dissociative states as flashbacks, depersonalization, and derealization.

The distinction between these states and those experienced in narcissistic character disorder is still somewhat unclear. Some theorists hold to the view that persons are more vulnerable to PTSD when the preexisting self-structure and self-object relations are less well-developed (e.g., Moses, 1978). Others hold that severe trauma can disrupt the self even without a preexisting vulnerability (e.g., Bard & Sangrey, 1986; Parson, 1984; Ulman & Brothers, 1988). In Chapter 7, we elaborate our own views on the relevance of self psychology concepts to understanding unique post-trauma reactions.

Cognitive Theories

Horowitz's Information Processing Model. Mardi Horowitz (1975, 1976, 1979), a pioneer in the area of stress response syndromes, has attempted to explain PTSD within a cognitive theory of information processing. The emphasis in this model is on the impact of trauma on cognitive schemas and the role of control (defenses) in regulating the processing of information. The three basic propositions of this theory are as follows:

> 1) Active memory storage has an intrinsic tendency toward repeated representation of its contents, 2) This tendency will continue indefinitely until the storage of the particular contents in active memory is terminated, and 3) Termination of contents in active memory occurs when cognitive processing has been completed. In effect, then, active memory contents would follow an automatic completion tendency. (Horowitz, 1975, pp. 1461-1462)

In essence, this theory proposes that until the traumatic event can be integrated into existing cognitive schemas, the psychological representations of the event are stored in active memory, which has an intrinsic property of repeated representation. Repetitive phenomena include intrusive thoughts and images about the trauma that are accompanied by waves of intense, uncomfortable emotions. Denial and emotional numbing often follow these states, serving as a defense against becoming emotionally overwhelmed. Horowitz (1974) writes:

> After these first emotional reactions and physical responses, there may be a period of comparative denial and numbing. Then an oscillatory period commonly emerges in which there are periods of intrusive ideas or images, attacks of emotions, or compulsive behavior alternating with continued denial, numbing or other indications of efforts to ward off the implications of this new information. Finally, a phase of working through may occur in which there are less intrusive thoughts, less uncontrolled attacks of emotion with greater recognition, conceptualization, stability of mood, and acceptance of the meaning of the event. (p. 769)

The typical phases of response following a trauma are thus believed to include outcry, oscillations of intrusion and denial, transition, and integration (Horowitz, 1979). In this model, Horowitz has elaborated on Freud's (1939/1964) repetition compulsion model and extended this work to include contemporary cognitive models of stress and coping (Lazarus, 1966).

The Shattering of the Assumptive World. In recent years, a number of researchers have discussed how victimizing life events can disrupt or alter an individual's basic assumptions about self and world (Epstein, 1985, in press b; Janoff-Bulman, 1985; Janoff-Bulman & Frieze, 1983; Roth & Lebowitz, 1988; Roth, 1989). The underlying premise of Janoff-

Bulman's work has been derived from Epstein's (1985) cognitive-experiential self-theory which "assumes that the essence of a person's personality is the implicit theory of self and world that the person constructs" (p. 283). Within this theoretical tradition, Janoff-Bulman (1985) has focused on three major assumptions that are disrupted by trauma: the belief in personal invulnerability, the perception of the world as meaningful, and the perception of the self as positive. In more recent work, she has found empirical evidence that victims are more likely than non-victims to view the interpersonal world as malevolent, the self as unworthy, and the world as random (Janoff-Bulman, 1989a). The "illusion of invulnerability" (Perloff, 1983) has been described as a basic assumption that allows individuals to underestimate the likelihood of experiencing misfortune. As Janoff-Bulman and others have pointed out, this illusion can be adaptive to the extent that it protects an individual from anxiety about future life events and maladaptive to the extent that it prevents the individual from behaving in appropriately self-protective ways.

Epstein (in press a), in an elegant formulation of traumatic stress reactions, describes the disruption of self and world assumptions in trauma, including

> the degree to which the world is regarded as benign versus malevolent, the degree to which it is regarded as meaningful (including predictable, controllable, and just), the degree to which others are regarded favorably rather than a source of threat, and the degree to which the self is regarded as worthy. (p. 2)

Epstein postulates that the disruption of these schemas or conceptual systems has a destabilizing effect on the entire personality, producing a state of disequilibrium characterized by symptoms of PTSD. He suggests that in order to reestablish equilibrium, the individual must develop a modified theory of reality that can assimilate the trauma.

Most recently, the parallels between theories derived from social cognition research, such as the ones described above, and object relations theory have been elaborated by Westen (1989). The parallels between these theories and our own were described in Chapter 2.

Biological and Behavioral Models

Biological Theories. As previously noted, a biological conceptualization of PTSD has a long history, dating back to Freud (1920/1953) and Kardiner and Spiegel's (1947) conceptions about war neurosis. In recent years, Kolb (1983, 1984, 1988), building upon the earlier work of Dobbs and Wilson (1960), has described a subgroup of Vietnam veterans with chronic and delayed PTSD who exhibit a conditioned emotional response to combat stimuli. In support of this model, Kolb and his colleagues have demonstrated that emotional responses of fear become conditioned to stimuli associated with the traumatic event. For example, Vietnam veterans were found to exhibit high levels of physiological arousal when exposed to combat sounds, such as a helicopter taking off. This conditioned emotional response continues to be elicited by conditioned stimuli and by the presence of emotions similar to those of the conditioned emotional response.

In a similar vein, van der Kolk (1988) has advanced a model of trauma that hypothesizes biological alterations in response to trauma. This model is based upon the animal model of inescapable shock (IS) and presumes that IS produces a massive secretion of a variety of neurotransmitters followed by depletion of these neurotransmitters. This is believed to result in receptor hypersensitivity that is then associated with biological overresponsiveness to a variety of trauma-related stimuli. This biological disruption is believed to be correlated with certain symptoms of PTSD, such as intrusive reexperiencing, nightmares, flashbacks, addiction to trauma, dissociative episodes, and other clinical phenomena. We direct the reader to van der Kolk's work for a description of the specific biochemical underpinnings of these response patterns.

Behavioral Theories. Behavioral theories are based upon both classical conditioning paradigms and two-factor learning theory. Learning theory has been used to explain the persistence of symptoms of anxiety, avoidance, and biological hyperarousal associated with PTSD. According to classical conditioning theory, the experience of threat is an unconditioned stimulus (UCS) that evokes the unconditioned response of anxiety and fear (UCR). Previously neutral stimuli which become associated with the UCS (threat condition) become conditioned stimuli (CS) and acquire the capacity to produce conditioned responses (CR). This model presumes that the conditioned fear response is directly linked to the particular circumstances surrounding the traumatic event, with stimulus generalization occurring over time. Consistent with instrumental learning theories, persons learn to avoid cues that evoke the conditioned fear response. Gradually, the avoidant behaviors that develop in response to conditioned stimuli are negatively reinforced by a reduction in anxiety, thus making this pattern very resistant to extinction.

Recent evidence suggests that persons who avoid opportunities for extinction are likely to experience more severe long-term distress (Wirtz & Harrell, 1987). This two-factor learning theory has been most widely discussed in relation to Vietnam veterans (Keane, Zimering, & Caddell, 1985) and rape victims (Kilpatrick, Veronen, & Resick, 1982). This position has been supported in the longitudinal research on long-term reactions to rape. Kilpatrick, Veronen, and Resick (1979) initially asserted that fear and anxiety responses persist in some victims because they are classically conditioned by the rape experience. This model has found empirical support from a number of studies. For example, in one study, the most highly feared stimuli initially after the rape were rape cues (e.g., knives, genitals) and attack vulnerability cues (e.g., being alone, darkness) (Calhoun, Atkeson, & Resick, 1982). Furthermore, there was evidence that over time, these fears tended to generalize to stimuli that became associated with the original trauma. In a study of children who had experienced a lightening strike disaster in which one child was killed, there was evidence that fear reactions tended to overgeneralize to trauma-related stimuli, such as sleep, noise, and storms (Dollinger, O'Donnell, & Staley, 1984).

Overall, the behavioral and biological theories provide a model for understanding a subset of post-trauma symptoms with the added benefit of delineating systematic treatment interventions targeted at reducing anxiety and avoidant patterns. These treatment paradigms will be reviewed in Chapter 12.

Learned Helplessness. A learned helplessness paradigm has often been used as a way of conceptualizing post-trauma reactions which include chronic depression, passivity, and futility. Walker (1977–1978) was one of the first to propose this paradigm to explain the behavior of battered women. Seligman (1975) originally hypothesized that learned helplessness results when people believe or expect their responses will not influence the future probability of environmental outcomes. According to Seligman, this process

> reduces the motivation to control the outcome, interferes with learning that responding controls the outcomes, produces fear for as long as the subject is uncertain of the uncontrollability of the outcome, and then produces depression. (p. 56)

Subsequently, the reformulated attributional theory of learned helplessness hypothesized that mere exposure to an uncontrollable event is not sufficient to produce helplessness (Abramson, Seligman, & Teasdale,

1978). Rather, it is the expectation of uncontrollability of future outcomes that results in learned helplessness. This is consistent with predictions from social learning theory (Rotter, 1954).

Within the area of victimization, Peterson and Seligman (1983) have agreed that a learned helplessness paradigm may be useful in understanding certain reactions to victimization, especially those involving depression and passivity, while other psychological theories may have more utility for explaining other response patterns. Furthermore, they warn against overgeneralizing those findings from controlled laboratory experiments to natural settings. In summary, while this theory may be useful for conceptualizing some victim responses, it is not a comprehensive enough model to account for the variability in victim responses across a variety of traumatic situations.

PARALLELS BETWEEN CONSTRUCTIVIST SELF DEVELOPMENT THEORY AND OTHER THEORIES

This brief review of the various theories of post-trauma reactions describes the wide range of conceptualizations that have been offered to account for the complex phenomena associated with post-trauma reactions. Each theory or model helps explain different aspects of these reactions, with some models, such as the behavioral and biological ones, generating clearly defined treatment paradigms and others providing more general frameworks for conceptualizing the phenomena. We do not intend to critique these various theories in any depth. Rather, we present these theories as a context for understanding the roots of constructivist self development theory.

Essentially, CSDT is a bridge theory which integrates clinical insights from object relations theory and self psychology, and research in social cognition. The cognitive portion of our theory parallels the trauma theories of Epstein (in press a), Janoff-Bulman (1985, 1989a), Horowitz (1986), and Roth (1989). We extend their work by describing both distinct and overlapping core schemas that we believe are most fundamental to the trauma survivor. Although we find these models to be quite valuable, our own list of central need areas that are disrupted has held heuristic value for us in our own clinical work.

One issue our theory addresses is the variability in victims' schema changes resulting from trauma, an area that Janoff-Bulman (1989a) acknowledges is poorly understood. Our theory brings in the notion of psychological needs as forming the basis for core schemas about self and world. In essence, we propose that disruptions in schemas are most disturbing to individuals when they occur in need areas that are most central to them. While Epstein's (1985, in press a) model takes into account the important relationship between needs and schemas, the role of needs is not central in his formulations.

In addition, we address the issue of the inner life of the individual, including affect regulation and other capacities of a cohesive and stable self. These concepts, drawn primarily from a self psychology perspective, parallel the self psychology focus of Parson (1984, 1988) and Brende and Parson (1985). In utilizing these concepts, we have attempted to define ego resources and self capacities in a way that provides a common language for researchers and clinicians, and particularly those without a background in self psychology. The bridge we have made across self psychology, object relations, and social cognition research serves to integrate concepts from diverse traditions in ways that are clinically meaningful.

Although our theory does not focus exclusively on the characteristics of the stressor, we are mindful of the shared meanings of certain traumas. We also wanted to include in our work a greater focus on the meanings of the social and cultural context, an area that has yet to be fully developed in the trauma literature.

Our theory also addresses the ongoing debate regarding the centrality of imagery or avoidance in post-trauma syndromes. The centrality of imagery is most common in certain psychoanalytic formulations, including Horowitz's (1986) work while avoidance patterns are given greater importance in classical conditioning models (e.g., Keane, Zimering, & Caddell, 1985). Although we lean toward the models that view traumatic imagery as a hallmark of trauma, we also attempt to account for patterns in which avoidance predominates. In this way, our theory closely matches that of Roth and Cohen (1986) in their individual differences perspective on approach-avoidance coping styles.

We believe our theory presents a coherent and clinically useful way of conceptualizing individual differences in responses to trauma. We address this issue below.

INDIVIDUAL DIFFERENCES IN ADAPTATION TO TRAUMA

We attempt to integrate diverse theories and concepts in such a way as to provide a heuristic model that focuses on individual differences for purposes of assessment and intervention.

Addressing individual differences in any theory of human adaptation is a complex issue that theorists have struggled with for many years (e.g., Adler, 1927; Allport, 1946, 1962; Underwood, 1975). In describing the two approaches to understanding human behavior, Allport (1946) borrowed the terms idiographic to describe a focus on what is distinctive and unique about the individual and nomothetic to describe a focus on universal, general laws of behavior. He believed that there was a place for both research traditions in psychology, but argued in favor of more emphasis on the idiographic methods as better means to predict and understand individual behavior. Although a number of creative methods of systematically studying whole persons have emerged (e.g., Shontz, 1965; Shontz & Rosenack, 1985), psychology as a whole has continued to favor the nomothetic tradition. Within the field of traumatic stress, there is a growing trend toward understanding individual differences in human adaptation to trauma.

In her work on children of Holocaust survivors, Danieli (1985) writes:

> the heterogeneity of responses to the Holocaust and to the post-Holocaust life experiences in families of survivors-implied here in the proposed taxonomy-is in part, intended to guard mental health professionals against the grouping of individuals as "survivors," all of whom are expected to exhibit a single "survivor syndrome." (p. 297)

We strongly agree with Danieli's statement regarding the importance of avoiding the tendency to view all trauma survivors as suffering from a similar syndrome. While it is indeed valuable, especially in the early evolution of a field of study, to develop broad frameworks for understanding the features that distinguish PTSD from other syndromes, it is equally important to develop theories that integrate these general laws with an understanding of and respect for individual differences and uniqueness among whole persons. There is a very positive trend in the field toward developing taxonomies that integrate both traditions (e.g., Green, Wilson, & Lindy, 1985). Constructivist self development theory is an attempt to bridge these diverse traditions by building upon previous works to formulate new ways of understanding individual variations in adaptation to trauma.

4. The Disruption of Psychological Needs and Related Cognitive Schemas

The adversities to which we are accustomed do not disturb us.
Claudian
In *Eutropian*, BK ii, 1.149
(Source: Stevenson, 1964)

SCHEMAS AND BEHAVIOR

A basic tenet of constructivist self development theory, drawn largely from developmental social cognition theories, is that complex cognitive representations of self and others underlie much of an individual's interpersonal behavior. In recent years, a connection has been made between social cognition theories and object relations theory (see Westen, 1989, for a comprehensive review of the relation between these two theoretical and research traditions). Westen describes the commonalities as follows:

> both are interested in the way mental representations of the self and other people (whether called "object relations" or "person schemas") are constructed and encoded, in the cognitive and affective processes brought to bear on these representations, and in the way these psychological processes mediate behavior. (p. 15)

The construct "schema" underlies the social cognition tradition, a construct that is largely derived from Piaget's cognitive developmental theory (1971). According to Piaget, human beings develop increasingly complex cognitive structures over their life span. These cognitive structures consist of schemas, which Piaget described as basic structures of action that form a pattern for experience. In recent years, schemas have been broadly defined as assumptions, beliefs, and expectations about self and world. Segal's (1988) definition of schemas is that they

> consist of organized elements of past reactions and experience that form a relatively cohesive and persistent body of knowledge capable of guiding subsequent perception and appraisals. (p. 147)

57

consist of organized elements of past reactions and experience that
form a relatively cohesive and persistent body of knowledge capable of guiding subsequent perception and appraisals. (p. 147)

Janoff-Bulman, who has written extensively about the disruption of
one's most fundamental schemas about self and world resulting from
trauma, defines schemas as

. . . an abstracted knowledge structure, stored in memory, that
involves a rich network of information about a given stimulus
domain. Schemas serve as preexisting theories that provide a basis
for anticipating the future and guide what we notice and remember,
as well as how we interpret new information. (1989a, p. 115)

Thus, schemas enable individuals to organize their life experiences
in ways that help them comprehend their world. This framework has
much in common with Rotter's (1954) social learning theory. Within
this theory, Rotter describes as a central construct "expectancies," which
include the expectations persons hold about their behavior and the
behavior of others. We consider these expectations to be a specific type
of schema. According to Rotter (1954), the individual's behavior is a
result of his or her expectancies for various outcomes and the importance
or value he or she places on the expected outcomes, in the context of
the psychological situation, or meaningful environment. Constructivist
self development theory focuses on those schemas that relate to psychological need areas. We view these schemas as the cognitive manifestations of psychological needs. Life experiences with both gratification
and frustration of needs shape the individual's beliefs, assumptions,
and expectations in relation to those needs. See Figure 1 (p. x) for a
depiction of the relation among schemas, life experiences, and psychological adaptation.

In his biosocial theory of personality, Gardner Murphy (1947) spoke
about the channelization of needs, a process whereby specific needs
become increasingly differentiated and individualized. This process takes
place throughout the individual's life as needs are channeled toward
certain objects, people, or experiences within one's meaningful environment. Murphy and Rotter believe that needs become increasingly
differentiated and unique over the life span. Rotter proposed that
expectancies (or schemas) related to these (and other) needs become
increasingly specific and individualized. These views form fundamental
assumptions underlying constructivist self development theory.

Individuals develop schemas related to all of their life experiences;
the schemas we focus on have particular relevance to understanding

the trauma survivor. An earlier version of this part of the theory is presented elsewhere (McCann, Pearlman, Sakheim, & Abrahamson, 1988; McCann, Sakheim, & Abrahamson, 1988).

The following major assumptions underlie this portion of the theory.

1. Individuals develop schemas that include beliefs, assumptions, and expectations in fundamental need areas. These schemas are the cognitive manifestation of psychological needs that are affectively laden. Most often, schemas operate at an unconscious or preconscious level of awareness. They develop as a result of one's life experiences, within a meaningful social and cultural context.

2. Schemas develop within the core areas of frame of reference, safety, trust/dependency, independence, power, esteem, and intimacy. They develop in relation to oneself and others. We consider the need for a meaningful frame of reference to be a broader need than the other six. Schemas related to this need, which include attributions about causality of events and one's general orientation to the future, will have a more generalized effect than other schemas upon one's psychological experience.

3. Over time, these schemas become increasingly unique to the individual, and may be generalized across life experiences or specific to certain situations or contexts. This concept is equivalent to Rotter's (1954) notions about generalized versus specific expectancies. The most general schemas for experience are likely to be most resistant to change (Epstein, 1985, in press b).

4. Individuals may develop positive or negative schemas within these areas. Various feelings, thoughts, and behaviors are associated with these schemas.

5. Just as life experiences shape or reinforce the development of positive or negative schemas, so too can these schemas be disrupted by life experiences that are discrepant with them. In the ordinary course of one's life, new information about the self and the world is assimilated into one's existing schemas. When a situation occurs that cannot be "fit" into existing schemas, an accommodation or change in schemas occurs. If the discrepancy between one's existing schemas and life experiences is extreme and perceived as threatening, the event is psychologically shocking. If this discrepancy occurs within a need area that is central to the individual, the event will be experienced as traumatic.

6. Individuals often seek out experiences that confirm their schemas, even if these experiences confirm schemas that others
might view as negative. Individuals may seek confirmatory
experiences because it is the only way they can make sense of
life experiences or because they believe it can protect them
from disappointment or retraumatization. In this way, schemas
can also shape one's interaction with others and the world.

These propositions are consistent with the cognitive work of Julian
Rotter (social learning theory; 1954), George Kelly (personal construct
theory; 1955), Aaron Beck (cognitive theory of depression; 1967), Jean
Piaget (structural theory; 1970, 1971), James Mancuso, whose motivational theory (1977) synthesizes the work of Kelly and Piaget, Seymour
Epstein (cognitive-experiential self-theory; 1985), and Michael Mahoney
(cognitive constructivism; 1981; Mahoney & Lyddon, 1988). These theories all focus on the individual actively making sense of life experiences
through the development of complex cognitive structures (which Piaget
and Beck have called schemas); these schemas enable individuals to
organize, interpret, and respond to life experiences.

According to Mancuso (1977), individuals select, interpret, and assimilate information from new life experiences in a way that provides
the best fit with their cognitive structures by maintaining affective arousal
at a moderate level. This view is consistent with the converging evidence
that schemas influence what individuals attend to and how they assimilate information. For instance, the research reveals that individuals
whose self schemas are negative ignore positive information and remember more negative information about themselves (e.g., Greenwald,
1987). In essence, schemas create biases in how information is perceived,
classified, or stored (e.g., Goldfried & Robins, 1983). The optimist with
rose-colored glasses will be likely to organize, interpret, and respond
to life experiences as if they were positive and life-affirming, while the
pessimist who wears dark shades will resist viewing similar events in
a positive or hopeful way. Although people don't always behave in
ways that are consistent with their attitudes (Ajzen & Fishbein, 1977),
there is evidence that individuals do often seek confirmation of their
beliefs and expectancies.

The previous discussion is meant to provide a context for understanding both the impact of trauma on one's schemas and the way
schemas color individuals' experience and interpretations of traumatic
life events. The assumption that trauma disrupts schemas is integral to
our understanding of the traumatic experience. A similar view has been

taken by Janoff-Bulman (1985), who proposed that trauma disrupts an individual's three basic assumptions about self and the world. These assumptions include the view of oneself in a favorable light; the belief in personal invulnerability; and the belief in a meaningful, orderly world. Most recently, Janoff-Bulman (1989a) described these assumptions as follows: benevolence of the world, meaningfulness of the world, and worthiness of self. She describes these schemas as higher order conceptual systems or postulates that are most fundamental and pervasive. In the ordinary course of life, it is the lower order schemas (e.g., I am a good athlete) that change while in trauma the higher order schemas (e.g., I am a good person) are disrupted, an experience that has profound emotional and interpersonal effects. In line with our own thinking, Epstein (in press, a), Fine (1988), Horowitz (1979), Janoff-Bulman (1985), and Roth and Lebowitz (1988) have described this disruption in schemas about self and world as one of the hallmarks of trauma. Similarly, Lifton (1976) discussed trauma as disrupting one's primary life symbols, including symbols of life and death.

In a recent validity study of the World Assumptions Scale, Janoff-Bulman (1989a) found that three factors discriminated victims from nonvictims: relative to nonvictims, victims tended to view themselves less positively, believe that chance or randomness accounts for unfortunate outcomes, and view the interpersonal world as less benevolent. Finally, Taylor and Brown (1988) have reviewed the literature affirming the value of illusions in the maintenance of positive mental health. In this review, they cite evidence that illusions are associated with the ability to be happy and to engage in productive or creative work. This is believed to have such an effect because the illusions provide a filter through which individuals can "distort" information in a positive direction. The concept of illusions has much in common with our concept of schemas.

We extend this work to focus on schemas that are closely tied to central human needs, including one's overall frame of reference. In essence, we propose that trauma disrupts one's central needs and alters, disrupts, or disconfirms one's beliefs, assumptions, and expectations in those central need areas. For some, this disruption is equivalent to driving on unknown roads without a map and perhaps without control over the steering.

While it is certainly not universally true, it is also possible for trauma to result in a positive restructuring of schemas. Janoff-Bulman (1989a) makes the observation that there is significant variability in victims' schemas after a trauma. For some, the enduring schemas are pervasive, generalized, and negative. For others, it is possible to regain a more positive view of self and the world, along with an awareness of the limitations of these assumptions.

We believe that one explanation for these individual differences is the degree to which emotionally significant schemas are altered by the experience. Janoff-Bulman (1989a) cites research suggesting that emotionally significant schemas are more accessible than more neutral schemas. We believe that emotionally significant schemas are those that reflect central needs prior to the victimization. For example, if needs for recognition and esteem from others is particularly important for an individual, schemas related to self-esteem are more likely to be emotionally significant and thus more vulnerable to disruption. In this sense, our theory extends the previous thinking by proposing a new way to understand individual differences in response to trauma. In this chapter and subsequent ones, we provide clinical material in support of these hypotheses.

In the following sections, we review the importance of these schemas and describe their relevance to the trauma experience.

DISTURBED SCHEMAS RELATED TO CENTRAL NEEDS

Frame of Reference

Frame of reference is the supraordinate need within constructivist self development theory. This concept is comparable to Janoff-Bulman's (1989a) and Epstein's (in press b) schemas related to a meaningful (just, predictable, and controllable) world. By definition, a traumatic experience affects one's frame of reference. Frame of reference includes perspective, meaning, and other overarching constructs. Within the area of trauma, we consider the especially important aspects of frame of reference to include one's frameworks for interpreting experience (or schemas), including customary ways of making sense of events (causality), orientation toward the future (hope), and usual source of reinforcement (locus of control). While these may vary somewhat within persons across situations, we posit that most individuals exhibit reasonable stability in each of these areas, and, further, that traumatic experiences will affect all of them, leading, through processes of assimilation and accommodation, to changes in frame of reference. The extent (in both the sense of breadth and longevity of effect) to which frame of reference schemas are altered by trauma is determined by several factors, including previous trauma history, post-trauma recovery environment, and immediacy of psychotherapeutic intervention.

We focus here primarily on the disruptive or negative effects of trauma upon frame of reference. However, for some individuals, a traumatic experience can lead to a reappraisal of priorities and values which may result in positive life changes. A near miss with death often has the effect of forcing an evaluation of how one spends one's time, and can transform persons in positive ways. A woman whose family was almost hit by a train while driving together in a car reported that the family subsequently examined their commitments and priorities and realized the importance of their relationships with one another; she described it as an "existential transformation." These individuals are less likely to come to treatment than those for whom the impact of trauma is primarily negative.

In the following sections we discuss specific disruptions to one's frame of reference.

Attributions of Causality

> He was ill a long time. But it was not the horrors of prison life, not the hard labour, the bad food, the shaven head, or the patched clothes that crushed him . . . It was wounded pride that made him ill. Oh, how happy he would have been if he could have blamed himself! He could have borne anything then, even shame and disgrace. But he judged himself severely, and his exasperated conscience found no particularly terrible fault in his past, except a simple blunder which might happen to anyone. He was ashamed just because he, Raskolnikov, had so hopelessly, stupidly come to grief through some decree of blind fate. . . . (Fyodor Dostoyevsky, 1944, *Crime and Punishment*, pp. 524–525)

The search for meaning in one's experiences has been widely discussed in the trauma literature (e.g., Frankl, 1963). One fundamental question that victimized persons ask is "Why did this happen to me?" (Figley, 1983; Janoff-Bulman, 1985). The search for causality is thought to relate to the strong human need to believe in an orderly, predictable universe in which events happen for a reason. There is evidence that victims of sexual trauma often blame themselves and that this is associated with feelings of guilt, shame, and rage at themselves (Roth & Lebowitz, 1988). The just world hypothesis (Lerner & Miller, 1978) states that individuals need to believe in a just world in which people get what they deserve and deserve what they get.

In recent years, the coping literature has focused on the attributional correlates of coping among victims of misfortune as researchers discovered that many victims ask themselves "Why did this happen to me?" Janoff-Bulman (1979) originally distinguished between character-ological self-blame (where the person blames a non-modifiable aspect of his or her character) and behavioral self-blame (where the person blames some modifiable aspect of his or her behavior) and suggested that behavioral self-blame was associated with higher self-esteem and perceptions of future avoidability of victimization, a more adaptive strategy because it enhanced beliefs about personal control. Miller and Porter (1983) distinguish among types of self-blame observed in victims of violence: blame for causing the violence, blame for not being able to modify the violence, and blame for tolerating the violence. As the research in this area becomes more sophisticated, various types of self-blame and their adaptive significance in different types of trauma will become clearer.

Clinically, one observes many people struggling with this question, trying out different alternatives, and seeking a resolution. For many, answers to this question never emerge. For some, putting aside the question and acknowledging the randomness of human tragedy are acceptable. For others, the search for causality may become an obsession that haunts and torments them. In our experience, sole survivors of death missions in Vietnam are often obsessed with this question, a phenomenon that has been linked to survival guilt (Lifton, 1976) and self-punishing behaviors (Glover, 1988). There is some evidence in the literature that unsuccessfully searching for meaning may be associated with less adaptive functioning than giving up the search (Silver, Boon, & Stones, 1983).

Hope

> Life as we know it has ended, and yet no one is able to grasp what has taken its place. . . . All around you one change follows another, each day produces a new upheaval, the old assumptions are so much air and emptiness. That is the dilemma. On the one hand, you want to survive, to adapt, to make the best of things as they are. But, on the other hand, to accomplish this seems to entail killing off all those things that once made you think of yourself as human. Do you see what I am trying to say? In order to live, you must make yourself die. That is why so many people have given up. For no matter how hard they struggle, they know they are bound to lose. And at that point it is surely a pointless thing to struggle at all. (Paul Auster, 1987, *In the Country of Last Things*, p. 20)

We believe that schemas concerning hope are tied to all the other schemas. Mahoney (1981) defines hope as "a generalized expectation of or trust in the satisfactory value of future experience" (p. 111). Pruyser (1987), following the French existentialist Gabriel Marcel, prefers the term "hoping," in order to emphasize the process nature of the construct. Pruyser's more literary definition includes the notion that hoping "is a response to felt tragedy, and is the positive outgrowth of a tragic sense of life" (1987, p. 465). He goes on to state that hoping "allows a person in distress to assume . . . that some benevolence is active somewhere" (p. 470).

Disturbed generalized schemas in a number of need areas are likely to be accompanied by a profound loss of hope, associated with a painful state of demoralization, depression, and pessimism. Within the trauma literature, there is some evidence that child survivors may become more pessimistic about the future, manifested in such phenomena as a foreshortened sense of future (e.g., Kazdin, Moser, Colbus, & Bell, 1985; Terr, 1983a, 1983b).

Trauma survivors who enter therapy are likely to have some hope for something better or they would not come to therapy. Yet the difficulties that accompany the adaptation to trauma, including the painful accommodation to a new reality, can result in a loss of hope, even in the most optimistic persons. A major component in frame of reference, hope must be instilled in therapy in order for progress to be made in building positive schemas in other areas. An accurate assessment of the client's ongoing ability to sustain a hopeful attitude toward the future and appropriate interventions to restore hope are essential to progress in other areas.

Locus of Control. Rotter (1966) originally defined locus of control as the individual's belief that reinforcement comes from internal or external sources. Since that time, locus of control has become one of the most widely used (and misused) psychological constructs (Rotter, 1975). Its importance to trauma is this: One common outcome for a trauma survivor is to move from looking to external sources for positive reinforcement (e.g., with respect to intimacy schemas, believing that his main happiness comes from relationships with others) to looking to internal sources (e.g., believing that meaningful connection with others is impossible). Conversely, a highly internal individual who experiences a trauma may move from an internal locus of control (e.g., with respect to safety schemas, believing she can make herself happy by keeping herself safe) to an external orientation (e.g., believing she is unable to protect herself and only others can ensure her safety and happiness). What separates locus of control from the six other, specific need areas is its generalized scope: A traumatic experience may shift one's schemas in several need areas from a more internal to a more external focus (or vice versa).

Safety

> *Caligula:* Then why wish to kill me? *Cherea:* I've told you why; because I regard you as noxious, a constant menace. I like, and need, to feel secure. So do most men. They resent living in a world where the most preposterous fancy may at any moment become a reality, and the absurd transfix their lives, like a dagger in the heart. I feel as they do; I refuse to live in a topsy turvy world. I want to know where I stand and to stand secure. (Camus, 1958, *Caligula*, p. 51)

This brief excerpt from Camus's *Caligula* underscores the centrality of safety or security needs to human beings, a theme that has been discussed by numerous personality theorists (e.g., Maslow, 1970; Sullivan, 1940). The belief in safety or invulnerability from harm is clearly a central illusion about the world (Janoff-Bulman, 1985). The illusion of safety is central to maintaining a positive attitude toward future life experiences and preventing crippling anxiety and phobic avoidance. If one were to focus on all the inherent dangers of the world, expecting the worst, one would be unable to function or to take risks that are essential to life and growth. The "frozen fear" or paralysis that has been described in the trauma literature (e.g., Symonds, 1975, 1976) is an outcome of the shattering of this basic sense of security. The illusion of safety allows individuals to feel capable of protecting themselves from danger and harm in a world that is potentially dangerous and unpredictable.

Within the trauma situation, a victim of some sudden, unexpected life disruption, be it a rape, other crime, or environmental disaster, must come to terms with two harsh realities of life: that the world and other people are sometimes dangerous and threatening, and that regardless of the precautions one takes, one cannot always protect oneself against harm. The rape literature suggests that women who are raped are likely to have their perceptions of safety radically altered in contrast to women who avoided rape and that a more radical change in safety schemas is likely if the woman was assaulted in a situation she had previously defined as safe (Scheppele & Bart, 1983). The findings from this study suggest that safety schemas are more likely to be shattered if the individual held illusions of safety prior to the assault. In another study of parents who experienced the murder of a child, Rinear (1988) found that one-fourth feared for their own safety and almost one-half feared for the safety of their children, which was interpreted as indicating a destruction of assumptions about personal invulnerability.

Many people develop "rules of safety" that provide them with a sense of comfort and security. Depending upon how strong this need is for the individual, the rules of safety may be rigid or flexible. To some degree, these rules of safety may be regarded as illusory in that they are ultimately fragile. However, the positive value they hold for many individuals cannot be disputed. Consider for example the case of Lee, a burglary and crime victim for whom security had always been a central concern.

> This young mother of two had always been mindful of the need to take precautions against harm to her family. On the summer evening when the traumatic event took place, Lee discussed with her husband whether it was safe to leave a window slightly open to cool the house that had been sweltering in 90-degree heat. After debating the issue, they opted to leave the window slightly ajar, inadvertently providing the opening for a break-in, resulting in their being robbed and raped in the middle of the night. Not surprisingly, Lee was severely traumatized by the experience, as her need for safety had been violated, and she blamed herself for violating her own rules of safety. Her husband, for whom security was less central, appeared to recover rapidly when the couple installed an alarm system in their home. Lee, on the other hand, continued to be plagued by tremendous anxiety and acute symptoms of distress. Even with the alarm system in place, she feared that the system would be faulty or that the burglars would become angry when the alarm went off, killing the family in fear and anger. (This case is described in more depth in Chapter 14.)

This case vignette underscores both the potential impact of trauma on safety schemas and the importance of previous safety schemas and security needs in shaping an individual's unique response to trauma. In those cases where safety schemas are badly shaken, one might expect certain feelings, thoughts, and behaviors, including anxiety and startle reactions, avoidant or phobic reactions, physiological hyperarousal to trauma-related stimuli, nightmares, intrusive recollections of the threat, and intense fears about future revictimization. On a positive, adaptive note, the individual may develop new rules of safety that serve to restore, at least partially, the illusion of safety and invulnerability to harm and may help protect the person from future harm. On the negative side, the individual may be unable to restore positive safety schemas until he or she receives appropriate interventions specifically targeted at resolving this issue. We discuss the assessment of these concerns as well as treatment strategies in Chapters 8 and 9.

Trust/Dependency

> What loneliness is more lonely than distrust?
>
> George Eliot
> *Middlemarch*, Bk. v., ch. 44
> (Source: Stevenson, 1966)

The central need for support from others and the expectancy that other people can be relied upon to provide this support are of critical importance in the maintenance of positive mental health and healthy relations with others. Erikson (1963) described the development of trust in others versus distrust as the first central task of psychological development. The ability to trust oneself, one's own perceptions and judgments, is in our view a more advanced cognitive-developmental task, but an equally important one. In the words of Emerson in *Self Reliance* (1865), it is important to "trust thyself: every heart vibrates to that iron string" (p. 49). It is indeed a lonely and frightening world if one is unable to trust others to respond to one's needs for support and care or to trust oneself as one would a good friend.

At the same time, it would be foolhardy to trust completely and without reservation, for not all people or self-judgments are equally reliable. Learning how to integrate trust and distrust with regard to both self and others is clearly a complex developmental task that requires a balance of positive and painful learning experiences. The optimist must sometimes balance his or her hopeful attitude with the realities of a sometimes harsh, uncaring world. So, too, one would hope that the pessimist could acknowledge that not all human beings are unreliable. Most likely, early or traumatic experiences of abandonment, betrayal, and disappointment with regard to one's dependency needs are critical to shaping generalized, negative schemas within this area. These negative schemas are often confirmed again and again, creating a resistance to reexperiencing the painful disappointment that might accompany trusting again.

The trauma literature is filled with clinical descriptions of damaged trust schemas within persons who have been victimized. This includes the distrust felt by incest victims who were betrayed by an adult upon whom they relied for protection and support (e.g., Finkelhor & Browne, 1985; Gelinas, 1983), the rape victim who learns that men can be violent and predatory toward women (Roth & Lebowitz, 1988), and the Vietnam combat veteran who experienced a profound shattering of his idealism as a young man in an untenable war (Wilson, 1980). What this literature has not addressed fully is how one might assess these trust schemas in an individual in the context of a unique life history. Furthermore, too little attention has been given to the profound shattering of self-trust that can also occur when someone finds his or her own judgments or perceptions invalidated. A brief case example will highlight the importance of negative trust schemas among trauma victims.

> Laura, an incest survivor in her mid-30s, had experienced violent, degrading, and cruel sexual abuse at the hands of several adult male relatives. From high school on, she had these experiences confirmed through abusive relationships with a series of men, many of whom initially appeared charming and supportive. Her attitude toward trust was, "Only a fool will let herself trust anyone. People are out to hurt you if you give them a chance." This overgeneralized negative schema kept her from allowing friendships into her life, resulting in a lonely, bitter existence.
>
> Paradoxically, she evidenced profound yet disavowed needs for support, as suggested by a continual search for a man to take care of her emotionally and physically. Although she bitterly degraded all men as "creeps and losers," she continued to succumb to the considerable charms of men who appeared to be strong, but were seeking power through abuse of women. This phenomenon appeared to relate to a severely damaged sense of self-trust, an inability to trust her own perceptions about who is trustworthy and who is not. She often made reference to her own lack of judgment in such statements as "I always manage to pick the losers" and "I feel like I'm blinded by their charm, even though another part of me probably knows better."

In this case, the combination of generalized, negative trust schemas with respect to self and others was associated with repeated revictimization.

In another case of a young woman who was raped after walking alone to a store late at night, issues of self-trust also became central.

Margie is a successful professional woman in her late 20s who had previously trusted her ability to make self-protective judgments, an ability that had contributed to keeping herself and her family safe. When this slight, yet tragic, human error resulted in the devastation of crime and violence, Margie became paralyzed by indecision, unable to believe that she could ever again determine when and how she could keep herself and her family safe through her own trust in herself.

The unique expressions of schemas and the resulting psychological and behavioral outcomes must be understood within the context of the whole person and his or her unique life circumstances. The feelings and behaviors we observe to be commonly associated with negative trust schemas regarding others are bitterness, chronic anger at people, an avoidance of close relationships, a repudiation of dependency needs because of a fear of betrayal or abandonment, and a pervasive sense of disappointment and disillusionment in others.

With respect to disrupted self-trust, the individual is likely to display one of two patterns: excessive caution and paralysis in the face of life decisions because of excessive self-doubt aimed at self-protection, as in the case of the rape victim, or a tendency to make "bad" decisions because one does not expect to be able to exercise appropriately self-protective judgments, as in the case of the incest victim who marries an abusive man. Most individuals with disruptions in trust schemas will experience the terrible loneliness noted by George Eliot.

Independence

> Yes, as my swift days near their goal
> 'tis all that I implore
> Through life and death a chainless soul
> With courage to endure

Emily Bronte
The Old Stoic (1846), st. 3
(Source: Bartlett, 1980)

In the poem *The Old Stoic*, Bronte describes the strong needs among human beings for independence ("a chainless soul") and for power to face life's obstacles with endurance and inner strength. The centrality of needs for both independence and power has been described by numerous personality theorists (e.g., Adler, see Ansbacher & Ansbacher,

1956; Sullivan, 1940). We differentiate independence from power in the following way: We define independence as the need to control one's own rewards or punishments or to be in control of one's behavior and destiny, while power is the need to exert control over one's environment. In this respect, independence schemas relate primarily to oneself while power schemas relate primarily to others or to the world in general. We discuss power schemas in the next section.

In *Childhood and Society*, Erikson (1963) described the differentiation of autonomy from self-doubt as the second developmental task of human beings. The need to rely on oneself, to be independent, is a theme throughout literature and philosophy. In Ibsen's play *"The Enemy of the People"* (Black, 1928), Dr. Stockman, a man who remains independent and true to himself despite pressures from others to conform, proclaims "The strongest man in the world is he who stands most alone" (p. 164).

Persons who experience degradation and humiliation at the hands of their tormenters or who are swept along helplessly by the capriciousness of fate often describe a profound identification with the terror of helplessness, which produces a diminution of self-esteem and sense of efficacy in the world (Bandura, 1977). The victim of a random act of violence may rail against himself or herself: "Why did I submit so helplessly? Why didn't I fight back?" The fact of their "frozen fear" (Symonds, 1980) and life-preserving passivity is unbearable. Although their helplessness and submission may have been the only option open to them and may have ultimately saved their lives, this produces an impossible dilemma that is in conflict with the deeply rooted need for independence.

In a case described previously, Lee, the young suburban mother who was raped and tortured in her home, described the physical rape and violence as the least traumatic aspect of the experience, for this was something she could reconcile in her mind. What obsessed her through intrusive images and nightmares was the anxiety and terror of her helplessness and paralysis during the approach. As she lay in bed in the middle of the night, wondering whether she had heard a noise downstairs, whether to act to get help or to remain silent to avoid harm, she experienced the most devastating experience of this central dilemma. Although she and her husband were held at knife point and tied up in ropes, and, indeed, a struggle could have resulted in violence, she persisted in ruminating "Why didn't I call 911? Why didn't I scream out or struggle? Why didn't I have a gun at hand so that I could blow them away?" The extent of her rage and despair at being forced into this predicament was the legacy of her tormentors. In the words of Donna, another rape victim who was also tied up and helpless,

> It doesn't matter that he tied me up and I couldn't move. I understand intellectually that I had to submit. But you have to understand, it was me that this happened to. The me that has always fought against the violence and oppression of my alcoholic family was shattered at that moment. Emotionally, I can never accept that I allowed this to happen to me.

Donna had very high needs for independence that created tremendous problems after the rape because she was unable to feel compassion toward the damaged self that she no longer experienced as strong, powerful, and independent.

Power

In *Power and Innocence,* Rollo May (1969) described power as a "fundamental aspect of the life process" (p. 20). Within the literature on trauma, there is ample evidence that power and powerlessness are central themes for persons who are traumatized. The "illusion of control" (Langer, 1975) is a schema that can be destroyed in trauma survivors. Krystal (1978) described the infantile helplessness and psychological paralysis of persons who had experienced catastrophic life events, such as the Nazi Holocaust. The invasion of one's body and personal space against one's will has been described by Finkelhor and Browne (1985) as a central "traumagenic dynamic" of disempowerment. The tragic figure of Joseph K. in Kafka's (1937/1969) *The Trial* is a prototypic victim who is overpowered by forces beyond his control and understanding as he is arrested and detained for no apparent reason. He becomes helpless, cannot assert himself, and lacks the strength to protest his persecution. In the end, he passively accepts his fate even though he has done nothing wrong. He resigns himself to death on a lonely street corner, a degrading fate in which he dies alone "like a dog; it was as if the shame of it must outlive him" (p. 286).

In a case of a Vietnam veteran, described elsewhere (McCann, Sakheim, & Abrahamson, 1988), themes of power or dominance were central. This Marine officer took great pride in protecting his comrades through his powerful leadership in his unit. When his unit was given the command to engage in a dangerous search and destroy mission, his strong need for power gave him the strength to fight this order all the way up to the top. He was defeated and incarcerated for insubordination when he stuck to his principles, refusing to obey orders and to expose his men to unnecessary risk. While he was helplessly raging against his superiors in military prison, he received the news that his entire unit had been destroyed while on the mission after a bridge blew up. This man, whose maturely expressed need for power had always served as an important source of pride and mastery, was demolished psychologically as his unit was demolished physically. He lost his fighting spirit, becoming a shell of his former self, no longer caring whether he lived or died.

Again, the meanings of power for the individual must be understood within the context of the whole person and his or her unique life history. Some common response patterns found among persons for whom this central need is severely disrupted are passivity, submission, or lack of assertiveness, which may resemble what Seligman (1975) originally conceptualized as learned helplessness. For others, like the Vietnam veteran, danger-seeking may persist as a search for mastery through seeking situations in which to attempt to reassert one's power (e.g., Blank, 1989).

Esteem

> It may be called the Master Passion, the hunger for self approval.
>   Mark Twain
>   *What is Man?* (1906), Ch. 6
>   (Source: Bartlett, 1980)

The belief in one's own worth or value has been described as a fundamental need across many theories of personality (Maslow, 1970; Rogers, 1959; Sullivan, 1940). The above quote represents one of our criteria for healthy self-esteem: the ability to value oneself, to understand and know oneself, to enjoy the inner experience of relating to oneself, to enjoy hope and faith in oneself as one lives one's life. The early psychoanalytic thinkers suggested that self-esteem resulted from the process of internalization (e.g., Dewald, 1969). Kohut (1977) focused on self-esteem regulation as essential to the development of a stable and cohesive self-structure.

In our view, the belief in one's value (or "self-esteem") is rooted in the psychological need for recognition or validation. All humans need to feel valued and respected by others. This experience of positive valuation and recognition is internalized within the deepest parts of the self. The person who has a healthy expectation for positive self-esteem will relate to the words of Walt Whitman in *Song of Myself*: "I celebrate myself, and sing myself and what I assume you shall assume.

For every atom that belongs to me as good belongs to you" (Ellman, 1976). In this poem, Whitman lyricizes and celebrates the self. Rather than representing a narcissistic self-focus that precludes genuine relatedness, a sense of connection with all human life is an outgrowth of this valuing of oneself. It is clear that positive self-esteem schemas relate quite directly to the ability to maintain positive self-esteem, which we described previously as a self capacity.

As with psychological needs, there are cognitive schemas associated with self capacities. For example, someone who cannot tolerate strong affect may hold a series of related beliefs such as, "I can't let myself cry. I can't stand to feel afraid. I'd rather die than experience my feelings. I will disintegrate if I feel my feelings." In our explications of constructivist self development theory, we have chosen to focus on only the schemas related to psychological needs. But, within the need area of esteem in particular, we become aware of both the existence of schemas related to self capacities and the interrelation of needs and self capacities.

Trauma can have profound effects on a person's self-esteem. The empirical literature has verified this effect among victims of rape (e.g., Roth & Lebowitz, 1988; Veronen & Kilpatrick, 1980), incest (e.g., Gold, 1986), domestic violence (e.g., Mills, 1984), and other crime (Krupnick, 1980), as well as other seriously stressful life events (Janoff-Bulman, 1989a). Much of this literature focuses on self-esteem as a global construct, with few operational definitions or descriptions of unique victim responses. The impact of trauma upon self-esteem will depend, in part, on the person's capacity to regulate self-esteem. A brief case example underscores the different processes involved in self-esteem schemas.

> Donna, a 35-year-old divorced female, was suddenly attacked by a strange male while hiking in the woods. She was tied up and forced to have sex with him. She apparently dissociated during most of the rape. When she regained consciousness, the man was saying very cruel things to her, including, "You bitch. You liked this, you wanted this, you deserved this." Those words played themselves over and over in her mind after the rape and during the next three months.
>
> When Donna came for therapy, she was plagued by a severe depression, suicidal thoughts, and paralyzing symptoms of acute PTSD. When she was eventually able to share what had happened, she was able to reflect on why those words had such a damaging

impact on her. Apparently, her alcoholic father had been emotionally cruel to her as a child, repeatedly telling her that she was no good, was undeserving, and would never amount to anything. When the rapist used the same words, she described "feeling as if I were a child again, and that somehow I had deserved to be punished by him."

As she made this connection and fully expressed her feelings about this, she was able to return to her adult self-esteem, which had been strengthened by much inner work and some previous therapy. Because her self-esteem had been repaired from childhood, Donna had the inner resources to recover from the damage the rape had on her self-esteem. (A more detailed case presentation is offered in Chapter 14).

Lee, the other rape and burglary victim described above, was also told many cruel things, almost the same words, when she too was tied up. However, because her self-esteem schemas had always been positive, Lee was not terribly impacted by these words. What they did mean to her, instead, was that she had to face the horror that cruel, sick people could want to hurt her and her family, whom she knew to be undeserving of such treatment. For her, a shattering of her schemas related to safety and esteem for others was much more focal than for Donna.

The other central part of the need for esteem is esteem for others, a need to recognize the inherent worth and goodness of other human beings. This concept is equivalent to Epstein's (1985; in press b) and Janoff-Bulman's (1989a) fundamental schemas related to the benevolence of other people and the world in general. An optimistic view of human nature reflected in such a need was originally espoused by the humanists (Maslow, 1970; Rogers, 1959), a view that is in sharp contrast to the more pessimistic view of Freud (1961/1930).

We believe that some degree of integration and reconciliation must occur in the dialectic of good and bad, worthiness and unworthiness, both within the self (as suggested by object relations theorists such as Mahler, Pine, and Bergman [1975]) and in relation to other people. Westen (1989) cites evidence that people diagnosed as borderline personalities tend to view other people as malevolent and that traumas that occur in the post-oedipal years are associated with the development of severe character pathology. Thus, maturity and psychological well-being are also intricately connected to one's internalized and consciously expressed valuations of other people, and are important dimensions to understand in relation to the trauma survivor.

These brief examples underscore the complex relation among trauma-related events, the self, and previous history. Again, understanding the individual's interpretation of experiences through his or her unique filters is of utmost importance. Lee, who was raped by a man of a different race, experienced a greater impact within the area of esteem of others. She was filled with angry feelings that generalized to racism. This decreased esteem for black males seemed to be tied to an earlier childhood experience in which she was nearly attacked by a black male in her neighborhood but was rescued by a neighbor.

Furthermore, Lee also experienced diminished esteem for others in her community, largely because of the careless or unhelpful responses of the community at large. For example, her best friend at work made the careless comment, "I heard that houses where this has happened become a magnet for other incidents," never stopping to consider that the survivor was still living at the house and was overcome by crippling fear each evening. After she experienced a number of such hurtful comments, Lee told the therapist,

> I'm beginning to lose my faith in other people, even my friends. They just don't understand and if I talk about it, I risk having them say things that will hurt me. I just feel like withdrawing from everyone except you and my husband.

We have found this desire to withdraw to be most common among persons who have many experiences with a cruel, uncaring, indifferent world, such as the Vietnam warriors fighting an unpopular war, who found themselves maligned as "losers" and "baby killers" upon returning from Vietnam (Lifton, 1973). Persons for whom post-trauma reactions are particularly cruel and damaging experience what Symonds (1980) has termed a "second injury." Common psychological effects of damage to self-esteem are depression, self-destructive thoughts or actions, guilt, shame, self-blame, substance abuse, and, sometimes, dissociative reactions. Within the other-esteem area, likely responses include bitterness and anger toward people, withdrawal from others, and isolation.

Intimacy

> I have been a stranger in a strange land
> *The Bible:* Exodus, 2:22

We have described the desire for belonging and connection with other human beings as central to positive mental health. Many personality theorists (e.g., Maslów, 1971) have discussed the importance of human connection. Erikson (1963) described the resolution of intimacy versus isolation as another central developmental task of young adulthood. The importance of the attachment bond between children and their caretakers has been well documented by developmental theorists (e.g., Bowlby, 1969; Harlow, 1974). Recent theories of adult development, particularly within the psychology of women, have stressed connection and relatedness as a developmental task as important as that of separation-individuation and autonomy (Jordan, 1984).

This need for intimate connection with others is very fragile and can be easily damaged or destroyed through insensitive, unempathetic, or cruel responses by others. When human relationships become associated with loss, pain, and agony, it is difficult to maintain a sense of connection with others as the risk to oneself is too great to bear. The death of close friends in Vietnam is believed to be particularly traumatic for the adolescent warrior because of the intense attachment bonds established among the peers at that developmental stage (Haley, 1985; van der Kolk, 1985). Similarly, victims of sexual trauma report a sense of isolation and alienation from others (e.g., Roth & Lebowitz, 1988). Furthermore, if the world at large is cruel, unempathetic, or blaming, as was the case of the returning Vietnam veteran, it is difficult to maintain a sense of belonging in the world (Lifton, 1973). Lifton (1979) described the "broken connection" that entails the severing of bonds of identification with other human beings that can occur in traumas that devastate the community. Erikson (1976) also wrote about the loss of communality that can occur among survivors of a widespread community disaster.

The above quote from the Biblical book of *Exodus* depicts the person who experiences the intense alienation of feeling like a stranger in a strange land. Yet, in the words of William Blake "Everything that lives, lives not alone, nor for itself" (Source: Smyth, 1953, p. 74). People need other people and need to feel a sense of belonging to some place, community, or person (e.g., Bellah et al., 1985).

The shattering of schemas related to intimacy is nowhere more apparent than in persons who have experienced traumatic losses or a painful withdrawal by loved ones or society. In situations of extreme loss of meaning and pervasive death, as in Hiroshima after the devastation of the atomic bomb, John Hersey (1963) described survivors wandering around aimlessly, unaware of each other, with eyes of the walking dead.

For many victims, the traumatic loss of loved ones is at the root of this shattering of intimate bonds, resulting in an intense fear that allowing themselves to love again will only result in suffering.

In the words of a Vietnam veteran nurse who experienced a series of traumatic losses, including the loss of a brother in Vietnam combat, the loss of the men she had grown attached to during the war, and the tragic loss of her husband in a plane crash after the war, "the part of me that loved, that felt connected to anyone, died. I no longer feel nor do I have the ability to really care." This person, who is described in Chapter 9 in the section on intimacy, was most afraid that caring, feeling again, could lead to self-disintegration if she experienced another traumatic loss. She characterized herself as merely existing, with no emotion or passion. When her relationships were passionate, as new relationships often are, she fled with terror.

These fears were indeed based on some reality in her past history. After the losses during Vietnam, including the traumatic loss of her younger brother, she coped by becoming numb and disconnected. After the war, she married her childhood sweetheart, allowing herself to take another chance at loving, for his love for her touched her heart deeply and reawakened her longing for connection. When he tragically died in a plane crash two years after an idyllic marriage, she became psychotic for six months and was locked away in a back ward of a VA hospital. When she was released, she was a shell of her former self, and she described the death of the life force inside of her that is the source of all love and connection.

Although each case history must be understood in its uniqueness, there are some commonalities that we have observed among those who have had their schemas for intimacy disrupted. These include a sense of inner emptiness, a chronic state of psychic numbing and emotional detachment, a fear of closeness which has become associated with traumatic loss, and a terrible, pervasive sense of loneliness and alienation. For some, the loss of connection extends to their own internal relationship with themselves. In these cases, the person may describe an inability to be alone and to tolerate his or her own sense of disconnectedness internally, relying on other people for a sense of inner fullness and support. Unfortunately, this is a need that cannot be met by others, often resulting in even greater disappointment in and disaffection from others.

SUMMARY

In this chapter, we described the schemas that relate to one's frame of reference, including causality, hope, and locus of control. We also described schemas that relate to the psychological needs for safety, trust/dependency, esteem, independence, power, and intimacy. These schemas, which develop in relation to self and others, arise from a unique personal history and shape the way an individual experiences a traumatic event. In some cases, the person will experience a trauma as confirming negative schemas. In other cases, the traumatic event will disrupt or alter previously positive schemas. The complex relation among life experiences, schemas, and psychological adaptation must be understood within the context of the whole person and the social and cultural environment. We will discuss the assessment of these areas and the specific interventions designed to impact negative schemas in Chapters 8 and 9.

Part 2

CLINICAL ASSESSMENT AND INTERVENTION

5. An Overview of Therapeutic Strategies

In this chapter, we provide an overview of clinical applications of constructivist self development theory to trauma survivors. We describe here the general principles underlying our treatment paradigm, to be elaborated in subsequent chapters.

OVERVIEW OF PSYCHOTHERAPY WITH SURVIVORS

Here, we provide a general overview of our conceptualization of post-trauma therapy. Although we present this material in a sequence which might appear to represent stages of therapy, we do not mean to imply that the work is done in a strict sequence; rather, there is fluid movement among these areas as therapy unfolds.

ASSESSMENT

Assessment is an ongoing process in therapy that continually shapes and guides treatment. The progress or lack of progress in therapy provides additional information that is fed back into the assessment-treatment planning process.

Assessment of Life Experiences
Assessment of the previous history and of social and cultural context is an aspect of assessment that is common to work done with non-trauma psychotherapy clients. This, of course, includes an exploration of the client's early and most significant experiences and the context of those experiences. Through this work, the clinician begins to develop hypotheses about the individual's self capacities, ego resources, and psychological needs. In addition, with clients who have experienced traumatic

events as adults, the therapist can begin to form hypotheses about the possible extent of psychological damage caused by the trauma, based on discrepancies between the way the client describes himself or herself in younger years and the way s/he presents now.

> For example, Sylvia, a client in her mid-50s, reported in early sessions growing up in a home where the mother was clearly struggling to meet her own emotional needs and unable to provide the nuturance and care her children needed, while the father was emotionally distant. Her description of her childhood home helped the therapist to begin framing hypotheses about Sylvia's possible difficulties in soothing herself, her low self-esteem, and strong conflicts about trust/dependency.

We emphasize the social and cultural context because it shapes the individual's experience of the trauma as well as of himself or herself. Chronic poverty, experiences of racism or sexism, and other more subtle forms of discrimination or abuse provide the context for individuals' schemas about self and others.

> For example, Karen, an incest survivor in her mid-20s, grew up in an impoverished home. She believed that her abusive father could have given the family more material things than he did, but that he withheld his paycheck as another form of torture. This evolved into a belief that people who have things (material and emotional) enjoy seeing others suffer, a background theme which tempered the therapeutic relationship throughout the first year of therapy.

A sensitivity to the meanings of these issues to the client should guide the therapist's explorations and interventions in order to avoid revictimizing the client through subtle, and perhaps unconscious, victim blaming.

> For example, Linda was an attractive incest survivor in her mid-30s. Linda had been taught by her abusive grandfather that it was her physical attractiveness combined with her seductive behaviors that led to the sexual abuse. As often happens, her behavior at times elicited responses from others which confirmed her view of herself as seductive. Her male therapist found her attractive and used supervision to explore his confusion about her behaviors, which were increasingly provocative over the first several therapy

sessions, including her style of dress and her detailed descriptions of her masturbation behavior.

The assessment and treatment of the traumatic experience occur simultaneously with the assessment of the self, with one exception. If the self capacities or ego resources have been severely disrupted by the trauma, or were very weak before the trauma, they must be strengthened prior to in-depth exploration of the traumatic experience.

Exploration of the traumatic experience includes a thorough understanding of the central trauma(s) for the individual and the impact on the self development and psychological adaptation. The clinician will gradually learn about the specific nature of the traumatic experience, its characteristics and themes. The characteristics of the trauma refer to the specific nature of the trauma (rape, incest, etc.), the details surrounding the events (what led up to the event, how and when it occurred, what ensued), the duration and intensity of the trauma, and the traumatic themes. The traumatic themes refer to the victim's central experience of the trauma, including, for example, betrayal, powerlessness, stigmatization (Finkelhor & Browne, 1985), defilement, or subjugation (Ochberg, 1988). The specific nature of the trauma and its themes often suggest important disturbed schemas. Thus, to a large extent, the individual will experience, construe, and remember the trauma in terms and images that are consistent with his or her psychological needs and schemas. We discuss this in more detail in Chapters 8 and 9.

Over the course of treatment, the clinician and client will explore the imagery and verbal components of the traumatic memory. The imagery component includes the client's visual images of what happened and the related affect. The verbal component includes whatever the client remembers about what was said to him or her or what s/he thought about during or after the event. As a prelude to the exploration of these components, which we call memory work, the clinician must assess the degree to which the memories are repressed or within conscious awareness and the degree to which they are fragmented or whole, as these are clues to how painful this material will be for the client. For example, some incest survivors come to therapy without knowing they were abused; instead, they may present with chronic depression, anxiety, loneliness, or anomie, or with behavioral expressions of distress such as chronic substance abuse.

The assessment of life experiences will be discussed in more depth in Chapter 6.

Assessment of the Self

This is the ongoing process of building a psychological picture of the person both before and after the traumatization. First, the clinician assesses the self capacities and ego resources. The self capacities, drawn from a self-psychology perspective (Kohut, 1977), are central to an individual's ability to master traumatic memories both cognitively and emotionally. The self capacities reflect the individual's ability to regulate self-esteem. The ego resources refer to the psychological reserves of the person that enable him or her to manage relationships with others and negotiate external demands.

We believe, as do others (e.g., Bard & Sangrey, 1986; Parson, 1984), that trauma can violate the self, disrupting self capacities and ego resources and thus diminishing the individual's ability to cope. Furthermore, we believe that the self capacities must be strengthened for the individual to tolerate the painful emotions and thoughts associated with memory work and to tolerate the accommodation of cognitive schemas to a new reality. The therapy process may be the first occasion many survivors have had to let themselves feel the losses inevitably associated with trauma, to feel the anger toward a specific abuser or toward the world or their god for allowing the traumatic events to happen. In addition, an accommodation of schemas is often a loss.

> For example, Jill and Rodney, whose daughter was murdered by her fiancé, had to manage their enormous grief, their fury at the perpetrator, and their loss of a former belief in an orderly or predictable world in which they were able to protect their children from serious harm. A systematic assessment of the ego resources and self capacities guides the clinician's interventions so they are respectful of the person. We present a model for this assessment in Chapter 7.

The second part of the self assessment is the development of an understanding of the psychological need structure of the individual. We view seven needs as salient for trauma survivors. They are frame of reference, safety, trust/dependency, independence, power, esteem, and intimacy. As noted earlier, by definition trauma disrupts frame of reference and other central needs. A disrupted need will be a more pressing concern for the person, becoming what Murray (1938) called a focal need. A full exploration of the individual's most salient or focal needs enables the clinician to respect these needs in the therapy process, to help the client restore or develop a balance among needs, and to enhance the client's ability to meet central needs in constructive ways in the future.

> For Lulu, safety had never been a particularly central concern. After she was raped in her home, however, she became obsessed with her physical safety and that of her female friends. She was unable to invest any energy in meeting her needs for connection or independence because she was too fearful of future assault and preoccupied with ensuring everyone's safety.

The cognitive expressions of needs are schemas, or the beliefs, assumptions, and expectations about self and others that enable individuals to organize and process their life experiences. These schemas are subject to disruption by trauma. The extent of the disruption or generalization of the negative schemas is a reflection of psychological adaptation. More generalized disturbed schemas in a number of areas are evidence of more psychological distress than fewer or more specific disturbances. Furthermore, the psychological disturbance is likely to be greater and the recovery process more prolonged if disturbed schemas exist within a weak or compromised self.

> For example, Jenny was raped by a man she met in a bar one evening. Because of her unique psychological nature, she was able to tell herself, "I was a jerk to trust some guy I met in a bar. I'll never do anything crazy like that again." But Catherine, another woman raped by a man on their first date, generalized her negative schemas in this way, "Only a tramp would let this happen to her so I must be a tramp." Catherine, whose self-esteem had never been especially strong, had a more difficult recovery process than Jenny.

There should be ongoing assessment of whether the individual seems to be moving forward through the processes of assimilation and accommodation, or is stalled or regressing. Piaget's theory suggests that the two processes should remain relatively balanced, with an imbalance resulting in disequilibrium. For example, it is potentially maladaptive to hold rigidly to schemas that no longer fit reality, just as it can be maladaptive to allow positive schemas to remain permanently shattered by traumatic events.

> An example of the former style is in Fred, a victim of a serious assault, who continued to travel on foot to dangerous parts of his urban hometown alone at night, refusing to accept that this be-

havior was in any way risky. Another assault victim, Bob, demonstrates the second point: his adaptation included a complete abdication of his former faith in humans as potentially valuable and trustworthy.

In Chapter 9, we describe the assessment of needs and schemas and the relation between disrupted needs and schemas and self development.

Adaptation and Coping

The individual's presenting problems and symptoms can be assessed within five areas of adaptation: emotional, cognitive, biological, interpersonal, and behavioral. Wherever necessary, immediate steps should be taken to protect the client from serious danger, and medical attention should be sought for biological problems. In the psychotherapy process, these symptoms should be explored and understood as representing the person's best efforts to cope with the trauma and its aftermath.

The therapy process should include an ongoing analysis of the costs and benefits of the two coping orientations, approach and avoidance. We utilize Roth and Cohen's (1986) model of approach-avoidance as a paradigm for understanding these coping processes in adaptation to stressful life events, including trauma. For example, according to Roth and Cohen, approach is beneficial if it involves increased assimilation of traumatic material but is costly if it results in overwhelming affect and intrusive imagery. Avoidance produces benefits if it allows the dosing of traumatic material and is costly if the traumatic memories remain unassimilated. In general, Roth (1989) presents a therapy paradigm that is similar to our own. In this view, the ideal therapy situation aims toward gradual approach and integration of traumatic memories and associated affects. Although the individual may at times avoid threatening material, these retreats are temporary and ultimately facilitate eventual approach and mastery.

We believe that the costs and benefits of these different processes are largely a function of the current strength of the ego resources and self capacities, the current balance of psychological needs, and the current adaptiveness of schemas. Roth (1989) takes a similar view when she acknowledges that while the goal of approach and integration is desirable, integration may not be possible for persons with limited social or psychological resources. This implies, of course, the importance of ongoing assessment of these aspects of the self in order to determine when to encourage approach and when to encourage avoidance or withdrawal from traumatic material.

TREATMENT PLANNING

A coherent, theory-based treatment plan will evolve over time, always subject to revisions, as part of the ongoing process of assessment. The treatment plan will include one's preliminary goals for therapy as well as the strategies and interventions designed to achieve these outcomes. Formulation of the treatment plan includes the following considerations.

Long-term vs. Short-term Work

The issue of long-term versus short-term work has traditionally been linked to the dimensions of acute versus chronic symptoms. The management of acute trauma, such as a single-incident rape or other crime, has traditionally been undertaken from a crisis intervention perspective (e.g., Burgess & Holmstrom, 1974). Marmar and Horowitz (1988) describe the phases of stress recovery as outcry (fear, sadness, and anger), denial experiences (numbing and avoidance), intrusive experiences (unbidden thoughts and images), working through (facing reality), and relative completion of response (going on with life). In acute cases, when the stressful event is not too severe, these theorists recommend time-limited psychotherapy (12 weeks), whereas they suggest that complex or chronic cases of PTSD may benefit from time-unlimited psychotherapy (Horowitz, Marmar, Weiss, DeWitt, & Rosenbaum, 1984; Marmar & Freedman, 1988; Marmar & Horowitz, 1988).

We view the issue of long-term vs. short-term psychotherapy somewhat differently. We do not focus on the nature of the event to determine duration of therapy but rather on the unique individual who has experienced a particular degree of disruption in self development. We use the following general guidelines to assess the likely length of treatment.

Short-term Therapy (Up to Six Months). Short-term therapy, including crisis intervention, is often indicated when the following conditions exist:

1. The memories of the trauma are accessible to conscious awareness, although distressing, and are recent and perhaps nonthreatening enough to be experienced as whole memories rather than fragments that have become repressed.
2. The self capacities are relatively free from major disruption, allowing the person to access traumatic memories without suffering severe psychological distress, such as crippling fear and anxiety. The ego resources are strong enough to allow the

person to engage in the therapeutic processes of introspection and exploration.

3. The central psychological needs are minimally disrupted, needs are reasonably well-balanced, and there is a history of being able to meet central needs in acceptable ways.

4. The cognitive schemas are minimally disrupted and disturbances are not overgeneralized.

Susan, a rape victim in her mid-20s, is someone with whom we predicted and accomplished a short-term intervention. She had fairly well-developed self capacities and ego resources. She found her relationships and her work rewarding. She had always been interested in personal growth, at various times exploring yoga, psychology, and philosophy. In about six months, she had worked through her terror and rage about the rape, had resumed normal social and work behaviors, and was beginning to think about taking some courses at the university.

Long-term Therapy (Six Months to Three or More Years). Long-term therapy is usually indicated if:

1. The traumatic memories are largely fragmented and partially or completely out of conscious awareness and/or the individual cannot talk about the memories without being overwhelmed by affect.

2. The self capacities and ego resources are severely disrupted or impaired, whether due to the intensity of the traumatic experience or to previous developmental assaults to the self, such as a severe failure in empathy from caretakers, early loss of attachment figures, or abuse.

3. The central psychological needs have been disrupted by the trauma, resulting in an imbalance among the seven needs which leads the individual to attempt to meet particular needs inappropriately or unsuccessfully, or there is a strong historical imbalance of needs or inability to meet needs in constructive or mature ways.

4. Cognitive schemas in a number of areas are disturbed; negative schemas are overgeneralized or are not balanced by more positive schemas.

5. There is a self-protective resistance to the accommodation or change in schemas that is necessary for continued psychological growth.

Gwen, for example, was someone for whom we predicted long-term therapy. In fact, her therapy lasted almost three years. A mugging was the precipitant of the therapy. Over the course of treatment, the fact that she had been raped during the mugging began to emerge. This fact had been inaccessible to Gwen for the first year of treatment. In addition, her mother had died when Gwen was six years old, and Gwen's father relied heavily upon Gwen for help with the younger children. This resulted in disrupted dependency/trust needs and schemas. She had a rather rigid style which kept her firmly planted in the present; she rarely sought out opportunities for personal growth. The therapy allowed her to understand and resolve the mugging/rape as well as to begin to explore the possibility of being taken care of by others at times. The beginning of termination was clearly indicated when Gwen announced that she was considering exploring alternatives to her career as a nurse.

Although we agree that the more severe and prolonged traumatic events (e.g., childhood incest, extended war trauma, torture) are more likely to be associated with a need for longer-term therapy, we do not believe there is a clear-cut relation between characteristics of the trauma and the need for short- vs. long-term therapy. We have encountered some incest survivors and Vietnam veterans who have benefited from short-term therapy and some crime or accident victims who needed long-term therapy. In essence, this assessment should be made by focusing first on the systems of the self and only secondarily on the nature of the traumatic events.

Supportive and Uncovering Approaches

Supportive and uncovering approaches are interwoven throughout the therapy process and reflect the assessment of the self capacities and current adaptation. Different approaches are warranted at different times in the therapy depending upon the psychological concerns and processes that are dominant at the time. The following general guidelines can be used to determine when supportive vs. uncovering approaches are indicated.

Supportive Approaches. Supportive approaches (e.g., stabilization, education, empathetic soothing, cognitive control strategies, etc.) are warranted when:

1. The memories of the trauma are intrusive, producing acute distress, and cannot be approached in a way that promotes cognitive and emotional mastery.

2. The self capacities are severely compromised, resulting in poor affect tolerance or an inability to soothe and calm oneself, to be alone, and to regulate self-loathing.
3. Self development is regressive, e.g., the individual is reverting to maladaptive forms of behavior such as acting out, suicide, or extreme withdrawal.
4. The processes of assimilation and accommodation are not balanced, creating a state of disequilibrium or rigid entrenchment in dysfunctional patterns.

Uncovering Approaches. Uncovering techniques such as approaching and integrating repressed or fragmented traumatic memories through revivification or hypnosis, reexperiencing and healing painful feelings, exploring unconscious cognitive schemas and meanings, and making connections between life experiences and psychological adaptation are called for when the following psychological processes are dominant:

1. The memories of the traumatic experience are to some degree fragmented and/or out of conscious awareness.
2. The self capacities are strong enough to allow the person to approach traumatic memory fragments gradually in a way that allows the person to master them emotionally and cognitively.
3. The individual is ready to process the powerful and painful emotions associated with accommodation, or a change in schemas.
4. There is an appropriate balance between approach and avoidance and between assimilation and accommodation such that there is a movement toward acknowledgment and integration of all aspects of the traumatic memories.

Integrating Self Work and Memory Work

Self work refers to the strengthening of the self capacities and ego resources. Memory work refers to the recovery (where necessary), exploration, and integration of traumatic memories. The interweaving of self work and memory work takes place in the context of the following considerations:

1. The memory work should always occur within the context of a relatively stable self. Over the course of the memory work (e.g., when repressed, painful memories are being uncovered), self capacities may become temporarily compromised. For example, the affect can become overwhelming or self-esteem

regulation impaired, thus necessitating the integration of specific self-building techniques into the memory work.

2. Self work should predominate if the individual is unable to tolerate strong affect, is overcome by self-loathing, is acting out self-destructive impulses, or is otherwise manifesting disturbances that are interfering with functioning.

STABILIZATION

Managing Acute Symptoms of Distress

Clients who are experiencing suicidal thoughts which they cannot manage or who have attempted suicide may need to be hospitalized in order to stabilize before psychotherapy can begin or during the course of therapy. Clients with acute symptoms of anxiety or depression must be assisted in mastering these symptoms before they can engage in or continue the process of therapy. Crime victims may need to establish a safe physical environment before they can move on to talking about the trauma. Behavioral and psychopharmacological interventions can be useful in helping individuals to stabilize enough to engage in the psychotherapy process. These special clinical issues will be discussed in Chapter 12.

Building an Alliance Based on Respect for the Individual

Our therapeutic approach is to be as involved and engaged with trauma victims as is possible without violating therapist-client boundaries. A classical analytic neutrality may be appropriate for treating neurotic disorders and during some phases of work with traumatized persons. However, most people who are traumatized want and need to experience a relationship with a real, warm, concerned human being who is actively involved with them in an empathetic, responsive way. Lindy (1988) describes the initial discomfort of analytically trained therapists working with Vietnam veterans when they discovered that a much more active, open stance was necessary for building an alliance with these clients.

In our experience, severely impaired incest survivors and Vietnam veterans are especially sensitive to any signs of phoniness and distance in therapists and require an open, honest, direct approach in order to build trust (Figley, 1988). These clients, like troubled adolescents, may at times require extended periods of "hanging out" or doing things together that do not closely resemble the face-to-face work of traditional psychotherapy.

> For example, Lawrence was a Vietnam veteran with serious disruptions in his ability to trust others and an almost completely disavowed need for connection with others. For the first year of therapy, he stayed at the surface with the therapist, asking her as many questions as he answered about himself. One day Lawrence came to a session with juggling balls, offering to teach the therapist to juggle. Lawrence stated that he wanted to give the therapist something in exchange for what she had given him. The two spent a few minutes at the beginning of each of several subsequent sessions with Lawrence in the role of teacher. This marked a turning point in the therapy; after that time, Lawrence engaged in more in-depth exploration of his strong unmet dependency and intimacy needs than the therapist imagined he ever would based on the first year of treatment.

We are not suggesting that the therapist throw away all neutrality, since a balance between involvement and neutrality is necessary, but, particularly in the initial alliance-building stage of therapy, the therapist should convey hopefulness, a willingness to be involved, a capacity to tolerate painful affects and memories without either distancing or overreacting, a sense that s/he is a real person, a sense of compassion and understanding for the victim's unique experience, and a clear sense of direction in the work that is before them.

Educating the Client About Trauma and Therapy

We value the psychoeducational approaches to dealing with trauma that have been advocated by many authors (e.g., Parson, 1984; Scurfield, 1985). Our approach to education of clients includes the following goals:

1. Normalize the person's reactions by educating about what PTSD is, the way trauma reactions are manifested in different people, the fears that people commonly have when they experience these symptoms (e.g., going crazy, losing control, regressing), and the prognosis with appropriate treatment, given the individual's background and resources. Bibliotherapy, which involves suggesting readings related to the individual's trauma experience, can be a useful adjunct in the early stages of therapy.
2. Educate individuals about the approach-avoidance processes of post-trauma reactions by saying something like,

"Some days you may feel numb (deadened, like your feelings have died) and the next day you may feel that you're back to your normal self. Then suddenly something will happen inside you or outside of you that will trigger a memory. You may find yourself flooded with painful images of what happened and intolerable feelings. It is perfectly normal to fluctuate between these two very different states. As we learn more about how and when you experience these different states, we will gradually work to make the extremes less intense and painful for you."

Providing a Framework for What to Expect from Treatment

It is important that the therapist discuss the course of therapy with the individual, including preliminary predictions about the length of treatment, treatment approaches, and potential obstacles (e.g., Figley, 1988). For example, the therapist should discuss the various goals of therapy (e.g., stabilization of acute symptoms, exploration of the traumatic memories, etc.) and the projected time frames for meeting these goals. It is equally important to provide a realistic expectation of what the client might expect as a result of treatment. It is impossible to remove the traumatic experience from the individual's past or from memory. It is impossible to restore completely the pretrauma frame of reference. Yet with appropriate treatment, many clients can expect to recall their traumatic experiences with less terror or rage, for example, than they may feel at the beginning of therapy.

Inspiring Confidence in the Therapist and Therapy Process

Traumatized individuals are often ambivalent about entering therapy. The reasons for this are many and may include a fear that they will be violated again or that the therapist won't be able to help them. One of the early tasks of therapy is thus to begin to build a sense of hope about therapy. This will be essential to motivate the individual to invest in a process that will undoubtedly be painful and difficult. In our experience, clients seem to develop confidence in therapists who are honest about what to expect from therapy, are respectful of the client, have a sense of direction about the therapy, and convey a sense of calm and hope throughout the sessions.

STRENGTHENING OF SELF CAPACITIES AND MOBILIZATION OF EGO RESOURCES

The self work focuses primarily on the following goals: strengthening self capacities that are compromised by the trauma or other developmental assaults; mobilizing existing resources that can enable the person to tolerate the painful integration of traumatic memories; and encouraging movement toward the future rather than a regressive clinging to the past. As part of the self work, the individual is encouraged to focus inward, on the self, and to identify and build upon strengths. Development of underdeveloped parts of the self is encouraged through such techniques as imagery, spending positive time alone, and other self-nurturing behaviors. The general and specific techniques for self building will be addressed in Chapter 7.

RESTORATION OR CREATION OF A BALANCED NEED STRUCTURE

Another fundamental aspect of post-trauma therapy is the exploration of the unique need structure of the individual. This process includes identifying needs that have become disrupted as a result of the trauma and the current ways in which those needs are being gratified or frustrated. Many individuals, particularly those whose sense of self is damaged, are not consciously aware of their psychological needs. Thus, the first step in this process is identifying the most important needs and their role in motivating the person to behave in characteristic ways. This is done primarily by listening for and exploring themes that relate to the seven need areas. The next step is discovering how the individual can learn to meet the central needs as well as bring other needs, which may have become focal as a result of trauma, into balance. This begins with learning how the individual currently meets these needs, whether these avenues are constructive, and whether they are still open to him or her.

> For example, Paula, an accident victim with a strong need for recognition or esteem, had been able to gratify this need through her outstanding performance as an amateur athlete. Because this path was blocked, Paula and the therapist worked to find other ways Paula could feel proud of herself, as well, of course, as exploring the early origins of this strong need.

The process of restoring a balance among needs is closely tied to interventions focused on exploring and challenging disturbed schemas.

RESTORATION OF POSITIVE SCHEMAS

This aspect of therapy is closely linked to the exploration of needs because the schemas of interest within constructivist self development theory are those that relate directly to psychological needs. The disruption of psychological needs is reflected in disturbed or overgeneralized negative schemas in the seven need areas. For example, schemas such as, "Nothing makes sense anymore," or "The future feels totally bleak" reflect disturbances in frame of reference. Schemas such as, "It's stupid to trust anyone" reflect disturbances in the need for trust/dependency.

The first stage in this process of restoring positive schemas is uncovering the disturbed schemas, often unconscious, as they are manifested directly and indirectly through characteristic themes, feelings, and behavior patterns. A client who expresses, for example, her belief that she could never feel close to anyone is manifesting disturbed intimacy schemas. This may come out only indirectly through the revelation of a lifetime without friends or intimate others.

The next phase of work is discovering how positive schemas that have been shattered might be restored. For example, a trauma survivor whose need for independence has been disrupted may be encouraged to view coming to therapy as taking charge of her life and may also be encouraged to resume control over those parts of her life where it is still possible and appropriate.

The disturbed or overgeneralized negative schemas are then gently challenged by first exploring the resistances to changing these inner models of self and world. For example, in the case of disturbed intimacy schemas, the therapist might ask, "I wonder if you could imagine yourself ever having a close friend?" This often meets with resistance, as an alteration in core schemas (or accommodation) can be psychologically shocking unless it takes place gradually and in the context of a strong therapeutic alliance. Thus, the therapist must accept the client's inability to entertain the possibilities the therapist proposes at first without trying to persuade or convince the client.

INTEGRATION OF TRAUMATIC MEMORIES

The memory work should always be interwoven with the processes described above. The memory work consists of gradually encouraging the client to talk about what happened, in detail, including what s/he felt or thought at the time and what s/he feels and thinks now about the images s/he recovers.

For example, when Molly, an incest survivor, reported a nightmare in which a faceless man grabbed her in a darkened room, the therapist gently encouraged her to talk about what she felt as she talked about the nightmare; exactly what the room, the man, and she herself looked like; what they said to one another, and so on.

When the whole memories are not available consciously, they may be accessed through hypnotherapy and other uncovering techniques. This should be done only in the most nondirective fashion.

For example, in a hypnotherapy session with Irma, an incest survivor, the therapist suggested Irma return to a time in childhood that was important to her in some way. Gradually Irma became aware of another person in her childhood bedroom. The therapist guided the uncovering in a nondirective way, using such questions as, "What's happening now?" "What do you see?" "What are you doing?" "Is the other person still there?" "Can you see who it is?" Because of the individual's vulnerability to suggestion during hypnosis, it would be inappropriate and perhaps even unethical to ask directive questions such as, "Is it your father?" "Is he making you do something you don't want to do?"

Uncovering techniques should be used only after the client and therapist agree that the client is ready to discover the hidden material. The therapist must respect and explore the client's resistances to using hypnotherapy, and must take care not to replicate the traumatic situation by bringing forth overwhelming affect and a state of helplessness (Parson, 1984). An important aspect of this is checking with the client after a hypnotherapy session (both that day and in the next session) about how s/he felt about the material uncovered. Less direct methods of regulating the uncovering of traumatic material include paying attention to changes in the client's willingness to open up, missed sessions, or more overt signs of distress such as reports of panic attacks, nightmares, suicidal behavior, and so forth.

Techniques to facilitate controlled approach and avoidance can be used during and between sessions where hypnotherapy is utilized as the client indicates how well s/he is managing the emerging memories. Approach techniques that can be used between sessions include self-hypnosis or self-guided imagery, visiting the scene of the traumatic event, talking with the perpetrator or, for example, with the mother if the father was the abuser, reading popular books for trauma survivors, and so forth. Avoidance techniques that can be used between sessions include imagining leaving the painful images in the therapist's office, staying busy, spending time with friends who will not demand that the client talk about the event, self-hypnosis whose focus is on feeling safe, listening to soothing music, and so forth. This process will be described in more detail in Chapter 10.

IDEAL THERAPY OUTCOME

The following general goals of post-trauma therapy are based on constructivist self development theory:

1. The individual will be able to explore the meanings of the traumatic event at will, experiencing emotions that are appropriate to the situation without being overwhelmed.
2. The self that has been damaged or disrupted as a result of trauma will be restored over the course of post-trauma therapy. Specifically, the self capacities should be strengthened and the ego resources mobilized to enable the individual to maintain a stable sense of self-esteem while gradually tolerating the painful emotions, thoughts, and images associated with recollections of the trauma.
3. The psychological need structure of the individual will become more balanced. As individuals become able to meet needs that were disrupted by the trauma, these needs will represent less pressing concerns. Important psychological needs that were neglected as a consequence of the trauma will regain importance in the person's life.
4. Overgeneralized negative schemas will become less rigid and maladaptive and more positive schemas will emerge. The traumatic memories will ultimately be assimilated into the individual's schemas about self and world, and the necessary accommodation will take place through a grieving process followed by acceptance of new inner representations of or schemas about self and world. Although painful, the accommodation of previous schemas to new realities is growth-producing.
5. As the individual works through the traumatic material, there will be an appropriate balance between approach and avoidance and between assimilation and accommodation. In other words, all of these psychological processes will be utilized where appropriate, with the psychological benefits outweighing the costs.

CONCLUSION

In this chapter, we have given some general principles of assessment and intervention based on constructivist self development theory. The following chapters describe, in greater detail, the processes and techniques utilized in achieving these broad therapeutic goals.

6. Assessing Personal History, Traumatic Events, the Social and Cultural Context, and Social Support

In this chapter, we discuss the assessment of significant life experiences of the traumatized individual, including personal history, characteristics of the traumatic life events, and the social and cultural context. This assessment helps the clinician and client understand the development of the individual's self capacities, ego resources, needs, and schemas, as well as providing the context for the meanings of the trauma. In addition, we include a brief discussion of the importance of others' responses to the victim.

PERSONAL HISTORY

While we generally begin to build a picture of the individual's history early in treatment, clients who are in distress may not be capable of providing historical information in initial sessions. Clients who are distressed will experience questions they perceive as irrelevant as a failure in empathy, starting therapy off on a bad footing. The following guidelines for history-taking assume that the individual is not in crisis, and is prepared to answer questions about the past. This information may of course be collected over the course of several sessions, and grows throughout therapy as new material emerges.

In Parson's (1988) model of therapy for post-trauma self disorders, the first phase of therapy is the "clinical-psychohistorical inquiry," an important phase in the self-reparative work. With regard to this process, he writes,

> It seeks to make meaningful connections between and among persons, things, emotional states, and cognitions experienced by (the survivor) at conscious, preconscious, and unconscious levels of awareness, historically and currently (p. 262).

101

Our approach to history-taking is consistent with our understanding of persons: While we are interested in events in the individual's life, we are most interested in whatever the individual considers important. Because we view the individual's psychological experiences as both the motivation for and the focus of change, we are less interested in the historical accuracy of the client's report than in the meanings s/he ascribes to whatever s/he reports and the associated feelings.

We emphasize the importance of narrative rather than historical truth (Spence, 1982), that is, the client's interpretation of life experiences and what is most central to him or her, rather than an "accurate" accounting of the events as they actually occurred. Yet we are aware of some problems associated with this approach. First, some adult clients who have or believe they may have experienced childhood abuse are very anxious to know exactly what happened. It is likely that memories of early abuse are composites of actual experiences (Orne, 1986). The legal issues involved in this complex matter are obviously different from the clinical issues; the former are addressed by Orne, Whitehouse, Orne, Dinges, and Nadon (1989). As Orne (1986) points out, the client's account has psychological meaning and truth, whether or not it is historically accurate.

In our experience, clients who struggle with this issue eventually come to understand that their experience of being abused, neglected, or otherwise violated during childhood must be worked through; worrying endlessly about exactly what happened is in many cases a defense against confronting the traumatic imagery and corresponding feelings.

A second hazard to the therapist (which is not unique in victim cases) is another aspect of narrative truth: As listeners, we tend to interpolate and make the client's statements into a coherent narrative (Spence, 1982). This can lead us to assume that we understand rather than to clarify and probe for further details. While it would be disruptive to question every nuance of every statement, as therapists we should remember that our own experience provides the context for what we are hearing and attempt to remain aware that our client's context is likely quite different from our own.

Any of the myriad psychosocial history questionnaires may be used for the initial interview. We tend to use a fairly nondirective interviewing approach, although we attempt to cover the major areas covered by most standard psychosocial history interviews. Our approach is differentiated from others in that we use our theory to guide our listening for themes. Thus, we follow up on anything that the client volunteers which might relate to the self capacities and ego resources, to the development of psychological needs and schemas, or to the subjective experience of trauma. This can be done with a list of the self capacities, ego resources, and needs at hand until one becomes familiar with them.

The important areas to explore, based on the theory, are the seven need areas. Thus, the following themes should be explored fully: those related to attributions of causality for traumatic events and orientation toward the future (frame of reference), vulnerability to harm (safety), being cared for or supported (trust/dependency), relationships (intimacy), feelings of self-worth or ideas about the value of others (esteem), taking care of oneself or individuation (independence), and being in control of or exerting influence over others (power).

The following intake questionnaire is based on one presented by Wolberg (1977, pp. 404–405), but we have modified it to reflect our own view of important areas to cover with trauma survivors in the first few therapy sessions. We have included some material taken from the Menninger Foundation (1984) Test Packet, an instrument developed originally by Appelbaum and Katz (1975) to collect data prior to the first visit.

NEW CLIENT QUESTIONNAIRE

Presenting Problem
Presenting problem (in client's words).
>   History and development of this concern (trauma presentation).
>   (If the client cites a traumatic experience as the presenting problem, the following material may have to be collected over an extended period of time, as the client comes to trust the therapist enough to talk with the therapist about what happened.)
>
>   Exactly what happened? (In cases of childhood abuse, it will be important for the client eventually to be able to explain in detail what happened. This, however, may not happen until well into the therapy process.)
>
>   When? (How old was the client, how long ago, how often, for how long a period of time, especially with respect to childhood abuse)
>
>   If abuse, was/is it ongoing, multiple episode or was it a one-time incident? If an adult client is currently being abused, the therapist should attempt to assess the client's safety and need for protection. With a child client, legal requirements for reporting should be observed.

Who was/were the perpetrator(s)? (Here the therapist should be aware of the possibility of multiple victimizations. After the client responds to this question, the therapist should inquire in a matter-of-fact manner whether there were other abusers in the client's history.)

Has the client ever told anyone about what happened before? If so, what was the response?

Other complaints or symptoms

Physical/biological
Emotional
Cognitive
Behavioral
Interpersonal

History and development of these concerns

When did the problem begin?
Under what circumstances?
What does the client believe produced it?
What treatment has been tried?
What does the client hope to gain by coming to therapy?

Previous psychological/emotional difficulties

As a child
As an adult
Any hospitalizations?
At what period does client believe himself/herself to have been completely free from emotional disorder?

Effect of current disorder on present functioning

Effect on physical health, appetite, sleep, and sexual function
Effect on work
Effect on family and other relationships
Effect on interests and recreation
Effect on community relations

Evaluation of presenting problem

Evidence of disrupted psychological needs
Evidence of disrupted or negative schemas
Evidence of compromised self capacities or ego resources
What is the client's attitude toward the problem?
What coping strategies has s/he tried? How successful have these been?

Etiologic Factors

> History of family medical problems
>
> Family history of psychiatric disorder, including alcohol abuse
>
> Family social history: genogram, exploration of early psychological environment and relationships with parents and siblings

Significant events, particularly traumatic events, in the past history, including traumatic separations, accidents, early or recent losses, chronic or life-threatening illnesses, childhood neglect, crime, etc. witnessing or engaging in violence (this last item is especially relevant to victims of childhood abuse and war veterans)

Precipitating factors in present environment

> Details of any recent traumatic experiences
>
> Other current psychosocial stressors

What brings the individual to therapy at this time?

Inner conflicts, evidence of imbalance among needs

Early memories: what are the client's earliest memory, happiest and most unhappy memory of childhood?

Personality Strengths and Limitations

Level of maturity: physical growth, educational achievement and school progress, sexual maturity, marriage, parenthood, social relationships, community involvement

Evaluation of self capacities and ego resources (detailed in Chapter 7)

Evaluation of psychological needs and schemas in the seven areas

Interests, hobbies, ambitions

Although we consider all of this information important to gather in the course of the early interviews, our approach is to follow the client through the material as he or she presents it without imposing a structure. Some of the information in the suggested interview presented above may not come forth until well into therapy. The statistical data can be obtained through an initial written client questionnaire. We prefer to collect the other material in an unstructured interview as this also provides an excellent early opportunity to learn about what is important to the client. However, putting this material into a written questionnaire certainly has value: Appelbaum and Katz (1975) showed that their written Test Packet provided data that were highly comparable with both diagnostic inferences based on one to three psychiatric interviews and full psychiatric examinations, including extensive psychological testing, and that the Test Packet often added significant information to the other two methods of data collection.

Others have developed questionnaires for use with trauma survivors which are useful for structuring data collection (e.g., Courtois [1988] for incest victims; Keane, Fairbank, Caddell, Zimering, & Bender [1985] for Vietnam combat veterans; Meyer & Taylor [1986] for rape victims). Most recently, for the purposes of learning both what traumatic life events the client has experienced and, perhaps more important, how distressed the client is about these events, we have developed the TSI Life Event Questionnaire (Pearlman, McCann, & Johnson, 1990a). This is an 80-item questionnaire that asks respondents to note both whether they have experienced a wide variety of traumatic life events and how much that experience distresses them now. Because of the sensitive nature of this material, we generally do not ask clients to complete this questionnaire until a therapeutic bond exists and the client is deemed to have sufficiently well-developed self capacities to tolerate any strong feelings that the questionnaire may evoke. Our preference is to have the client come to a therapy session a bit early to complete the questionnaire so that resulting feelings can be addressed with the therapist.

The following excerpt from part of an initial interview with a client illustrates our approach with someone who does not bring up trauma as a presenting problem. The client is a 35-year-old married mother of three children. She came in expressing distress about her marriage, in which she felt degraded by her husband and overwhelmed with responsibility for children and household in addition to her full-time job. (We note parenthetically the avenues the therapist is exploring in the interview.)

Therapist: Tell me something about your family.

Rosa: I have two brothers. My parents always thought boys were better than girls, so they were little kings and I was the slave.
(Possibility that the client was abused by brothers. Possible power or independence issues.)

Therapist: Did your brothers treat you like a slave?

Rosa: Oh no, they thought it was awful, the way my parents treated me, but they were nice to me.

Therapist: How did your parents treat you?

Rosa: Well, my father always told me I was worthless because I was fat. I'm still fat so I guess I'm still worthless. *(Low self-esteem.)*

Therapist: Is that what you feel about yourself?

Rosa: Well it's hard not to when everyone tells you that all the time. That's what my husband says too. If I'd just lose weight . . . that's what everyone says to me all the time. Even my mother.

Therapist: Tell me something about your relationship with your mother.

Rosa: She was always mean to me. Nothing I did was ever good enough. She told me I was dumb.

Therapist: What was that like for you? *(Exploring self capacities and feelings of self-worth.)*

Rosa: It was awful. Still is. I just try to ignore her and do my best. *(Sign of some strength in ego resources; exploring where this might have developed.)*

Therapist: I sense a lot of determination in you.

Rosa: You bet. I have to keep going, for the kids' sake. My younger son is just like me. He's real sensitive so I have to show him "Mommy can do it, and so can you." *(Signs of independence.)*

Therapist: Tell me about your relationship with your son.

Rosa: Oh, we're very close. When things are bothering him, he talks to me first. He'd never talk to his father. His father just ranks on him. *(Possibility of father abusing son.)*

Therapist: Ranks on him?

Rosa: I mean, he acts just like another kid. It's like having two 4-year-olds. When Bobby is watching TV, his father will walk in and switch the channels just to annoy him.

Therapist: Is that typical of their relationship?

Rosa: No—sometimes it's worse. He reminds me of my own father. Not that Ralph (her husband) has ever hit Bobby. . .
(Possible child abuse.)

Therapist: Did your father hit you?

Rosa: Sometimes, yes, sometimes he did. *(tears)* I'm trying to put that behind me. Ralph tells me I hold on to things, live in the past. I'm trying not to do that.

Therapist: And yet it seems like a hurt that's still with you.

Rosa: Yes. I know I shouldn't let it bother me. But it does.

Therapist: Of course it does. Until you are able to talk about what happened and make sense of it and feel and express the feelings that go with it, it probably will continue to bother you.

Rosa: I've wanted to talk about it for so long but Ralph won't listen.

Therapist: Can you imagine letting yourself talk about painful or difficult things?
(Exploring dependency needs.)

Rosa: Well, I think I can . . . maybe here . . . but I have to pull myself together so I won't be a mess for the kids.

Therapist: For the kids?

Rosa: Yeah, I mean, I'm their only parent really.

Therapist: And what about your own needs?

Rosa: There's never been anybody to take care of me *(crying)*. Sometimes I just want to lock the door and crawl under the covers.

Therapist: Tell me about that fantasy.
(Exploring abuse possibilities.)

It should be clear from this brief example that history-taking is an integral part of therapy. Using this approach, it may take some time for "the facts" to emerge. Yet, in our experience, taking a history in this way is a powerful means of building rapport with the client, and the important information does unfold over time. Over the course of three such sessions, it became clear that the client's father had abused her physically and sexually, and that both parents had degraded her throughout her childhood. Furthermore, the therapist established that Rosa had conflicts about her own unmet dependency needs which she only felt able to meet at the expense of meeting her power needs.

THE TRAUMATIC EVENT

While our approach focuses largely on the individual's psychological experience of the traumatic event or events, we also view as important the events themselves, as reported by the client, for several reasons. First, the client's report of the events is, of course, a subjective account, revealing as much about the client as it does about the events. Second, some clients who are presenting with trauma-related concerns will likely (although not invariably) want to focus on the trauma in early sessions; to ignore this for more purely psychological or other historical material would be an empathic failure on the part of the therapist. (Other clients, however, may be more comfortable talking about historical or "safer" material until they begin to trust the therapist.) Third, the client must eventually talk about what happened as part of the process of resolving the psychological experience of the trauma. The recollection, elaboration, and discussion of the memories constitute an important part of the healing process. Fourth, the impact of the trauma will be revealed in part through the client's description of what happened. Finally, the client's account of what happened will begin to give the therapist a sense of what is missing or repressed, the extent to which the memories are fragmented, and the client's ability to tolerate the affect associated with traumatic memories. Thus, this portion of the history-taking is in part diagnostic.

It is important that the therapist demonstrate at the outset that he or she is willing and able to listen to the client's account of what happened. There may not be people in the client's support network who are willing to listen or who are able to encourage the client to talk as much as he or she needs to about the event. Early inquiry about the event as the client perceives it demonstrates the therapist's understanding that the client experienced something important and distressing, validation that may be very important to the individual. It also conveys the message that the therapist fully expects the client to have feelings about and be affected by what happened. This will help normalize the client's distress and may provide some early relief.

Here we emphasize exploring the event as the client perceives it and encouraging but not pressing the client to talk about it because the discussion of the event may well raise painful feelings and open the client to retraumatization if the exploration is not done in a gentle, empathic manner. This means that the therapist must not distract the client with questions that divert him or her from whatever is salient to the client. This will be illustrated in the example below.

Another reason for attending to the details of the event is that some research has shown a relation between characteristics of the stressor and adaptation. In their studies of two populations that had survived major disasters, a group of researchers (Gleser, Green, & Winget, 1981; Green, Grace, & Gleser, 1985) showed that bereavement, threat to life, and exposure to the grotesque predicted severity of symptoms at two-year follow-up. In a study that included individuals who had experienced a variety of stressors, Wilson, Smith, and Johnson (1985) also found support for a relation among loss of a significant other, degree of life threat, and severity of post-traumatic stress disorder symptoms. In another study, Wilson and Krauss (1985) found that the best predictor of intrusive imagery among Vietnam veterans was exposure to scenes of injury or death, as well as psychological isolation upon returning from the war. Similarly, Brett and Mangine (1985) found that greater exposure to combat among Vietnam veterans was associated with greater disturbances in intrusive imagery.

More specifically, Laufer, Brett, and Gallops (1985) found the following correlations between post-trauma symptoms and exposure to combat: Symptoms of PTSD were significantly related to exposure to combat and witnessing of abusive violence; witnessing abusive violence was associated with reexperiencing phenomena; and participating in abusive violence was related to denial and numbing.

More generally, others have found that combat exposure is significantly related to severity of PTSD among Vietnam veterans (Foy, Sipprelle, Rueger, & Carroll, 1984). With regard to other survivor groups, Maida, Gordon, Steinberg, and Gordon (1989) found that victims of a major fire who had lost their homes exhibited more symptoms of depression two to four months after the fire than did those whose homes were damaged but not destroyed. While McCahill, Meyer, and Fischman (1979) found no differences in rape victims' short-term reactions, they did find at one-year follow-up that victims of more brutal rapes were having greater psychological difficulties.

The overwhelming evidence suggests that the extent of exposure to certain trauma-linked stimuli is powerfully associated with subsequent adaptation. Yet this finding is not universal. Studies that found no relation between the nature of the traumatic events and post-trauma psychological functioning include studies of rape survivors (Atkeson, Calhoun, Resick, & Ellis, 1982; Frank, Turner, & Stewart, 1980; Kilpatrick, Veronen, & Best, 1985; Ruch & Chandler, 1983) and incest survivors (Courtois, 1979).

In general, we believe that the clinical value of such research findings is to generate preliminary hypotheses about possible relations between type of trauma and the individual's adaptation. For example, observing that a Vietnam veteran evidences almost no intrusive symptoms while showing pronounced denial symptoms might lead the clinician to speculate that this client may have participated in abusive violence. This hypothesis would lead the clinician eventually to explore repressed or unexpressed memories, as well as deeply buried pain or disturbed schemas. Conversely, this hypothesis might give the clinician some way to begin to understand the expression of seemingly unwarranted extremely negative schemas about self and/or others.

One of the dangers of this type of research is that it may mislead the therapist whose client adapts in ways that are contrary to research findings. For example, we have worked with individuals who were exposed to what might be called "milder" forms of trauma, such as being fondled by a coworker, who developed full-blown PTSD. In contrast, other survivors who experienced very severe traumas, such as concentration camp confinement, may be adapting very well with the exception of circumscribed areas of functioning. In summary, we suggest that this type of research guide the exploration rather than lead the clinician to make judgments about what is a "typical" response.

We present the following segment of an early interview to illustrate our approach to this portion of the history-taking. In contrast to the previous example, this client identified a traumatic history as the presenting problem. This is the first interview with a 21-year-old female incest survivor.

Therapist: Tell me something about what brings you to therapy.

Janice: I've been working on understanding what happened to me when I was a little girl. *(tears)*

Therapist: It looks like you're hurting a lot.

Janice: Yes. I'm so angry at them I can't stand it. Why didn't they protect me?

Therapist: Your parents.

Janice: Yes . . . they knew it was happening, they must have, but they didn't stop him.

Therapist: When you feel ready, it will be helpful for you to tell me a little about what happened.

Janice: It was my cousin. The things he made me do. *(sobbing)* Why didn't I stop him?

Therapist: You wish you could have stopped him.

Janice: But he was bigger and I was afraid of him.

Therapist: Yes, of course you were. Tell me more about this feeling.

Janice: Well, he was so powerful. Everyone in the family looked up to him. Even my parents were a little afraid of him. That's why it went on for years.

Therapist: How old were you when it began?

Here, because it was an initial interview and because the client was having great difficulty containing her emotions, the therapist chose to follow her lead into the content of what happened. In a later interview or with a client who was not in such great distress, these same client statements might have been followed up with therapist responses designed to reveal the meanings to the client or to explore disrupted schemas.

SOCIAL AND CULTURAL CONTEXT

A third important piece of the assessment process is exploring the social and cultural context. Within this we include

(1) the meanings that society ascribes to the particular event of which the client is a victim

(2) the historical and social circumstances and meanings of the event, and

(3) the individual's experience of his or her position in society as described by demographic variables such as socioeconomic status, race, and gender.

We view all three of these aspects of context from the point of view of their meanings to the client and the resulting context which they provide for the traumatic experience and the recovery process.

Social Meanings of the Event

We discuss some of the shared meanings of particular events in Chapter 13. Here we wish to emphasize the importance of exploring the client's perceptions of the meaning the event has for others. For example, rape survivors often struggle with thoughts about whether they in some way colluded, brought on the assaults, or encouraged the perpetrator. As Roth (1989) points out, the cultural meanings associated with rape may become incorporated into schemas related to what it means to be a woman in this society. These questions reflect, in part, views held by others about sexual assault and objectification of women.

Similarly, the victim may adopt overgeneralized negative schemas related to the event and/or the perpetrator, more simply termed prejudices. For example, one crime victim who was assaulted by a young black man began to feel unsafe around all blacks. This overgeneralized negative schema, or racial prejudice, was reinforced by her support network which held racist views. It is important that therapists gently and gradually challenge whatever racist, sexist, or other prejudicial schemas clients hold as they work toward helping clients develop constructive ways of understanding what happened. Whenever the therapist hears material about what other people think or confusion in the victim about responsibility for what happened, it signals the need to explore the victim's thinking about how others might perceive what happened and associated issues of shame and stigma.

In subcultures which place a higher premium on self-determination, victims may have greater difficulty retaining their sense of self-worth. The victim is, indeed, often perceived in this culture as someone who is a failure, a loser (Bard & Sangrey, 1986). Few people want to be associated with a loser because it would diminish their own sense of self-esteem, as well as disrupting their illusions about their own invulnerability. The impact of societal attitudes toward Vietnam veterans, who were perceived as losers by the culture at large, has been widely discussed (e.g., Figley, 1978). This phenomenon of blaming the victim was first described by Ryan (1971) and continues to be an important issue in understanding how the victim perceives the attitudes of the larger culture.

Historical Context

Nowhere is the historical context as important as in understanding the trauma of war, terrorism, or genocide. Those clinicians who work with Vietnam or Korean war veterans, Cambodian refugees, or Holocaust survivors are painfully aware of the social disdain and/or cultural persecution symbolized by these events. Clinicians must understand something about the historical and cultural context of the Vietnam war, the killing fields in Cambodia, the reign of Hitler if they are going to work effectively with these populations and understand the profound past and present impact of these events on the client's life as well as the lives of his or her cohorts. The client's place in history, his or her understanding of this historical context, and the meaning this has are of utmost importance in understanding who this person is and how he or she experienced the trauma. For example,

- Does the victim feel like a pawn of historical forces beyond his or her control?
- Does s/he feel continued anger for the damage this has done to his or her life and the lives of others of the same generation or cultural group?
- Does s/he ever regret being born into this era or being a member of his or her cultural or religious group?
- Does s/he identify with any aspects of this history, does s/he continue to feel stuck in the time in history when the event occurred?

Here we would also add the usefulness of an awareness of the effects of sexism in working with victims of sexual assault, of an awareness of the drug culture in working with families of drug-related homicide victims, and so forth. The meanings of the historical and social era are inextricably bound to the meanings of the traumatic event for the individual; understanding this context is an essential part of aiding the victim in the recovery process.

Placing a traumatic event in historical or social perspective may be part of the healing for some survivors. For example,

Sandra, a rape victim and long-time feminist and social activist, viewed the sexual assault as further evidence of social dysfunction. This enabled her to talk publicly about what happened, to work to change medical examination protocols for rape victims, and to empathize with the perpetrator (whom she also viewed as a victim) to the extent that she could transform her anger from an immobilizing force to a motivator for continued activism. Her ability to place the trauma in a social context helped her to transform the victimization into meaningful activity.

For one Vietnam veteran, however, the effect was the opposite.

For many months Michael, a 41-year-old two-tour Vietnam combat veteran talked about how enraged he was at the middle-class college students who evaded the draft and thus the war, a sentiment that is not uncommon among Vietnam veterans. The societal support for the antiwar movement embittered him, creating a sense of painful alienation from society. He acted out his anger related to the historical-social context by going into bars where he could provoke and, at times, assault peers who represented those who had resisted the war.

Young and Erickson (1989) make an additional point about the current cultural context as post-trauma recovery environment. They note that American culture has been in rapid transition since World War II, and that such cultural transition makes the development of individual identity more difficult. In addition, the reconstruction of one's identity after a traumatic experience is doubly difficult in a culture that is evolving so rapidly.

THE INDIVIDUAL IN SOCIETY

Social class, race, and gender are fundamental parts of an individual's identity. These strongly shape one's experience, in part by shaping others' responses, thus contributing to the individual's sense of himself or herself. Understanding the unique and shared meanings of demographic characteristics is another essential part of understanding the person.

Social Class

Although social class is a strong factor in determining one's life experiences, its importance is often neglected by psychologists (Albee, 1982). Social class underlies experiences which shape cognitive schemas, and in this way is fundamental to one's psychological experience of self and others. For example,

Rosalie, an incest victim and ACOA in her early 30s, came from an impoverished family in which the father never held a steady job and the nine children were often deprived of the basic necessities of life. Her social class background translated into specific meanings, including a sense of not being good enough, of being treated "like dirt" by her peers. This resulted in very low self-esteem, disrupted dependency needs, and a corresponding strong need for independence. These experiences led to a pervasive sense of deprivation and distrust that made it difficult for her to expect much of herself, other people, or the world. The feeling of being held in contempt by the larger culture set the stage for the sexual victimization, which she interpreted as further evidence that she was worthless.

In another case, that of a teenaged girl from an upper-class, educated, professional family, we see a variation on this theme. In this case,

Julia, a teenager, was extremely reluctant to acknowledge the continuing abuse at the hands of her father. This was not only because of her deep sense of shame, guilt, and loyalty toward her dad, but also because of the values that she had internalized. These included a strong need to present herself in a favorable light in the community and to preserve the family's reputation as community leaders. In this case as well, the meanings of social class had a profound impact on the individual's experience of the traumatization.

In general, we recommend that the clinician make an assessment of the family's social and cultural background by doing a genogram in which family occupational and educational status, cultural background and norms, and family traditions are fully explored. The meanings of the victimization in the context of the intergenerational background are very important clinical data. The literature on the intergenerational transmission of certain personal and interpersonal problems among children of survivors is a fascinating area that is receiving increased attention. For example, the discovery of social and personal problems among some children of Holocaust survivors (Danieli, 1985; Freyberg, 1980), some children of Vietnam combat veterans with PTSD (Kehle & Parsons, 1988), and other families of survivors (Figley, 1983) is extremely important. Within constructivist self development theory, we approach this phenomenon in terms of understanding the impact of the meanings of social and cultural background upon the development of the person's self, central psychological needs, and schemas.

Race

We will briefly discuss the case of a black female victim to highlight the importance of racial issues.

> Brenda, a divorced black woman, was brutally raped by an unknown black male. Racial issues pervaded the unique meanings this event had for her. Brenda was fiercely independent, and had always viewed vulnerability and emotionality as signs of weakness. In describing this strong need, she often said that "Black women can't afford the luxury of emotions like white women. I've had to fight for everything I have and I don't have room in my life for these indulgences" (referring to the indulgence of experiencing and expressing feelings in therapy). This strong need for independence translated into high achievement needs and she was at the top of her field professionally.
>
> However, the cost of this achievement for her, as for many successful women, was that she could find few male peers who had achieved a similar degree of success with whom to have an intimate relationship. A continuing source of problems for her was that she felt enraged because she believed that "black women always have to pay the price for the inadequacy of black men."

In the case of Brenda, we also see the complexity of social class and gender interacting with race. The man who raped her was from a different social class, someone she viewed with contempt. It is important to assess the meanings of race for the individual, how it shapes his or her view of self and others, the impact this has upon psychological needs and schemas, and the relation of all of this to psychological adaptation. Although Brenda had few overt symptoms of PTSD, she suffered the cost of diminished capacity to feel, to allow herself to be vulnerable or intimate with any man.

At another level, racism pervades and complicates the psychological issues experienced by members of both the majority and minority cultures. In a racist society, members of minority races are victims of prejudice and discrimination. This can lead to the development of disturbed schemas about trust and safety which impede the growth of a therapeutic relationship, particularly between client and therapist of different races. Therapists must be aware of their own stereotypes about members of different racial groups in order to avoid retraumatizing clients, and in order to avoid making assumptions which neglect the individual or in any way undermine that person's dignity.

Ethnicity

Different cultures hold different views about therapy. In working with trauma survivors, therapists must be aware of the value the culture places on independence, intimacy, trust, and so forth. These issues come to the fore, in particular, in working with groups such as Southeast Asian survivors who may not view psychotherapy in the same way as Westerners do (Kinzie, 1989; Lee & Lu, 1989), or with other nonmajority ethnic groups (Parson, 1985).

These issues are also present with clients who have a strong ethnic identification. For example, a client who has a strong sense of her Irish heritage struggled for over a year to allow herself to talk to her therapist about problems of neglect and abuse in her family because of a deep sense, which she identified as rooted in her Irish background, that families should keep their troubles to themselves. Parson (1985) provides an excellent discussion of the importance of attending to the meanings of the ethnicity in trauma work.

Gender

The importance of gender socialization and trauma has primarily been addressed in the feminist literature on violence against women. Much has been written about the impact of sexism on a woman's view of herself, her sense of efficacy in the world, and her psychological needs (Gilligan, 1982; Miller, 1976). In recent years, more attention has focused on the role of male gender socialization in the development of dysfunctional personal and relationship patterns. O'Neil (1981) has identified these patterns as including restrictive emotionality; success, power, and competition issues; and restricted sexual and affectionate behaviors. These gender issues are important to consider in working with victims of both sexes. For example, it is important to understand how the person experiences his or her gender socialization and the meanings this has as a context for the victimization.

Too little attention has been paid to the relation between gender socialization and coping processes among victims. Recent evidence of gender differences in schema change among victims suggests that male victims are more likely to view the world as random and other people as more malevolent than do female victims (Janoff-Bulman, 1989a). Janoff-Bulman suggests that women may be less likely to view others as malevolent because of their strong need for connection and intimacy.

In much of our work with couples who have been crime victims, as well as with families of Vietnam veterans, gender issues often play a large role. For example, many times we observe the husband of a crime victim couple coping in a very different way than his wife. This sometimes includes the man demonstrating a need to take action to resolve the problem rather than valuing the process of emotional expression. Those men who are unable to restore a sense of power are likely to be depressed, an observation that is consistent with the Janoff-Bulman (1989a) finding that victimized men tend to be more depressed than victimized women and that this appears to relate to a post-trauma belief in a random, unpredictable world. The woman often feels devalued for being so emotional and unable to "bounce back" while the husband feels frustrated that he cannot "fix" their problem with logic and instrumental behaviors. Unless family or couples therapy is a part of treatment, these differences may result in increased marital problems and slower individual progress. Clearly, these issues are not unique to traumatized persons. However, they are of central importance in understanding the different ways that people construe trauma and its aftermath.

In summary, we view the social and cultural context as extremely important in understanding the meanings of trauma for individuals. A fruitful area for exploration in the future is the impact of culture, race, gender, and ethnicity on individuals' schematic representations of self and others, an area that has not been fully addressed in the literature (Westen, 1989).

SOCIAL SUPPORT

The post-trauma environment, including social support and others' reactions to the victimization, has received much attention in the literature (e.g., Figley, 1986; Green et al., 1985) since Symonds (1980) first wrote about the "second injury" among victims. Within this context, it is important to explore the victim's perceptions of the "support" others are providing and whether it is helpful or hurtful to the recovery process. One should not assume that a person is receiving helpful or even adequate social support just because he or she reports having a loving group of family and friends who have rallied around after the trauma. As we have emphasized in all other areas, social support is the individual's psychological experience of others' helpfulness rather than some objective or observable phenomenon. The therapist who carefully and thoroughly explores the client's support network may be shocked to learn about the thoughtless things people say in their attempts to be supportive.

An example of one such well-intended but harmful reaction reported by numerous rape victims is the attempt to minimize the victim's sense of shame by saying such things as, "He didn't really mean to hurt YOU personally, he was only venting his anger against all women." Time and time again, rape victims we have seen express outrage at this unthinking statement. As one of them retorted angrily, "What did she mean, it wasn't personal! He raped and assaulted ME. What could be more personal than THAT?" A variation on this theme is for others to ponder the reason the victimizer did what he did, clearly an intellectualized defense that protects the bystander but injures the victim. As one rape victim put it, "I don't care whether he was beaten black and blue as a child. It doesn't matter. It still doesn't make it okay."

Other victims respond to more or less subtle pressures to pull themselves together and go on with their lives by retreating from their friends and families. As one crime victim put it, "Everyone seems so relieved when I'm doing a little better and it seems to upset them when I talk about what happened. I don't want people to get sick of me because I keep talking about the same thing." It is thus important as part of this exploration to validate the victim's reactions to the reactions of other people as well as to remind the victim that it is important to the healing process to resolve his or her feelings about others' often hurtful reactions.

For example, when victims complain that "No one understands" or "Even my friends and family are getting sick of me talking about it," they need to be validated in this hurtful experience. Indeed, even the most well-meaning supporters often do not truly understand, nor can they, unless they have been similarly traumatized. Furthermore, we have observed the tolerance level of most people for others' pain to be quite limited. People do, indeed, become tired of hearing others talk about their problems because they feel helpless and want to make things better. If the client can begin to understand this process as well as his or her own reactions to it, these reactions may lose their power to produce a secondary injury.

Again, the unique meanings to the victim must be understood. One accident victim with strong independence needs found the experience of being taken care of by her family to be enormously distressing. Other victims with strong trust/dependency needs may find it distressing when people in their social network fail to call with offers of help. Working with clients to help them understand and then express to others what they need in the wake of a trauma is an important part of the healing process.

SUMMARY

In summary, we have described general guidelines for assessing the personal meanings of traumatic life experiences, the social and cultural context, and social support. Although our methods for assessing these areas have much in common with standard psychosocial history-taking, it differs from others in that it is guided by constructivist self development theory. That is, we view the process of history-taking as another opportunity to learn more about the unique client and his or her self capacities and ego resources, needs, and schemas. We use the theory to guide our explorations and to provide a framework for conceptualizing a complex psychohistorical picture of one person's life. In subsequent chapters, we discuss in more depth the applications of this assessment process to treatment planning and intervention.

7. Assessing and Strengthening Ego Resources and Self Capacities

The self capacities and ego resources, like the other aspects of the self, contribute to the unique experience of trauma and to its resolution. In Chapter 2, we refer to the self as the seat of the individual's identity and inner life. In essence, the ego resources and self capacities serve to regulate one's interpersonal interactions and to regulate self-esteem and affect. We refer the reader again to Table 2.1 (p. 14) to see how the self capacities and ego resources fit into constructivist self development theory. Table 2.2 (p. 17) also provides a list of the self capacities and the ego resources. In this chapter, we focus on assessing strengths and deficits and addressing the deficits in these areas.

As a context for the importance of this area, we will provide a theoretical link among the self, cognitive schemas, and traumatic memories, a view that integrates self psychology, object relations, and social cognition theory. In an article synthesizing psychoanalytic developmental theories and social cognition, Westen (1989) provides a cogent description of the connection between the self and schemas:

> Self-representation or self-schema refers to a relatively circumscribed, periodically activated cognitive-affective representation of self. . . . Self-system refers to the entire system of self-representations which are associatively connected with each other, with specific episodic memories, and with other kinds of representations (such as semantic-conceptual, motoric, and affective). (pp. 47–48)

Thus, Westen takes a view similar to our own by attempting to integrate analytic notions of the "self-system" with social cognitive views of schemas about self and others.

There is evidence that severe character pathology, which we view as

122

a serious disorder of the self (Kohut, 1971), is associated with severe traumatization. For example, there is evidence for a relation between borderline personality disorder and a childhood history of severe abuse (e.g., Herman, Perry, & van der Kolk, 1989; Westen et al., 1990). In severe character pathology, such as borderline personality disorder, theorists have described serious deficits in self-esteem regulation, affect regulation, and chronic instability in interpersonal relations (e.g., Kohut, 1971, 1977).

Westen (1989) also cites evidence that borderline personalities show an attributional style which is not reducible to developmental differences, but may have resulted from abusive experiences that occurred in the post-oedipal years. This attributional style includes a view of other people as malevolent, untrustworthy, and overpowering. Furthermore, there is some suggestion that among clients with a borderline diagnosis, disturbed schemas may be affect-centered. That is, when these individuals are flooded with affects they cannot regulate, this activates more distorted schemas or representations of self and world.

Westen's work supports our own view that severe traumatization can produce both serious impairments in self capacities and seriously distorted schemas about self and world. The clinical significance of this is that clients with disruptions in self capacities may well be experiencing a concurrent activation of unconscious, disturbed schemas about self and world. These schemas can be activated by traumatic memory fragments that may be unconscious.

For example, an incest survivor who inexplicably becomes overwhelmed by negative affects between sessions and who is unable to soothe and calm herself may well be experiencing an activation of disturbed self schemas related to feeling "like a whore," schemas that are activated (although out of conscious awareness) when she has sex with an older, married man. These schemas can activate unconscious memory fragments, whether imagery or other schemas. In other words, disturbed schemas and their relation to past trauma may be unconscious because they have the potential to create affective overload and disruptions in self-esteem regulation. The complexities inherent within this view are many and will be addressed in this and subsequent chapters.

The ongoing assessment of self capacities and ego resources has important implications for treatment planning and intervention. This assessment will help the clinician gauge the client's readiness to engage in memory work, the therapeutic work directly related to approaching and resolving the traumatic experience. The following areas should be explored throughout post-trauma therapy:

- The ego resources and self capacities the client brings to therapy;
- The extent to which early experience inhibited or supported the development of the ego resources and self capacities; and
- The extent to which traumas in childhood or adulthood have disrupted ego resources and self capacities.

We refer to the therapeutic task of strengthening the ego resources and self capacities as "self work." The major goals of self work are to support, enhance, and/or create the ego resources and self capacities necessary to tolerate the painful affects and meanings of the trauma, to create or restore a cohesive and positive sense of self-esteem, and to enable the individual to resume progressive self-development. The extent and nature of self work will vary from one individual to the next.

The clinician should keep in mind that self capacities are relatively fluid, except perhaps in serious personality disorders, and can be temporarily disrupted by trauma and subsequent stressors. For example, a rape victim who is normally able to soothe and calm herself may be less able to do so when facing a situation that resembles the rape, or when she is overwhelmed by affect, as she might be when testifying in court. This process may be linked to the emergence of traumatic memories that activate schemas connected with feelings of shame and self-hatred.

In addition to indicating the individual's ability to tolerate the work of therapy, the assessment of self capacities and ego resources helps the therapist to determine the length of treatment, and to decide whether an exploratory, uncovering approach or a more supportive approach aimed at stabilization is indicated in the initial phases of treatment. The treatment plan will evolve as the clinician learns more about the client over the course of therapy.

With regard to this assessment goal, the following questions are important to explore:

1. Does the individual evidence diminished self capacities and ego resources in many areas of his or her life or are the disruptions circumscribed?
2. Have these disruptions to the self occurred as a result of chronic trauma or failures in empathy, which extend far back in the individual's history, or do they appear to stem from more recent traumatic experiences?

The client who manifests a chronic history of severely underdeveloped self capacities and ego resources will probably require long-term and initially self-reparative therapy (Parson, 1988). The emphasis here is on building the self capacities in order to develop a more stable and cohesive sense of self and to decrease the dysfunctional behavior patterns that arise from an undeveloped self. If a client's view of self or the world has become extremely distorted through prolonged or chronic traumatization, one must expect that the change will be very slow. In contrast, the victim who presents with more circumscribed and acute disruptions in the self resulting from a recent trauma may respond more quickly to short-term interventions aimed at bolstering existing self capacities and ego resources.

THERAPIST ASSESSMENT OF SELF CAPACITIES AND EGO RESOURCES

We have developed a structured process to assess the ego resources and self capacities of therapy clients based upon our clinical work. The following list of ego resources and self capacities was derived, in part, from our interpretation of self psychology theory (Kohut, 1971, 1977) and from the work of Murray and Kluckhohn (1953). While we are not strict self psychology theorists, we believe there are concepts derived from self psychology that can be useful in understanding the experience of trauma survivors. The work of Brende (1983), Parson (1984, 1988), Parson and Brende (1985), and Ulman and Brothers (1988) represents classical self psychology theory as applied to the experience of trauma. Our purpose is to distill these concepts in a way that will be comprehensible and meaningful for clinicians from a variety of theoretical backgrounds.

In reviewing the literature, we have been struck by a lack of clear or consistent definitions of these constructs. It is our hope that our preliminary attempt at such definitions will offer a common language for understanding the self-reparative processes in post-trauma therapy. We discuss each capacity and resource in some detail in the second part of this chapter, entitled "Strengthening the Damaged Self."

We are aware that the following method of assessing ego resources and self capacities is very subjective and is confounded by the therapist's own level of training, experience, and self-understanding, which will influence the extent to which the therapist knows the client. The purpose of developing definitions is to allow clinicians to work with these constructs, with a longer-term goal of developing less subjective, more valid assessment methods.

The self capacities and ego resources are aspects of the personality which are assets to the individual. They develop over time through internalization of significant others, direct learning, and attempts to gain positive reinforcement from valued others. We distinguish self capacities from ego resources as follows: The self capacities enable the individual to maintain a cohesive sense of identity or self and to regulate self-esteem, while the ego resources enable the individual to negotiate the world outside himself or herself, including relationships and life tasks.

We further break down the ego resources of interest to constructivist self development theory and trauma into two groups: those whose primary importance is to facilitate the therapy process and those whose primary purpose is to enable individuals to protect themselves from further harm. Whether or not these distinctions or our preliminary definitions are valid or reliable is an empirical matter, which we plan to explore in our future research on constructivist self development theory. For clinical purposes, we have found it to be a useful way of organizing our own thinking about clients' psychological assets, both as a guide to strengths that can be mobilized during therapy and as a way to identify areas that require development before and during the memory work. We present our assessment guide below. For clarity and simplicity, we use masculine pronouns here to refer to the client being assessed, with the understanding that this process applies equally to male and female clients.

Ego Resources

Intelligence. A person in whom intelligence is well-developed is bright; is able to apply his mind to an abstract problem; and is able to think, speak, and write coherently and logically.

A person in whom intelligence is a poorly developed resource may not be particularly bright; may be unable to apply his mind to a problem; may customarily use concepts whose meanings are vague, undefined, or meaningless; and may not be able to think, write, or speak clearly, coherently, or logically. He may be unable to generate alternatives or respond readily to requests for clarification or further information.

Awareness of Psychological Needs. A person in whom this is a well-developed resource has a strong sense of what is important to him and can readily discern which course of action will most likely result in his needs being met. This person often bases his actions on an assessment of the probability of the actions gratifying important needs. This person probably has a well-developed system of values which he tries to integrate into his daily living. He may hold a goal of personal development and accomplishment suited to his circumstances and capabilities.

A person whose awareness of psychological needs is poorly developed may not feel comfortable with the idea that he has needs, or may not be able to identify anything that he values beyond survival or perhaps making others happy. He lacks a clear internal guide to his behavior. He may have difficulty understanding why he is so unhappy at times, or he may experience life as confusing and unrewarding.

Ability to Introspect. A person in whom this is a well-developed resource has the capacity for self-detachment and analysis and insight into his own motives, evaluations, and emotional responses.

A person whose ability to introspect is poorly developed may have little capacity for self-analysis and little insight into his motives, evaluations, and emotional responses.

Willpower and Initiative. A person in whom this is a well-developed resource is able to initiate creative or purposeful activities, is able to do what he has resolved to do, is able to persist in the face of difficulties, is able to complete a prescribed or elected course of action, and is able to resume a task after failure. He may exhibit a "fighting spirit" in the face of obstacles, responding positively to appropriate personal challenges.

A person in whom willpower and initiative are poorly developed may be unable to take initiative in purposeful activities, may be unable to do what he resolves to do, or may be incapable of committing himself to a course of action. He is often unable to persist in the face of difficulties and gives up easily.

Ability to Strive for Personal Growth, to Recognize and Move Toward What is Healthy for Oneself, with Appropriate Regard for Others. A person in whom this is a well-developed resource seeks personal growth and development, even when the hurdles are substantial. He is capable of recognizing and moving toward what will be good for him in the long run.

A person in whom the ability to strive for personal growth is poorly developed may appear hopeless and report feeling helpless in the face of minor or moderate life difficulties or obstacles. This person may be easily discouraged, may present seemingly endless barriers to progress, and may appear to the therapist as quite resistant to change.

Ability to View Oneself and Others from More Than One Perspective. A person in whom this is a well-developed resource can generate alternative explanations for the behavior of self and others, is able to view his difficulties in a larger context, and brings humor to bear as a coping mechanism, but not as a rigid defense. This person may laugh readily and see irony in situations.

A person whose ability to take perspective is poorly developed rarely experiences the humor in life, may be so deeply embroiled in his problems that he has no perspective or sense of a larger context, and has difficulty imagining that there is more than one possible motive for a particular behavior.

Empathy. A person in whom this is a well-developed resource is able to emphathize with another's experience and is capable of altruistic or unselfish behavior. He is capable of experiencing and expressing genuine concern for others in a variety of interpersonal relationships, as well as for others whom he does not know personally.

A person in whom empathy is a poorly developed resource may feel a sense of entitlement and resentment toward others whom he may view as existing solely to meet his needs. Alternatively, this individual may hold rigidly to the role of helper, caretaker, or director in relationships, demonstrating an inability to understand the meanings of helping to the other.

Awareness of Boundaries Between Self and Others. A person in whom this is a well-developed resource rarely assumes others think or feel as he does, has the capacity to be aware of his impact upon others, rarely infringes upon others' time and space, and rarely wears out his welcome.

A person with a poorly developed awareness of boundaries seems unable to distinguish between his own feelings or thoughts and those of others, often experiences his wishes or needs as someone else's mandate, and may feel others should know what he wants without overt communication.

Self Capacities

Ability to Moderate Self-loathing. A person in whom this is a well-developed capacity seems to be able to hear criticism and use it constructively, without becoming depressed or overgeneralizing it. He appears able to acknowledge his personal limitations without becoming critical of or destructive to himself.

A person with a poorly developed ability to moderate self-loathing may overgeneralize criticism about his behavior to a denunciation of himself. He may experience another's inattention as a direct rejection. He may constantly seek validation of his worth, and failing to receive this, he may experience self-loathing or engage in self-destructive recriminations. He may lapse into self-loathing when unacceptable feelings emerge.

Ability to Tolerate Strong Affect. A person in whom this is a well-developed ability does not fear experiencing strong feelings, whether positive or negative, and expresses a wide range of feelings readily and appropriately.

A person with a poorly developed ability to tolerate strong affect may avoid various situations or topics of discussion for fear of experiencing strong feelings. He is very likely to engage in substance abuse or other forms of emotional anesthesia. He may become overwhelmed or frightened or act out when strong emotions are aroused.

Ability to Be Alone Without Being Lonely. A person in whom this is a well-developed resource enjoys time spent alone and is able to take pleasure in solitary pursuits such as reading, painting, writing, and listening to music.

A person with a poorly developed ability to be alone without feeling lonely may experience great anxiety at the thought of being alone and go to great lengths to avoid being alone. When alone, this person may feel he doesn't exist; he may engage in self-destructive behaviors, including substance abuse; he may feel compelled to call friends, family members, or the therapist; or he may feel an intense need to escape the situation.

Ability to Soothe and Calm Oneself. A person with a well-developed ability to soothe and calm himself is generally able to comfort himself when distressed. Methods employed will vary from time to time and may include but not be limited to walking in the woods, taking a bubble bath, drinking a cup of tea, listening to music, seeking support from others, and engaging in positive self-statements.

A person whose ability to soothe himself is poorly developed may fear intense affect because of a fear of not being able to help himself recover readily; may find it necessary to contact others as the exclusive means of restoring calm when upset; often works himself up even more when distressed, perhaps by focusing on the negative aspects of the stressor or by generating negative self-statements.

CASE ILLUSTRATIONS OF SELF ASSESSMENTS

Two brief case examples will illustrate the importance and methods of assessing the ego resources and self capacities in the initial stages of therapy. In the first case, the client had moderately strong ego resources, but, through years of extreme abuse, her self capacities had been severely compromised. In the second case, we see a woman with considerable ego resources and self capacities who demonstrated circumscribed areas of disruption resulting from a more recent trauma.

The first case involved Betsy, a 42-year-old woman who was referred for outpatient therapy after a three month admission to a psychiatric hospital. Her presenting problems, even after extended inpatient treatment and antidepressant therapy, included severe, disabling depression, suicidal behaviors, nightmares, sleep disturbance, anorexia, chronic anxiety, agoraphobia, and a marked decline in occupational and social functioning. She had been the victim of extreme emotional and physical cruelty by her husband over the previous 10 years, as well as having been the victim of marital rape and a violent stranger rape. It should be noted that the disclosure of the rapes did not occur until much later in treatment, when she was able to begin tolerating the overwhelming affects and meanings associated with these events. The client came into the first few sessions in a state of acute distress manifested in suicidal fantasies; severe anxiety, including tremors and hyperventilation; and a profound psychological paralysis.

The following clinical vignette illustrates the assessment of ego resources and self capacities in the initial stages of therapy.

> Betsy: (*Crying and shaking*) I just want to die, I'm falling apart, I feel like I'm going to crawl out of my skin. I can't eat, I can't sleep, I can't function. The only way out is death. Then maybe I can get some peace.

> Therapist: I can see how much you are suffering—the pain is overwhelming. I want to understand who you are and what has hurt you so badly so that we can work together to help you regain what you've lost.

Betsy: That's just it. I don't know if anyone can help me now. I don't exist, I've been reduced to a non-being. I'm just an empty shell, dead, destroyed.

Therapist: I imagine you have been very badly traumatized to feel that your self has been destroyed, to feel like you don't exist as a real person.

Betsy: *(sobbing)* I have been hurt and betrayed and abused for so many years like an animal—no, worse, like an insect that someone stomps on over and over again. After awhile you stop feeling and are reduced to a non-being.

Therapist: It must be terribly sad and painful to feel reduced to a non-being. Tell me—are there times when you are able to experience yourself as a real person? *(probing for the extent of self fragmentation)*

Betsy: *(Head in hands)* Not anymore. I used to feel like a person before my husband became so cruel. I loved my work, I felt competent, I was a good mother. Now I hate what I've become because I'm not able to cope at all.

Therapist: When you are alone with yourself and feeling distressed, are you ever able to find relief from your pain? *(probing for the capacity to soothe and calm the self or to be alone without being lonely)*

Besty: I can't bear to be alone. I'm filled with so much disgust and hatred for myself, I'm just overwhelmed with feelings of wanting to destroy what I have become. When this happens, I just start to shake all over and cry and cry. Nothing can console me.

Therpaist: That must be terribly lonely and very frightening. Are there any people in your world who are able to provide some comfort, who are there when you need them? *(exploring capacity for mature relationships)*

Besty: I'm completely alone in the world. My husband made sure I had no friends over the years and my family—well, they're still alive, but inside, they're really dead to me too. People don't seem real to me anymore, it's been so many years.

Later, in another session, she revealed a recurrent nightmare in which she was crucified on a cross with angry people mocking her, as in Christ's passion play, and then was made to suffer having her breasts, arms, and legs cut off so that she was reduced to something subhuman and despicable, as in Kafka's (1962) *Metamorphosis*.

This case illustrates someone who has endured years of torture and helplessness which eventually eroded almost all her ego resources and self capacities. Betsy demonstrated serious deficits in her ability to moderate self-loathing, to soothe herself, to tolerate being alone, to be aware of her own needs, and to demonstrate will power and initiative. On the positive side, she did possess high intelligence which had previously allowed her to attend college and pursue a career in business. She had the ability to introspect, and somehow had maintained an ability to empathize with others, which eventually enabled her to establish a friendship with two other women.

In Betsy's case, the therapy took place over a three-year period and involved considerable self building until she had the inner resources to integrate and put to rest the traumatic memories. Furthermore, the therapy focused on uncovering and working through extremely disturbed, overgeneralized schemas related to self-esteem and the view of others as malevolent (esteem-others), untrustworthy (trust), and dangerous (safety), schemas that were linked to painful affects and a complete withdrawal from interpersonal relationships. Building ego resources that would enable her to protect herself from future abuse was also an essential part of the process as she continued to be at risk while living with an abusive husband.

The following case example provides an illustration of a woman with more circumscribed deficits in self capacities which were disrupted after a brutal, single-incident victimization. Two weeks after a vicious, degrading rape by a stranger, Donna, a single woman in her 30s, came into therapy after experiencing a rapid decline in functioning, characterized by nightmares, flashbacks, panic attacks, severe depression, suicidal thoughts, and uncontrollable crying. In the second session, Donna began by talking about how depressed and overwhelmed she had felt all week.

Donna: I really lost it at work today. I feel so ashamed.

Therapist: Are you able to describe what you experienced?

Donna: A delivery man came to drop something off. I've met him before, I know he's an okay guy . . . but he reminded me of the rapist. I dropped everything I was doing and had to go outside. I started to shake and cry uncontrollably, I just couldn't calm down.

Therapist: Of course, you must have felt very frightened. Every woman feels frightened when she encounters someone who reminds her of the rapist. Can you help me understand what was going on in your mind at the time?

Donna: I had a flashback of the rapist hitting me and knocking me out. When I woke up my hands were tied and he was telling me, "You slut, you deserve it." I kept thinking to myself, maybe he's right. I know it's not right, but that's the same message my father used to give me when I was in high school, that I was a no good tramp who didn't deserve anything.

Therapist: Remembering his words, you felt as though you were unworthy, undeserving?

Donna: Yes, it was like I was overcome with self-hatred.

Therapist: And when you remembered your attacker's words, it was like you went back in time to when you were a young girl and your father made you believe you were undeserving, even though all these years you have struggled to prove to yourself that she was wrong.

Donna: Yes, I guess you're right. It is like I'm a little girl again in some ways and I hate being like this, I hate myself for overreacting like this.

Therapist: You feel like you're overreacting to be afraid and yet you were understandably afraid when you were reminded of the man who hurt you, who degraded and humiliated you.

Donna: I just feel I should be able to handle it better, shouldn't get so overwhelmed. I hate myself when I'm like this.

Therapist: I understand how you don't want to feel so overwhelmed; no one would. But you've been badly hurt, only a few short weeks ago. Is it so difficult to be compassionate toward yourself when you experience all these very understandable feelings?

Donna: I just can't accept that I'm not handling things and that I'm still falling apart. I've always been a strong person and I can't tolerate being so weak and unable to handle my feelings.

Therapist: Then that's something we have to work on together, yes?

In the case of Donna, we see a woman who, despite a difficult background, possessed many ego resources: a sense of humor, intelligence, awareness of her needs, and a fighting spirit that reflected highly developed willpower. Although her ability to regulate self-esteem (self capacities) had been fairly strong, negative esteem schemas (described in detail in Chapter 14) emerged which were linked to the previous emotional abuse by her father. The verbal degradation during the rape activated these unconscious schemas, causing her to regress to a state in which she temporarily lost the ability to regulate affect and moderate self-loathing.

One clinical picture we have observed which is of interest to us is that of individuals who have very strong ego resources coupled with impaired self capacities. Often these survivors, who present as bright, competent, and high-functioning in many ways, can give the impression that they are able and ready to move steadily toward the approach and integration of traumatic memories. In these cases, it is tempting to follow the client's lead to move into painful material early in therapy. The result is that these clients quickly retreat from therapy or become increasingly symptomatic between sessions. We have made this error a number of times with certain clients. Only when we began fully exploring the internal capacities for affect regulation and self soothing were we able to discover that the capacities necessary for successful memory integration did not exist.

We bring up this point because it is important not to assume that an individual with considerable resources who presents as high-functioning will have a corresponding strength in the self capacities. In this regard, we find the distinction between ego resources and self capacities to have heuristic value in guiding us in the pacing of approach in a way that will protect the individual from becoming retraumatized.

STRENGTHENING THE DAMAGED SELF

Here we will describe the type of interventions we have found helpful in building, restoring, and mobilizing the self capacities and ego resources. First, we will discuss general principles underlying self-reparative work. Next, we will describe interventions which can facilitate the development of specific ego resources and self capacities.

Solidifying the Alliance Through Supporting the Self

The development of a therapeutic alliance is viewed by many as central to the beginning stages of therapy (e.g., Wolberg, 1977). Many theorists have discussed the important role of accurate empathy, responsiveness, warmth, and concerned involvement in forming a working alliance (Greenson, 1967). We now address the ways our conceptualization of self-building can guide the clinician in forming a working alliance.

We believe the client's strengths should be acknowledged openly through direct feedback early in therapy. For example, the therapist might say something like,

> Your sense of yourself has clearly been hurt by your experience (the rape, crime, other abuse) and it's going to take some time to heal these wounds. However, what I've learned so far about you is that you appear to be an intelligent person who has a great deal of initiative and willpower, who has the capacity to care about others, and a strong desire to overcome what happened (citing here the client's specific strengths). These considerable strengths make me hopeful that you will be able to recover.

By framing this feedback in the most hopeful manner, the clinician is able to help the client mobilize his or her ego resources and to build hope as she or he undertakes the sometimes long and often painful process of post-trauma therapy. When clients have suffered an extreme diminution of self capacities, this should also be acknowledged and normalized as a condition that is often associated with traumatization.

In summary, the therapist builds the alliance by

1. acknowledging the individual's strengths and weaknesses;
2. conveying hope about resolving areas of deficit and a respect for areas of strength;
3. expressing a commitment to working collaboratively with the person, with respect for his or her defenses; and
4. being as open as possible about the course of treatment, what it may or may not involve, the time frame, and any concerns one imagines the client might have.

With respect to the latter issue, it is important to give clients a realistic sense of what to expect about the course of treatment, what they might experience over the course of therapy, and a general time frame. This, of course, derives from a thorough assessment of ego resources and self capacities. Clients often experience this process as reassuring; by addressing early concerns about the treatment itself, the therapist is demonstrating empathy and responsiveness.

Respecting the Individual's Pacing

It is also important to convey to clients that the therapist does not intend to retraumatize them or cause them unnecessary pain by going too fast, and that he or she wants them to feel free to discuss any concerns or feelings about the therapy process. In order to encourage clients to discuss their reactions to the therapy process, we try to make a point of "checking in" with the client toward the end of the session or after a particularly painful piece of work. Questions such as, "How are you feeling about the work we have done today?", "Are you feeling comfortable with this?", and "Are we going too fast?" convey a respectful attitude toward the person that strengthens the alliance. This process is particularly important with individuals who have limited self capacities, as the risk for retraumatization within therapy is significant. With clients who are having a very difficult time regulating affect and/or imagery after sessions, it may be helpful to agree to stop 10 minutes before the end of each session not only to check in but also to talk about what the client can do to comfort and care for herself or himself over the hours and days ahead.

Some clients will express concerns about going too slowly, some motivated by a desire to feel better, others by a sense that the ability to do the work faster is related to their own independence or self-esteem. The therapist must help these clients not to push themselves so hard that they are retraumatized by overwhelming the available ego resources and self capacities. Specifically, the therapist must be alert to signs that the individual is pressing ahead with the memory work too rapidly, before the self capacities are sufficiently strong. Signs of this include sudden increases in anxiety-related symptoms, panic states, increased nightmares or flashbacks, increased self-destructive behaviors, and so forth. In most cases, these disturbances are associated with affectively powerful and disrupted schemas that are activated as traumatic memories emerge. As with any clinical issue, it is important to explore with these clients their apparent need to press ahead and its associated meanings. Reframing a slower pace can be helpful.

> For example, with an incest survivor, a social worker with high independence needs who felt more pressure as she approached age 30 to "put this behind me and get on with my life," the therapist took the stance, "You can do many things well for yourself, but one area you need to grow in is in your ability to be gentle with and take care of yourself psychologically. This will be important for you as a role model as you become a clinical supervisor and a mother" (both goals held by this woman).

Finally, it is important also to anticipate a client's concerns about therapy, such as it taking too much time, costing too much money, or not being helpful. As one addresses the manifest concerns that are presented, one must also listen for the symbolic meanings of such concerns. For example, in bringing up the issues of fees, is the client expressing suspicion about the therapist's motives? By bringing up issues about therapy not being helpful, is she or he expressing a concern about being damaged beyond repair, a hopeless case? The therapist must attempt to address the underlying fears, which may at times manifest themselves in treatment resistances. We discuss assessment of resistances and techniques for working them through in Chapter 11.

The preceding comments suggest the importance of building a therapeutic alliance through acknowledging and understanding the person's self capacities, ego resources, and deficits; conveying an attitude of concern and respect for the person; educating him or her about all facets of PTSD and about therapy as a way of instilling hope; increasing trust in the therapist gradually; and normalizing the client's reactions so that they are less frightening.

Self Work as a Prelude to Memory and Schema Work

As implied previously, the type of self work that will be necessary depends on the specific self capacities and ego resources that are impaired and the extent of impairment. First we describe some general principles of self work and then we address interventions aimed at strengthening the ego resources and self capacities.

In general, we find Kohut's (1971, 1977) framework helpful for conceptualizing how individuals internalize a responsive, empathetic human being who is respectful of their needs and ego resources. We have found several notions from self psychology useful in our work with trauma survivors. We use simplified versions of these concepts in our theory for heuristic purposes.

Kohut's concept of "positive mirroring" is valuable in its implication that the therapist reflects back to the client a more positive, and less distorted self-image. The therapist does this by conveying a sense of respect for the person's dignity, an empathetic understanding of the wounds to self-esteem that have been endured, and a valuing of the person with all his or her strengths and weaknesses.

In referring to empathy, we do not refer merely to the Rogerian techniques of reflection and paraphrase. Rather, we agree with Kohut (1971, 1977) that the empathy must be finely attuned to hearing, knowing, and responding to the client's deepest fears, conflicts, and needs. This process of empathetic interpretation, along with soothing responsiveness, is one which requires a solid theoretical basis for determining the timing and content of interpretations. A warm, caring listener can be empathetic, nonjudgmental, and reflective, but the experienced therapist does more. By being strong enough to delve into the inner world of the victim, he or she is able to hear and not merely to listen, to know without simply parroting what the client already knows. To be attuned to the client's unique inner world, the therapist must be willing to delve into the depths of the frightening world of the victim. The therapist must learn and understand, through empathy, the client's inner experience of terror and estrangement from self and others. In order to accomplish this, the therapist must walk with the client where the deepest and seemingly intolerable hurts have been experienced, offering gentle words of encouragement and gradually leading the client through the process of self-healing. The effects this can have on the therapist's own psyche are described elsewhere in the context of our theory (McCann & Pearlman, 1990).

Parson (1988) refers to the therapist as a "container" for the survivor's inner world of affective turmoil. The therapist must confront and absorb some of the perceived "poisons" inside the client, just as the ancient Shaman absorbed the illnesses of others during the process of healing and transformation (Frank, 1974). The therapist must have a map to guide them in this difficult journey, with the hope and wisdom to coax the client out of the darkness and chaos of the violated inner world. The assessment and conceptualization serve as this guide, with the first area to negotiate being the self. The self that is damaged must be restored to its former wholeness or, for some people, the functions of the self that have never been developed must be created, expanded, and integrated.

Below, we offer specific guidelines for helping trauma victims restore the wholeness and unity of the self through the strengthening of the self capacities and ego resources.

STRENGTHENING EGO RESOURCES

In the following sections, we describe the ego resources that are important to working with trauma survivors, focusing on approaches to developing, mobilizing, and using these resources. We have described ego resources as assets that enable the individual to negotiate the world outside of himself or herself, including relationships and life tasks. We also distinguish between two types of ego resources: those whose primary value is to help the individual to benefit from a therapeutic process of reflection and introspection, and those whose primary value is to enable the individual to protect himself or herself from harm. Of course, all of the ego resources are helpful to the individual in many ways; we make this distinction because it can be useful to the clinician.

Ego Resources Important to the Recovery Process

The following ego resources are especially helpful to the therapy process and recovery from trauma:

1. Intelligence;
2. An awareness of one's psychological needs;
3. The ability to introspect;
4. Willpower and initiative;
5. The ability to strive for personal growth;
6. The ability to view oneself and others from more than one perspective;
7. The ability to empathize with another's point of view.

These ego resources are valuable assets that clients bring to therapy, assets which can be acknowledged, mobilized, or bolstered as the individual embarks on the difficult journey of posttrauma therapy. One major way the therapist can mobilize the existing ego resources of the client is through reflection, honest feedback, and modeling, as well as through other methods described below.

Intelligence. The therapist must be respectful of the intellectual capacities of the individual, using language and conceptualizations that are matched to the client's verbal and conceptual abilities. It is important to avoid using jargon or language that will be experienced as distancing. It may be appropriate to use language that matches the client's style, if this comes naturally to the therapist. If this is not comfortable for the therapist, the client may experience these attempts as false. Ideally, the therapist should strike a balance between his or her natural language style and that of the client, remaining alert to any possible mismatch and its implications. Statements or interventions that are too abstract or complex for a particular client will not be helpful.

At the other end of the intelligence continuum, clients who are overintellectualized may be defending against painful feelings. This defense must not be challenged prematurely. Ideally, the therapist should discover interventions suited to the client's particular intellectual level and style. Some clients enjoy reading, and may find self-help books useful. To suggest this to other clients may be a failure in empathy.

Awareness of Psychological Needs and Ability to Introspect. An understanding of one's psychological needs is the basis for connecting behaviors and feelings that might otherwise seem unrelated or incomprehensible. It is an invaluable asset in the therapy process, since trauma inevitably results in a disruption of psychological needs and their gratification. Self-awareness will also help the client discover new ways to satisfy his or her needs in the aftermath of the trauma. These ego resources can be shaped gradually by initially educating the client about the therapy process, gradually developing the process of self-reflection, and modeling this through discussing the therapy process itself. Helping clients understand the connections among their behavior patterns and making explicit the connection between life experiences and feelings help the client develop these resources. Many clients find journal writing very useful in developing the ability to introspect.

Willpower, Initiative, and the Ability to Strive for Personal Growth. These ego resources are closely linked, yet conceptually distinct. Initiative refers to the ability to undertake endeavors, to try new things, to pursue beginnings. Willpower refers to determination, persistence, and the ability to persevere in the face of difficulties. The ability to strive for personal growth is the application of willpower and initiative to one's own development. In addition, it implies a sense of direction or vision for oneself. Willpower and initiative can be strengthened by the therapist who points out the person's courage and strength in enduring traumatic events and in seeking therapy, as well as acknowledging or praising the accomplishment of small steps toward healing and growth. The ability to strive for personal growth relates to the individual's sense of hope about the future and determination to persist through the often painful therapy process.

The therapist can mobilize movement toward personal growth, both in individuals whose self capacities are intact and in those for whom this resource is impaired, by conveying a sense of optimism and realistic hopefulness. The therapist may gently encourage the client to begin to resume normal activities, to explore barriers to growth and change, and to confront painful memories and feelings. With clients with a strong fighting spirit, the therapeutic challenge is to help clients to allow themselves time to heal. Often, these individuals put pressure on themselves to move ahead too quickly, leading to frustration and a sense of failure.

In contrast, individuals with a diminished ability to strive for personal growth can pose a difficult challenge to the therapist, as they often present as perpetually hopeless. In these cases, the therapist must be extremely patient, set very low minimal goals, and avoid trying to convince the client s/he is making progress. The therapist's enduring acceptance of the client and steadfast belief that the client can grow will eventually be internalized by the client.

Perspective and Empathy. Some traumatized persons may have temporarily lost their ability to view themselves and others from more than one perspective, while others may never have developed it. This resource will be very helpful to the trauma survivor as s/he searches for the reasons for the traumatic experience, a process we discuss later in relation to frame of reference and causal attributions.

Perspective-taking is also helpful to survivors who have close relationships with their abusers. For example, some incest survivors who have done a good deal of memory work and recalled the abuse, put together the feelings and images, experienced and worked through many of the feelings, and began to develop ways of understanding what happened and why, may at some point want to resume or develop a positive relationship with, for example, the abusive father. One piece of this may be to work with the client to help her understand the father's family of origin and his possible motives for the abuse. This should not be construed in any way as an attempt to justify the abuser's behavior; rather, if done at the initiative of the client, it can be a way of coming to understand what happened and developing some empathy with the perpetrator so a relationship can be developed.

The ability to view oneself and others from more than one perspective can be developed by gentle questioning by the therapist and speculation about alternatives to the client's attributions and evaluations. The therapist must be very sensitive to the client's response to these probes so as to prevent or resolve any perceived failure of empathy on the part of the therapist.

Perspective is essential to the ability to empathize; empathy can be described as the ability to view oneself or others with kindly understanding. The ability to empathize with oneself, with one's vulnerabilities, is related to the capacity for self-soothing; viewing one's experience with understanding can be a way of forgiving oneself for being victimized. Many trauma survivors blame themselves for what happened; to the extent that this tendency becomes harshly self-critical, it will inhibit the healing process.

Another form of perspective-taking is humor. Humor requires the ability to step back from one's experience and look at it from a different perspective. Over the course of therapy, this resource can be encouraged through modeling the appropriate, nondestructive uses of humor in the therapy. As such, it can serve people well both as a means of comforting themselves and as a way of gaining some distance from their pain.

Ego Resources Important to Self-protection

The ego resources discussed in this section enable survivors to protect themselves from harm. These resources are as follows:

1. The ability to foresee consequences;
2. The ability to make self-protective judgments;
3. The ability to establish appropriate boundaries between self and others;
4. The ability to establish mature relations with others.

We have observed that these ego resources tend to be compromised in survivors of prolonged trauma. In these cases, the trauma often occurred in childhood, and included continual violations in boundaries as well as invalidation of their perceptions and judgments. We will discuss the clinical implications of this below.

The Ability to Foresee Consequences and to Make Self-protective Judgments. These ego resources can be invalidated by powerful others, as in the case of early childhood abuse, or in individuals whose attempt at self-protective judgments failed, as in the Vietnam veteran who blames himself for a tragic error in judgment. In the first case, the clinical task is to help the individual begin to articulate and be attuned to his or her own perceptions and judgments about other people and situations which may or may not be safe. This growing ability to make sound judgments can first be tested in the therapy relationship and then in one's life. This resource is related to schemas related to self-trust and will be discussed in more depth in Chapters 8 and 9.

For the adult who suffers a diminished ability to foresee consequences and make self-protective judgments, it is important to learn to accept that one's judgments are not infallible and to begin to reevaluate past mistakes in judgment in a more compassionate light. This obviously relates to empathy, a resource discussed above. Resuming making small judgments and taking small risks, first in safe situations like the therapy and gradually beyond the therapy relationship, will eventually restore or develop the client's self-confidence in this area. In addition, s/he may learn to make these judgments in light of revised schemas resulting from the trauma; for example, a rape victim who once felt comfortable walking around her neighborhood alone at night can eventually develop a new understanding of where and when she can feel safe.

The Ability to Establish Appropriate Boundaries Between Self and Others. This is an important ego resource which has been written about extensively in the object relations literature (e.g., Horner, 1986, White & Weiner, 1986). An understanding of how the client experiences and manages closeness and distance may reveal a need to build or repair this resource. For example, the therapist can explore what the client experiences when s/he feels others (including the therapist) are too close or too distant. The presence and level of development of this resource relates to the individual's sense of himself or herself as a separate and complete person, as well as his or her ability to enjoy time alone.

If the individual fears disintegration when alone, or feels incomplete without some other person present, s/he may feel compelled to be with others at all times. If, on the other hand, the client feels threatened by intimacy, s/he may retreat from relationships. The ability to tolerate and regulate distance and closeness, then, obviously determines the individual's ability to have mature relationships with others. This ego resource has clear connections to intimacy schemas, which we discuss in Chapters 8 and 9.

The individual who is most likely to experience difficulty in this area is one who, during early stages of development, has suffered violations of boundaries, including the invasion of his or her bodily space. Survivors of such violations may have difficulty establishing appropriate boundaries in the therapy, as well as in other relationships. Seeking closeness and yet fearing the loss of boundaries, they may struggle with conflicts related to closeness and distance. Some survivors may become involved in exploitative relationships, often because they are unable to protect their own boundaries or unaware that they have the right to do so. These individuals must discover, first through the therapy relationship and later in other relationships, that they are responsible for and capable of establishing boundaries and protecting themselves from violations.

Other survivors may experience the need to define rigid boundaries between themselves and others because boundaries that were violated previously resulted in death or severe harm. This is evident in some Vietnam combat veterans who are very sensitive to any sign that their boundaries will be violated. The ability to establish boundaries is related to safety and independence schemas, which we discuss in Chapters 8 and 9.

The Ability to Establish Mature Relations with Others. The healing process is assisted by the individual's ability to obtain support from others who will validate his or her worth, especially during the difficult process of working through the traumatic material. In addition, the ability to give to others in the context of an ongoing relationship is healing for many individuals. The ability to establish mature, mutual relations may be compromised in persons who were not allowed to form appropriate relationships with their parents, perhaps because the child was par- entified or otherwise exploited. In addition, this resource can be disrupted by trauma in persons in whom it was previously well-developed, especially if they experienced disruptions in trust or intimacy schemas.

The ability to establish mature relations can be restored through the development of the relationship with the therapist, who responds to the client's needs in an empathic manner and maintains appropriate boundaries. The therapist can also help the individual deal with prob- lems in other relationships, thereby supporting the development of mature relationships. This ego resource relates to dependency/trust and intimacy schemas, discussed in Chapters 8 and 9.

STRENGTHENING SELF CAPACITIES

Constructivist self development theory proposes that disrupted self schemas are related to need areas that are central to the individual. For example, persons for whom the need for recognition or esteem from others is salient may experience the trauma as an assault on their sense of worth. In contrast, the person for whom independence is salient may be more likely to experience the trauma as disrupting self schemas concerning invulnerability and strength. Furthermore, in accordance with self psychology theory, the individual's ability to tolerate affect, soothe the self, and enjoy time alone are all related to the maintenance of a cohesive, stable, positive self-concept, which is what we refer to as self-esteem. The therapist must be attuned to specific deficits in self- esteem regulation, under what circumstances this occurs, and how this is tied to psychological needs and schemas.

Constructivist self development theory posits that individuals regulate self-esteem through the self capacities. These capacities are listed in the greater context of the theory in Table 2.2 (see p. 17). Building and strengthening self capacities is a gradual process, and will be slow when there is extensive self work to be done. Here we describe techniques that can facilitate this process.

The Ability to Regulate Affect

The ability to be aware of and tolerate one's own strong feelings is clearly an essential capacity if therapy is to proceed. Many trauma victims are terrified of affect because it is potentially overwhelming; Krystal (1978) points out that some adults automatically shut down affect before it becomes disintegrative and overwhelming.

There are two aspects to developing this capacity. One is the exploration of the many meanings strong affect has for the individual, of the fears and fantasies related to experiencing strong affects, and of the past events which engendered these meanings. Furthermore, it is important to discover the relation between disturbances in affect regulation and the activation of unconscious, disturbed representations of self and world. The other aspect is working in a direct way to help the individual build his or her ability to overcome these fears, to neutralize and tolerate affect. We interweave these two aspects of the work of developing affect tolerance.

It is important that the therapist demonstrate that s/he can tolerate the client's strong feelings. In self psychology terms, the therapeutic holding environment (Winnicott, 1965) or container (Parson, 1988) allows the client to feel soothed and to internalize the therapist's calming presence. In social learning terms, the client observes the therapist responding calmly to the client's affect and observes the therapist's confidence and expectation that the client can eventually do this as well, and over time the client develops the expectation that s/he can tolerate affect and that the therapist will reward him or her for doing so. To the extent that the client expects and values this reinforcement, s/he will eventually learn to tolerate affect.

Many people respond to the use of metaphor in describing these fears. For some, the fear of affect is analogous to having one's finger in a dike, holding back the strength of the water that has built up to intolerable levels behind the dam. Others will use metaphors of a flood, a storm, an avalanche, a tidal wave, or other images of the overpowering forces of nature out of control. Still others may have a sense of a deep or bottomless pit or well, from which they might never emerge once they have peered into the depths. Individuals for whom power or independence is a central need may be especially fearful of strong affects. The experience of strong affects may activate unconscious negative self schemas related to viewing one self as weak, helpless, or damaged.

The client's metaphors for affect can be used to help the client conceptualize and experience affect in a less threatening way; transforming the image can help the client transform his or her inner experience. For example, if the client imagines a flood of water breaking through the dam, the therapist might suggest that the client imagine allowing the water to begin to seep through in droplets so that the flow of water is very gradual. Tolerating and neutralizing small amounts of affect are the goals with persons with limited or diminished affect tolerance.

Guided imagery can also be productive, using the metaphors or images that are natural to the person to begin experiencing affect in a safe, protected place where there are escape routes and a supportive guide. If a client is overwhelmed by affect and appears to be in danger of self-fragmentation, offering controls and temporary distancing techniques can be useful. For others, transitional objects, symbolic of others' caring presence, may be an important source of comfort during times of distress. For example, one early childhood torture victim who had periods of disintegrative anxiety at night when reexperiencing the terror of the abuse discovered that holding onto a teddy bear, symbolic of the therapist's care, was soothing and comforting when she was flooded with affect.

Other examples include encouraging the client to imagine himself or herself facing the storm, flood, etc., with the therapist or another supportive companion offering a lifeboat or rope to help the client return to safe ground. Other healing images include not fighting the waves, the flood, etc., but rather "going with it" as suggested by paradoxical techniques for overcoming other anxiety disorders (e.g., Beck & Emery, 1985). Beck and Emery outline a 5-step program that includes helping clients to accept and go with the anxiety rather than fighting it, observing the anxiety as if it were separate from oneself, acting as if one is not anxious, and so forth, until the anxiety disappears. Other cognitive techniques involve helping the client to master the anxiety about strong affects calmly, without triggering a panic reaction. Such self-statements as, "You're going to be okay" or "We'll get through this" can be helpful as a supportive strategy.

Another part of developing affect tolerance is helping the client to back away when she or he is becoming overwhelmed, giving the message (whether directly or indirectly) that the client can be in control of his or her affective states. This obviously relates to the ability to soothe and calm oneself, to be discussed below.

The Ability to Soothe and Calm Oneself

The capacity to soothe and comfort oneself is critical to developing affect tolerance as well as to moderating the destructive impact of self-loathing. This capacity is related to Jordan's (1984) concept of self-empathy. Jordan wrote:

> [In self-empathy] the observing, often judging, self can then make contact with the same aspect of the self as object. This could occur in the form of having a memory of oneself in which the inner state at that time had not been fully integrated because it was not acceptable. To be able to tolerate the affect of that state in a context of understanding becomes a kind of intrapsychic empathy which can actually lead to a lasting structural change in self-representations. (1984, p. 9)

Often, when we ask clients to describe in detail the self-statements they make when they are distressed, we learn that clients can be unmercifully cruel to themselves when they experience affects they experience as threatening or bad, such as rage, anxiety, and helplessness. This failure in self-soothing or self-empathy can exacerbate such feelings, leading to intolerable affective states that individuals feel compelled to avoid. Hymer's (1984) self-in-conflict model of trauma suggests that the unconscious, vulnerable self-representation often becomes disavowed and split off from the conscious, invulnerable self-representation. In this case, the individual may experience self-loathing, the antithesis of self-empathy, a state in which manifestations of the vulnerable self, such as fear and helplessness, emerge.

The therapist's ability to be genuinely soothing, as one would with a child in deep distress, is critical to enhancing this self capacity. Therapists who enjoy children might imagine how they would comfort a distressed child. Often, this comfort is communicated nonverbally, with empathetic sounds accompanied by an expression of warmth and care in the eyes of the therapist. With regard to nonverbal communication, it is important that the therapist be careful not to convey inadvertently that she or he feels sorry for the person. The meanings this has for the individual should be explored and understood; it is important to convey warmth without looking pained or sympathetic rather than empathetic. Sympathy only reinforces the view that one is despicable, weak, or helpless, while genuine empathy takes away the destructive power of self-loathing.

Ultimately, a therapeutic goal should be to help the individual gradually develop the capacity for self-soothing during states of affective distress. For example,

> One therapist taught a victim of an attempted homicide, who was overwhelmed by terrifying flashbacks accompanied by panic attacks, to make self-soothing statements rather than fighting desparately against the rising panic. Initially, the woman looked in the mirror and talked to herself while she was not upset, saying kind and loving things to her reflection. She practiced this several times a day, saying to herself such comforting statements as, "You're going to get through this, it's going to work out, you're a good person." When she had her next flashback, she was able to calm herself, greatly reducing the intensity and duration of the panic attack.

The capacity for self-soothing can also be enhanced through drawing upon the client's ability to empathize with others. For example, the therapist might ask the client to imagine the experience of someone who has undergone a similar traumatic event. The following scenario was presented by the therapist to a rape victim who was furious at herself for a "failed enactment" (Lifton, 1988), when she was helpless and unable to fight back:

> Try to imagine a woman who is enjoying a walk in the park on a lovely spring day. Perhaps she is having pleasant thoughts about future plans or just enjoying the peaceful feeling that comes from being surrounded by nature. Suddenly, a strange man emerges from the bushes and puts a knife to her throat, commanding her to be quiet or be killed. She is paralyzed with fear and must comply with his command to lie down on the grass. She wants to scream or fight back but she keeps thinking that he will kill her and that she will never see her family again. She is brutally raped and left for dead. When help finally arrives, she is shaking and disoriented with fear. When she finally returns home, she is obsessed with the thought, "Why didn't I fight back? Why didn't I scream for help?" If you were a friend of this woman, how would you respond to her? (This scenario should be modified to reflect the failed enactment of the particular client.)

At this point, most individuals, drawn into the metaphor, will say, "But he held her at knife point, she only did what she had to in order to survive." The therapist might then respond, "But shouldn't she have fought back? If she was really a strong person, might she have been able to do something to prevent the rape?" As this dialogue continues, the client's compassion for the victim is activated. Once this occurs, the therapist can say something like,

> And how is what happened to you any different from what happened to this woman? Isn't it also the case that you didn't fight back because it was the only thing you could do to save your own life (using the client's words). Why is it so difficult for you to feel compassion for yourself in the same predicament?

This technique for enhancing self-empathy can have powerful effects. For example,

> One Vietnam veteran who was unmerciful toward himself when he failed in any way, no matter how slight his failure, was a compassionate counselor for young people at his church. One day when he was overcome by intense self-loathing resulting from a minor failure, the therapist asked him whether he could imagine himself counseling a young person who had made the same mistake. With great warmth, he described how he would handle the situation by gently instructing the boy and helping him to do better in the future. After a bit, the therapist asked, "Is it so difficult for you to imagine showing the same compassion for yourself as you clearly show for this child?" In the next session, the veteran talked about revealing his vulnerability to a friend, and asking for help, something that had always been incredibly difficult for him.

The Ability to Be Alone Without Being Lonely

Winnicott (1965) originally wrote about this capacity. More recently, Horner (1986) wrote,

> An individual's capacity to be alone without being lonely or depressed is nourished by inner ego resources that build upon the good me-you image of the stage of symbiosis and culminate in what psychoanalysts refer to as object constancy around the age of three. Object constancy refers to the enduring nature of the psychological connection with the mother—and later, with im-

portant people in general, when they are gone or when they are not actively meeting one's needs. The inner world of ever-present intimacies which continue to nourish and sustain us when we are alone frees us to choose to be alone or to live alone. (1986, p. 88)

Furthermore, she writes,

the capacity to be alone also comes through the process of learning to do for the self what mother once had to do. After a time, the young child outgrows his need for his teddy bear or blanket and develops within himself, at a symbolic level, ego resources for the kind of comforting that he derived from external sources. (1986, p. 89)

The process of developing this capacity is twofold. First, the individual must develop an awareness of self; this includes valuing oneself, having dialogues with oneself, and spending time alone. The therapist must gently help the individual focus on the self by listening to his or her inner messages, by writing in a journal, and by spending time alone. Time alone may be brief at first, and can be easier initially while one is engaged in calming or creative activities, such as listening to music, painting, or reading. For many of the victims we work with, journal writing is very valuable, as are other creative expressions such as writing poems, drawing, and creating or playing music. Some theories of creativity suggest that imaginative productive activities can facilitate the important process of "self-creation" (Mangione, 1989).

Second, the individual must develop the capacity to connect with supportive images of other people, including the therapist, when alone. One guided imagery technique often discussed in the literature (e.g., Brown & Fromm, 1986) is to have the individual create a safe, comforting place in his or her mind where she or he can be spontaneous, say whatever comes to mind, be surrounded with objects that are soothing or comforting, such as books or paintings or images of loving people. Often, people will pick a beautiful spot near a beach or in the woods, or a cozy, beautiful room. Next, the therapist can guide the client to explore some aspect of the self symbolically, through the use of metaphor. This might be the core self (Gergen, 1968) or the ideal self (Rosenberg, 1979). Within the guided imagery, one can explore both who one is and who one hopes to become, learning and understanding himself or herself from a new perspective.

In work with individuals whose ability to use visual imagery is highly developed, the therapist can suggest that the client picture some aspect of himself or herself taking another shape or form, such as an object or an animal. This technique can enable the person to begin exploring those aspects of the self that were previously hidden. The varieties of these techniques are only limited by the therapist's and client's imaginations and willingness to explore new avenues for growth. Overall, the most important attitude to convey is that one can become a good friend to oneself, a companion to rely on in good times and bad, and an important source of inner strength and calm.

With regard to the goal of enhancing internal object constancy, which Horner (1986) connected to the ability to be alone without being lonely, there are a variety of ways one can learn to internalize the loving, caring images of others. For most victims we work with, there has usually been at least one person who they felt really loved or cared for them sometime in their lives.

> For example, Brenda, a 42-year-old incest victim, described feeling constantly lonely and disconnected from others, in part because she associated dependency with weakness and feared that people would betray her. After about six months of therapy, she had the insight that she worked so hard and kept herself so busy because she could not tolerate being alone. This state was intensely uncomfortable, leaving her feeling empty and bereft whenever her activity level dropped.
>
> The therapist asked her if she could conjure up the image of someone whom she had felt loved by and whom she had loved. She was able to remember her deceased aunt, the one and only person who had loved her unconditionally. She then became very sad, remembering the loss of her aunt, and quickly pushed the feelings away because she associated sadness with weakness.
>
> *Brenda:* I can't feel any love for her or her love for me.
>
> *Therapist:* Where did all that love go?
>
> *Brenda:* The love died when she died.
>
> *Therapist:* Can you imagine that love is still alive somewhere inside of you, contained in the wonderful memories you have of your aunt?
>
> *Brenda (sobbing):* But if I have the memories, I feel so sad and I hate feeling sad.

More therapeutic work followed that focused on her resistance to affect and her self-loathing when she perceived herself as weak. At the end of the session, the therapist gave an indirect suggestion.

Therapist: Perhaps during the week you will find yourself remembering your aunt, her loving face, the ways she talked to you, the things you did together. And when you have these images you will feel some deep sadness for this loss. And yet, you will also have a glimpse of her love, a love that will warm your heart and make you feel less alone.

In the next session the client reported that she had thought about her aunt during the week, when they had worked in the garden together and talked about life. She was able to tolerate the intense feelings of grief and discovered that she also felt a spark of love fill her entire being. She then commented, "It's strange but this week, I feel calmer, less alone than I've felt in a long time."

In general, the internalization of soothing objects and the development of a relationship with oneself is a central self capacity that, as with the others, must be developed before work on the traumatic memories can proceed in any depth.

The Ability to Moderate Self-Loathing

This capacity relates perhaps most closely to one's ability to maintain a positive sense of self-esteem. The individual who has a more stable sense of self-esteem will be better able to integrate criticism or to tolerate rejection. Another potential stimulus for self-loathing is the emergence of unacceptable thoughts or feelings. Most often, this is tied to the activation of unconscious disturbed schemas that are associated with painful affects. The experiences that have the potential to lead to self-loathing will differ across individuals, according to salient need areas. For example, an individual with a strong need for independence may become self-critical, angry, or depressed when dependency needs emerge or when someone questions his or her ability to take care of himself or herself. In this case, disturbed self-schemas related to helplessness may be activated and will need to be uncovered and worked through over time. In another individual with strong needs for safety, this self-loathing might emerge when she experiences intense fear. Here, disturbed schemas related to safety, such as the belief that one is uniquely vulnerable to repeated victimization, may be activated.

Individuals who have experienced prolonged or early trauma or who have endured continuous, severe criticism or neglect may live in a constant state of self-loathing. In working with such persons, the therapist must be careful not to present too discrepant a challenge to the client's belief that s/he is worthless, bad, or damaged. We discuss this in detail in Chapters 8 and 9, in the sections on disrupted esteem schemas. Here we focus on ways of increasing the individual's ability to tolerate criticism.

As with any aspect of the client's experience, the therapist must convey understanding. In this case, this means empathizing with how painful it is when the client experiences self-loathing. Beyond this, there are various aspects of increasing the ability to moderate self-loathing. Some of this work is exploratory, exploring how the individual experienced criticism in childhood, how parents conveyed displeasure, and how the individual now experiences criticism. Another aspect of this work is cognitive, helping the individual to hear what is being said rather than overgeneralizing any faintly negative statement to a complete renunciation. Here the therapist's task is to work with the client to understand exactly what was said, to begin to examine what might have been intended, and to consider the source of the comment, and to not personalize everything that is heard. Another aspect of this work involves increasing affect tolerance, which we have discussed in some detail above.

Shame is often associated with self-loathing. We have seen a number of clients who prefer to continue in relationships they detest rather than attempting to change the relationship, which may lead to intolerable feelings of shame. Again, working at two levels is helpful. One level is an exploration of the person's history of shame, how parents may have induced shame in the client in childhood, the direct and indirect messages conveyed during early years about misbehavior or inadequacy, and the past and present meanings of shame to this individual. The other level is more cognitive, helping individuals, to understand the costs and benefits of various behaviors and to accept the possibility of living with some feelings of guilt or shame without generalizing these feelings to their overall sense of self-worth.

Trauma survivors who feel some responsibility for the traumatic event may have particular difficulties in this area, even if the ability to moderate self-loathing was well-developed prior to the traumatic event. This has been most apparent in our work with parents whose children have been harmed or with people who felt some responsibility for a sibling who met with disaster. Again, it is essential to empathize with the client's feelings of responsibility while also gently challenging the beliefs that lead to these feelings.

SUMMARY

We have attempted to provide a framework for assessing the ego resources and self capacities. This assessment provides a context, within which the clinician and client can explore and strengthen the self in the service of integration of the traumatic memories and resolving disturbed schemas about self and world. Although we have chosen to organize these concepts separately for the purpose of clarity, we keep in mind that human beings are whole beings, not composites of variables. Thus, the assessment and exploration of the self must always be seen as a process of understanding a whole individual who has interrelated strengths and vulnerabilities.

8. Assessing Disrupted Psychological Needs and Related Schemas

In our clinical work, we have developed indirect and direct methods for exploring central needs and schemas which offer valuable insights into the client's inner experience and serve as useful therapeutic tools. This work can be integrated throughout the therapy process, and used as a reference point for progress in later stages of treatment.

ASSESSING CENTRAL PSYCHOLOGICAL NEEDS

Assessment of psychological needs is a matter of diagnosis and inference, rather than of behavioral observation (Murray & Kluckhohn, 1953). It is a difficult yet essential part of the therapeutic process. Identifying the client's salient psychological needs will inform the therapist about both where and how to intervene. The salient disrupted need areas are those that must be restored through the therapy process. These needs also determine how the clinician can shape interventions so they are most effective.

The exploration of psychological needs should be an ongoing process in therapy with trauma survivors. The three stages of this process are exploration of (1) the degree to which each need is salient or focal, (2) the degree to which trauma has disrupted central needs and created an imbalance among the needs, and (3) the individual's awareness of his or her needs.

Another interesting and important aspect of needs assessment is learning about patterns of needs and the interaction among needs. We do not address this topic in this book, although we are aware of its importance. The clinician may benefit, however, from keeping in mind questions about how certain needs may interrelate.

155

From the very first contact with the client, the therapist should listen for themes related to frame of reference, safety, trust/dependency, independence, power, esteem, and intimacy. Clients who express in various ways that independence, for example, is important to them will need to understand therapy as a process of regaining control over their lives, while those who express needs for trust/dependency will likely connect with the therapist and engage in the therapeutic process more readily if therapy is framed as a place to receive support and encouragement following a traumatic experience.

Therapists who experience early resistance from clients may be intervening in ways that are inconsistent with the individual's psychological need structure. For example, early encouragement to express feelings of vulnerability may be very threatening to clients with a strong need for independence.

Another part of the process is to identify needs that have been disrupted by the trauma. Again, this can be done by listening for themes reflecting thwarted needs. This is often revealed in material related to frustrations in one's life or relationships. Statements such as, "I'm not the kind of person who asks other people to do things for me. I can't stand having to ask for help since I've become disabled," or "I can't stand feeling like I can't go out of my house at night," or "I feel so alone all the time now, even when I'm with friends; I never felt like this before" can be illuminating. At this point, the clinician might state, "It sounds like you feel your needs for independence (or safety or intimacy) are threatened." This can lead to further exploration of the disrupted needs through such questions as, "What does it mean to feel secure, independent, etc. In what situations in your life have you felt secure, independent, etc.? In what situations have you felt blocked or frustrated in getting these needs met?" Discussions of psychological needs are often gateways to powerful emotions. These explorations can help clients express and understand feelings that might otherwise be difficult to access.

The next part of the process might involve asking the person whether s/he can think back to a time in life when these basic needs were met. Next, the clinician can explore situations and relationships in which these needs were frustrated. If the needs have been frustrated, explore what life circumstances were associated with this (e.g., alcoholic family, lack of validation by parents, emotional neglect, etc.). If there appear to be any changes in the individual's need structure over the life span, try to help the person identify the major forces that were operating to change or disrupt these needs, being alert to any connection to traumatic life events.

Next, one can explore the needs that are less important now. For example, is an apparently diminished need for intimacy the result of being fearful of losing people or is it a result of never feeling really cared for or connected to anyone? The relation between these needs and cognitive schemas can be explored by asking whether the individual believes s/he can get these needs met in the future. If the individual expresses negative schemas, explore why s/he holds these beliefs and how s/he would feel if they were different, in what situations it might be more or less likely, and what it might feel like to imagine getting these needs met in the future. This latter question often produces powerful emotions as well as areas of resistance that will need to be worked through as part of therapy.

Through this process, clients will gradually develop an awareness of their salient psychological needs. For some individuals, needs may not be well differentiated. This can result in vague, generalized life dissatisfaction. The process of helping individuals develop and understand their psychological needs can facilitate the differentiation process, placing the individual in a position to attempt to meet important needs in appropriate ways. Individuals who have little sense of their own psychological needs can be encouraged to develop this sense through guided reflection upon what is important to them, what experiences bring them pleasure, how they spend leisure time, the importance of friendships, of time alone, and so forth. The therapist can act as interpreter for the client who, for example, might state s/he has no needs except to make others happy; this might be explored as a reflection of disrupted intimacy, esteem, or trust/dependency needs. The enjoyment of solitary pursuits such as playing the piano, working in a job in which one relies little on others, and so forth might reflect central independence needs.

Finally, trauma survivors often experience an unsettling imbalance of needs. For example, an individual may suddenly, as a result of an assault, experience extreme anxiety and obsessive thoughts concerning safety. Every situation may be a painful reminder of his or her vulnerability to loss or harm. To the extent that such imbalances block the individual from engaging in regular activities or from peace of mind, they should be addressed promptly in therapy. This may mean taking a more active role with trauma survivors who are in crisis, such as working with a rape victim whose safety needs are paramount to suggest she find a place to stay where she can feel safe, or working with an

accident victim with high independence needs to help him find ways
to begin to restore his sense of control within his life.

ASSESSING COGNITIVE SCHEMAS

An important area of research based in constructivist self development
theory involves the assessment of disrupted cognitive schemas. The
McPearl Belief Scale (Pearlman, McCann, & Johnson, 1990b) consists
of several statements within each need area. Respondents are asked to
note the degree to which they agree with each item on a six-point
Likert scale. The scale yields scores indicating the extent of schema
disruption within each need area. As this book goes to press, scale
validation data are being collected both by ourselves and by our colleagues around the country. The authors will gladly provide the scale
and research results to interested persons.

Because of the theoretical relation between schemas and needs (see
Chapter 4), the exploration of schemas is related to the exploration of
needs. Some indirect methods of exploring schemas include listening
carefully for themes that relate to the seven need areas of frame of
reference, safety, trust/dependency, independence, power, esteem, and
intimacy. Like needs, schemas may not be readily accessible at a
conscious level; they generally operate at a preconscious (Epstein, in
press a, in press b) or unconscious (Westen, 1989) level. The centrality
of these schemas will be revealed as certain themes reemerge in therapy
and as the client expresses his or her most pressing concerns. The
trauma themes, or psychological experiences related to characteristics
of the traumatic event, combine with the individual's personal history,
psychological needs, and cognitive schemas to paint the unique picture
of the meaning this event has for this individual. Certain trauma themes
are often related to disruptions in particular schemas, although they
will always have unique meanings for the individual.

Frame of Reference Schemas

Disturbed Schemas Related to Frame of Reference. All human beings have
a need to discover a meaningful frame of reference (Fromm, 1955), "a
stable and consistent way of perceiving and comprehending the world"
(Hall & Lindzey, 1978, p. 171). Epstein (in press a) refers to this as a
need to "assimilate the data of reality into a cohesive, relatively stable
conceptual system" (p. 1). Schemas concerning attributions of causality,
hope for the future, and locus of control are (Rotter, 1966) related to

this fundamental need. Themes and concerns reflecting disturbed frame of reference schemas include the following:

- The belief that the trauma was an inevitable outcome of one's tragic fate;
- The belief that the world is no longer meaningful or coherent;
- The belief that the world is unpredictable, dangerous, and un-controllable (Epstein, in press a);
- An obsessive need to search for answers to the question, "Why me?";
- The belief that chance factors or randomness account for un-fortunate events (Janoff-Bulman, 1989a);
- A generalized sense of disorientation or loss of meaning;
- A sense of demoralization, pessimism, or hopelessness;
- An extreme or exclusive internal or external orientation, reflected in an absolute belief that rewards can come only from within or from outside oneself.

Trauma Themes Related to Disturbed Frame of Reference Schemas. By definition, trauma will alter one's frame of reference because it requires accommodation or bending of schemas. Certain experiences are asso-ciated with greater disruptions in this area, such as:

- The experience of a trauma that is perceived as extremely non-normative relative to one's peers or one's former experience (e.g., murder of a child);
- The violation of one's most basic values;
- Being the object of random, impersonal acts of violence;
- The sense of being singled out as the object of violence while others are spared;
- The experience of repeated victimization.

Exploration of Disturbed Frame of Reference Schemas. The following questions are useful guidelines for the therapist exploring disruptions in this area:

1. What does the client understand about why the traumatic event(s) happened to him or her?
2. How generalized are the disturbed frame of reference schemas? That is, has the inability to make sense of this event resulted in an overall sense of meaninglessness, disorientation, or de-

spair, or is the client continuing to struggle constructively with this issue?

3. Does the client grapple with a variety of attributions about what happened, each with different emotional implications? To what extent are these attributions adaptive or maladaptive?

4. To what extent is the client distressed by his or her inability to formulate a meaningful answer to questions of causality?

5. To what extent does the client feel hopeful about the future, about his or her ability to resume meaningful relationships and constructive activity?

6. Has the individual come to rely entirely upon others for positive reinforcement or, conversely, has s/he come to believe that his or her only life satisfactions can come from within?

Safety Schemas

Disturbed Safety Schemas.   Persons for whom disturbed safety schemas are central will often reveal the following recurrent themes or concerns:

- A sense of unique vulnerability to future harm;
- Chronic anxiety or vigilance in strange or threatening situations;
- Concerns about being able to protect oneself in the future from specific or vague threats;
- A sense of danger that has overgeneralized to a number of life situations;
- A belief that one is a "magnet" for danger or harm;
- Compulsive behaviors aimed at enhancing safety, such as sleeping with a weapon;
- Avoidance of certain situations that symbolize danger.

One Vietnam veteran expressed this powerfully by quoting the Beatles' song title, stating, "Happiness is a warm gun." A woman who was raped in her bed reported to her therapist she had slept on the couch for the 10 years since the rape.

Trauma Themes Related to Disturbed Safety Schemas.   The trauma themes likely to be associated with disturbed safety schemas are the following:

- Violation of or harm to one's home, property, loved ones, or person;
- Near-death experiences or threat to one's life or a loved one's life;
- Immersion in danger;

• Exposure to situations of extreme terror.

Exploration of Disturbed Safety Schemas. The following questions should be explored over time as the therapist assesses how central safety is for the client.

1. What is the significance of safety for this individual? How generalized are the concerns for safety (e.g., do they extend to all areas of the person's life or are they restricted to certain domains)?
2. Are there certain situations in which the person feels particularly insecure or vulnerable?
3. When do these feelings usually arise?
4. What is it about these situations that makes him or her feel afraid (vulnerable, insecure)?
5. Is the person able to discern situations involving genuine threat to himself or herself or does the person overreact to situations with low probability of harm?
5. What kinds of thoughts or images go through the person's mind when he or she feels this way?
6. Are there other times in his or her life when s/he has felt the same way?
7. How does s/he handle these situations? Have any of these methods been more or less helpful in the past?

The latter questions are aimed at exploring both adaptive and maladaptive coping mechanisms such as seeking support, comforting oneself, creating a safe place, withdrawal or avoidance, gradual exposure to trauma-linked stimuli, relaxation techniques, creating behavioral or cognitive diversions, etc. It is very important to refrain from challenging any coping processes, no matter how maladaptive they may appear, until it is clear what they mean to the client, how they relate to central needs, and the implications of changing these patterns. This issue will be discussed in Chapter 9 on treatment interventions.

Trust/Dependency Schemas

Disturbed Trust/Dependency Schemas. Persons with disturbances in the area of trust or dependency may reveal the following themes or life issues:

• The experience of feeling betrayed or abandoned by others;

- The expectation that other people will disappoint them or let them down;
- The fear that others will make a fool of them;
- A devaluation of themselves when they perceive themselves to be needy or demanding;
- The expectation that people will hurt them if given the opportunity.

Trauma Themes Related to Disturbed Trust/Dependency Schemas. The trauma themes associated with disturbed trust schemas include the following:

- Abandonment;
- Betrayal and broken promises;
- Unresponsiveness or active resistance to having needs for support acknowledged or met;
- Humiliation resulting from dependency.

Exploration of Disturbed Trust/Dependency Schemas. Within this area, it is important to assess the following issues:

1. What is the meaning of trust for the individual? For example, does s/he interpret trusting or depending upon others as "bad" or "stupid" because to do so only results in hurt or disappointment? Does s/he interpret as pathological any signs of dependency, such as making small requests of others or acknowledging that s/he needs the support of other people?
2. Is the individual able to differentiate between situations in which it is unwise to trust and those in which it makes sense to trust? Is the inability to trust or depend upon others overgeneralized or limited to specific people?
3. Does s/he evidence an "all or none" attitude toward trust, believing that you trust completely or don't trust at all? Is s/he able to size up situations in order to trust others gradually or does s/he set other people up to fail him or her by trusting too much too soon?
4. Does s/he seem to engage in relationships that are seriously unbalanced, with one person providing far more support than the other?
5. What kind of feelings are associated with these issues?
6. What life experiences are linked to these disturbances and what impact has this had on the person's life?

Independence Schemas

Disturbed Independence Schemas.   Persons with disturbed independence schemas often present with the following themes or concerns:

- A general devaluation of the self for being weak, helpless, vulnerable, needy, dependent, a baby, etc.;
- Statements about how important it is that they resolve difficult situations or be strong enough to cope with any crisis on their own; a reluctance to ask anyone for help or to acknowledge that they need help from others;
- A desperate need to be self-sufficient and free from restrictions;
- A dread of helplessness or vulnerability.

Trauma Themes Related to Disturbed Independence Schemas.   The following trauma themes are often related to disturbed independence schemas:

- Restriction of freedom;
- Loss of mobility;
- Helplessness to act on one's own accord;
- Humiliation associated with weakness or vulnerability.

Exploration of Disturbed Independence Schemas.   The questions to keep in mind in this area are the following:

1. How did independence come to be so important for the person? For example, is this need a reaction to being devalued or disappointed when s/he allowed himself or herself to be dependent?
2. Does s/he find it hard to distinguish between the human need to be cared for or comforted and infantile needs that s/he experiences as weak and bad?
3. Are there situations where s/he will allow himself or herself to be vulnerable or does s/he expect to be strong and capable under any and all circumstances?
4. Is the individual able to be compassionate toward himself or herself when s/he is feeling vulnerable, afraid, weak, etc. or does s/he experience self-loathing if s/he perceives that s/he has failed to be independent?
5. What costs has this had for the person in his or her life and in what way has it been adaptive?

6. How did the trauma(s) s/he experienced compromise this need for independence or the expectation that it would be met?

As we discussed earlier, fears about dependency/trust may be reflected in an extremely high need for independence and self-devaluation when one fails to live up to these expectations.

Power Schemas

Disturbed Power Schemas. To some degree, all human beings have a need for power, which we define as the need to direct or exert control over others or the environment. Clearly, for some people this need is more central than for others. The mature expression of power needs is leadership. The less mature or healthy expression of this need is taking advantage of or oppressing others. Themes and concerns reflecting disturbed power schemas include the following:

- A belief that one cannot control future outcomes in interpersonal relationships;
- The belief that one must be in control of others;
- The belief that others desire or expect to be dominated, controlled, or oppressed.

Trauma Themes Related to Disturbed Power Schemas. The following trauma themes are likely to be associated with disturbed power schemas:

- Forced placement in the role of oppressor (such as committing war atrocities or committing sexually abusive behaviors at the direction of another person);
- Entrapment, imprisonment, subjugation, helplessness vis-á-vis others; forced submission;
- Inability to protect others when in a legitimate leadership role (e.g., a parent whose child is hurt or killed or a military leader whose troops are harmed).

Exploration of Disturbed Power Schemas. The major issues to explore in the therapy process are these:

1. Is the client able to exert power in any relationships, what are the outcomes, and how is this power expressed?
2. Does s/he have difficulty recognizing opportunities to share power in relationships?

3. Are there certain relationships in which power struggles are a central concern?
4. Does s/he try to express interpersonal power in maladaptive ways, e.g., being manipulative, making suicidal gestures, becoming aggressive instead of assertive?
5. Is s/he aware that s/he is capable of exerting control over others under some circumstances or is the belief in powerlessness pervasive and overgeneralized?
6. Does s/he manipulate or oppress others? Does s/he become anxious when not in charge of others?

Esteem Schemas

Disturbed Esteem Schemas.   All human beings have a fundamental need to feel valued, appreciated, recognized, and acknowledged. For some, however, this need is more salient. In addition, people need to experience a fundamental sense that others are valuable and worthy of respect. This of course is the foundation of trust of and intimacy with others. Themes and issues reflecting disturbed esteem schemas include the following:

- References to the self or parts of the self as bad, damaged, flawed, or evil;
- The belief that one is responsible for destructive actions or events;
- Expressions of profound guilt or unworthiness;
- The belief that trauma occurs because of something about the victim. We refer to this phenomenon as the "negative Midas touch." This is commonly revealed by such statements as "Everything I touch turns bad" and "There's something inside me that is a magnet for evil";
- The belief that other people are basically bad, evil, or malevolent.

Trauma Themes Related to Disturbed Esteem Schemas.   The trauma themes likely to be associated with disturbed esteem schemas are:

- Degradation;
- Defilement;
- Rejection;
- Blame and devaluation;
- Perception of one's own moral failure;
- Second injury through stigmatization.

Exploration of Disturbed Esteem Schemas.   The primary issues to explore are as follows:

1. To what extent is the person able to balance these painful schemas with more realistic or positive views of himself or herself?
2. Does s/he possess the capacity to soothe and calm himself or herself when feeling bad about himself or herself, or does s/he engage in self-punishing behaviors?
3. Are there significant people or activities in his or her life that provide recognition, validation, or respect?
4. Is the individual able to acknowledge his or her positive (stable) attributes or is s/he dependent on external sources of validation?
5. Has there ever been a time when s/he valued others? Are there any individuals whom s/he respects and values?
6. Are these negative schemas related to the trauma, and if so, in what ways?

Intimacy Schemas

Disturbed Intimacy Schemas.   The central themes and issues related to this area are as follows:

- Feeling lonely, cut off, alienated;
- Feeling like the part of oneself that cares for others has died;
- Frustration or sadness at feeling disconnected from even those people who appear genuinely loving;
- A sense of alienation from the world at large, which is sometimes expressed by statements such as, "I feel like I'm from another planet" or "There's no place on earth for me."

Trauma Themes Related to Disturbed Intimacy Schemas.   The following trauma themes are often linked to disturbed intimacy schemas:

- Traumatic loss of an attachment figure, including death or other abandonments;
- Loss of community or community supports;
- Betrayal or abuse by an important attachment figure;
- The perception that one is different from one's peers, feeling like a freak or an outcast, because of the traumatic experiences.

Exploration of Disturbed Intimacy Schemas.   The specific questions to keep in mind throughout the therapy process are the following.

1. Has the client ever been able to experience a sense of connection and intimacy with others, and if so, with whom and under what circumstances? If not, what seems to be standing in the way—are other people perceived as unresponsive or is s/he unable to let other people into his or her emotional life?
2. Is the loss of connection tied to traumatic losses in his or her life and if so, what fears are there when s/he imagines loving again?
3. Is the loss of connection specific to certain situations, as in the sexual abuse victim who experiences this only in sexual relationships, or has it become generalized to all relationships?
4. Is there a longing for deeper connection with others or has s/he given up out of fear or bitterness?
5. Finally, is there a sense of connection with others, whether people or spiritual beings, that offers support and sustenance or does s/he experience the world of inner relationships as empty or dead?

In summary, the assessment of needs and schemas is a central process in posttrauma therapy that is interwoven with therapeutic interventions focused on building the self and working through the traumatic memories.

9. Resolving Disturbed Schemas

In this chapter, we provide guidelines for therapeutic interventions that follow from a systematic assessment of central disrupted needs and schemas. First, we describe general principles for guiding the process of schema change and transformation. Next, we describe specific interventions aimed at gently challenging disturbed schemas in the seven need areas.

A METAPHOR FOR THE THERAPEUTIC PROCESS OF SCHEMA CHANGE

The Allegory of Plato's Cave

The process of therapy can be likened to the process of enlightenment, where initiates emerge from the darkness of a distorted state of mind to one in which they are transformed by a fresh, truer view of themselves and the world. The allegory of Plato's cave from *The Republic* (Jowett, 1968) is a metaphor for the process of healing and recovery. Here we offer excerpts from this masterpiece as a context for later sections on the therapy process. Our own psychological analysis follows certain segments.

> And now, I said, let me show in a figure how far our nature is enlightened or unenlightened: Behold! Human beings housed in an underground cave, which has a long entrance toward the light and as wide as the interior of the cave: here they have been from their childhood, and have their legs and necks chained, so that they cannot move and can only see before them, being prevented by the chains from turning round their heads. (p. 376)

Plato goes on to describe how the prisoners are unable to see the world outside, but have come to believe that the shadows on the wall represent reality. The cave can be viewed as a metaphor for the experience of traumatization. Here, the persons are prisoners, being unable to view the world or themselves in a clear light because they are chained to the walls from childhood. The victims see, as if through a glass darkly, a distorted view of self and humanity that has become their unique reality.

Plato next describes the process people undergo when they move from a state of unconsciousness or unenlightenment to consciousness and insight.

> And now look again, and see in what manner they would be released from their bonds, and cured of their error, whether the process would be naturally as follows. At first, when any of them is liberated and compelled suddenly to stand up and turn his neck round and walk and look toward the light, he will suffer sharp pains; the glare will distress him and he will be unable to see the realities of which in his former state he had seen the shadows. (p. 377)

The process of enlightenment (insight) described here is a difficult one which initially causes deep pain and anguish. This section of the metaphor underscores the need to respect and understand how painful this process is for victims and to recognize that altering one's views about self and the world cannot occur instantly. Instead, a gradual process occurs which is less psychologically shocking for the victim. Plato goes on to write that, initially, the released prisoners will hold onto their previous world views, being unable to assimilate a new vision of reality.

Resistance is represented here, for in resistance the individual clings to his or her former reality with a passion. Although the person has begun to come out of the cave into the light of greater awareness, he or she resists the therapist's attempts to point out a new reality. This process is so shocking and painful because the therapist is presenting a new view that is discrepant with the former view of self and the world. Despite how restricting it was to be chained to the walls of the cave, this old reality was known, and thus safer, less threatening. Plato goes on to paint a vivid picture of what happens if the person is faced with the new reality too abruptly, through force or confrontation:

> And if he is compelled to look straight at the light, will he not have a pain in his eyes which will make him turn away to take

refuge in the objects of vision which he can see, and which he will now conceive to be in reality clearer than the things which are now being shown to him? (Reply) True, he said. And suppose once more he is reluctantly dragged up that steep and rugged ascent, and held fast until he is forced into the presence of the sun himself, is he not likely to be pained and irritated? When he approaches the light his eyes will be dazzled, and he will not be able to see anything at all of what are now called realities. (p. 377)

The importance of gradually presenting discrepancy between old and new realities is the major theme of this passage. Dragging individuals into the light suddenly or forcefully will blind them psychologically. They will be disoriented, pained, and irritated. Thus, confrontive approaches which push too hard and too fast are likely to have the opposite result from what is desired. The person is traumatized and retreats back into the safe haven of his or her former life. How then does Plato suggest that persons change and integrate new insights?

[Reply] Not all in a moment, he said. He will require to grow accustomed to the sight of the upper world. And first he will see the shadows, next the reflection of men and other objects in the water, and then the objects themselves. Last of all he will be able to see the sun, not turning aside to the illusory reflection of him in the water, but gazing directly at him in his own proper place, and contemplating him as he is. (pp. 377–378)

Here we see the gradual process of accommodation as the person moves from blindness to catching a glimpse of the new reality. Plato's allegory of the cave thus offers us a fresh view of the meaning of schema transformation among traumatized persons, a process that will be described subsequently.

Restoring Balanced Needs and Positive Schemas

A star looks down at me,
And says, "Here I and you
Stand, each in our degree.
What do you mean to do,—
Mean to do?"
I say: "For all I know,
Wait, and let time go by,

> Till my change come,—"Just so."
> The star says: "So mean I:—
> So mean I."

Waiting Both
Thomas Hardy
(Puk, 1978)

Here we describe general guidelines for restoring or creating a balance among needs, challenging disturbed schemas, and restoring or building positive schemas. As in Plato's cave, the victim who has grown accustomed to darkness, who has been deprived of basic needs, who has had his or her self-image and view of the world shattered or distorted, will find it psychologically shocking to be forced out of the darkness into the light, particularly if this process does not take place gradually and very gently. Furthermore, there will be a period of time during which the individual will resist any interventions that challenge his or her disturbed schemas or which threaten to uncover disturbed, affectively powerful schemas that are unconscious. The changes that are brought about by trauma are themselves shocking and most trauma survivors require time before they are prepared for additional change, even if it is positive. The Thomas Hardy poem reminds us of the importance of patience and time in the process of change.

Finally, it is important to remember that the most disturbed, affectively painful schemas may be activated but out of conscious awareness because of the threat they pose to affect regulation (Westen, 1989). Furthermore, the client may reveal these disturbed schemas symbolically or behaviorally at first. With regard to this issue, Westen (1989) writes

> a concept of self as seductress is surely active when a victim of sexual abuse finds herself compelled to seduce older, married men, or when she finds herself inexplicably depressed during a love affair, but it may well not be conscious. . . . [However], she could only begin reporting the self-as-seductress schema after much tremendously painful work in the context of a therapeutic relationship. (pp. 16, 18)

The above quote underscores the importance of building a strong alliance in a safe environment before survivors can uncover and reveal schemas that are associated with painful affective states, such as shame and self-loathing.

We do not condone so-called "confrontive" approaches because they are often experienced as hostile, challenging, and intrusive. Therapists often utilize these techniques without being tuned in to the individual's self capacities and psychological needs, thus risking a retraumatization of the client who is not ready to assimilate these new ideas into existing meaning systems. Furthermore, we do not advocate techniques which are aimed at cognitive restructuring of disturbed schemas as the primary focus of therapy. Although encouraging clients to view their experiences in new ways is important, we agree with Roth (1989) that early cognitive behavioral interventions may impede the process of gradual approach and integration of traumatic memories by giving clients the message that thinking about the traumatic material is dangerous.

In this regard, it is essential to help clients regulate an appropriate balance between approach and avoidance (Roth & Cohen, 1986) as they gradually learn to acknowledge and integrate the painful affects connected with disturbed, activated schemas. We do not mean to imply that the therapist should never be direct, or move the client toward growth, or challenge the client. However, these interventions, as all others, must be planned within the context of the client's capacities, respectful of the client's dignity, and based in an understanding of the client's current therapeutic need rather than, as is sometimes the case with such interventions, a result of the therapist's frustration.

The following principles are useful as a general guide to helping clients change gradually, as well as motivating them to integrate these changes into the self.

1. The major focus of treatment should be, above everything else, to be respectful of the individual's central needs and their meanings to the individual. For example, if an individual is experiencing high needs for support, the therapist should not challenge him or her to become more independent, just as one would not challenge an individual with central independence needs suddenly to become more dependent.

2. The individual should be encouraged gently to explore the adaptive value of his or her disturbed schemas. For example, a person may be distrustful and unable to depend on others because s/he is afraid of being hurt and betrayed, just as a person may feel disconnected and unable to love because s/he is terrified of another traumatic loss. The defensive value of certain needs and schemas thus must be understood and explored thoroughly before they are challenged. This should be the case even if the therapist perceives these disturbed needs and schemas as maladaptive to the individual. Although the needs and schemas may be maladaptive in

the person's current life, it is important to keep in mind that they served an adaptive function at some point and may be perceived by the individual as essential to his or her psychological well-being.

3. It is also important to remember that seemingly positive life experiences, such as establishing a relationship with a caring, supportive person or reaching out to others, may be very threatening to some people because of the challenge this may pose to their central needs and schemas. In this instance, accommodation would be necessary for the individual to bend his or her schemas to fit a new post-trauma reality. For example, within the area of self-esteem, it could be potentially devastating to an individual to hear from the therapist that s/he is not to blame and is really a good person. The possible reasons for this are many, but might include the fact that the damaged esteem is a protection against rage against others (thus threatening affect tolerance, etc.) or that it is a control strategy that enables the person to make sense of an otherwise incomprehensible event (Janoff-Bulman, 1979). Likewise, the experience of the therapist as a caring, warm person may be, in some ways, more psychologically discrepant than if the therapist lived up to the individual's expectation of being disappointed in all relationships. Returning to Plato's metaphor, the goal should be to have the person gradually gaze at the shadows before staring straight at the sun. This generally means that discrepancy should be presented in tolerable doses, allowing the person to accommodate to a new reality by gradually altering disturbed schemas. If this process takes place too quickly, the person will flee from therapy or become avoidant.

4. The most disturbed or disrupted schemas may be largely unconscious and may be associated with powerful affective states. Although we describe schemas as beliefs, assumptions, and expectations, it is important to keep in mind that individuals may have conflicting sets of schemas within certain areas, one set which is consciously accessible and the other which is largely unconscious. Most often, the most damaged schemas are those that emerge at first only symbolically or indirectly through behavioral reenactments or repetitive life patterns. Thus, these disturbed schemas, often associated with shame, fear, or rage, will often be made conscious and expressed only within the context of a safe and trusting therapeutic relationship. A premature exploration or inter-

pretation of these unconscious schemas will produce distress and possible withdrawal from therapy.

5. Finally, it is important to be flexible with one's treatment approach, varying the style and pacing of interventions to be closely attuned to the unique self capacities and needs of the individual as well as to his or her current psychological struggles. Although our general approach to therapy tends to be broadly psychodynamic and interpersonal, we sometimes find it helpful to utilize techniques from other approaches as they are useful in intervening with specific disturbed schemas. At times, an eclectic approach may reflect a lack of clarity about what one does or how one conceptualizes cases. However, this is not the case when one has made a thorough assessment that is derived from a coherent theoretical framework.

In the following sections, we offer clinical vignettes in which disturbed schemas are explored and provide suggestions for interventions focused on restoring positive schemas in specific areas.

FRAME OF REFERENCE

Case Example of Disturbed Frame of Reference Schemas

A central aspect of memory work is struggling with the individual's attributions of causality, which we relate to the need for a frame of reference. Most often, the focal question becomes, "Why did this happen to me?" (Figley, 1983; Janoff-Bulman, 1979). As each memory fragment is recovered and processed, this question continues to be a pressing concern for many trauma survivors.

> Ralph, a 40-year-old Vietnam veteran, was obsessed with discovering the reason that his entire unit, except for himself, was destroyed on a mission. It was intolerable for him to consider that this was a random event because he could not accept life events as unpredictable and uncontrollable. His obsession was whether, in the minutes before the ambush, he had missed some clue to the impending disaster. He was haunted by the question, "Did I screw up?" In the following interview, Ralph struggles to make sense of what happened:

Therapist: Try to tell me exactly what you remember right before the boat was blown up.

Ralph: I remember being on lookout. Everything was incredibly quiet. I was looking out toward the jungle. When we were on lookout, you could hear the enemy breathing, that was how charged up we were.

Therapist: And do you remember hearing anything?

Ralph: I didn't hear anything. It was so quiet.

Therapist: And then what happened?

Ralph: The next thing I remember was hearing the rocket come toward the boat. It was so fast, it was like it was happening before we even had any warning.

Therapist: What happened next?

Ralph: I don't really know. I only know what they told me later. I guess I was blown out of the front of the boat and everything else exploded. They were wasted (*tears began to form in his eyes*).

Therapist: I can only imagine the pain you must have felt to learn that your whole unit had died.

Ralph: (*Angrily*) It just doesn't make any sense. It shouldn't have happened. In the Navy, these things don't happen on river patrol. We had the big guns. It was like we were set up.

Therapist: Tell me more about that.

Ralph: It was like they were just waiting for us. But I should have heard something, I should have been able to sense they were there.

Therapist: But every time we've gone over your memory, you didn't hear anything, there was no warning.

Ralph: Yeah, but how do I know I wasn't off that day and that I screwed up because I was off?

Therapist: Is there any way you can check that out with yourself?

Ralph: I keep going over it again and again in my mind and I can't find anything.

Therapist: Then perhaps the truth is as you remember it: The enemy was waiting for you and you had no warning that they were going to attack.

Ralph: I find that hard to accept. It doesn't make any sense. We were the biggest, the best. We always told ourselves that we would never die because our unit was the best.

Therapist: And yet, even among the best units, men were killed and it doesn't make a lot of sense.

Ralph: It sure doesn't. It makes me think that the world is a pretty screwed up place if you do your best and you get blown away anyway.

Therapist: It must be painful to accept that the world sometimes doesn't make any sense and that terrible things happen, even when we do everything we can to prevent them from happening.

Ralph: But I still don't understand why I was the only one to survive. If that's true, then I should have died too.

Therapist: Then I guess we need to keep trying to understand what this means to you and how you can someday find peace with this question.

In Ralph's case, his disturbed schemas regarding frame of reference, unaddressed for 20 years after the war, led to a generalized feeling of unworthiness, a belief that he has a terrible power to destroy everything in his path, and a sense of meaninglessness and hopelessness about life in general.

As Frankl (1963) and others have pointed out, working through these questions of causality and meaning is essential to transforming traumatic experiences; this is central to the healing process.

Within the coping literature, people have written extensively about the relation between attributions of causality and mood (e.g., Abramson, Seligman, & Teasdale, 1978; Beck, 1967). In the trauma literature, Janoff-Bulman (1979, 1982) and Wortman (1983) have explored the adaptive significance of self-blame among rape victims. These writers have focused on attributions as control strategies that help people cope with stressful life events. While there was early evidence that self-blame might be adaptive for victims (Baum, Fleming, & Singer, 1983; Bulman & Wortman, 1977; Chodoff, Friedman, & Hamburg, 1964; Janoff-Bulman,

1979; Timko & Janoff-Bulman, 1984), this has not been borne out by later research (Meyer & Taylor, 1986).

Janoff-Bulman (1979) proposes a useful distinction between behavioral and characterological self-blame to sort out these mixed findings. Additional clarification can be obtained by examining individuals' causal attributions in the context of their self development. By uncovering the unique meanings of attributions of causality for each individual, the therapist can begin to assess whether self-blame is useful or destructive in each specific situation. We believe that individuals who have impaired capacities for affect regulation and moderating self-loathing are most vulnerable to a destructive impact of self-blame. Conversely, individuals with strong resources and capacities who have high needs for independence may find behavioral self-blame strategies comforting.

In general, individuals must resolve disturbances in frame of reference schemas, both those concerning causality and those concerning hope, in their own way and in their own time. As with the other areas, we do not advocate directly challenging these schemas, particularly at an intellectual level. Rather, we see the therapist's role as working with the client to understand the various meanings of these schemas and gently exploring other interpretations. As the therapist and client examine these schemas time and time again in the light of their current understanding, a new frame of reference gradually emerges. At all times, the therapist is merely a guide; he or she has a general map but the client will need to fill in the details in ways that are unique to him or her.

SAFETY

Case Example of Disturbed Safety Schemas

The following excerpt of an early session with Matilda, an incest survivor in her 20s, is an example of how to listen for and explore themes concerning safety. The clinical presentation was one of generalized, nonspecific anxiety; social isolation; a history of revictimization by abusive men; and chronic depression. There were no overt intrusive symptoms, nor had Matilda consciously remembered the details of the incest until she saw the movie *Something about Amelia*, which led her to enter therapy. In the fourth session, Matilda was talking about how isolated and alone she felt and yet how difficult it was for her to be in social situations with men:

Matilda: It's hard to describe. Sometimes I become nervous, not myself when I'm around strange men, like I just want to run away.

Therapist: Can you tell me about the last time you felt this way?

Matilda: Um, I was at a cocktail party at work with some people from the company. I knew a few people but a lot of them were strangers. This strange man came up and started talking to me, asking me about myself. I got real nervous, felt kind of shaky, and then excused myself to go to the bathroom.

Therapist: So you were feeling anxious, shaky. Do you remember the thoughts that were going through your mind at the time?

Matilda: I don't really remember. I went into the bathroom and put on some makeup to try to calm myself down.

Therapist: Yes, go on.

Matilda: I do remember saying to myself, "You really know how to pick them." I felt crummy, like I wanted to go home.

Therapist: When you thought, "You really know how to pick them," what did you mean by that?

Matilda: Well, I guess I was thinking that he's probably like a lot of men I've known, bad for me.

Therapist: In what way?

Matilda: I guess because he would hurt me, do something bad to me.

Therapist: How might he hurt you?

Matilda: I don't really know, but somehow he'd figure out how to get to me, he'd find out where I'm vulnerable.

Therapist: Tell me more about that . . . how would he know how to hurt you?

Matilda: Well, maybe because it's like I'm wearing a sign on my back saying, "Kick me." These kind of guys just seem to gravitate toward me. If I let down my guard, they'll take advantage.

Therapist: What does that mean to you?

Matilda: I just become defenseless, like I'm a little girl who can't stand up for herself.

Therapist: You feel like you couldn't protect yourself?

Matilda: No way, I've never known how. Bad things just keep on happening to me with guys and I don't know how to make them stop.

Therapist: I imagine that makes you feel very vulnerable and unsafe. It's understandable then that you would want to avoid situations that make you feel like that.

Matilda: Yeah, I guess I've felt that way most of my life, like there isn't any safe place in the world for me.

Therapist: That must be a very painful and scary feeling. Can you tell me more about some of those other times when you've felt unsafe?

In this session, the therapist was alert to potential concerns about safety, probed into the schemas that had developed in this area, and began to establish links between these feelings and specific events in the client's life. The therapist also made a mental note that the client was implying a diminished capacity to establish appropriate boundaries between self and others in order to protect herself. Furthermore, she hypothesized that these disturbed schemas might be linked to disturbed schemas related to trust and power. This hypothesis generation and testing is a continuous part of the assessment process.

Individuals who are experiencing concerns in this area need a way to enhance feelings of safety within themselves and their social environment. For persons in acute distress, direct interventions designed to decrease anxiety and enhance security are essential. The person should first be asked whether any safe places exist currently within or outside of the person. For example, is the client feeling safe only at home or while with other people but not when alone? What situations make him or her feel particularly unsafe or threatened?

Kilpatrick, Resick, and Veronen (1981), operating from a classical conditioning paradigm, suggest that fear and anxiety reactions among rape victims are often cued to specific environmental stimuli that are associated with the circumstances of the rape. For example, a victim might feel anxious and vulnerable in the presence of men who are drinking alcohol if the rapist was intoxicated during the rape. The thorough assessment of this area should provide clues as to where and how to intervene.

Cognitive techniques focused on self-calming and self-talk are useful, as is validating the person's need to do things that are calming, nurturant, or pleasurable. This can range from having contact with close friends several times a day to taking a warm bath when one is anxious. Techniques aimed at enabling the person to "go with" the anxiety, rather than fighting it provide a useful paradoxical intervention that has been found to be helpful among persons with other anxiety disorders (e.g., Beck & Emory, 1985).

With persistent anxiety reactions associated with avoidance of trauma-linked stimuli, it may be useful to employ a classical conditioning paradigm to conceptualize and a psychoeducational model to intervene. For example, with many acute victims who have generalized fear reactions, we find it useful to explain how fears become generalized and how reinforcing the avoidant patterns by giving in to the fear can be counterproductive. Some rape or other crime victims find it distressing to find their fears generalized to all men, or certain types of men, often experiencing this process as "irrational." Education about how fear and anxiety responses become conditioned to certain stimuli and how the pattern of avoidance reinforces the fear is often helpful in normalizing these responses and providing a rationale for gradual exposure.

The work can then proceed to developing a program of gradual exposure based on the principles of systematic desensitization, a technique researched by Keane in his work with Vietnam veterans (e.g., Keane & Kaloupek, 1982). We usually allow the individual to structure his or her own program with some guidance and checking in with the therapist about progress.

Hypnotherapy and imagery work can also be a useful adjunct to therapy in which one can create a safe place internally, neutralize perceived dangers symbolically, and hold onto the feeling of safety during the week. For some people, particularly those who are very independent, active mastery can be very useful, such as changing the locks on one's doors, taking a self-defense class, etc. For many veterans with severe PTSD, having a gun is often essential to feeling safe. Although this is not a coping strategy we advocate, we nonetheless believe it is counterproductive to challenge this method unless the person is suicidal or violent. The therapist can work with the client to retain the gun legally, safely, and symbolically, if the client feels a gun is essential to his or her safety. Overall, there are many useful techniques for enhancing the sense of safety, particularly if the self-capacities have been strengthened and the individual is able to garner support for safety needs in his or her environment.

TRUST

Case Example of Disturbed Trust Schemas

Sara, an incest victim in her mid-20s from a working class background, came into treatment with profound feelings of loneliness, isolation, depression, chronic anger at people, and general dissatisfaction with her life. Early in treatment, we explored her chronic anger and disappointment with people in her life:

Sara: I'm angry because people keep messing with me. I can't count on them for anything. I should know better by now that I can't depend on anyone but I still keep trying and getting hurt.

Therapist: Can you think of recent times in your life when you've felt this way? I want to understand what this means to you and how this has hurt you.

Sara: Yeah, last weekend I was feeling really down and lonely, I had nothing to do. I called a friend and asked her to come over and she said she would, after she did something else. I made dinner and cleaned up my apartment. Then the bitch calls me and tells me she got tied up with some guy at a bar and couldn't come over.

Therapist: I imagine you felt very hurt and disappointed in her for letting you down like that.

Sara: Yeah, at first I was hurt but then I was really furious. I should have known better than to trust her. I'm the fool for letting her get into my life.

Therapist: You feel like you're a fool for trusting her to be there for you?

Sara: Yes . . . I'm a fool for allowing myself to believe that she would follow through, that it was okay to think that she was going to come through for me. I just don't let myself do that very often.

Therapist: How come?

Sara: Because most of the time people just screw you. I don't trust most people, and when I try, here's what I get. It just proves to me that it's better to trust no one, no way.

Therapist: I gather from what you're saying that you've been badly hurt when you've trusted other people, depended upon them.

Sara: Well, that's the story of my life. I guess I can't expect it to be different.

Therapist: Most people need someone they can count on, someone they know will be there when they need them. Where was it you learned that people can't be trusted?

Sara: (sarcastic laugh) On my mother's knee, I guess. She was never there when I needed her, she was too spaced out or sick a lot, just left me to hang out with my brothers and stepfather.

Therapist: And what about with them?

Sara: (becoming tearful) Well, I thought my stepdad was my buddy, he and I used to hang out together a lot and then, well when I was about 7 or 8 it happened, you know . . . .

Therapist: He abused you?

Sara: (shamefully looking down) Yeah . . I just can't talk about it yet.

Therapist: That's okay. I'm not going to push you to talk about it before you're ready. I understand there are a lot of scary feelings involved. For now, it helps us just to understand how you've been hurt through the betrayal by your stepfather and many other people. That makes it very scary to allow yourself to trust anyone again, probably even me.

Sara: (looking up with a little smile) Yeah, how did you know?

As might be anticipated, this particular client had a very difficult time engaging in therapy; she would resist the process by putting on a tough exterior that said, "I don't need anyone." In Chapter 11 on resistances and working through the transference, we will come back to this issue.

As mentioned previously, some persons with disturbed trust often fear being let down or betrayed by others or fear that they will be helpless and weak if they allow themselves to depend on others. Other persons may feel a very strong need for support and dependence, attempting to have this need gratified in their relationships. For the individual who has disturbed dependency needs coupled with disturbed schemas related to trust, the therapy should be aimed at exploring the following areas: why it is so frightful to trust, be dependent, etc., and what would be the major (perceived) risks of allowing this to happen. Working through resistances to changing the client's framework is an essential component of therapy. For many people, these fears have some basis in reality and it is indeed frightening to consider opening oneself up to be hurt again. However, for the most part, these schemas are distortions that have developed over time and which are often inappropriate to many current life situations.

Working through the fears and the resistances involves gradually introducing discrepancy to the beliefs that trust is always dangerous or that dependence is inevitably a sign of weakness. Sometimes people can be encouraged to imagine, through guided imagery or hypnosis, under what conditions they might be able to be dependent or trusting and how this would feel. Often, these techniques bring a flood of affect as the person gets in touch with his or her deep longing for support from others and the hurt s/he has experienced relating to frustration of these needs.

It is also helpful to present to the client the possibility of learning to trust gradually, in small doses. Clients with very disturbed schemas in this area frequently evidence an all-or-nothing approach to trust, setting up impossible standards of trust for other people. For example, the individual is often hyperalert to any signs of untrustworthiness, such as one incest victim who "wrote off" people she first met if they did not respond well to her disclosure that she was an incest victim. Not surprisingly, few people knew how to meet this test, particularly outside the context of an existing relationship. Thus, learning how to balance trust and distrust and to modulate one's closeness or distance to others is critical to learning to build healthy trust schemas over time.

Furthermore, the standards of trust individuals set up should be gently challenged if they are distorted or unrealistic. For example, one Vietnam veteran often abandoned long-time acquaintances if they cancelled any engagement, even, as once happened, if the person was in a car accident and was not to blame for not keeping the appointment. Thus, learning how to trust requires that the individual make better discriminations about trust versus distrust, trusting where it is appropriate and not trusting when it is inappropriate.

SELF-TRUST

Another important set of schemas are those related to self-trust. These schemas are related to the ego resource involving the ability to make self-protective judgements. This resource underlies the individual's ability to trust his or her own judgment, to be aware of signals of danger in interpersonal relationships, and to meet dependency needs in non-destructive ways. A case example of an incest victim who was abused emotionally and physically by her husband illustrates the importance of the development of positive self-trust schemas.

> Carla, a woman in her 30s, complained of being unable to know how to avoid men who might hurt her. She had generally avoided relationships with men after the sexual abuse by her alcoholic father, but then married a man who was also an exploitive, abusive alcoholic. After her divorce from him, she was paralyzed with fear that she would make the wrong choice again, ending in a total withdrawal from heterosexual relationships.

Excerpts from one therapy session illustrate how disrupted self-trust schemas are gently challenged by the therapist.

Therapist: What is it you don't want in a man?

Carla: A man who drinks too much, appears to be sincere but is inconsistent, appears caring and attentive only when he needs something, and who is overdependent and needy.

Therapist: Is there anything appealing about this type of man initially?

Carla: He can be very giving when he wants something. He can also be very attentive at first, when he actively pursues me.

Therapist: At what point might there be some warning signs that all is not okay?

Carla: Well, he would start to become very possessive of me, wanting to spend all his time with me, not wanting me to see friends. Then he would want me to be there for him all the time, and get angry if I didn't do what he wanted. He would also start to make promises he wouldn't keep.

Therapist: Do you think you would recognize these qualities in a man if you saw them now?

Carla: Oh yes! I would be able to sense it if I felt these things again.

Therapist: And how long do you think it would take before you became more cautious?

Carla: Now, I think I would put up with it for about a week!

Therapist: Then perhaps your judgment is better than you are aware.

Carla was clearly emotionally impacted by this intervention and returned the next session to say at the outset,

> I've been thinking a lot about what you said the last time. I guess, in thinking back on my life, I have made progress and do know how to sense if a man is bad for me. I have picked good friends and can pick out nice qualities in women. I've just been so afraid that I couldn't do that with men. I really couldn't when I was a young woman but I've learned a lot since I was younger. I guess maybe I do have better judgment and should trust myself more.

This brief case illustration underscores the importance of probing into this area by exploring the extent to which the individual can make good judgments, the subtle cues s/he picks up on, how s/he evaluates those cues, and finally, how s/he tests his or her judgments against reality. In this case, the client had better judgment than she thought she had and merely had to be validated in this ego resource. For others whose judgment is seriously impaired, it may be necessary to be more educative, first teaching the person what it means to be self-protective and how this is helpful, and then testing out new skills by carefully tuning in to subtle and not-so-subtle interpersonal cues. For example, the following questions can encourage the survivor to develop these resources:

- What is it about (this person) that makes you uncomfortable?
- In previous relationships, were there any warning signs? What were they?
- What kind of feelings do you have inside that are signals to you that something isn't right?
- What is it you sense about me (the therapist)? What does this tell you?
- How can you check it out with respect to me? To others?

Exploration of this area can help the individual gradually develop the confidence to listen to his or her "gut" feelings and test them out in new relationships, including the therapeutic relationship.

INDEPENDENCE

Case Example of Disturbed Independence Schemas
The following clinical example of Donna, a rape victim in acute distress, illustrates disturbed independence schemas.

Donna: I've been depressed on and off all week, crying a lot. I hate it. It makes me feel like such a baby.

Therapist: Like a baby?

Donna: Yeah, a baby is weak, helpless. I cry all the time, sometimes even at work, and it's embarrassing because I've never cried in front of other people before.

Therapist: You feel like a baby because you cry and are sad?

Donna: I feel very disappointed in myself. . I'm not in control of myself or my life anymore.

Therapist: It's important to feel in control?

Donna: Yes, I'm very independent, have always needed to be in charge of myself. I've worked hard all my life to get my life together, to be strong. I thought I should be able to deal with this and go on.

Therapist: I understand how difficult it must be for you to feel so vulnerable and hurt when all your life you've tried so hard to be strong and independent. And yet, even the strongest people feel terrible pain and sadness when they're violated and hurt in the way that you have been.

Donna: I guess it's hard to be compassionate toward myself. I can understand other people reacting like this, but not me. It's very hard for me to feel like I can't handle something. I even find it hard to ask my friends for anything.

Therapist: What is difficult about that for you, asking for something you need?

Donna: Well, growing up in an alcoholic family . . . when I was a child, whenever I asked for things, they let me down. I had to be independent to survive.

Therapist: Of course you did, learning that people wouldn't be there if you needed them, learning to rely only on yourself. And yet, all people need comfort from others, and there are times in life when a person feels so badly hurt that she can't do it alone.

Donna: I guess so. It's the first time in my life I've ever felt this way. I guess after all these years it's just hard for me to feel any different.

Therapist: Of course it is, and we will have to work together to help you be kinder to the self that was badly hurt and is still suffering.

Donna: I just never wanted to be a crybaby, a whiner.

Therapist: Perhaps somewhere you learned that being vulnerable is a dangerous thing. Whom have you known in your life that you considered a crybaby, a whiner?

Donna: My mother, she was always a crybaby, complaining about everything, she was so weak she couldn't handle anything at all. I just couldn't respect her at all and I never wanted to be like her.

Therapist: So what you're telling me is that when you were a child
            you developed a distorted view of what it means to be
            dependent. You saw your mother being dependent but also
            weak and helpless, and of course, you never wanted to be
            like that. Is it difficult to see the difference between you
            and your mother? She was hurt but gave up, wasn't able
            to cope. You've fought to cope all your life and from what

            you've told me about yourself, you've done a good job of
            it. Is it hard to see that feeling sad and depressed after your
            rape is not the same as being like your mom?

Donna: I guess when you put it that way, I can see that I'm not
            the same. I have always been a coper, a fighter. I just want
            to be that way again.

Therapist: You will, in time, after the wounds heal and all these painful
            feelings are worked through.

In the next session, the client reported feeling less depressed and
overwhelmed, with a glimmer of hope that she wouldn't always feel
this way. A more detailed description of this case follows in Chapter
14. This brief example illustrates the importance of tuning in to a central
need, understanding its meaning, respecting the person's viewpoint,
and beginning the process of gently challenging the disturbed schemas.
This will be explored in more depth subsequently.

In the previous section on assessment of needs and schemas, we
suggested that persons with strong needs for independence often devalue
the self that is perceived as weak, helpless, dependent, or vulnerable.
The therapist must understand how these needs have been threatened
and how positive schemas can be restored. Often, these clients find it
difficult to engage in therapy because they associate therapy with a
potential threat to their independence. This fear may manifest itself in
being afraid to cry or be vulnerable in therapy because of a profound
fear of losing control or appearing weak. Initially, the therapist must
validate the need for independence by assuring the client that s/he
will be in control of the therapy process and that s/he is a very strong
person for having the courage to enter therapy instead of giving up.
    Furthermore, it is important to understand how independence became
so important to this individual. The exploration of early family history

and subsequent relationships will often reveal how this need became central for the individual. For some people, independence may have been valued and reinforced in their family of origin. For others, the need for independence may have arisen from a disappointment of their dependency needs or by experiencing disdain for those viewed as weak and helpless. Often, these individuals had one significant person in the family who was devalued, such as a mother who was helpless, weak, and passive in relation to a strict or authoritarian father. Independence thus becomes a way to avoid a dreaded identification with the devalued parent.

Furthermore, a striving for independence may have been the only way to fight one's way out of a dysfunctional or enmeshed family system. Often, these individuals find it difficult to acknowledge their needs for support and help from others. Emotional expression, particularly vulnerability, is perceived as dangerous. These distortions must be gently challenged through such techniques as reframing and working through the resistances to being vulnerable. In essence, the individual must recognize that he or she can maintain his or her independence while allowing for human frailties.

One technique which is useful for these individuals, previously described in Chapter 7 on treatment of the self, is that of eliciting compassion for the self that is wounded. Often, these individuals are able to have compassion for other people's suffering but not for their own. Conceptualizing that people can be both strong and vulnerable, independent and needing of support, tough and tender, is the first step in the process of resolving distortions in these need areas. If the expectancies for independence are unrealistically high, then the therapist can gradually present discrepancy by such gentle yet challenging questions as, "Do you feel that to be strong means never to cry or feel vulnerable?" and "Is it difficult to imagine that some of the strongest people also feel deep pain, just as you do, and that this strength allows them to master these feelings rather than avoiding or denying them?" With regard to the self capacities, these individual must learn to self-soothe and moderate self-loathing as they integrate a more realistic view of strength and independence.

Guided imagery or hypnosis can be useful in promoting a sense of independence and self-power as individuals gradually confront their deepest feelings in a scenario where they have control over the pace and timing of this process. For example, a highly hypnotizable client may devise his or her own controls as s/he faces painful memories, such as creating a spaceship that can travel to and from painful places, with built-in controls for regulated approach and avoidance. As part of this process, the therapist can gently encourage the person to acknowledge his or her own strength in charting unknown territories with strength and perseverance.

POWER

Case Example of Disturbed Power Schemas

A brief case example describes Clarisse, a 45-year-old woman who was the victim of early childhood physical and emotional abuse, extreme parental discord, and a marriage to an abusive, alcoholic husband, with several instances of marital rape. She presented for therapy after a bitter divorce from her husband, feeling chronically depressed, lethargic, and unmotivated, and experiencing many somatic complaints that could not be diagnosed medically. She did not report her chief concern as a history of abuse, nor did the previous abuse appear to be discrepant with her expectations. Instead, her chief concerns were "being walked all over" by her five unruly children and being mistreated by a married man who was "playing games" with her. The following clinical vignette, in the first few weeks of therapy, offers a glimpse into the inner experience of a woman who had given up trying to exert control over others in her environment, with significant effects on her mood and life satisfaction.

Therapist: You said that you're feeling tired, worn out. Can you say more about what that is like for you?

Clarisse: I'm just tired of everything. I come home and the kids are screaming, the house is a mess, and I feel sick all the time. All I ever want to do is sleep. I went to the doctor again, but he can't find anything wrong with me.

Therapist: Do you have any thoughts about what might be going on with you?

Clarisse: I think I'm just worn out by life. All my life, it's been one struggle after another, first my parents' craziness, then my ex's, now my kids, who are driving me crazy.

Therapist: It feels like life is too much of a struggle?

Clarisse: Yeah, I'm tired of fighting. I feel like I've been fighting my whole life.

Therapist: In what way?

Clarisse: First there was my family . . . you know my dad was pretty mean to us kids and also to my mother . . . there was a lot of fighting and yelling . . . and then I walked back into the same situation with my ex . . . he was always pushing me around, until I finally got fed up with it. Now it's the kids and Fred (her married lover) who think I should be at their beck and call and that they can walk all over me.

Therapist: You feel that people walk all over you?

Clarisse: You bet! I'm the biggest pushover there is, it's like I have a sign on me that says "Walk all over me."

Therapist: Is it difficult for you to assert your own needs, to tell people that you don't like it when they walk all over you?

Clarisse: Huh! What needs! I don't have needs anymore. I don't know how to stand up for myself, I just give up and people know they can get away with it.

Therapist: Are there any situations in your life where you feel more powerful and in control?

Clarisse: Not really, even my 6-year-old is more powerful than me; he bosses me around all the time just like the others do.

Therapist: I can understand how you might feel fed up with all of that. Can you imagine it being any different for you?

Clarisse: It's hard to imagine, I guess. I know some women that are stronger, their kids know who's in charge. I'd like to be like that but I never really have.

Therapist: What do you think makes it so difficult for you to be in control, to assert your needs?

Clarisse: I guess I don't really believe it would work. I don't expect a lot anymore, I just do what I have to do to get by and the rest of the time I just want to escape.

Therapist: I imagine it might feel very painful to try to be more in control and then to discover that even that didn't work.

Clarisse: Yeah. I guess at some point I figured it was just easier to give up, to go with somebody else's program.

Therapist: Would you like that to be different?

Clarisse: Yeah, but I don't know how. I'm sick of doing what I'm doing. I'm just getting worn down by all of this.

Therapist: Then maybe that's something we can work on together. First, I guess we need to discover what some of your needs really are.

Clarisse: Sounds good to me. How do we start?

In this brief vignette, we see a woman who has been "beaten down" by all the circumstances in her life. Her healthy needs for power have been thwarted continually, a pattern which is common among battered women (Walker, 1977–1978). As a result of these experiences, she has given up psychologically, a condition of learned helplessness in which she no longer expects that she can exert control over people or her environment (Abramson, Seligman, & Teasdale, 1978; Seligman, 1975). The result was depression, low self-esteem, futility about the future, and passivity in relation to other people in her life who continued to abuse or otherwise take advantage of her. This type of pattern may be most amenable to the experience of empowerment, a concept that has been widely used in the feminist literature on victimization of women (e.g., Russell, 1986).

Clarisse presented with very little awareness of her own needs, a reflection of a poorly developed sense of self. In this case example, we find the therapist beginning the very gradual process of presenting alternative expectations to her disturbed schemas and providing hope that things might be different than she expects.

Initially, the therapeutic work must focus on strengthening those self capacities and ego resources that have been compromised by years of abuse or helplessness. In our experience, these individuals often have an impaired ability to know their own needs as distinct from other people's. Furthermore, they often describe being devoid of a sense of self or personhood. When asked what they feel they need for themselves or who they are, they often respond by saying, "I don't know" or "I'm not able to have needs of my own." Thus, the first therapeutic task is creating a self, through exploration of psychological needs and encouraging the individual to value and respect herself or himself as a unique, autonomous person. The thorough assessment of needs may be particularly important in the early stages of therapy. Likewise, continually identifying and labeling the individual's needs as s/he describes feeling frustrated, blocked, or depressed is an important prelude to learning to exert power over others or the environment.

As within the other areas, it is important that the therapist avoid prematurely challenging the expectation that the individual cannot control outcomes. Too great a discrepancy can be unsettling to clients and they will often indicate that they feel misunderstood by the therapist. Thus, it is critical to first empathize with the experience of helplessness, understanding fully how the person perceives his or her power in relation to other people. As part of this, the therapist must fully tune in to the terrible frustration that is experienced when attempts at control fail, as well as to the attributions individuals make about why this is happening. Often, individuals will talk about feeling weak, helpless, like a pushover or a wimp, or produce other derogatory self-descriptions. The extent to which this has become an integral part of the self-representations must be understood and taken into account as the therapist intervenes in this area. Individuals who have internalized a negative self-view in this area will be more resistant to changing these views than those who find themselves temporarily paralyzed after a victimization but report a previous history of being able to be appropriately dominant or interpersonally powerful.

The next phase of therapy will involve gently encouraging clients to explore, first through fantasy or imagery, and then in real life, scenarios in which they exert more power with others. An integration of techniques from assertiveness training may be useful as individuals role-play situations in their lives in which they hope to assert their own needs for power. As part of this process, the therapist should be tuned into how this new behavior feels to the person, what fears s/he may have about what might happen, and any resistances to becoming more powerful. Individuals may fear that they will fail at their attempts, that other people will resist them, or that they will be rejected by others. These and other fears must be understood, explored, and gradually tested out in reality as the individual makes attempts at changing his or her behavior. Small attempts should be reinforced as the therapist acknowledges how difficult it is to change deeply ingrained patterns.

These changes can sometimes seem insignificant to the therapist unless there is accurate empathy for what this means to the person. For example, an abused or dominated woman who tells her husband that he is capable of getting himself a cup of coffee when he demands one or who moves into another bedroom after a verbal assault may be doing something that is radically different from lifelong patterns of submissiveness and helplessness. Often, clients are amazed when such new behaviors result in positive outcomes and their sense of self is bolstered as they discover that they can identify and assert their needs. The gradual shaping of new patterns through exploration of needs, strengthening a sense of self, working through resistances to changing schemas, and, finally, gradually encouraging attempts at controlling outcomes will ultimately result in new, more rewarding patterns that enhance self-esteem and feelings of mastery.

ESTEEM

Case Example of Disturbed Esteem Schemas

The following case example provides a look at John, a 39-year-old Vietnam veteran who experienced profound self-loathing, followed by blackouts and self-destructive acting out. In the fourth month of therapy, John described experiencing a dissociative episode during the week, followed by severe depression and remorse. In this session, the extent of his damaged self-esteem was revealed and a link was made to specific war traumas that he had never talked about. In the following vignette, the client was describing what had happened to him the previous week.

> *John:* I don't really know what happened. I went home after work and my wife was angry about something, she was yelling at the kids, and then started accusing me of never being around when they needed me, the same old garbage.

> *Therapist:* Do you remember what you were feeling or thinking at the time?

> *John:* Really tight, wound up, like I do when I'm about to explode. I told her to get off my case and she was screaming at me about how I'm irresponsible, never help out.

> *Therapist:* Do you remember what happened next?

John: No, things get confusing then. I remember storming out of the house, getting into the car. The next thing I remember was that I was walking in the woods, I was filthy, dirty, I think I had fallen into a stream or something. I finally found a road and then started walking; it seemed like hours. Finally, I recognized where I was and was able to find my car.

Therapist: I imagine you must have felt very frightened.

John: Yeah, I was scared. I didn't know what happened to me, I just don't understand why I keep screwing up.

Therapist: What do you mean, keep screwing up?

John: I don't know . . . everything I touch turns to shit.

Therapist: Help me understand what this means to you.

John: *(tears in his eyes)* I just seem to destroy everything that's good.

Therapist: *(gently)* How so?

John: I've screwed up my marriage, my kids, everyone I've gotten close to has been badly hurt.

Therapist: How is it you feel that you have hurt people close to you?

John: It's just something in me. They go away, they disappear, something bad happens.

Therapist: What makes you feel it's something in you that causes people to go away?

John: I wish I knew, it just keeps happening, it has to be me.

Therapist: It really hurts when it keeps happening.

John: *(puts his head down, begins to cry)*

Therapist: Can you tell me what happened that hurt you so badly?

At this point, the client revealed a trauma in Vietnam in which his best buddy was blown up by a mine. John was in charge of the unit and had gone out earlier to check for mines. He was supposed to go into the jungle first but was held back by someone. His friend wanted to go ahead and John was concerned but thought it was okay. He was sobbing continuously as he told this story.

> John: I went in right behind him but he was blown up, wasted. I screwed up. . . . *(angrily)* I should have been more careful. It should have been me. It was MY responsibility and I was always so careful.

> Therapist: *(softly)* I'm so sorry this happened. I can only imagine the agony you must have felt to see your best friend die, the grief, the pain. And yet what I'm hearing also is that you felt responsible for his death, as if you should have been able to prevent it, or that it should have been you that died.

> John: It should have been me. I fucked up, it was me. It's always me.

> Therapist: And so throughout your life, as you've held onto this memory, you have felt again and again that you are guilty of terrible things. And it's so difficult to remember how much you loved him and how you would have done anything to protect him, to save his life.

> John: *(bitterly)* Yeah, I loved him. He was the first person I ever loved and look what happened, I destroyed him, just like I destroy everyone else.

Ultimately, the survivor guilt and ensuing self-loathing were resolved through a lengthy process of recapitulation, grief work, and finding compassion for the self that was able to love and care, the man who did the best job he possibly could. Furthermore, later in the session, the therapist discovered that the intense self-loathing and guilt were precipitated when John was accused of being irresponsible, a painful assault to his sense of self-esteem as well as to his strong needs to be responsible and to protect others.

In an excellent article on resolving survivor guilt, Williams (1988), makes the point that directly challenging the sense of guilt is likely to be fruitless until the affects underlying the guilt are acknowledged and worked through. Williams describes a number of approaches that can be useful in resolving survivor guilt, such as helping the individual recognize he or she did the best possible job under the circumstances, clarifying how much time the person actually had to act, and discovering as many positive aspects of the individual's behavior during the trauma as possible. This work must not be done prematurely, however. If the client feels the therapist does not fully understand the extent of his or her self-loathing, these interventions will be experienced as a failure of empathy.

As with all the areas, resolving disturbed esteem schemas must take place in the context of a thorough understanding of the whole person, the strength of the self-capacities, the person's central needs, and the meanings of esteem for this individual. It is well known that traumatic experiences, as well as those that involve neglect, failures in empathy, or lack of validation, can result in varying degrees of disturbances in self-esteem. For some, the damage is circumscribed or balanced by positive esteem schemas. For others, the damage is pervasive, becoming a central issue for the individual, creating disturbances in his or her intrapersonal and interpersonal relations.

The therapist must first explore with the client the specific ways in which needs for esteem and recognition have been thwarted through harmful, invalidating life experiences. As the memories of specific instances are reviewed, the therapist should ask the question, "How did you make sense out of what happened?" Often, persons with damage in this area will report shame and remorse for their own behaviors or will attribute causality to some aspect of themselves. The literature on the adaptive significance of self-blame strategies has been mixed, with some authors suggesting that behavioral self-blame can enhance feelings of control (Janoff-Bulman, 1979), while others have not found support for this as a useful coping strategy (Meyer & Taylor, 1986).

Conventional wisdom holds that self-blame is always destructive in that it leads to decreased self-esteem. However, given the ambiguity in the scientific literature, we prefer to focus on the unique meaning that self-blame holds for the individual. Thus, it is important to explore the feelings that are associated with self-blame or negative esteem schemas as well as the adaptive significance this may hold for the individual (Tennen, Affleck, & Gershman, 1986). Furthermore, it is important to ascertain whether other attributions of causality have been entertained, such as blaming others or circumstances. There is some recent evidence in the social psychology literature that other-blame is associated with less adaptive functioning (Tennen & Affleck, 1989). This finding also runs counter to the conventional lore, at least in the rape and incest literature, which implies that assigning blame where it belongs (e.g., to the perpetrator, society, etc.) is the way to resolve self-blame.

Overall, the findings derived from research on groups of people are not necessarily applicable to unique individuals. Thus, in accordance with constructivist self development theory, the special meanings self-blame has for individuals, the resistances to changing these meaning systems, and its relation to psychological adaptation must be understood thoroughly before the therapist challenges any esteem schemas, despite how maladaptive they appear on the surface.

Negative esteem schemas, such as the belief that one brought on the abuse, may serve a protective function against feeling anger or rage toward others who perpetrated the harm. In our view, it is not desirable to probe for anger prematurely, especially if the self capacities are not sufficiently developed to tolerate potentially overwhelming affects. Strengthening the self capacities is often an essential part of restoring positive esteem schemas. The individual's relationship with herself, her internal images of herself, her ability to modulate feelings of self-loathing and shame, and her compassion for herself are important aspects of positive esteem schemas. Furthermore, the individual's ability to seek out validating relationships is important as many victims find themselves retraumatized by the invalidating statements of others.

Learning how clients perceive others' attitudes and interprets others' statements toward them is important in order to work through any distortions. For example, some individuals with negative esteem schemas will misinterpret other people's comments as critical, blaming, or devaluing, thus confirming their negative view of themselves. The perception these individuals hold about how the therapist views them is also an important component of working through these issues in the transference. Overall, the goal is to help individuals develop a more balanced view of themselves which contains realistic appraisals of both strengths and weaknesses as well as of some illusions about themselves which can be protective of self-esteem (e.g., Taylor & Brown, 1988).

As discussed previously, some individuals with negative esteem schemas need to become as compassionate with and forgiving of themselves, of their own human frailty, as they can be with other people. The techniques described earlier that include self-soothing, experiencing empathy for the wounded self, constructive self-talk, and learning to value all parts of the self are extremely valuable for building self-esteem. In particular, teaching the client to recognize and validate himself or herself through such techniques as imagery or creative projects such as a self-esteem collage can be valuable adjuncts to traditional therapies.

ESTEEM FOR OTHERS

Another set of esteem schemas concerns esteem for others. The need to value others and view them in a positive light is essential to positive interpersonal relations. When someone has experienced harm intentionally inflicted by another, or when others have failed to help a victim, schemas concerning the worth of others can be damaged. For children who have been abused by those responsible for protecting them, positive other-esteem schemas may never develop. Such beliefs as "People only want to hurt you" or "People are basically evil" reflect damage in this area. Such beliefs become evident early in the therapy process, as they make it difficult for the client to form a trusting relationship with the therapist.

To the extent that they are overgeneralized, these beliefs can be challenged gently through exploring with clients whether they have ever observed any positive intent or behavior in anyone, whether they can imagine anyone wanting to be helpful, and of course in the therapy relationship, whether they experience the therapist as malicious or evil. By gently pointing out instances in the client's experiences in which another person behaved in a positive or helpful way, the therapist can gradually help the client develop alternative ways of viewing others. The overgeneralized schemas can be challenged by exploration of the traumatic circumstances in which they developed. In summary, it is important to recognize that damaged esteem schemas can be altered only gradually, because these beliefs arose in the context of trauma and serve some adaptive purpose, despite the costs to the individual.

INTIMACY

Case Example of Disturbed Intimacy Schemas

The following clinical vignette offers an example of someone for whom a damaged sense of intimacy is central. This case involves Darlene, a 36-year-old widow who was a nurse in Vietnam. Although she functioned well professionally and presented with no intrusive symptoms or subjective distress, she complained of feeling numb, cut off from other people, and empty inside. After years of avoiding talking about her Vietnam experiences, she came into therapy. This was, in part, precipitated by the termination of a destructive relationship. In the second session she touched upon intimacy themes. After Darlene discussed the loss of a recent romantic relationship, the therapist asked how she felt about it.

Darlene: I don't feel anything, really. I know I should, but I don't. I put things behind me and I move on.

Therapist: So it's difficult to feel, even when you lose someone you care about. What has that meant for you in your life?

Darlene: I have no friendships, no intimacy. I have no social life at all.

Therapist: How do you understand that?

Darlene: I always screw them up.

Therapist: What comes to mind when you say that?

Darlene: My relationships always start off being passionate, but then I back off. It becomes too close and then I just run. After I leave, I have no feelings for them at all, I just avoid them.

Therapist: Perhaps it's difficult to experience the feelings of loss, sadness. I imagine that perhaps you've been badly hurt in this area.

Darlene: I turned off my emotions in Nam. The first day in country I thought it was real easy. Then the second day, I was dealing with body bags. I kept saying to myself, "No, no. This isn't real." I stood there crying and I just wanted to go home. . . . Then certain people would get to you . . . there was this one kid in the ICU. He was badly hurt but he was conscious the whole time. We developed a relationship, I felt really connected to him. I became hysterical when he died. After that, nothing made me feel that way again. After a few months, I had no feelings. I just drank and smoked pot and got numbed out. I was afraid to talk about it to anyone.

Therapist: What were you most afraid of if you talked to someone, if you let your feelings out?

Darlene: I was afraid if I started crying, I'd lose control, I'd go crazy. I've gotten weird about death. When my husband died in a plane crash a few years ago, I felt nothing, was just cold, frigid. I can say the words but there are no feelings. I just don't seem to care anymore.

Therapist: Sometimes when people experience a traumatic loss, the feelings are so painful that they just shut down. I imagine it must have been devastating to have someone you had grown close to, whom you cared about, die on you. And so over time you felt dead inside, like you couldn't feel for anyone or expect to be connected with anyone again.

Darlene: I just can't afford to feel that way again. I can't imagine ever getting close, taking that risk again. Anyway, I'm not sure those feelings could ever come back to life.

Therapist: It's understandable that you would feel that way. And yet I believe that although you feel dead inside, deep down inside there's still a caring person with real human feelings just like anyone else. I am hopeful that over time, as we mourn these losses together, you will be able once again to experience being fully alive. *(At this point, tears began to form in the client's eyes.)* I also imagine that as you feel this sadness now, it might feel very scary.

Darlene: Yes, it does. I'm just so afraid of being overwhelmed.

Therapist: Of course, you are. Then we'll have to take it slowly, and in a way that's not overwhelming for you.

In this case, the therapist was also alert to the client's fears about losing control and being vulnerable, themes associated with disturbed independence schemas. The therapist also predicted that this woman would have a very difficult time feeling connected to the therapist, an issue that will be explored further in Chapter 11 on transference and resistance.

One pattern associated with disturbed intimacy schemas involves an individual who has established appropriate and meaningful attachments in the past, but has then experienced the traumatic loss of one of these attachments. A second pattern involves the individual who has never been able to form mature and satisfying attachments to others. This pattern is often associated with a history of emotional neglect and unresponsiveness, described by some clients as the experience of "not being seen." Each of the patterns has different implications for therapy that we will discuss below.

The individual for whom the first pattern is predominant, as in the case of Darlene, often longs for an intimate connection with others but is fearful of his or her vulnerability to loss. An important step in the therapeutic process is to begin exploring the specific meanings of attachment for this individual. For example, the therapist might ask, "What do you imagine would happen if you were to allow yourself to love again?" This exploration will often yield responses such as, "I would always be afraid that something would happen to that person" and "I don't think I could ever really give myself fully in fear that I would be devastated again." The therapist might then explore the client's fantasy of what it would mean to experience another loss.

Often individuals will express a diminished belief in their ability to cope with another loss, such as the fear that they would be shattered. In our experience, this fear often is tied to previous unresolved losses, and most specifically, the experience of "impacted" grief (Shatan, 1974). One of the costs of unfinished mourning is that the disavowed affect is viewed with dread. Clearly, in order to work this through, the individual must gradually develop the affect tolerance necessary for grief work to be productive rather than retraumatizing.

The individual for whom disturbed intimacy schemas resulted, in part, from extreme unresponsiveness or emotional neglect will present with a different set of issues. In this case, the healthy development of intimacy needs has been thwarted, resulting in an inner state of disconnectedness and isolation. Often these individuals do not express overt distress about their lack of connection. These are the clients who say they prefer being alone or their only wish is to live in a cabin in the woods away from civilization. For them, the work will need to focus on the experience of forming a relationship with the therapist. This process will often involve long-term work in which a connection is gradually built through accurate responsiveness and attunement on the part of the therapist.

For many individuals, this experience of disconnection is associated with affective numbing and alexithymia. The important work of Krystal (1988) on alexithymia and trauma is valuable for understanding how affective states gradually become verbal, desomatized, and differentiated. For these individuals, this process must precede the formation of mature attachments, since one cannot become attached without learning first how to identify and tolerate one's own emotional states.

One last important issue is respecting the client's values related to intimacy. Often we've found our own values about intimacy and the importance of connection discrepant with those of our clients, most often Vietnam veterans who have given up on the world of people. In our experience, it is important to be respectful of the individual's wish for solitude, while continuing to understand this in the context of that individual's history.

GROWTH-PRODUCING CHANGES IN SCHEMAS

In this last section, we want to acknowledge that trauma can also alter schemas in positive, growth-producing directions. Koss and Burkhart (1989) cite examples of this in their excellent analysis of the experience of rape:

> Through the process of cognitive re-appraisal, several positive outcomes are possible including: healthy questioning of beliefs about the meaning and direction of one's life, discovered ability to maintain a sense of competence under trying circumstances, heightened sensitivity to horror and dehumanization, and the development of strong convictions. (p. 33)

Other authors have written about how trauma can enhance one's appreciation for life and for one's relationships, as well as producing the realization that one is strong, a survivor (e.g., Brown, Feldberg, Fox, & Kohen, 1976; Veronen & Kilpatrick, 1982). To the extent that new schemas emerge through adversity, these new schemas may be more resilient than those before. Some examples of the positive transformation of schemas involve those survivors who transform their victimization into a gift for others or the world. The many therapists in the field of traumatic stress who were themselves victims of trauma are an example of how trauma can be transformed in a meaningful way. For others, a more profound faith in their God and in the spiritual dimensions of life can provide this transformation. Understanding and appreciating the many ways that schemas can be transformed will help therapists guide the survivor into new meanings and growth-producing understandings.

10. Resolving Traumatic Memories

In this chapter, we synthesize the literature on posttrauma memory work and provide guidelines for assessment and specific interventions for recovering and/or therapeutically managing traumatic material so that memories can ultimately be integrated into the person's experience.

ASSESSMENT AND EARLY EXPLORATION

Assessing the Characteristics of Traumatic Memories

The assessment of the characteristics of traumatic memories should be an ongoing process in posttrauma therapy. Early in treatment, it is important to explore whether the client has any conscious recollection of the traumatic events and to what extent the memories are repressed or accessible, whole memories or fragments, tolerable or distressing, and intrusive or avoided. This assessment is an important prelude to the exploration of the specific content and meanings of traumatic memories. If, because of inadequate self capacities, it is premature to explore the specific content of memories, it is nonetheless important to begin an assessment of the memory systems early in the treatment process. The importance of this exploration is twofold. It can help the therapist develop a preliminary treatment plan (e.g., hypnosis, guided imagery, or other uncovering techniques versus techniques to manage intrusive imagery), as well as helping the therapist to anticipate resistances to exploring or uncovering these memories.

As described previously, the memory system includes verbal and imagery systems (Paivio, 1986). An exploration of these different systems is another important part of the assessment process.

Exploring the Verbal System of Memory

In assessing the verbal system of memory, the therapist might probe for the following information:

- What is the first thing you remember about what happened? What happened next? What is the last thing you remember happening?
- Can you clearly remember the sequence of events or the time frame? Do you ever experience any missing pieces in your memory?
- *(If the verbal memory is fragmented)* Do you feel the need to find out exactly what happened? What aspect of the experience is most important for you to remember *(time frame, dates, sequence, etc.)*?

We explore this latter question because for some individuals there is a pressing need to complete a coherent picture of what happened, while for others this is less important.

As a prelude to this exploration, those clients who are avoiding the traumatic material should be reassured that they don't have to reveal any recollections that are too distressing. If the individual evidences nonverbal signs of distress, the therapist should gently explore what the person is experiencing and then ask if he or she feels comfortable sharing this with the therapist. If affect is expressed, it is likely that the imagery system of memory was evoked, which involves a different type of assessment.

Exploring the Imagery System of Memory

The therapist can explore the imagery system of memory with the following types of questions:

- When you remember what happened, do you see any images or pictures in your mind?
- Can you share with me exactly what pictures you see in your mind?
- Can you see colors? Can you what you were wearing? Can you visualize or sense any other objects or people around you?
- Are you aware of any smells, sounds, bodily sensations?

As more vivid and elaborate detail emerges, memory fragments that have been repressed may become accessible. The exploration of imagery is very powerful, most often opening up intense affect, and should be done only when the person is ready. Some indications that the client is not ready to delve further into the imagery are as follows:

- There is a flood of affect that is frightening to the client;
- The exploration of imagery has produced a severe exacerbation of reexperiencing symptoms and subjective distress;
- The self capacities are not strong enough yet for the person to tolerate the affect without disintegrative anxiety or destructive acting out;
- In the sessions following this exploration, the client is late, misses an appointment, or suddenly talks about terminating therapy.

In a later section, we discuss indications that a client is ready to share traumatic imagery. If it becomes apparent that the client is not ready for this work, the therapist can move into the emotional realm, with the goal of working through any emotional reactions, providing soothing or support, and working through fears about approaching the memories.

Exploring Affect as a Prelude to Imagery Exploration

In the area of affect exploration, it is important to explore the following:

- What kinds of feelings were you having at the time or are you having now?
- Are you experiencing the feeling in a particular part of your body?
- What happens inside you when you experience these feelings?
- When you experience these feelings, are you able to comfort yourself?
- Are you afraid of what might happen if you talk about these memories? What do you imagine might happen?
- What would be the worst thing you could imagine happening?
- Is there anything that could make it easier to talk about?

The following excerpt from a clinical interview provides examples of this exploration in the early stages of therapy. This case involves Marinda, an incest victim in her early 30s, who only recently began thinking, after being exposed to media presentations on the topic, that she might have been a victim of incest. It became clear that Marinda became extremely anxious when she discussed the topic of incest in the therapy. The therapist was respectful of her need to avoid the subject and acknowledged that it was probably too early to discuss the details of what happened. However, the therapist chose to assess the characteristics of the memory system as a basis for future treatment planning.

Therapist: I understand that it's still too painful to imagine talking about the details of what happened. However, it would be helpful if I can begin to understand how much you do remember about what happened and the way you experience these memories. You don't have to share any of the specific details if you're not ready. Do you feel up to this today?

Marinda: I guess I can talk in general. I just can't talk about what happened yet.

Therapist: That's okay. Just let me know if at any time you're feeling uncomfortable.

Marinda: Okay.

Therapist: You told me that a few months ago you were reading an article in a magazine about a woman who had been abused by her stepfather and that you suddenly had the thought that this had happened to you. Before you read this article, did you have any similar thoughts?

Marinda: Not really, just that I remember hating my stepfather after I went into junior high. I also didn't date any boys in high school because I was afraid of them. I didn't know why.

Therapist: Did you have any thoughts about why, either then or later in your life?

Marinda: (pause) Well, one time I remember my stepfather walked in the bathroom while I was taking a bath and he didn't knock. The way he was looking at me was weird and then he suddenly left.

Therapist: Do you remember how you felt when that happened?

Marinda: Now that you say that, I remember feeling really strange, kind of scared. (She began looking down at the floor).

Therapist: I have a sense that you are experiencing very strong feelings now as we talk about this.

Marinda: Yes, I feel weird, like I want to run away and hide.

Therapist: Of course, I understand this is very difficult for you. Sometimes these questions stir up other memories that are very uncomfortable. We don't have to go on if you don't want to.

Marinda: No, I guess I'll be okay. It's just that these pictures that don't make sense keep going through my mind and then they're gone. It's weird.

Therapist: I imagine it feels unsettling but that's the way memories sometimes come to mind, in little pictures or thoughts that may not make any sense right now. Does this sound like what you're experiencing now?

Marinda: Uh huh. One picture I have is a man standing over me while I'm in bed at night, but I don't know who it is or what happened. Sometimes I have other pictures that don't make any sense.

Therapist: What kinds of feelings or sensations do you experience when these pictures comes into your mind?

Marinda: It's awful, a sick feeling in my stomach. Sometimes it feels like I have a stomachache or like I'm going to throw up. Sometimes when I have other thoughts it feels like my vagina is burning . . . I just want to run away. Usually I just try not to think about it until the feelings stop.

Therapist: That's understandable as those feelings must be very uncomfortable. What do you imagine might happen if you allowed yourself to stay with the feeling?

Marinda: It's scary, like I would fall apart, break into little pieces.

Therapist: I imagine then that it's very frightening to experience these feelings. We'll just take it slowly and talk about things as you feel ready.

Marinda: I hope so.

Therapist: You have concerns about this?

Marinda: Well, sometimes the thoughts pop into my mind whether I like it or not.

Therapist: I know it's difficult to tolerate these memories but its very normal for the memories to be experienced like that. We'll just have to work on the feelings each time that happens.

Marinda: I guess I just can't really believe it, even now. It's like a bad dream. Sometimes I feel like I made it up or I dreamt it. I just don't want to think I let something so disgusting happen to me.

Therapist: I understand how you might feel that now. However, if you were sexually abused by your stepfather, he is the responsible party. I know it will take a while for you to really come to believe that and that we will have to work on how this has made you feel about yourself.

This session provided important preliminary information about the characteristics of the memory system and the client's subjective experience of the memories. In this case, Marinda revealed that the memories had been totally repressed until stimulated by a magazine article, that most of the memories were probably still repressed but that avoidance was no longer working, that the memories were experienced as fragmented and unbidden, and that the emotions surrounding the memories were very distressing.

With regard to the imagery system of memory, it was also evident that Marinda was primarily experiencing strong emotions associated with fragmented and largely incomprehensible visual images. The verbal system of memory was not currently accessible, meaning that she had no clear knowledge of what happened or the sequence of events. This type of assessment provides information that is valuable in later stages of therapy, including overcoming resistances and working through the memories.

Overall, the therapist should always convey respect for the client's inner experience and readiness to begin exploring traumatic memories. Often, the fears that are expressed relate to conflicted need areas, such as the fear that one will lose control, be overwhelmed, and so forth. In this regard, the memory exploration should always take place within the context of an understanding and respect for the client's existing self capacities and central needs.

This exploration will reveal important information about the memory systems that can later form the basis for treatment planning and intervention.

Assessing Readiness to Approach Traumatic Memories

In reading some of the clinical literature on therapy with trauma survivors, one might form the impression that trauma survivors readily discuss their traumatic memories in therapy or that survivors make full disclosures once they are encouraged to do so. In our experience, this is not often the case, unless an individual has experienced a recent, discrete trauma. If that is the case, the natural tendency toward avoidance has not yet become an entrenched pattern and memories are not yet repressed or dissociated from affects. Many survivors are ambivalent about discussing the details of traumatic memories, particularly those connected to the imagery system of memory. Often, particularly in early stages of therapy, clients will describe the events to the therapist without actually delving into the imagery. For example, Juliette, a rape victim in her teens, shared the following details of her assault in the first session:

> I was walking to my car in a mall parking lot and these two men came up to me. One of the men suddenly grabbed me and pulled me into the car. Both men raped me and threatened to kill me if I screamed. Finally, it was over and I ran to get help.

In this case, Juliette was not really describing a whole memory. Rather, she gave an account that reflects the verbal system of memory. While the details were accurate, the imagery and affect were as yet not fully experienced. For example, Juliette had yet to describe the horror she experienced when one of the men looked into her eyes and taunted her with ugly words about how she was "a slut, a deserving bitch." Nor did she share the segment where one of the men smeared her face with his semen and laughed at her. She did not share the horrifying thoughts that went through her mind about dying when they held the knife to her throat. These and other devastating details only emerged when she had developed the sufficient inner strength (e.g., affect tolerance and self-soothing capacities) to face the powerful emotions and meanings associated with these terrible images.

In her case, the meanings of each image had to be understood as it disrupted central schemas about self and world. The themes of degradation and humiliation activated disturbed esteem schemas, while the terrible helplessness she endured was a threat to her self-image as a powerful, competent young woman who could protect herself from harm, themes related to both independence and safety.

The direct and in-depth exploration of imagery and associated meanings is thus essential in posttrauma therapy. Although this is restating the obvious, we are aware in our own work that therapists may fail to probe for imagery in sufficient depth for a number of reasons. These include:

- A misconception that a detailed, verbal account of a trauma represents the whole memory;
- A reluctance to probe into areas that are clearly painful for the client;
- The client's tendency to avoid talking about imagery directly, keeping the discussion at a cognitive level;
- The therapist's unconscious defenses against hearing powerful imagery, which is emotionally evocative for the therapist as well.

Even experienced clinicians must pay careful attention to the extent to which they probe into imagery, as clients are inclined to protect themselves (and possibly the therapist) by avoiding the disclosure of this most central aspect of the traumatic experience, inhibiting complete resolution of the trauma.

Assessing Readiness to Explore Imagery

In this section, we offer general guidelines for assessing whether a client is ready to begin sharing and working through the traumatic imagery. The therapist should begin this process by probing gently into the imagery and assessing carefully how the client reacts. If the client continues to give a factual, nonemotional report, the therapist might comment on this and suggest that perhaps it is too painful to share the images at this point. Some indications that the client is ready to be guided gently into an exploration of traumatic imagery are as follows:

- The therapy appears to be primarily cognitive intellectual understanding with more dominant than affective processing;
- A specific memory is repeatedly discussed with no sign of emotional relief;
- The client shares a central traumatic memory, noting it is significant, with little accompanying emotion;
- The client has evidenced a capacity to self-soothe and to regulate affect associated with reexperiencing phenomena.

This part of the assessment offers important information about how to proceed with memory work and the resistances and fears that must be worked through before this can be accomplished. Probing into imagery before clients indicate readiness is clearly countertherapeutic and, in fact, can be retraumatizing.

THE DISCLOSURE OF TRAUMATIC MEMORIES

To point out that many survivors must be asked directly about traumatic material if they are to disclose it may be stating the obvious. This issue has been discussed most often in cases involving the uncovering of early and repressed memories of childhood physical or sexual abuse. In our experience, this general principle extends to all phases of memory work, from initial disclosure to later sharing of the most painful aspects of the memories. Not only must the therapist encourage disclosure initially, but the issue must be revisited, at the therapist's initiative, many times, as openings arise during the therapy process. We raise this point here to remind the reader that encouraging the disclosure of traumatic material in a way that is respectful of the client's needs is often a complex and delicate process.

The following case vignette describes the complexity of striking a balance between respecting the client's defenses and conveying an interest in hearing about traumatic material:

> Marta, an incest victim in her mid 20s, came to therapy because of chronic feelings of depression, low self-esteem, and sexual dysfunction in her marriage. A few months into therapy, Marta revealed that she had been sexually abused by her stepfather from the ages of 12 to 16. Over several sessions, Marta and the therapist talked about the memories of the abuse and the concomitant feelings and thoughts about it. After a few sessions, Marta indicated that she no longer wanted to talk about the abuse and the therapist respected this wish, suggesting that Marta might want to bring it up at a later point in time when she felt more comfortable.
>
> This therapeutic approach was consistent with a nondirective stance in which the therapist allows the free associations to guide the exploration. The therapist then followed Marta's lead to move into current areas of dysfunction, exploring current life issues in considerable depth. Over the next six months, Marta never brought up the incest memories and the therapist chose not to bring it up out of respect for Marta's defenses.
>
> When Marta needed to terminate therapy because of a move out of town, she and the therapist reviewed the course of therapy.

During these termination sessions, Marta brought up the one issue in therapy that had bothered her all along. She said, "After I talked about what happened with my stepfather, you never brought it up again. I thought this meant you didn't think it was important so I never talked about it again, even though it was on my mind. I guess I needed you to encourage me to talk about it even though I wanted to run from it."

This therapeutic error, occurring early in one clinician's work with survivors, taught her an important lesson which led to the following guideline with regard to this issue: One should always be respectful of a client's wishes to back away from traumatic memories. Nonetheless, the therapist should periodically acknowledge that this has happened and check in with the client about how s/he feels about the possibility of further disclosure. This might involve being somewhat more directive, saying something like

> Since we last talked about (the traumatic material), I've noticed that you haven't brought it up again. I want to respect your need to bring this up when you feel ready. However, I'm also interested in knowing how you're feeling about this and whether there are ways that I can make it easier for you to talk about in here.

Often, the acknowledgment of the wish to avoid coupled with the message that the therapist is ready and willing to hear more facilitates eventual approach. In some instances, we have observed that survivors will begin sharing previously undisclosed aspects of the trauma soon after they are told that their avoidance will be respected. Individuals with strong needs for independence or power may especially need to be reassured that they will not be led, however subtly, into talking about certain material unless they choose to talk about it.

Anticipating and Resolving Resistances to Disclosure

It is also important to anticipate and explore resistances to disclosing traumatic material. The particular resistance is generally tied to the client's unique self, needs, and schemas, an issue that we discuss in Chapter 11. The following resistances are some that often emerge over the course of memory exploration:

- The fear that one will not be believed;
- The concern that the memories may not be real (e.g., that they are only dreams or fantasies);
- The fear that the therapist will be repulsed and disgusted;

- The fear of one's own reactions to the memories, including overpowering rage and aggression or a loss of control over one's emotional states;
- The fear that one will regress to a childlike state, becoming vulnerable, weak, or helpless;
- The concern that talking about the memories will not help or, indeed, will make things worse.

As the therapist explores these resistances to disclosure, a common theme may emerge, as in the case of one rape victim who was terrified of revealing the detail of what happened:

> I'm afraid that I might fall apart if I talk about it in detail. I try to push away some of the images because if I don't, I might begin crying and never stop. I don't think I can stand the pain.

This led into a discussion of this survivor's strong needs for self-control and her association of emotionality to vulnerability and psychological frailty, a very common area of fear among survivors with strong needs for independence. The fear that one will not be able to tolerate the affect without becoming overwhelmed is also particularly salient for clients for whom this self capacity has been compromised or was never developed.

Other clients might report that they feel terribly ashamed when sharing the memories and are concerned that the therapist will be shocked or perceive them as bad or blameworthy. This might reflect the fear that esteem schemas will be disrupted further if images associated with defilement, degradation, or perceived moral failure are revealed. In yet other cases, clients may be fearful that an in-depth exploration of memories will cause a flood of images that won't stop, a somewhat realistic fear if they have avoided disclosure in the past and have made the appraisal that they won't be able to cope.

The therapist must anticipate these concerns and normalize these fears in order for the memory work to be constructive. An educative framework can help the client normalize his or her resources and enhance a sense of hope about proceeding. As clients will often not verbalize these concerns directly, the therapist should be proactive by making statements such as, "Many survivors experience (these concerns) and I'm wondering if these might be concerns for you." The therapist may also want to be explicit about his or her approach to working with traumatic memories, such as allowing time to "dose" or back away, processing emotional reactions and cognitive meanings of the event fully before proceeding, and building the inner resources that will make this work possible. It may be important to reassure clients that they will never be pushed to talk about more than they are ready for and that if the memory work is causing too much distress, the therapist will work with them to discover ways to decrease their distress. The respect that is conveyed to the client during this process is often essential to building trust, solidifying the alliance, and creating a safe therapeutic environment.

Discouraging the Disclosure of Traumatic Memories

In our clinical work and from clients' feedback about their current or previous therapies, we have learned about subtle ways that therapists inadvertently discourage or inhibit the disclosure of traumatic memories. Although some of these errors are very blatant, others are more subtle and should be monitored closely, even by experienced clinicians.

1. Conveying distress or sympathy (rather than empathy), verbally or nonverbally, may suppress further disclosures. For example, the therapist who leans forward to listen to a particular memory or who registers distress on his or her face may frighten or overwhelm certain clients who may experience this as an indication that they have upset the therapist because the disclosure is so terrible. Many clients will say that they do not want to feel "pitied" by the therapist. Most often, a calm but empathetic tuning in leads to a decrease in distress. Conveying too much feeling will often cause clients to shut down. In this regard, we feel it is valuable to explore, on a continuing basis, the meaning of the therapist's response to the client. Most often, we believe that empathy is expressed nonverbally, through one's eyes and presence. This is expressed in the words of one sexual abuse victim who wrote the following in a journal to her therapist:

I can see the pain I express to you in your eyes of understanding, in a simple acknowledgment of, "Uh huh . . ."

2. The therapist must be aware of signs that he or she has "shut down" or become emotionally distant or numb during a client's traumatic disclosure. These reactions may be subtle and out of the conscious awareness of the therapist. Feeling emotionally untouched by the client's disclosure, moving into questions that relate to factual aspects of the experience, daydreaming, clockwatching, and so forth often indicate emotional distancing. Subsequently, the client, unconsciously responding to the therapist, may distance and move away from the traumatic material as a way of protecting the therapist.

3. Prematurely assuming that the event was very distressing to clients by making statements such as, "This must have been very distressing for you" may be risky to the extent that the therapist is not yet aware of the meaning this has for the individual. For some individuals, such as those with high needs for self-control, a reflection that suggests distress may be frightening, connoting such things as fragility, craziness, etc.

Making references to the client being a victim, victimized, or damaged by what happened can also be risky to the extent that it may challenge the client's present need to deny the full implications of this event. There is evidence that "devictimizing strategies," such as comparing oneself to less fortunate others or not labeling oneself as a victim, can be very adaptive (e.g., Taylor, Wood, & Lichtman, 1983). For some clients, the growing awareness that they were victimized can be emotionally distressing and needs to be assimilated gradually. This is particularly true for individuals who have minimized previous traumas or for whom earlier traumas have been largely repressed. Overall, one should not challenge clients' conceptualizations of the trauma before understanding what this means to them.

4. Exploring seemingly unrelated early childhood material soon after the disclosure can convey the message that the trauma is not taken seriously by the therapist or that the therapist doesn't really want to hear about what happened. One incest victim who had been in therapy for three years with a more traditional psychodynamic therapist had repeatedly brought up her intrusive but fragmented recollections which suggested abuse by her father. The therapist interpreted this preoccupation with her father as a defense against talking about her damaged relationship with her mother. Not surprisingly, the client gradually learned to talk about what the therapist wanted to hear and left therapy without ever sharing her deepest concerns.

5. Prematurely attempting to assuage a client's sense of guilt and shame about his or her perceived role in a traumatic incident may also represent a failure in empathy that discourages the client from further disclosures. For example:

> Julie, a woman in her 40s who had been in therapy for several years with another therapist, had reported a shameful series of events in which she, her sister, and several male cousins in puberty had engaged in sexual activity. Because the children were about the same age, the therapist quickly assured her that she had done nothing wrong and that sex play among peers was normal. She

didn't reveal more details about what happened until years later in another therapy when the therapist suggested that this type of incident could be very distressing and traumatic for children. Only then did the client reveal the most shameful and traumatic components of the memory, including forced submission, humiliation, and degrading sexual acts.

6. On a more subtle level, the therapist might respond to a reported memory by probing only into its cognitive aspects, failing to probe fully into the related imagery and affect. This might occur for a number of reasons. One reaction that is particularly important to monitor is an unconscious desire on the part of the therapist to avoid being traumatized by the emotionally evocative imagery, which relates to a process we call vicarious traumatization (McCann & Pearlman, 1990). In our experience, it is also easy to become intrigued by the cognitive processing of memories and their meanings and inadvertently avoid the exploration of imagery. This is a countertransference issue which is discussed in McCann and Pearlman (1990).

THE THERAPEUTIC MANAGEMENT OF INTRUSIVE MEMORIES

Over the course of memory work, there are many crises that may be stimulated by a number of internal and external stimuli. It is essential that the therapist be aware of the possible precipitants for these crises, as well as having a preliminary understanding of their link to specific traumatic experiences.

As discussed above, both emotional and sensory experiences that in any way relate to the traumatic memory can stimulate intense emotional states which clients can experience as crises. In addition, the anniversary of the traumatic event or an important personal occasion (such as a birthday, holiday, or the loss of a loved one) can evoke strong reactions. Finally, media events such as reports of violence similar to that experienced by the client can provoke strong emotional responses. While any of these experiences might be manageable under ordinary circumstances, the trauma survivor, and especially the trauma survivor who is engaged in memory work, will likely react more strongly to such events. These reactions may include the emergence of intrusive memories.

The literature on posttrauma therapy offers many suggestions about the management of intrusive memories. Here, we synthesize this work and extend it by integrating these recommendations into our own conceptualization of intrusive phenomena.

Horowitz (1974, 1976) provided the first systematic treatment model for stress response syndromes, with guidelines for managing the oscillatory states of intrusion and denial. This approach has been elaborated in numerous treatment articles (e.g., Horowitz, Marmar, Weiss, DeWitt, & Rosenbaum, 1984; Marmar & Horowitz, 1988). The techniques Horowitz (1976) originally described include supporting the client in reducing environmental demands; encouraging appropriate rest and relaxation; decreasing environmental stimuli that arouse recollections; encouraging "dosing" in which the client changes focus, away from traumatic material, and then moves back to it; providing emotional support during the recollections; aiding in the temporary management of distressing emotions (e.g., the use of antianxiety medications on a short-term basis); and using such techniques as systematic desensitization.

In recent years, there has been evidence that direct exposure techniques, such as imaginal flooding, may be associated with a decrease in distressing intrusive symptoms. This technique, developed originally by Stampfl and Levis (1967), has been described in relation to PTSD treatment by Keane and his colleagues (Keane, Fairbank, Caddell, Zimering, & Bender, 1985; Keane & Kaloupek, 1982; Lyons & Keane, 1989). This approach is a variation of systematic desensitization and is aimed at reducing anxiety associated with traumatic recollections through direct exposure coupled with relaxation training. There is some evidence that this technique is efficacious in the treatment of some PTSD symptoms among Vietnam veterans (e.g., Foy, Donahoe, Carroll, Gallers, & Reno, 1987; Keane & Kaloupek, 1982) and in a case involving incest (Rychtarik, Silverman, Van Landingham, & Prue, 1984).

In the cognitive area, stress inoculation therapy has been suggested as a treatment of PTSD symptoms among rape victims (e.g., Kilpatrick, Veronen, & Resick, 1982; Veronen & Kilpatrick, 1983). This approach focuses on managing trauma-related anxiety through the use of relaxation techniques and cognitive techniques, including self-dialogue. Below, we offer some variations on these approaches that are consistent with constructivist self development theory.

Mobilizing the Capacities of the Self

Although most clients find traumatic recollections, particularly traumatic imagery, highly distressing and anxiety-provoking, we believe that this is especially so if the capacities of the self are diminished. The self capacities that are most relevant for modulating the potentially frightening impact of intrusive memories are those that regulate affect and soothe and calm oneself. We use this as a framework for understanding how to help survivors cope with and manage intrusions.

The capacity to regulate affect is closely tied to the ability to soothe and calm oneself. These capacities enable individuals to tolerate and modulate painful affective states and to restore inner calm and self-control. We discussed ways of strengthening these capacities in Chapter 7. Here, we focus on mobilizing these resources through a variety of cognitive techniques to cope with traumatic imagery. We conceptualize this process from a self-psychology perspective, but utilize techniques from the cognitive-behavioral tradition. The overall goal of these approaches is to help clients learn to tolerate the anxiety and other strong affects associated with traumatic imagery, while attempting to soothe and calm themselves. The cognitive-behavioral techniques reviewed above have essentially the same overall goals. However, one distinction between these models and ours is that we focus more on individual differences in the self capacities for managing affects and calming oneself.

The following techniques are aimed at mobilizing these self capacities in the service of coping with intrusive memories. The first step in this process is to assess thoroughly the internal processes of the individual when s/he is flooded with traumatic imagery. This involves an in-depth exploration of what s/he is thinking while experiencing the images and the accompanying feeling states, as well as the metacognitions, or thoughts about what s/he is thinking and feeling. Most important, the clinician assesses the client's inner dialogue and learns about the content of this covert communication. In some cases, the client may be focused primarily on avoiding the anxiety associated with the imagery and will report little or no inner dialogue that is comforting. In that case, one can develop or mobilize the self-soothing capacity by encouraging the client to begin an inner dialogue that is calming and supportive. We describe this process as we applied it in a case of rape:

> Megan, a woman in her early 30s, came into therapy eight weeks after experiencing a mugging in which she was held up at knifepoint and told she would die if she resisted the ensuing rape. She had initially tried to handle things on her own but found that she was continuing to regress and suffer from terrifying nightmares and flashbacks, uncontrollable emotional outbursts, severe depression, withdrawal, and a rapid decline in all areas of functioning.

She had developed a fearful reaction to any recollections of the trauma and attempted to avoid trauma-related stimuli. Despite these attempts at avoidance, she continued to be flooded with traumatic imagery, making it impossible for her to function. Although she had told some friends and the present therapist the facts of the rape, she had never verbalized the more painful images.

Early in therapy the therapist assessed her resources, capacities, and needs. The assessment revealed a bright, competent woman with considerable resources and a strong need for independence. However, she appeared to have diminished capacities for self-soothing and affect regulation as a result of the rape. This was coupled with the self-loathing she experienced for being weak or out of control. As a result, she reacted to intrusive imagery by panicking, which resulted in further self-devaluation.

The first few weeks of therapy focused on encouraging her to replace her condemning self-statements with soothing self-talk such as, "It's going to be okay, you're going to make it, you're not going to fall apart." Paradoxical techniques involving going with the anxiety as opposed to fighting it were also encouraged in combination with self-soothing. Additionally, she was encouraged to hold herself when she was afraid, to take deep breaths, and to imagine that she was comforting a child in distress. This intervention is based on the observation that, initially, many people can imagine empathizing with a hurting child more easily than they can imagine empathizing with the vulnerable self. Another technique was conjuring up the image of her mother, whom she imagined making such comforting statements as, "It wasn't your fault. You're going to get through this." These and other techniques, coupled with the empathetic soothing of the therapist, produced a marked diminishment in distressing intrusive recollections by the end of the sixth session. Megan was able to return to work and was ready to approach the traumatic material directly without overwhelming anxiety.

Clearly, this case resolved itself so quickly because of early intervention in an individual with considerable psychological resources. In more difficult cases, such as persons who have been exposed to extreme, prolonged trauma that more seriously disrupts the self capacities, more lengthy self work is often necessary before memory work can proceed. This is described more fully in Chapter 7.

Taking Planned Vacations from Memory Work

Planned vacations from memory work are integral to most treatment models of trauma, a process that has been described as the "dosing" of traumatic material (e.g., Horowitz, 1976). This view is consistent with a biphasic view of PTSD in which there is a continual approach, working through, integration, and backing away from traumatic memories. At all times, clients are encouraged to explore coping strategies that enable them to dose traumatic material.

Clients often ask whether it is necessary to open up the painful memories in order to heal. One analogy provided in the literature that we have found useful with some clients is that of a wound that has formed a scab over an infection (Courtois, 1988). In order to allow the wound to heal properly, the scab must be removed, the infected material cleaned out, and the wound must heal. One client built upon this metaphor by expressing powerfully the importance of appropriate pacing:

> Sometimes you have to stop for a while in that cleaning-out process so that the patient doesn't bleed to death. Maybe you have to put a temporary bandage on until the bleeding stops. Then you can go back to the work of cleaning out the old infected material.

Focusing on here-and-now concerns in therapy and developing distractions for time outside of therapy such as exercise or other demanding activities can be valuable as a way of consciously backing away from the memories. The exercise and enhanced fitness program advocated by Ochberg (1988) may be valuable for increasing a sense of mastery as well as providing a needed break from traumatic recollections. For example,

> Ben was a Vietnam veteran who was often unable to sleep at night because of unremitting flashbacks and intrusive imagery. He found this most distressing because he felt immobilized and helpless in his chair at night. After exploring activities that might command all of his physical and mental energies, he recalled that he could spend hours working in his tool shed engaged in strenuous woodwork. This activity enabled him to experience a relief from the intrusive images as well as feeling less immobilized and helpless.

In cases involving severe intrusive recollections, it is counterproductive to allow continual processing of these memories in therapy. The danger of not regulating these experiences is that the client may continually retraumatize himself or herself, with accompanying physiological arousal states that can become addictive (e.g., van der Kolk, 1988). In addition, of course, the client will eventually become overwhelmed emotionally, leading to likely withdrawal from therapy.

Mastering Trauma-Linked Stimuli

Consistent with learning theory models of trauma (e.g., Kilpatrick, Veronen, & Resick, 1979), it is also helpful to encourage individuals to expose themselves gradually to trauma-linked stimuli which they have avoided. This is important because long-term avoidance of trauma-linked stimuli is associated with more severe long-term distress (e.g., Wirtz & Harrell, 1987). The therapist might suggest a program for systematic in vivo exposure as is used in the treatment of agoraphobia (e.g., Michelson, 1987) and described by some in the treatment of PTSD (e.g., McCaffrey & Fairbank, 1984). When we employ these methods, we favor gradual pacing over rapid pacing, an approach that is supported in the clinical research on other anxiety disorders (e.g., Michelson, 1987). We take a more unstructured approach to this process than do behavior therapists, encouraging individuals to regulate their own pacing of exposure. For example, rape or other crime victims with considerable resources and capacities may be able to give themselves weekly assignments involving graduated exposure, such as going to a park with a friend, taking a walk alone around their apartment complex, and ultimately going back to the scene of the crime. These techniques, coupled with enhanced capacities for self-soothing and anxiety management, can be very helpful in restoring a feeling of mastery.

Using Self-hypnosis and Waking Imagery to Regulate Intrusive Memories

The technique of creating a safe place where one is offered a respite from the traumatic imagery through self-hypnosis or guided imagery can be helpful for backing away from traumatic material. If the client is able to access symbolic imagery, s/he may find it helpful also to create a special place for the memories to be stored until s/he is ready to retrieve them with the collaboration of the therapist. Some clients prefer to create a place in the therapist's office, sometimes referring, for example, to a box on the therapist's desk or a file cabinet, where they can leave the memories; others may create a place in their own mind, such as a locked chest, to store the memories.

These techniques offer no long-term solutions, but may enable some clients to get temporary relief from the intrusions. The journal writing technique which is advocated in the treatment of incest (e.g., Courtois, 1988) can also provide a way for the memories to have a special place "outside" of the person. In a number of cases, clients have been able to write down memories in their journal and store them away until they are ready to bring them into therapy. For example:

Clara, a rape victims in her 20s, was too overwhelmed emotionally to share the most degrading parts of her rape. Over the course of a few weeks, she came to understand this as a need to protect herself from powerful feelings of shame and self-loathing for what happened. When she began to work this through, she expressed a desire to share what happened but felt too ashamed to tell the therapist face to face. Furthermore, she became too distressed when she began to approach the material. The therapist explored with Clara ways in which she might gradually move toward a direct disclosure. Clara came up with the plan to first write down the details at home without subsequently looking at what she wrote. At the first try, she became upset and tore up the piece of paper. The next week she was able to write it down without tearing it up and kept it enclosed in a wooden box. Ultimately, she was able to bring it to the therapist's office to be read but not discussed. This session preceded her reading her account directly to the therapist without becoming emotionally over-whelmed.

Transforming Memories Symbolically Through Imagery

Individuals who feel comfortable with guided imagery may begin to transform the traumatic images symbolically as a way of restoring a sense of control. Art therapy has been described as one technique that can facilitate the process of transformation and integration of traumatic imagery (Greenberg & van der Kolk, 1987). In this process, as with others, we convey a sense of trust in the client's own inner resources and encourage him or her to allow spontaneous mastery imagery to emerge. The initial directive might be to imagine changing the traumatic scene into one which will offer more control. For example:

Gloria, another rape survivor, was terrified at night by images of her attacker's face. She imagined him intimidating and frightening her. The therapist explored with her what it would feel like if she could imagine transforming her tormentor into something less threatening. Gloria spontaneously described turning him into a toad. She burst into laughter at the image and was able to use it to dissipate her tension when the scene reemerged in her memory.

As illustrated here, this technique often mobilizes the self resource of humor and makes the approach toward traumatic material less terrifying.

In general, the mastery of traumatic intrusions can be facilitated through a number of traditional and creative techniques. Overall, we advocate a stance that is respectful of the person's unique strengths and vulnerabilities, while mobilizing those resources that are most needed at the time. The integration of self work into this process provides a way of gradually building resources and capacities that will enable the individual ultimately to integrate the memories.

THE THERAPEUTIC UNCOVERING AND RESOLUTION OF REPRESSED MEMORY FRAGMENTS

In this section, we review the various techniques described in the literature which focus on uncovering and exploring repressed and/or fragmented traumatic memories. Most often, this work is necessary in clients who have experienced traumas in early childhood or young adulthood, traumas which have been buried and unexpressed for many years.

The History of and Rationale for the Use of Hypnosis and Guided Imagery in Posttrauma Therapy

Historically, hypnotherapy of PTSD has been based on abreaction or the free expression of repressed emotions. This use of hypnotherapy dates back to Janet (1925) and Breuer and Freud (1895/1955). Drug induced abreaction was commonly utilized in treating war neurosis in World War II (e.g., Grinker & Spiegel, 1945). The use of abreaction and catharsis was originally based in Freud's hydraulic model of personality which assumed that pent-up emotions were the root cause of traumatic reactions.

In recent years, the abreaction and catharsis models of hypnotherapy in the treatment of PTSD have been criticized for a number of reasons. Current thinking is that the primary emphasis of memory work should be on integration rather than an affective catharsis (e.g., Horowitz, 1973; Lindy, Grace, & Green, 1984; Parson, 1984). Abreactive techniques can precipitate overwhelming intrusive experiences and affect floods, re-traumatizing the client (Brown & Fromm, 1986). Other theorists have discussed the importance of regulating affects and their expression in order to enhance self-control (e.g., Horowitz, 1973; Lindy, Grace, &

Green, 1984), a process that is critical in the stabilization phase of posttrauma therapy (Parson, 1984).

This approach is consistent with our view that self work, including enhanced affect regulation, must precede the uncovering of traumatic memories. More recent reports of hypnotherapy among traumatized persons have focused on progressive uncovering, working through, and integration of traumatic material as the client is increasingly able to maintain control over the traumatic recollections (e.g., Brende & Benedict, 1980; Silver & Kelly, 1985; Spiegel, 1981, 1988). A detailed description of this type of hypnotherapy for PTSD can be found in Brown & Fromm (1986).

Brende (1985) and Brown and Fromm (1986) describe multiple uses of hypnotherapy and guided imagery depending upon the phase of therapy. Brende (1985) describes four cases of hypnosis: as a supportive technique, as an uncovering technique, as an abreactive technique, and as an integrative technique. Likewise, Brown and Fromm (1986) advocate deep relaxation and self-hypnosis during the stabilization phase and controlled uncovering during the integration phase. The use of these modalities should be determined by a number of factors: the willingness and readiness of the client, the phase of therapy, and the availability of considerable resources and capacities. The different approaches employed will be described further below.

Contraindications to and Cautions About the Use of Hypnosis and Guided Imagery

Contraindications.   A major contraindication to the use of hypnosis is low hypnotizability. Evidence suggests that about 60 percent of people are able to be hypnotized, although, through the use of Eriksonian methods for indirect hypnotic inductions it is possible to induce a trance state in almost all people (Brown & Fromm, 1986). There is also the observation that in some disguised cases of PTSD persons may have suppressed hypnotic ability in an attempt to ward off intrusive phenomena (Brown & Fromm, 1986). In some cases involving early childhood abuse and torture, we have learned that these survivors were controlled through hypnotic techniques. Needless to say, these individuals will experience hypnotic states as a terrifying recapitulation of the abuse experience and hypnosis should be avoided until this connection is severed.

Brown and Fromm (1986), consistent with other authors (e.g., Parson, 1984), also suggest that hypnosis is contraindicated in the stabilization phase of posttrauma therapy. Rather, self-hypnosis for relaxation may be adopted in order to decrease anxiety and internalize protective and soothing imagery. Spiegel (1988) describes the value of self-hypnosis as enhancing the individual's sense of self through self-care, a view that is very similar to our own.

A major contraindication for hypnosis as an uncovering technique is the existence of severely damaged or compromised self capacities. In these cases, we favor the use of waking guided imagery to approach repressed memories gradually. Furthermore, the salient needs of the individual must be understood and respected, with needs for safety, trust, and independence being most relevant to the use of hypnosis. Clearly, clients who do not yet trust the therapist or for whom trust schemas are disturbed will only be frightened by premature suggestions for the use of hypnosis. Likewise, a sense of safety and control within both the therapeutic relationship and the self must exist before this work is possible. As hypnosis requires considerable ground work, most often we do not ordinarily employ hypnosis for uncovering memories until many months into therapy.

Cautions. In using hypnosis, the therapist must be careful not to create "memories." In the vulnerable state of hypnosis, particularly good hypnotic subjects as well as clients who are feeling pressure to remember may "fill in the blanks" if the therapist provides too much direction (Orne, Whitehouse, Orne, Dinges, & Nadon, 1989).

We attempt to be as nondirective as possible in our hypnotic work, especially that aimed at recovering repressed memory fragments. For example, rather than saying, "Imagine your father in your room with you; what is happening?" we are more likely to say, "Go back to a time that was important to you in some way. Where are you? What is happening now?" Although the above example may appear very obvious, we have learned of many subtle ways in which therapists may become too directive in the process of hypnotherapy. Overall, we advocate a nondirective, open-ended stance in which we allow the client to produce the framework for the hypnotic session rather than providing too much direction.

Education About Hypnosis

As with other aspects of posttrauma therapy, the therapist explores the meaning of the uncovering techniques to the client and provides a conceptual framework for them. Initially, the client is asked for his or her associations to hypnosis, and misconceptions or fears are addressed directly. We generally describe hypnosis as an altered state of consciouness that is similar to other states of deep relaxation and focused attention, such as meditation. Most often, clients will express concerns about their ability to stay in control and to be influenced by hypnotic suggestions. Excellent resources exist for helping the clinician know how to frame this experience positively for the client (e.g., Edelstein, 1981). The rationale given for hypnotherapy will depend upon its intended purpose, whether for relaxation and self-soothing, exploration of hidden resources within the self, or the uncovering and integration of traumatic memories. This process of education and preparation often takes several weeks or months. In cases involving repressed or fragmented memories, we may raise the possibility of future hypnotic work early in therapy. A preliminary discussion enables the client gradually to become accustomed to this idea.

Using Hypnotherapy and Guided Imagery

For more detailed explanations of the use of hypnotherapy and guided imagery, we direct the reader to such comprehensive sources as Brown and Fromm (1986), Edelstein (1981), and Erikson and Rossi (1979). Furthermore, advanced training and supervision are essential for using this powerful tool in a helpful way.

In general, waking guided imagery is recommended initially to introduce relaxation and soothing imagery. In the early phases of memory work, guided imagery can be a nonthreatening way to gradually move toward uncovering traumatic memories. The client may be instructed to create a safe place in his or her mind where s/he is free to explore all aspects of the self. This approach is valuable because it supports the client's defenses and provides a protected way to begin delving into more painful material. Often clients will create a beach or country home where they are surrounded by beautiful, calming objects. Brown and Fromm (1986) also describe introducing transitional imagery at this point, such as being surrounded by supportive, trusted people such as friends or the therapist.

Initially, the therapist avoids delving into areas that might be associated with traumatic recall. A few sessions will focus on allowing the client spontaneously to evoke neutral imagery. Often, these seemingly neutral images will symbolically represent aspects of the repressed or split-off traumatic experience. For example:

> Marinda, the woman in her 30s previously described who presented
> with a disguised presentation of PTSD, gradually came to suspect

that she had been sexually abused as a child. After eight months of therapy and the establishment of a trusting relationship with the therapist, they began to use guided imagery and hypnosis as a way of beginning to explore repressed traumatic memories. After a few sessions in which Marinda was able to create a safe place in a beach home, spontaneous imagery emerged about a dark cellar where the shadow of a tall, menacing man was lurking behind the cellar door. When asked to explore this issue further, she revealed that the shadowy figure was attempting to lure a child down into the darkness of the cellar. Over several sessions, in which the guided imagery alternated with exploration of the feelings and meanings associated with the images, the trauma involving abuse by her father was revealed.

In this example, we underscore the importance of using the hypnosis and guided imagery first to establish an environment of safety within which the client can begin to explore the previously repressed or symbolic representations of the trauma. Through a gradual approach toward less disguised manifestations of the memories coupled with the processing of the affects and cognitions associated with the images, the client begins to confront the memories without becoming overwhelmed. If this process had not been very gradual, occurring within the context of a strong, trusting alliance, the client could have easily become frightened by the hypnotic induction and fled from therapy. Again, this process is aimed toward a waking integration and working through of the traumatic imagery, rather than toward affective abreaction. The exploration of affect through hypnosis can occur through the affect bridge method described by Brown & Fromm (1986).

A variety of hypnoprojective techniques can be useful to facilitate the experience of regulating the process. The theater and television techniques (Brown & Fromm, 1986), the split-screen technique (Spiegel, 1981; 1988), and the imaginary videotape (Silver & Kelly, 1985) can enable the client to experience increasing control over affects and images. Techniques similar to these that we have utilized include storing away the memories in a safe place, such as a treasure chest or computer disc, until the therapist and client choose to access them. If at any time during the process the client becomes overanxious, s/he can retreat from the images by exiting the scene temporarily, going back to the safe place, or concentrating on clearing his or her mind, coupled with deep breathing.

We don't recommend suddenly terminating a hypnotic session or leaving the scene permanently during a moment of high anxiety because it may reinforce avoidant defenses. Rather, the client is encouraged to discover alternative ways of establishing control and mastery. For example, as one client approached, in hypnosis, a room in which as-yet unconscious sexual abuse had taken place, she became overwhelmed with anxiety. The therapist suggested she go back to a place in the house where she felt safe, get in touch with her resources, and go back to the frightening room with some additional resources, such as her best friend, the therapist, her pet, or her adult self.

Consistent with our approach, Brown and Fromm (1986) also recommend that each hypnotic session end with a posthypnotic suggestion to remember only those things that will be most helpful or which the client is ready to remember.

Each phase of the work alternates with waking processing of the experiences in hypnosis. We strongly believe in letting clients be the guide to when they are ready to resume hypnotic sessions. Sometimes, clients will alternate sessions and at other times weeks or months may pass before they express a desire to resume this work. During these times, the therapist will help the client continue building resources and capacities, while assimilating the available memories into his or her cognitive schemas. These principles are illustrated in the case of Marinda as therapy proceeded from early exploration of the symbolic representations of trauma to approaching the material in less disguised form. The process of approaching memories and then fully processing them emotionally and cognitively is also described. This part of the therapy took place eight months into therapy:

> As Marinda's symbolic images of a man in the basement gradually became less disguised, she revealed a vivid memory of being down in the basement of her house. Using transitional imagery, she took the therapist along on these excursions as a way of calming and comforting herself. In one hypnotic session, a man who is not yet identified walks down the stairs. She is not frightened because she knows him. She recalls his big hands and recalls him coming up to her and lying down next to her. She becomes anxious and the therapist stays close to her, reminding her that what she is experiencing is only a memory and cannot hurt her. She is then able to remember the man putting his fingers inside her vagina. She begins to sob, crying out, "But why did I just let him, why didn't I fight back?" The next few sessions involved processing her feelings of terror and paralysis and learning that she responded to him because she felt he was in such terrible need.

A few weeks later we return to the basement where she focuses on the man's hands. The therapist explores her associations to this. She says, "My first thought is that they look like my father's hands, but I don't want to say that because I can't believe it is my father." Several sessions were spent talking about what this would mean to her, how she would feel about herself and her family if this were true. This led into a process of mourning for a family that could not ever respond to her emotional needs.

During the next two hypnotic sessions, we discovered one source of internal resistance to revealing what happened. Here, Marinda revealed that a little girl part of her lived inside of her and contained the memories. She was called the gatekeeper and her purpose was to protect the adult Marinda. This discovery of a split-off self-representation enabled the therapist and Marinda to understand how the memories had been protected for so long.

During the next few sessions she was able to recover other memory fragments and express her sense of vulnerability and aloneness as a small child. She was able to begin working through her self-loathing for having her body respond to the man's embraces. In a subsequent hypnotic session, she was able to embrace the little girl inside, holding and comforting her as she cried. This was a very moving session and Marinda reported feeling stronger afterward.

A few weeks later Marinda had a series of dreams about being raped by a man wearing a black mask. In one of the dreams the man was taunting her. In the next hypnotic session, Marinda tuned in to feeling very small and almost nonexistent, "peripheral." The therapist made the interpretation, "But you're not invisible—you're very much a person with your own feelings and needs." Marinda began to cry and talked about how the man would put her in a trance state before he abused her. She became frightened and she wanted to dissociate into the wall, as she had done as a child. The therapist touched her on the shoulder and said, "When I touch you now, you will remember that he has no power over you any more, he cannot mesmerize you any longer. You are here with me now and you are safe."

In the next session she reported a dream in which he began to mesmerize her but she fought back with all her powers. For the first time she realized, "I could hurt him back, I could retaliate." She was for the first time able to acknowledge angry feelings and this increased her feelings of strength. She then had a series of dreams in which her world was coming to an end or her childhood home was exploding. This led her into a process of mourning for the loss of innocence in childhood and a shattering of illusions about the family she had always longed for. After processing the grief for a period of weeks, she was ready to take the final plunge into deeper-level memories, confronting for the first time the reality of the sadistic and degrading abuse at the hands of her father. During the next six months, the therapy focused on incorporating the full meanings of the abuse into her existing schemas and hypnotic work was no longer necessary.

WORKING THROUGH RESISTANCES

The uncovering of traumatic memories occurs gradually and with respect for the client's defenses. We try to work with, rather than against, resistances, and the therapist always conveys a belief in the client's own natural healing abilities. In cases of complicated PTSD, the therapist acknowledges that the work will be slow and that there will be times when the symptoms intensify. These periods are handled by the techniques utilized in the stabilization phase, described above. One is likely to meet resistance when the client approaches a deeper layer of traumatic imagery, with the most painful, degrading, shameful experiences being processed well into the therapy.

Furthermore, the therapist must recognize that resistances occur when "core structures" or schemas are being threatened (e.g., Mahoney & Lyddon, 1988). These schemas are often reflected in the various themes associated with the traumatic memories. In the case of Marinda, the themes that emerged over the course of memory exploration included safety schemas related to violation to her person and loss of bodily integrity, trust schemas related to betrayal and broken promises, and independence schemas related to helplessness to act on her own accord, entrapment, and subjugation. Each memory that was uncovered was connected to disrupted schemas in one of these areas and had to be processed thoroughly. We describe the gradual accommodation or change from disrupted schemas to more positive or balanced schemas in Chapter 9.

Part 3

SPECIAL ISSUES

11. Understanding and Resolving Transference Reactions and Resistances

The major premise of this chapter is that individuals' transference reactions are determined by their central needs and schemas, a view that is consistent with classical conceptualizations of transference. The classic description of transference by Fenichel (1945) is as follows: In the transference the client "misunderstands the present in terms of the past . . . he 'transfers' his past attitudes to the present" (p. 29).

Similarly, Brown and Fromm (1986) define transference as

> a psychoanalytic term indicating that the client distortedly perceives, unrealistically feels about, and behaves toward his therapist according to the impressions formed about significant figures in childhood. He sees his therapist—who is part of his current world—through the tinted glasses of the past. (p. 209)

We integrate these traditional psychoanalytic notions of transference with social learning theory notions about expectancies. Westen's (1989) conceptualization of transference phenomena is most consistent with that of constructivist self development theory. In referring to transference as person-schema, he writes,

> To the extent that the manner, appearance, or status of the therapist resembles another person or exemplar of a social category, schemas relevant to that person or category are likely to be activated. (p. 62)

Thus, one of our uses of transference in this chapter makes reference to the activation of the client's unconscious schemas about other people in the therapy relationship. Westen's definition of transference as interpersonal expectancies is also in line with our conceptualization. With regard to this concept, he writes,

> Patients' reactions to the therapist often reflect their expectations about particular kinds of social interaction or interaction in general. The more generalized the expectancy, the more pervasive are likely to be its effects interpersonally, and perhaps the more recalcitrant it will be to change. When stressed, borderline personalities tend to shift into a malevolent object world, in which the interpersonal arena seems filled with victims and victimization. (p. 64)

This view of transference is consistent with our view that severely traumatized clients may expect the worst from their therapist, and that the more generalized these expectations (or schemas) are, the more likely they will have a deleterious effect on the therapeutic relationship unless they are understood and ultimately resolved.

Finally, Westen refers to the transference of unconscious wishes onto the therapist. This view is consistent with psychodynamic formulations. Here, Westen defines a "wish" as

> a cognitive-affective structure which includes a cognitive representation of a desired state and an anticipated affect associated with attainment of that state. (p. 65)

We will not address here the theoretical differences between a "wish" and a "need"; rather, we believe that a "wish" is activated when a central need area is also activated, whether consciously or unconsciously. Thus, the client who characteristically wishes to be taken care of, nurtured, or protected by the therapist may be reflecting central needs for dependency, while the client who typically wishes for admiration and validation from the therapist is probably reflecting a central need for esteem.

We retain the term transference because we believe it provides a useful framework for understanding clients' responses to therapists. We use the term transference to refer to the client's transfer onto the therapist of the client's expectations about other people or situations related to psychological needs that are central or conflictual for the individual. In a modification of traditional notions about transference, we agree with Lindy (1988) that transference reactions among trauma survivors do not always arise from childhood experiences; rather, they often arise from traumas the person experienced in adolescence, as in the Vietnam veteran, or even in adulthood.

Resistances often reflect important transference phenomena. We interpret resistances as arising most often from a perceived, if often unconscious, threat to central aspects of the person, including the subjective experience of self and one's fundamental self-world schemas (or beliefs and expectations about self and others). Although much has been written about the adaptive significance of positive schemas, little is currently understood about the adaptive significance of negative self or other schemas (Taylor & Brown, 1988). As implied in earlier chapters, we believe that disturbed schemas, no matter how maladaptive they may seem, serve defensive functions for the individual, protecting against perceived internal and external dangers. In this sense, we are proposing that disturbed self-world schemas may be analogous to other defenses of the ego as described in psychoanalytic theory (Freud, 1946).

We hope that the following discussion will provide a framework for predicting and working with unique transference reactions and resistances over the course of therapy with adult trauma survivors.

SELF PSYCHOLOGY CONCEPTUALIZATIONS OF TRANSFERENCE

The self-psychology literature contains extensive writings about the transference reactions of clients with disorders of the self (e.g., Brown & Fromm, 1986; Chessick, 1985; Kohut, 1977). Brown and Fromm (1986) discuss the different transference reactions in persons with narcissistic and borderline personality disorders. With regard to the narcissistic client, they suggest that a "selfobject" transference emerges in which the client's fragile self-esteem is dependent upon the positive mirroring and admiration of the therapist. When the therapist fails to offer this or there is a failure in empathy, the client's self-esteem plummets, resulting in depression. The borderline transference is characterized by boundary diffusion, splitting, panic states, and transient self-fragmentation. Chessick (1985), describing the self-psychology view of resistance, states that resistance arises when the client fears humiliation, rejection, or another selfobject failure that may fragment the self.

Self-psychology theory categorizes severe disorders of the self into narcissistic and borderline disorders. We prefer to assess clients descriptively, in terms of the nature and stability of the self schemas and the degree of development of the self capacities. One rationale for this approach is that in trauma victims, symptoms of severe character pathology may represent chronic, severe, and unresolved posttrauma adaptation (e.g., Briere, 1984; Scurfield, 1985). Furthermore, we believe that focusing on a personality disorder diagnosis can obscure the central issues involved in chronic forms of PTSD. We also believe that labeling trauma survivors as borderline often reflects the therapist's own countertransference difficulties with "difficult" or "resistive" clients. Finally, we find that our descriptive approach provides clinical information of direct relevance to the therapy process.

For these reasons, we prefer to make a complete assessment of each self capacity and ego resource in the context of the individual's unique history and trauma experience. We believe this is a more useful approach to understanding the client's inner world and is ultimately more respectful of the trauma survivor. In the following sections, we will describe our own formulations of how the transference reactions and resistances may be manifested in traumatized persons with serious deficits in self capacities.

TRANSFERENCE REACTIONS IN CLIENTS WITH IMPAIRED SELF CAPACITIES

The Therapist as a Threat to Vulnerable Self-esteem

Clients with an extremely vulnerable sense of self, as Chessick implies above, have a terrible fear that the therapist, as "selfobject" (someone upon whom the client depends for self-esteem regulation) who will disappoint or humiliate them as others have done in the past. These clients will be highly sensitive to perceived assaults to their sense of self and become depressed or rageful when the therapist fails empathetically. We believe that, most often, these individuals experience failures in empathy when the therapist makes interpretations, observations, or other statements that are either premature or experienced as an assault on the self. With regard to the issue of interpretation, Chessick (1985) writes

> Again, there is continuing emphasis on the proper tact, timing, and understanding on the part of the (therapist) of how an interpretation is experienced by the patient. (p. 136)

We agree with this formulation and suggest that if the client reacts with rage or other negative affects when an interpretation is made, then the interpretation was not truly empathetic, no matter how "correct" the therapist believes it to be. With regard to the "selfobject transference," Brown and Fromm (1986) write,

> At least for a while, (the therapist) must be the always available
> mother, who thinks so highly of her child and admires the child
> so much that the patient can begin to develop solid self-confidence.
> (p. 212)

In working with trauma survivors with extremely undeveloped self capacities, we are generally cautious about making any interpretations, but rather focus on maintaining a calm, stable, soothing therapeutic stance while providing a safe and supportive "holding environment" (Winnicott, 1965). During the early phase of the work with such individuals, we avoid being too active or delving into areas that may be too painful for the client, but rather let the client's material guide the process. If the client experiences a failure in empathy, the therapist nondefensively apologizes for the error and empathetically seeks to understand how the error was experienced by the client. In relation to trauma survivors, one must be very cautious about how one responds to material related to the client's sense of inner damage or unworthiness. Prematurely offering reassurances can be a failure in empathy; rather, tuning in to the feelings underlying these painful self schemas must precede any interpretations about their meaning.

The Therapist as "Container" for Intolerable Affects

Parson (1988) writes about the importance of the therapist being a "container" for the terrible affects the client experiences. Often, clients with severely impaired affect tolerance will unconsciously test in a number of ways the therapist's ability to contain the affect. One common way is by experiencing affective overload, such as intense rageful states, in the presence of the therapist. Another way might be for the client, early in therapy, to pour out horrible details of the trauma which are often associated with shame and self-loathing. The client will be reading the therapist's reactions very carefully to ascertain whether the therapist can tolerate these emotions or whether there is any indication, however subtle, of shock, dismay, or disgust. Lindy's (1988) articulate description of this process is as follows:

> [The veteran] tests his therapist's mettle; his capacity to survive
> the trauma when it breaks through. The therapist must not cower
> when horror reveals itself. (p. 225)

It takes a great deal of self-awareness and working with one's own countertransference issues to pass these tests, as overwhelming affects and exposure to material that is horrific can temporarily overtax the therapist's own self capacities. Again, it is critical to respond to these states in a calm, gentle, soothing way, through one's tone of voice and nonverbal demeanor. At times it is useful to address the client's underlying fears by saying something like,

> Perhaps you are wondering whether I will be able to understand
> and tolerate these terribly painful feelings, and memories, or whether
> I, as other people have, will be repelled or overwhelmed by them.

With regard to rage states, we often respond by tuning in to the underlying affects of hurt and vulnerability, by responding with such statements, "I imagine you have been badly hurt, betrayed, disappointed, to feel so much anger." Finally, the therapist should be aware that it will often take a long time for the client to internalize the therapist's empathy and develop trust that the therapist, and eventually the client, will be able to absorb and transform the intolerable affects.

In a discussion of these issues, Lindy (1988) makes the important point that setting a slow, careful pace is often essential to managing affect overload. In this regard, he writes,

> The veteran, perhaps with more foresight than his therapist, knows
> that trauma is always close to the surface. He scans his therapist
> to assess the leadership skills he possesses, his ability to set out
> a careful course, to proceed cautiously. (p. 225)

The issues of pacing and timing are clearly complex and cannot be fully elaborated here. However, we will say that one important way of regulating this process is to be very alert to any signs that one is going too fast. Even if a client pours out traumatic material with little prompting, this does not mean that he or she will not become frightened by the meanings or overwhelmed by the affect associated with these disclosures. This is particularly true if this occurs early in therapy, but may also hold true at later stages in therapy.

One way to monitor this process is to allow time at the end of such a session to explore fully how the client felt and what it meant to him or her to have made such a disclosure, how the client perceived the therapist's response, what the client imagines s/he might experience after leaving the therapist's office, and how the client might soothe or nuture himself or herself later. It is also helpful to let the client know that s/he and the therapist can work together to regulate the pacing of the uncovering process.

The Therapist as Soothing Other

Individuals who are unable to tolerate affects, to self-soothe, and to tolerate being alone become very dependent on the therapist to supply these self capacities or they may act out in ways that pose difficult case management issues. This may be expressed by calling the therapist frequently outside of the therapy hour or going into panic states during the therapist's vacations. The other troubling aspect of working with clients with serious self deficits is that they will often attempt to self-soothe through excessive drug or alcohol use, hypersexuality, or other self-destructive behaviors.

Most often, these clients come from backgrounds of severe and sadistic child abuse or they may have been massively traumatized in Vietnam or other cultural or social arenas. It is most likely that persons with strong dependency needs will adopt the former pattern, calling the therapist frequently, while those with stronger needs for independence are more likely to act out destructively, failing to call the therapist unless in an imminent life-threatening situation. In either case, if such behavior is frequent or extreme, the therapist may feel drained, worn out, or angry at the client. If these feelings are not monitored closely and discussed in supervision, the therapist is at risk for acting out by "forgetting" the therapy hour, being late, failing to return the client's phone calls, and so forth.

On a more subtle level, the therapist may tune out during therapy sessions with these individuals. The therapist may also suffer somatic reactions, as in the case of Jeb described by Lindy (1988). Lindy reported developing a severe headache after receiving a telephone message from Jeb, at whom he was unconsciously very angry.

We do not pose any simple solutions to these difficult clinical issues; clearly, such individuals will require long-term therapy in order to develop the capacity to internalize the empathetic therapist. These issues were addressed in Chapter 7. However, there are some responses that have been helpful in the short run as these self capacities are developing. We generally feel it is appropriate to gratify the client's wishes for merger by responding to telephone calls and being available, within limits, during times of crisis. This is particularly true when an alliance is being built and the client is testing whether the therapist will be there for him or her.

Our approach to these crisis calls is to make them as brief as possible, while conveying the following messages: "I'm still here; I understand how much pain you are in; let's find a way for you to calm yourself until we meet again; what do you need now in order to feel safe, calm, in control?" With some very damaged clients, such as persons with MPD, we have provided transitional objects, such as a book or the therapist's business card with the next appointment date written on it—something that will encourage object constancy; the ability to recognize that the therapist is still alive and present internally. It is important, however, that the therapist set sufficient limits on outside contact to avoid feeling so drained that she or he experiences annoyance, anger, resentment, boredom, or exhaustion. The therapist might say something like,

> I understand how difficult it is for you when you experience these painful states and how important it is for you to feel in contact with me. However, I too need my time alone so that I can be rested and present when we are together. I want to be there for you when you need me but I also believe that you have the internal strength to calm yourself when you are alone. How do you feel about working together to discover a way to do that?

Clearly, it is important to monitor the client's reactions closely, exploring any feelings of anger or rejection. Finally, it is also important for the therapist to state that s/he does want to be contacted in potentially life-threatening emergencies. With persons who are reluctant to call until they are in dire straits, it is important to explore the meanings of calling and to convey concern for the client's well-being. Gradually, as the relationship solidifies, we will gently broach the issue of the outside calls and explore ways that the person can calm and soothe himself or herself without the therapist's direct involvement.

TRANSFERENCE ISSUES RELATED TO CENTRAL PSYCHOLOGICAL NEEDS AND SCHEMAS

Transferences Related to Disruptions in Safety

Vietnam veterans are often acutely aware of the safety of the therapeutic relationship as well as of the physical environment. Lindy (1988) describes one transference theme among Vietnam veterans as

> ubiquitous danger-preoccupation with any aspects of the physical setting of the office or the environs which might indicate that a perimeter had been breached and that the veteran or doctor was in imminent danger of losing his life. (p. 242)

Lindy proceeds to articulate the central dynamics surrounding transference reactions related to safety concerns:

> An unusual and striking experience for many of us was to discover the nearly universal importance of the physical setting of our

offices and surroundings to these veteran patients. We were un-accustomed to seeing transference reactions being so physically attached to this particular element in the therapeutic frame, but we quickly learned to expect a series of questions and concerns related to space: Where were the doctor's chair and the patient's chair with respect to exits? What was the road to the therapist's office like? How dangerous was it? What unfamiliar or unexpected cue might indicate a change in environment, turning it from friendly to hostile? (p. 236)

In one of the cases presented in Lindy's (1988) *Casebook,* a veteran became agitated when the furniture in the office was rearranged so that passageway to the door was blocked. The therapist, understanding that the client's concerns about being blocked might relate to a specific trauma, was able to guide the client back to a central trauma in Vietnam. We imagine that most therapists who work with Vietnam veterans are sensitive to these issues and allow the veteran to position himself or herself in order to maximize his or her sense of security. This may involve rearranging the seating so that the veteran can sit against a wall and have free access to the door.

We have learned that many veterans are reluctant to go to the local vet center after hours because it is located in a dangerous part of the city. Fortunately, our own rural-suburban setting is perceived as much safer, although some have expressed concerns about the security system after hours. This theme may also emerge for rape or other crime victims who were assaulted at night or in a parking lot. For persons whose safety needs have been disrupted, the therapist must be sensitive to understanding these themes as they emerge in response to the physical environment.

With regard to safety issues within the therapeutic relationship, we have observed some common themes among persons for whom disturbed safety schemas are central. We describe these in the following sections.

The Therapist as a Threatening Force. In clients whose safety schemas have been devastated, there is often the unconscious fear that the therapist will in some way recapitulate the experience of threat and terror. In some extreme cases, most often with MPD clients, we have observed in the therapy hour clients experiencing flashbacks in which they believe the therapist is going to kill or harm them. These psychotic episodes are rare. They must be handled gently and firmly by anchoring the client to the present reality and to the fact that the therapist is not a tormentor but someone who is there to keep the client safe.

In a less dramatic way, safety themes will often emerge symbolically through dream material or other imagery. This symbolic material generally represents client fears directly related to some aspect of the original trauma. The client may also fear that the therapy process will in some way be injurious or harmful. Again, symbolic material related to themes of dying, drowning, being lost, being assaulted by strangers, and so forth is important to helping the client understand the meanings of previous traumatic experiences. Exploring the ways in which the person feels safe and unsafe with the therapist, in the sessions, in the physical therapy environment, outside of therapy, and so forth is essential to ultimately resolving disturbed safety schemas.

It is important to explore whether the client can imagine feeling safe and secure. This can lead into very fruitful discussions which help guide the therapy process. Often individuals will express the fear that if they were to alter their safety schemas, for example, becoming less vigilant and less attendant to all the dangers in the world, they would become more vulnerable to repeated trauma. As one crime victim expressed,

> What if I allow myself to let down my guard, begin to believe that I am safe, and then I get hurt? I could never forgive myself for allowing myself to be so stupid.

The therapist can follow this up by exploring the meanings of feeling "stupid" if one lets down one's guard, perhaps implying a belief that one is responsible for protecting oneself from all the dangers in the world. This exploration often leads into issues of blame and responsibility. Despite the conscious knowledge that the trauma occurred randomly or uncontrollably, there is often the deep-seated belief that something about oneself or one's behavior made one vulnerable to injury.

As we discussed in earlier chapters, sometimes individuals, particularly those who have experienced multiple traumas, will feel that they are magnets for harm. Others, such as Vietnam veterans who prided themselves on being good warriors, believe that truly competent warriors avoid danger; hence, if one was injured, one must have failed in some way. The logical extension of this type of belief is that "I have to be the best warrior I can now, alert to potential danger from all sources, at all times."

Because individuals generally need a frame of reference that includes a belief in an orderly universe, we do not advocate challenging these schemas prematurely. Rather, the therapist must tune into the affect that is associated with a change in these schemas while supporting appropriate and adaptive ways that safety needs can be met.

The Therapist as Violator of Sacred Boundaries. Boundary issues in the therapy most often arise with clients who have experienced past violations of physical or psychological boundaries, such as incest survivors or Vietnam veterans. These individuals may experience this issue in two ways: a difficulty in establishing appropriate boundaries in relationships or a rigid need for boundaries that precludes any closeness or intimacy.

In the first case, the client may attempt to test the therapist's ability to establish appropriate boundaries by unconscious attempts to violate client-therapist boundaries. The therapists at our institute have experienced working with incest survivors who are flirtatious, who want to be held or touched, who want to know personal details about the therapist's life, who complain that the therapist is too distant or impersonal, and so forth. We have heard all too many reports about therapists who gratified these often unconscious wishes with disastrous outcomes. The therapist who holds or touches the incest survivor, particularly when therapist and client are of opposite sexes, risks confirming the belief that sexual contact is inevitable. Although this may represent a wish, it is also that which is most dreaded.

For this reason, and also because we cannot know the meanings of such boundary violations for clients, we are very cautious about doing anything that may represent a boundary violation. In this sense, we adopt a traditional analytic stance which discourages touching, personal disclosures, and so forth. This, however, does not mean that we are cold, distant blank screens, as there are times when giving a nonsexualized hug at the end of a difficult session or revealing something about oneself can solidify the relationship. However, we do not bend these rules unless we know the client well and have thoroughly explored the meanings to him or her.

With regard to the Vietnam veteran who needs to establish rigid boundaries in order to feel safe, we have found it important to avoid getting too close too soon. For some veterans, physical or psychological closeness may represent a terrible threat, the threat of annihilation. Until the veteran has differentiated the therapist from the enemy, the therapist must proceed cautiously. The meanings of "coming too close" will vary from individual to individual but often relate to intrusiveness. For some, asking too many questions or being too directive will be experienced as intrusive. Again, learning to understand what represents a violation of boundaries and avoiding such errors will be essential to the therapeutic relationship; a serious error will result in a premature termination.

Transferences Related to Disruptions in Trust/Dependency

The Therapist as Untrustworthy or as Betrayer. Clients with disturbed trust schemas will often anticipate a violation of trust within the therapeutic relationship. Most often, we observe this to be true among survivors of early childhood abuse, Vietnam combat veterans, and other survivors who have experienced other human beings as untrustworthy and unreliable. Often these issues will not emerge directly but rather symbolically at first, until the alliance is strong enough for them to be processed openly. For example,

> Harry, a Vietnam veteran, had experienced numerous abandonments in his life. These included being sent a "Dear John" letter from his wife and having had his family clear out all his bank accounts and sell his belongings while he was in Vietnam. These betrayals of trust were compounded by being abandoned or betrayed by numerous people in his life after the war. Early in therapy, the therapist cancelled two sessions due to a serious illness that necessitated a hospitalization. Harry failed to show up for the next scheduled session.
>
> The therapist struggled over whether to call Harry or to wait for him to initiate contact. Choosing to call and inquire about the missed appointment turned out to be the wiser decision as the meanings of this unfolded over the course of therapy. Harry was eventually able to understand that he expected the therapist to abandon him after the therapist had been out ill, an expectation that was based on his experience of being abandoned when he was away at war. Missing the next scheduled appointment was an unconscious trust test designed to determine whether the therapist cared enough to reach out. Over the course of therapy, many other tests of trust emerged, all of which had to be made conscious and understood within the context of the evolving therapeutic relationship.

There are many possible ways in which disturbed trust can manifest itself symbolically in the therapy relationship. One subtle example is the client who pays for sessions in advance. For some, this may merely reflect a bookkeeping preference. For many, however, we have learned that this behavior reflects a need to protect against being abandoned by the therapist: If one pays in advance, then one can feel safe in knowing the therapist is committed to being there for that period of time.

Trust issues can also be reflected in fears of becoming too dependent on the therapist or on the therapy process. Clients with great difficulty tolerating their own dependency needs may feel particularly distressed when the relationship is intensifying and they find themselves increasingly reliant upon the therapist. If this issue is not openly addressed early in therapy, these individuals will often flee treatment, under another pretext. Anticipating these concerns and being alert to the symbolic manifestation of trust issues is often the best way to prevent such acting out.

As implied earlier, the period when trust is first developing is most crucial. The therapist may naively assume that this evolving trust is a positive sign; one may fail to recognize soon enough that this is precisely the time when these clients become most afraid, retreating back into old patterns. As with all the other areas, exploring the fears related to trust/dependency is essential to resolving these complex transferential issues. Often, individuals will express the fear that if they trust again they will be wounded again or that if they grow to be too dependent they will become helpless and needy. Learning that trust develops gradually and can be tested and developed within a stable relationship can help these clients learn to trust in less threatening ways.

Finally, it is important to be mindful that for some individuals, trust will never be fully possible or even desirable, as the experience of vulnerability is too discrepant with their needs. The therapist should respect this and refrain from encouraging the client to trust too much. One error is to encourage disclosure of difficult material prematurely. With individuals with disruptions in trust, getting too close too quickly will almost always result in a need to distance. If this is anticipated and processed early on, clients will learn that their needs for distance and closeness will be respected and that they will not be asked to become more vulnerable than they can tolerate.

Transferences Related to Disruptions in Esteem

The Therapist as Interrogator or Judge. Earlier, we discussed the sensitivity of some clients to being rejected, humiliated, or degraded by the therapist, an issue that clearly relates to esteem schemas. In this case, we are referring to the projection onto the therapist of the client's own worst beliefs about himself or herself, fearing that the therapist, as judge, will deem the client guilty of terrible crimes. We borrow the concept of therapist as interrogator from Lindy (1988), who describes a case in which a veteran began to panic during the session, saying he refused to be interrogated any longer. The meaning of this was then linked to an experience in which he was interrogated by an officer who treated him as the enemy following his shooting of a child. The central issue in these cases is the fear of being condemned by the therapist, confirming one's own beliefs that one deserves to be judged and convicted.

Again, we reassert that premature reassurances are likely to be more harmful than helpful, representing a failure in empathy for the internal experience of terrible guilt and badness. Instead, one must empathize fully with the painful affects associated with these self schemas and understand the client's fears of being condemned. For some, condemnation means that they must die or destroy the bad part of the self. For others, this fear may lead to an avoidance of repressed memories that will confirm the sense of badness. Ultimately, this issue will be resolved only through the development of a strong alliance in which the client experiences, at a deep emotional level, genuine and deeply felt compassion and acceptance by the therapist, an experience that is internalized through subtle nuances in the therapist's attitude as much as through any verbal means. Clearly, this internalization occurs slowly and only through the patience and constancy expressed by the therapist.

The Therapist as Victim of the Lethal Self. In Chapter 8, we discussed one disturbed esteem schema that may involve the belief that one is evil, malignant, and potentially lethal to all who are close to the person. We have observed this dynamic among Vietnam veterans who experience a deep sense of badness and evil for the terrible acts they feel they have committed. Others may have had this belief confirmed after the war as people close to them died or otherwise went away. In addition, this disturbed self-esteem schema is often present in children who grew up in deeply disturbed families who may have blamed them, explicitly or implicitly, for the abuse which they endured. Often, this self schema is deeply unconscious and will emerge only as the transference develops and the survivor begins caring for the therapist.

One needs to listen carefully for themes that relate to fears that the therapist will be destroyed, die, or meet with a tragic fate. The ways in which this theme is expressed are often very subtle. For example, one veteran, after a strong alliance had developed, would casually say to the therapist at the end of the evening session, "Have a safe trip home." Another veteran, upon learning that the therapist was going on vacation to the shore, said, "Be careful of the undertow." The exploration of the underlying meanings of these casual statements opened up powerful issues as the clients revealed the true basis of these remarks: a fear that anyone who came into close contact with them would die. Over time, it was possible to link up these meanings with specific traumas in which others died. For some, even after this work is accomplished, it may take a long time for these schemas to resolve. For one veteran, it was only after the end of his three-and-a-half-year therapy that he was able to believe fully that because the therapist hadn't died yet, perhaps he wasn't so lethal after all and thus might safely allow other people into his life.

Transferences Related to Disturbances in Independence

The Therapist as Caretaker. This transference issue is often most salient for clients whose strong need for independence is a defense against dependency needs. Some of these individuals will remain at a safe distance from the therapist, rebuffing any signs that the therapist cares for or is concerned about them. These individuals may have particular difficulty demonstrating any signs of weakness, such as crying during sessions or revealing painful material. Again we see this pattern most commonly in adults who grew up in dysfunctional families that could not be counted on for care and protection. In learning that his or her dependency needs were unacceptable to the family, the child also learns that such needs are unacceptable to himself or herself and transfers this belief onto the therapist. This can be expressed in concerns that the therapist is bored with the client, that the client feels as if all s/he does in the sessions is complain, and that the therapist will not like or respect the client if the client shows his or her dependency needs. These are the clients who at times state, "Of course you listen to me, but that's your job," implying both that the therapist is not genuinely interested and that no one else (who wasn't being paid to do so) would be interested in the client's concerns.

Here, as in other areas, reassurance is not useful. These individuals will need time to understand that the therapist is genuinely interested in and concerned about them, that the therapist can be counted on to be at the therapy hour every week and to attempt to understand the client's concerns, and that the therapist can respect the client even with an awareness of the client's dependency needs and wishes. Over time, this becomes internalized so that the client can begin to accept the simultaneous existence of dependency and independence needs and feelings of self-worth.

The Therapist as Controller. Clients who have a strong need for independence which is not mainly an outgrowth of disavowed dependency needs sometimes fear that the therapist will try to dominate, change, persuade, or otherwise control them against their will. These are often clients who were reinforced for independence as children and, through trauma, have found that their ability to take care of themselves is compromised in some way. It may take time for such persons to reveal any vulnerability in the therapy as they may fear that doing so would open them up to persuasion. These clients often negate the therapist's interpretations, although they may often make the same observations themselves at a later time. There is often a strong need for individualism, which may be expressed verbally or indirectly through personal presentation.

It is easy to mistake the presentation of this disrupted need for independence as a disrupted need for recognition/esteem because these persons may talk extensively about their accomplishments and capabilities. Careful probing can reveal, however, that such an individual is struggling to restore a sense of personal power and is holding the therapist at a distance by reiterating that, prior to the traumatic event, s/he was quite independent. The loss of independence through trauma heightens the client's sensitivity to further potential assaults to his or her independence need, and hence the defensiveness against the therapist's support. In these cases, the therapist must be very sensitive to the possibility that any supportive or mildly directive remark may be perceived as an attempt to coddle or control the client. Exploring the meanings of independence or the affect associated with the traumatic loss of independence will be fruitful in working through this transference.

Transferences Related to Disruptions in Power

The Therapist as Competitor for Control of Situation. Some individuals respond to a lack of power by attempting to control others around them. As a set of disrupted power schemas, this is reflected in the belief that one must control others. We often see this in adult survivors of child abuse who have vowed never to let others dominate them and can feel calm only when in a position of power over others. We also see this need for dominance in Vietnam veterans who experienced the traumatic loss of people for whom they felt responsible. This theme is often played out in the therapy by the client attempting to take control of the frame of the therapy, for example, by asking for a different appointment time than that offered by the therapist, by attempting to establish a different fee payment plan or schedule, or by requesting that some other aspect of the therapy be done differently.

One such client, a victim of long-term childhood physical abuse, insisted each week that he could not sit through 50 minutes without a cigarette, that therapy would be more useful to him if it were conducted outdoors where he could feel less confined, that he would prefer two 25-minute sessions per week to the customary 50-minute weekly session, and so forth. Over time, he was able to discover that he feared that if he went along with the therapist's rules, she would continue to ask for concessions from him and eventually he would again feel abused. Again, the best route to understanding the meanings of and eventually resolving these transference reactions is to be alert to any special client requests or concerns and to empathize with the client's need for control while continuing to explore schemas related to power.

The Therapist as Exclusive Controller of Situation. Another set of disturbed power schemas concerns the belief that one cannot exert meaningful or essential control over one's environment. These persons reflect the learned helplessness described by Seligman (1975). This disruption is common in battered women and may also be present in adult survivors of child abuse as well as in other persons whose attempts to exert control over their environments have failed.

Some clients respond to the therapist as if the therapist were harsh, authoritarian, or power-hungry. This can evoke a potentially dangerous countertransference reaction in the therapist, who may feel frustrated in his or her attempts to encourage the client to express appropriate control and influence in the therapy situation. A client with this disruption in power schemas often presents with an air of helplessness about various aspects of the therapy situation, viewing the therapist as a powerful authority figure. One such client was a 32-year-old woman, a survivor of extensive childhood physical and emotional abuse, who had disturbances in the areas of power and dependency. When the therapist would attempt to explore the client's feelings about frame issues such as the therapist's vacation and a fee increase, the client's initial response was, "It doesn't matter how I feel; you're going to do it anyway."

Again, the continuing exploration of the meanings of power and its relation to the abuse or trauma will eventually, although in many cases very slowly, lead to the resolution of this transference and the gradual development of positive schemas in this area.

Transferences Related to Disruptions in Intimacy

The Therapist as Potential Loss.   Individuals who have experienced the traumatic loss of loved ones, whether physically through death or symbolically through betrayal, are likely to have disturbed intimacy schemas which they may well transfer onto the therapist. These issues will arise through concerns about the loss of the therapist, such as those discussed above in relation to disturbances in esteem schemas. Pinpointing the meanings of such concerns (in this example, esteem vs. intimacy) is a matter of exploring in depth with the client his or her concerns about the loss of the therapist as well as the meanings of earlier traumatic losses.

One client, a woman who grew up in a severely dysfunctional family, expressed concern about what she would do if the therapist were to abandon her. This concern reflected disturbed schemas related to trust and intimacy. Early in the therapy, she felt she shouldn't depend on the therapist because the therapist might intentionally leave her by terminating the therapy relationship. As she worked through this fear and as her relationship with the therapist changed from one of dependency (in which she viewed the therapist as her caretaker) to one of connection (in which she viewed the therapist as a partner on her personal journey), her fear shifted to one related to intimacy, that is, would the therapist abandon her unintentionally, through death. The expressed concerns shifted from, "Do you love me?" to "Do you like me?"

Again, time and constancy on the part of the therapist are two essential ingredients to helping such a client internalize the therapist as a caring, concerned companion. Another piece of the work of resolving this transference issue is to help the client come to terms with the unpredictability of life events and gradually to realize that even the tragic loss of the therapist would not shatter the client permanently.

The Therapist as Friend. Individuals who have never had a close connection with anyone, as is the case for many adult survivors of child sexual abuse, may grow deeply attached to the therapist from whom they experience genuine caring, support, and acceptance. This can develop into a strong wish for closer contact or a broader relationship. It can be revealed symbolically in dreams in which the therapist plays the role of friend or lover, or more directly through questions about the therapist or about the therapist's opinions, values, and so forth. Again more indirectly, this is sometimes manifest by clients styling themselves after the therapist, in dress, speech, gestures, and so forth. Finally, clients may bring gifts or lend or ask to borrow books from the therapist as ways of broadening their contact and making the therapist into a friend.

These situations must be handled delicately, as an unthinking rejection of any of this material can result in a severe injury to the client's budding ability to connect with others. As in other areas, gently observing and exploring the meanings of these behaviors and empathizing with the wishes underlying them can lead to important material concerning past attempts at connection.

RESISTANCE

Traditional Conceptualizations

Freud's (1900/1953) original notion was that resistance is the conscious opposition to the recall of unconscious material, and thus an expression of struggle against the therapeutic process (and, by extension, against the therapist). Current object relations views of resistance flow from this view to the extent that they suggest that ". . . resistance must be defined in terms of the object relationship—as occurring within the therapeutic dyad, as something between the patient and the therapist that interferes with the flow of the therapeutic process" (Blatt & Erlich, 1982, p. 70).

Freud (1926/1959) later reconceptualized resistance as the unconscious manifestations of the individual's attempts to cope with intrapsychic conflicts, a shift which, as Dewald (1982) notes, recast resistance as a more benign process from the perspective of the therapist.

CSDT Conceptualization

Our own understanding of resistance draws upon both of these views. We understand resistance as a reflection of the client's attempt to protect himself or herself from pain in an area of psychological vulnerability. To the extent that the client believes that the therapist is trying to inflict pain or to bring about change against the client's will, resistances are an expression of "... fundamental distortions in the patient's modes of relatedness within a particular therapeutic relationship" (Blatt & Erlich, 1982, p. 71).

Within constructivist self development theory, we attempt to understand the meaning of resistance in terms of self capacities, psychological needs, and related core schemas. Our own view of resistance is most similar to that of Mahoney and Lyddon (1988), who write,

> From a constructivist perspective . . . resistance reflects natural and healthy self-protective processes that serve to protect the individual from changing too much, too quickly. In this view, resistance is a basic adaptive process that prevents core psychological structures from changing too rapidly and should therefore be worked "with" rather than "against." (p. 220)

Thus, in constructivist terms, resistance may occur when the therapy or therapist prematurely challenges "core psychological structures," such as capacities, needs, and schemas. For example, when the client begins to exhibit behaviors that suggest resistance to change, behaviors such as missing or coming late to appointments, not talking during sessions, shifting from talking about traumatic memories to talking about day-to-day events, or any of the host of behaviors traditionally understood as resistance, we attempt to assess first whether we have estimated the client's self capacities incorrectly.

With trauma survivors, resistance of this sort is most likely to emerge when we move prematurely into memory work (see Chapter 10) with clients who do not have sufficient ability to tolerate strong affect and regulate self-esteem. In addition, even the best-developed self capacities can be strained by the painful memory work necessary to the psychological healing of many survivors, particularly those of severe abuse or torture. Thus, when we observe a client retreating from memory work, we often interpret this "resistance" as a sign of self-protective functioning (Dewald, 1982), letting the client know that it is important now to shore up his or her reserves by returning to self work (see Chapter 7). Horner (1984) has also pointed out the importance of supporting the client's resistance when it is being used to protect the survival of the self. For example,

> Malcolm's younger brother had been tragically killed when both were children. Malcolm was working to understand the impact of this event upon his feelings about his parents. At one point, this

work became quite overwhelming as he began to realize he felt both that his father had failed to save his brother's life and that his parents had neglected Malcolm's needs as they withdrew into their grief surrounding the loss of their other son. After several intense sessions, Malcolm came in one week and chatted about his job, TV programs he had watched, and current local events. The therapist interpreted Malcolm's withdrawal from the painful material as a need to take a break and to rebuild the self-soothing capacities that had been the focus of the early part of therapy.

A second important aspect of understanding and responding appropriately to resistance is to discover which psychological need is being threatened. As Schlesinger (1982) points out, the emergence of resistance in the treatment is diagnostic, conveying to the therapist areas of sensitivity. Knowing the client's need structure is helpful in developing hypotheses here, but the observation of resistance can also help the clinician build a picture of the client's need structure. For example,

> Susan, a 30-year-old mother of two young children, had been in therapy for about two months when she began to reveal a history of severe childhood torture. Susan presented as a very independent woman with well-developed ego resources. She had rejected the therapist's soothing statements, stating on one such occasion that she could take care of herself. As the therapist gently guided Susan into the abuse memories, Susan grew very quiet and then missed a session. When the therapist probed into the meanings of this behavior, hypothesizing that it might be too early in the relationship for the memory work or that memory work might be too painful for Susan at this time, Susan stated that she could share the material if the therapist would sit next to her rather than across from her. A further exploration of this request revealed Susan's deep sense of shame related to her past as well as her strong desire to experience the therapist's supportive presence next to her. This was the first direct indication of Susan's strong disavowed dependency need.

In summary, in our work with trauma survivors, we have found it important to accept the resistance behaviors as a form of indirect communication (Schlesinger, 1982), and try to understand whether the message concerns the need for self work or the need to protect core psychological needs and related schemas that are being threatened.

12. Applying the Theory to Special Clinical Issues

Therapists who work with trauma survivors are likely to be familiar with a wide variety of difficult clinical problems. In this chapter, we demonstrate the application of constructivist self development theory to these problems. We have chosen this particular set of issues because they are either especially complex or emergent. The issues we discuss are self-destructive behaviors, including suicide and self-mutilation, substance abuse, reenactments, and aggressive and antisocial behaviors; affective disturbances, including depression, bereavement, anxiety and hyperarousal, and somatic disturbances; and interpersonal issues, including revictimization, sexual problems, and social support.

In addition, we discuss different treatment modalities that have been utilized with traumatized populations. These include crisis management, group therapy, family therapy, couples therapy, pharmacological interventions, spiritual counseling, and community outreach. We attempt to integrate findings from the literature into constructivist self development theory in order to shed new light on these issues.

SELF-DESTRUCTIVE BEHAVIORS

Suicide and Self-mutilation

As with any depressed or acutely distressed client, a careful suicide assessment is necessary if the client reveals any suicidal ideation. This includes finding out the details of the fantasies, how elaborate they are, what method is being considered, and whether there are any internal or external barriers to carrying out these thoughts. Among trauma survivors, these behaviors are often associated with depression, self-hatred, repressed rage toward others, feelings of despair and hope-lessness, guilt, and shame. From a Kohutian perspective (Kohut, 1977), these self-destructive behaviors may also be a by-product of a frag-mented self. In constructivist self development theory terms, this means that persons with impaired self capacities may be higher suicide risks. It is important to assess suicidal thoughts in relation to the individual's self capacities and psychological needs. One must explore the possible meanings of the suicidal feelings, reflected in the following hypotheses:

- Is the individual experiencing wishes to die because he or she is overcome by self-loathing and wishes to destroy the damaged part of himself or herself?
- Does the individual engage in fantasies of being reunited with loved ones who have died, representing an unresolved identi-fication with the dead?
- Do the person's suicidal wishes reflect a desire to punish himself or herself because s/he feels unworthy to live, as in cases involving unresolved survivor guilt?
- Are central needs, such as the need for esteem/recognition or dependency/trust, being thwarted, to the extent that the indi-vidual feels hopeless about finding anything other than despair in life?
- Do the suicidal thoughts occur only when the individual is alone and distressed, indicating possible disruptions in the self capac-ities?
- Are the suicidal thoughts connected to a sense of frustration with other people, reflecting a desire to seek revenge or to express rage and disappointment?

As with the other areas, this assessment needs to be made by em-pathetically exploring the meaning of the suicidal wishes and their connection to internal and external processes.

If it appears that the client may have difficulty controlling his or her behavior, a suicide contract may be necessary. Individuals who appear to be in imminent danger of harming themselves may require hospi-talization. This is a delicate and important matter; the way the therapist handles it will have enduring implications for the therapy relationship. Many suicidal clients respond positively to the suggestion that they need to be in a safe place until the current crisis is past in order to have the support they need to make it through a difficult time.

For others, however, especially those who have a long history of abuse, the notion of hospitalization seems incongruent because they do not view themselves as in crisis; they are chronically suicidal and do not view these wishes as discrepant with their usual internal experience. In such cases, the therapist must carefully explore the client's intentions, empathize with the hopelessness, and attempt to give some small sense of hope and connection which may sustain the client. However, these hopeful messages should not be so discrepant with the client's own sense of despair that the client will dismiss the therapist's hopefulness as naive and unempathic. The decision to hospitalize a client against his or her wishes must be considered in light of the client's overall best interest, and should be made only under the most dire of circumstances.

Self-mutilation or fantasies of self-harm have been noted among survivors of severe childhood abuse (e.g., Courtois, 1988). Biologically, self-mutilation may induce analgesia associated with the release of endogenous opoids as well as an altered state of consciousness (van der Kolk, 1988). In essence, this hypothesis suggests that some survivors may become "addicted" to self-destructive behaviors because they are reinforcing.

Clinically, we have observed that the desire to self-mutilate appears to be linked to affective states that cannot be managed through self-soothing or other nondestructive means of finding inner calm. Alternatively, this desire may be linked to the client's need to ground himself or herself in the present; the very real, here-and-now experience of physical pain that resulted from self-mutilation was the only way one incest survivor had of bringing herself out of flashbacks. Our experience is that the urge to harm oneself is often related to the emergence of traumatic memories outside of the therapy hour.

The most helpful interventions we have discovered have been a combination of working with the client to understand what prompted the current self-mutilation fantasies and desires, instilling hope that these distressing desires will eventually resolve, and helping the client to design a way of releasing the immediate tension, such as going out for a run or engaging in other strenuous activity for a brief period of time. Helping individuals who are experiencing flashbacks to discover other ways of reconnecting with the present is one way of eliminating the use of self-mutilation for this purpose. When these clients are not in crisis, the therapy should focus on developing the capacity for self-soothing.

Substance Abuse

There is strong evidence that substance abuse may be more prevalent in Vietnam combat veterans (particularly those who were exposed to atrocities or abusive violence) (Yager, Laufer, & Gallops, 1984), adult incest survivors (Briere, 1984; Peters, 1984), and battered women (Stark & Flitcraft, 1981) than in the general population. This behavior has been viewed as a form of self-medication, often as a way of managing the pain associated with intrusive memories. This has been conceptualized as a self-induced numbing among PTSD survivors. That is, individuals who are attempting to ward off overwhelming or guilt-inducing intrusive recollections may use substances as a way of shutting down painful affect associated with imagery.

We extend this thinking to include the possibility that the person is using substances as a substitute for diminished or inadequate self capacities, such as affect intolerance or impaired self-soothing. This idea is supported by research which suggests that negative emotional states are major determinants of relapse among persons with addictions (Cummings, Gordon, & Marlatt, 1980).

Doing psychotherapy with individuals who are actively abusing alcohol or other drugs can be difficult; many professionals and psychotherapists who treat substance abuse claim it is impossible. Indeed, for some trauma survivors, especially those who are heavily involved with chemicals, substance treatment may be essential before psychotherapy can be effective.

Taking a hard line approach to this problem, however, can be damaging to the therapeutic alliance, particularly in persons with high needs for independence. The therapist must weigh the extent of substance abuse against the client's ability to make use of psychotherapy. Gently setting limits on coming into sessions while under the influence of alcohol or drugs is usually effective, particularly if it is framed in the context of the individual's best interests. We gradually encourage clients who are not ready to accept that their substance abuse is a problem to look at the ways the substance abuse is creating difficulties in their lives, while also acknowledging the need for self-soothing and working on developing nondestructive alternatives. We also continually attempt to interpret and explore the meanings of this behavior, as with any other pattern, however maladaptive, that is serving some psychological purpose. For persons who have abstained from substances for a period of time, the emergence of traumatic memories may signal the threat of a relapse. Predicting this possibility and preparing for other ways to cope with negative emotional states is an important strategy with these individuals.

Where appropriate, we encourage clients to be actively involved in Alcoholics Anonymous or Narcotics Anonymous so as to have external support for sobriety while they are developing the necessary self capacities through psychotherapy.

Reenactments

Reenactments are a form of behavior through which an individual seeks (often unconsciously) to relive some aspect of the trauma. This phenomenon is sometimes referred to as an addiction to the trauma. As mentioned above, one biological model for understanding reenactment suggests that reexposure to trauma may release endogenous opoids which provide temporary relief from the stress (van der Kolk, 1988; van der Kolk, Greenberg, Boyd, & Krystal, 1985). Our own observations are consistent with those of van der Kolk (1988), who states that persons who are compulsively seeking to reenact the trauma often evidence compromised affect tolerance and the absence of verbal or symbolic control over their affective states.

Epstein (in press a) presents another model of reenactments which is consistent with constructivist self development theory. He suggests that individuals who are unable to integrate the trauma through accommodation or assimilation may alter their personalities to become congruent with the traumatic experience. He writes,

> voluntarily engaging in activities similar to those feared allows the individual to actively experience, in a controlled way, what was out of control and experienced passively during the trauma. When experiences similar to the trauma are defined as desirable, there is no longer the possibility of being traumatized in the same way again. (p. 34)

Epstein goes on to suggest that persons who "embrace the trauma" are those for whom the experience was particularly aversive and for whom a view of the self as helpless is especially intolerable. We concur with this view and suggest that reenactments may be a form of adaptation among individuals with high needs for power or independence compared with those for whom safety is more salient.

> For example, a prostitute with high power needs had been in treatment for some time before she revealed to her therapist that she was an incest survivor. Exploration of the meanings of prostitution revealed that indeed it was a reenactment through which she gained some sense of mastery. Despite the emotional costs of this pattern, she described it as an opportunity to make men "pay" for what they had previously taken from her without consent.

Furthermore, despite the degradation associated with prostitution, she stated, "I always know who is in charge."

Blank (1985, 1989) talks about the importance of therapists recognizing and, over time, interpreting reenactments as such to clients. The cases he describes from his clinical work with Vietnam veterans and torture survivors reveal that reenactments can be very subtle and symbolic in nature. For this reason, he suggests that even experienced therapists may miss reenactments, most often because they are unconscious and outside of the client's awareness. Likewise, Parson (1988) notes how the clinical literature often fails to fully discuss

> the multiplicity of nondramatic ways repetitive phenomena are replayed. Thus, the detailed information gleaned on the traumatic history is imperative in understanding the survivor's reenactment possibilities in human relationships with the wife or partner, children, boss, or subordinates, and in the transference. (p. 264)

We concur that reenactments can indeed be very subtle, often taking place outside the therapy hour. When reenactments are not dramatic and the client is unaware of the meanings of these patterns, the client will often not present this material spontaneously in the therapy hour. As Parson (1988) implies, a fruitful way of discovering such material is by exploring how survivors spend their time outside of therapy, with particular focus on any repetitive personal or interpersonal conflicts. For example, exploring an individual's relationship conflicts with his or her boss may reveal that he or she experiences explosive rage whenever s/he is given an order, an emotion that is tied to being dominated by an abuser in the past. Another example might be a Vietnam veteran who experiences profound self-hatred and self-punishing behaviors when he disappoints or lets down a friend, an affect that represents unresolved guilt for letting down a friend who died or was injured in combat.

Blank (1989) suggests that once these reenactments are interpreted, the symbolic behaviors and symptoms remit. In our experience, interpretation may not put an end to the behaviors if the reenactment has been gratifying central needs, and has therefore become reinforcing. In this case, working through the resistances to changing the pattern may become more focal.

Aggressive and Antisocial Behavior

There is some evidence that male victims are more likely than female victims to manifest aggressive or antisocial behaviors (Carmen, Rieker,

& Mills, 1984). This difference may be due, in part, to socialized sex differences (e.g., Russell, 1984). However, at least one study (Carroll, Rueger, Foy, & Donahoe, 1985) found that male Vietnam veterans with PTSD were more aggressive toward their partners than were male control subjects. Furthermore, among persons with Multiple Personality Disorder (MPD), an aggressive, hostile alter personality is often one manifestation of severe traumatization. Among all victims of violence, the therapist should assess whether there is aggressive or antisocial acting out toward other people or objects. Some victims will be reluctant to reveal these behaviors unless they are asked directly in a nonthreatening way.

For example, a common outlet for aggression among those who have observed or been victims of parental aggression is harsh punishment or abuse of their own children. In clients with this history, the therapist can probe into what behaviors the child displays that result in discipline, the exact nature of the discipline, whether any injuries have been sustained, and if so, what was the outcome. If patients reveal aggressive behavior, it is important to be aware that they may feel great shame and guilt about this. Often, if this behavior can be understood empathetically, the client will feel less need to defend such behavior. The therapist's empathy can allow the part of the client that wants to stop the abusive behavior to join with the therapist who must gently but firmly help ensure the safety of the client's children or others who may be victims.

Some severely disturbed MPD clients may abuse their children while an alter other than the one with whom the therapist usually meets is "out," so the client has no conscious awareness that s/he is abusing his or her children. For the safety of the children, the therapist must entertain the possibility that the client may unknowingly be harming his or her children, especially if the client reports dreams or hallucinations of children being harmed. We have found success in inviting clients to bring their children to a session so we can meet them; this gives the therapist an opportunity to observe directly whether the children appear to be in need of assistance, as well as helping the client, where necessary, with appropriate limit-setting and discipline, something most clients welcome.

We agree with Rollo May (1969) that abuses of power often arise out of powerlessness. We also concur with Kohut (1977) that aggression may be the by-product of a fragmented self or a serious narcissistic injury. The client's underlying feelings of powerlessness, or self-fragmentation must be explored in the light of these behaviors, with connections made to previous experiences of being the victim of violence. Finally, it is important to assess whether the individual engaged in aggressive behaviors in childhood or adolescence, whether there is guilt involved, and whether this behavior is ego-dystonic for the person. This line of questioning helps rule out sociopathy as a lifelong pattern, obviously a more difficult, if not impossible, condition to treat.

AFFECTIVE DISTURBANCES

Depression
The symptoms of depression, which include variations in sleep and appetite, and diminished energy level, ability to concentrate, or capacity for pleasure, must be understood in the context of the self, the psychological needs, the schemas, and the traumatic memories. For example, are the depressive symptoms linked to the activation of certain memories, and if so, are these memories stimulated by certain events in the person's internal or external world? Is the client aware of what stimulates the depressed mood? The following clinical vignettes offer examples of the different meanings depression may hold for the individual:

Abigail, an incest victim who had only fragmented images of her earlier abuse, became depressed in therapy as she and the therapist uncovered and pieced together memories of the abuse. It eventually became apparent that the depression was linked to feelings of self-hatred and self-blame, as she held herself responsible for having "seduced" her father. Furthermore, she eventually discovered that she had been told by her father that she would destroy and betray him if she ever revealed their "secret." Thus, as she came closer to sharing the dreaded secret, Abigail was plagued by guilt and the sense that she had a terrible power to destroy her father, a man she continued to protect throughout her life.

Jacob, a victim of a violent mugging who was physically injured during the assault, became increasingly depressed over the months following this trauma. He found it increasingly difficult to work and eventually left his job and was supported by social security disability payments, which increased his deep depression and hopelessness. In therapy, Jacob described himself as a hard-driving executive who prided himself on his success, his ability to exert influence over his environment, and his ability to be in charge of his own life and feelings, all suggestive of strong needs for power and independence. The helplessness he experienced during the mugging and afterwards as a result of his physical disability shattered his schemas and thwarted his needs for power and independence, resulting in feelings that he was weak, powerless, and out of control of his life.

John, a marine combat veteran who had served two tours in Vietnam, became severely depressed every spring. He would become immobilized, unable to eat or get out of bed, and spend his days sobbing. When he first entered therapy, he was unaware of what precipitated these episodes and had been treated unsuccessfully with antidepressants through the VA. Over the course of therapy, it gradually became apparent that he was experiencing an anniversary reaction of a very traumatic event in Vietnam in which his best friend was killed in a dangerous search and destroy mission, an event he felt responsible for because he gave the orders for the mission. After the death of his friend, he was removed from the field for a week due to severe depression in which he was immobilized and nearly catatonic. The recurrent symptoms of depression and the specific form they took were thus an anniversary reaction that recapitulated his deep feelings of guilt, helplessness, and unresolved grief.

These vignettes offer illustrations of the different meanings of depression, related to each individual's needs and schemas. Guilt, self-blame, loss and grief, self-hatred, and disrupted schemas for independence or power are among those dynamics often associated with depression. Understanding the individual dynamics underlying the depression provides a framework for intervention. In each case, the disturbed schemas that underlie the depressed mood must be explored, understood, and gently challenged in light of the client's present understanding of what happened.

For those clients for whom depression is a manifestation of disrupted schemas for power or independence, encouraging activities that facilitate a sense of efficacy is an important part of the recovery process. Furthermore, learning to view with compassion the child who did her/ his best under difficult circumstances, as described in Chapter 7, is often very meaningful for persons with a strong need for independence who feel disappointed in themselves. These treatment approaches are consistent with the cognitive behavioral therapy for depression described by Beck (1967, 1976).

Bereavement

The centrality of loss and bereavement to survivors has been discussed since the early studies of post-trauma reactions (e.g., Lindeman, 1944). In recent years, personal loss and bereavement have been associated with severity of response among survivors of disasters (e.g., Green, Grace, & Gleser, 1985; Milgram, Toubiana, Klingman, Raviv, & Goldstein, 1988). Although simple bereavement may overlap with traumatic states, there are important differences. Within the framework of DSM-III-R (APA, 1987), in order to qualify as traumatic, an event must be outside the realm of ordinary human experience and arise from human design. Within constructivist self development theory, trauma is differentiated from simple bereavement or nontraumatic stress by the definition of a traumatic experience as nonnormative or highly discrepant with expectations, which is consistent with the first part of the DSM-III-R requirement noted above.

Research on survivors of children who have been murdered, for example, suggests that there are multiple losses involved, including the death of a part of the self, the loss of a previously fulfilling role, and the destruction of the natural order of life, resulting in a shattering of one's frame of reference (Rinear, 1988). The shattering of the frame of reference is a permanent loss that has pervasive effects on all aspects of the self; coming to terms with this is an essential part of the later stages of therapy with trauma survivors. In our experience, the grieving process often begins by approaching the most conscious, most accessible, and least threatening material. As the client is increasingly able to tolerate the painful affects, gradually one moves on to explore the unconscious meanings of grief, often related to a profound shattering of frame of reference, including the loss of previously held self schemas.

In cases involving impacted grief (Shatan, 1974), the grief work is clearly more complex and protracted. Some clients experience a dread of affective overload if they allow themselves to acknowledge their sorrow. Often, individuals report fearing that once they begin crying, they will never be able to stop. We agree with Williams (1988) who suggests directly challenging this distorted belief by reassuring clients that no one has ever cried without stopping. The dosing of grief-related emotions is essential for allowing clients to overcome these fears.

An additional issue that is important to keep in mind is that clients with impacted grief reactions are more likely to have accommodated to a radical disruption in schemas, particularly those involving intimacy or trust/dependency. They may have concluded that connection is dangerous and that if they allow themselves to love again, pain and loss are the inevitable outcome. Working through these resistances to becoming connected again is crucial to resolving these disrupted schemas. This work often takes place initially within the therapy relationship, an issue that we discuss in some depth in Chapter 11.

Anxiety, Hyperarousal, and Intrusive Imagery

Behavioral treatments such as flooding and systematic desensitization have been reported in the treatment of symptoms of anxiety and physiological arousal among Vietnam veterans (Bowen & Lambert, 1986; Fairbank & Keane, 1982; Foy, Donahoe, Carroll, Gallers, & Reno, 1987; Keane & Kaloupek, 1982). These interventions are based on the assumption that the persistence of anxiety symptoms can be understood through learning theory principles. Specifically, avoidant responses are thought to be reinforced by decreases in anxiety and autonomic arousal following avoidant behavior. Imaginal flooding is an extinction-based procedure in which the client is presented with the cues for fear but is not allowed to engage in avoidant behaviors. In systematic desensitization (Wolpe, 1969), the client is gradually exposed to a hierarchy of anxiety-arousing imagery while actively maintaining relaxation. Both types of treatment have been shown to be efficacious in some cases of PTSD, although the findings are mixed and more carefully controlled treatment outcome studies are needed.

We have reservations about the use of flooding techniques with trauma survivors, a concern that has been expressed by others in relation to treatment of survivors of rape (Kilpatrick, Veronen, & Resick, 1982) and incest (Courtois, 1988). These reservations focus on the potential for retraumatizing the individual, particularly in those survivors for whom states of feeling helpless and out of control are very threatening, as in the individual with high needs for independence or power over the environment. We believe these techniques are also contraindicated in persons in whom the self capacities for affect regulation and self-soothing are limited. In a recent article about the use of implosive therapy, Lyons and Keane (1989) address these reservations and make the important point that this technique must be used in the context of a safe, supportive relationship and in conjunction with other techniques that facilitate effective coping. Furthermore, they make the point that direct exposure

> can be viewed as submitting maladaptive, trauma-related schemata to examination and challenging inflexible, incomplete views and unrealistic expectations the client may have. (p. 149)

In this respect, the goals of implosive therapy are consistent with our own, although we tend to favor less direct methods of encouraging exposure, as outlined in Chapter 10.

There is, however, evidence that victims of violent assaults, rape, and domestic violence who persist in fear and anxiety reactions are those who have been able to avoid exposure to situations that would enable them to extinguish these responses (Wirtz & Harrell, 1987). In this particular study, individuals at highest risk for persistent distress were those who had withdrawn from friends and other social activities. These findings support a classical conditioning paradigm which suggests that recovery must involve repeated exposure to attack-related stimuli in the absence of actual danger. The stress inoculation treatment advocated by Kilpatrick and his colleagues (Kilpatrick, Veronen, & Resick, 1982) is an intervention model which is respectful of the individual in that it combines gradual exposure with cognitive and behavioral coping techniques. With regard to this issue, we agree with Koss and Burkhart (1989) who write,

> Conditioning models, while having some heuristic value for immediate fear responses, do not address the individual variability in responses nor provide much conceptual utility for understanding coping processes adopted spontaneously by victims or provided through treatment interventions. (p. 30)

In our own work, we have found conditioning-based interventions effective as long as clients are encouraged to design and implement the exposure programs to meet their own needs, with the therapist serving as a resource rather than a director of this work. Understanding the individual's unique appraisal of potential stressors as threatening or harmful (Lazarus & Folkman, 1984) or, in our terms, transforming disturbed safety schemas, is more likely to be fruitful in ultimately resolving the persistence of anxiety reactions.

Somatic Disturbances

It is well-established that victims of rape (Norris & Feldman-Summers, 1981), childhood sexual abuse (Briere, 1984), domestic violence (Stark & Flitcraft, 1981), and other crime (Frederick, 1980), and those with Multiple Personality Disorder (Bliss, 1980; Braun, 1983) evidence more health problems and somatic concerns than the general population. There is now compelling evidence that long-term inhibition of thoughts and feelings about traumatic experiences is associated with long-term health problems (Pennebaker, Hughes, & O'Heeron, 1987) and that disclosure of both the event and the emotions surrounding it can reduce health problems and actually improve cellular immune functioning (Pennebaker, Kiecolt-Glaser, & Glaser, 1988).

It is thus extremely important to assess somatic concerns and health history among victims as well as to explore a history of victimization among persons who present with multiple somatic concerns but who have not revealed such a history. The type of somatic concerns may run the gamut from chronic muscle tension, ulcers, menstrual problems, and headaches to gastrointestinal disturbances, as well as a host of other stress-related problems. For the non-medical therapist, it is particularly important to explore what medical treatments have been sought for what conditions and to make appropriate referrals for consultations when necessary. It is our practice to refer all patients for a complete physical if they haven't had one in recent years or if chronic health concerns persist. We have found it useful to establish good working relations with local physicians who are open to learning about the issues surrounding trauma and somatic complaints.

Finally, it is important to convey an attitude of interest and concern about these complaints rather than to assume that they are outside the purview of non-medical therapy, as many emotional concerns will be revealed through somatic complaints. This is particularly true if the client does indeed have a chronic health problem or is suffering from alexithymia (Krystal, 1988). Given the association between inhibition and disease cited above, it is particularly important to encourage these individuals to explore a variety of ways to express undisclosed traumatic material. In their work with trauma survivors, Pennebaker and colleagues (Pennebaker, Hughes, & O'Heeron, 1987; Pennebaker, Kiecolt-Glaser, & Glaser, 1988) discovered that writing about the trauma had beneficial effects, supporting the value of journal writing for survivors who suffer from health problems. This may be particularly useful for persons who are alexithymic and cannot readily differentiate emotional states through talking therapy.

INTERPERSONAL PROBLEMS

Revictimization

One important finding in the literature is a strong association between early childhood victimization and repeated victimization later in life. This finding has been reported in some victims of domestic violence (Walker, 1985), childhood sexual abuse (Sedney & Brooks, 1984), and rape (Russell, 1986). Unfortunately, this finding has often been used to support subtle and not-so-subtle victim-blaming. In our own case conference on victimization, a therapist presenting a case of a woman who had experienced multiple victimizations since childhood unthinkingly made the statement, ". . . and she has continued to seek out relationships with abusive, alcoholic men in her adult life." Another clinician correctly took offense at the wording of this statement and pointed out that "no woman seeks out relationships with abusive men. Rather, a woman may be attracted to qualities that covary with abusive behaviors, such as machismo (Mosher & Sirkin, 1984), apparent physical strength, etc."

We believe that revictimization can stem from a number of internal or external dynamics. For example, a woman without a strong sense of self may be more likely to be attracted to men who are dominant and authoritarian. Decreased self-trust or ability to make appropriately self-protective judgments is often an important factor in creating a "blind spot" for abusive men. Likewise, a social and cultural context that supports or condones violence against women is likely a major factor in the perpetration of violence against women (Russell, 1984).

With clients who appear to be entrenched in a pattern of revictimization, most often those who have histories of early childhood abuse, we often uncover deeply held beliefs that abusive behavior is the norm. For example, women who repeatedly get involved in abusive relationships with men may not even define the man's behavior as abusive. That is, they believe that being hit, degraded verbally, sexually exploited, and so forth is to be expected in relationships with men. Other women may evidence a "looking for Mister Goodbar" pattern, allowing themselves to be picked up by strange men in bars who later abuse them. Gently challenging these assumptions and working with the client to develop a stronger sense of self, including the ability to establish appropriate boundaries and make self-protective judgments, is fundamental to reversing a pattern of revictimization.

Sexual Problems

Not surprisingly, there is empirical evidence for impaired sexual functioning, including fear of sex, arousal dysfunction, and decreased sexual satisfaction among victims of childhood sexual abuse (Feldman-Summers, Gordon, & Meagher, 1979), rape (Becker, Skinner, Abel, & Cichon, 1986), and domestic violence (Stark & Flitcraft, 1981). Furthermore, Vietnam veterans with PTSD have been found to evidence greater sexual adjustment problems than control subjects (Garte, 1986).

Like some of the other response patterns, patients will often not reveal their sexual dysfunctions unless this area is discussed in an open, matter-of-fact way by the therapist. The issues to be explored are the person's ability to experience satisfaction in sexual relationships, the frequency of sexual contact, the arousal level, the nature of sexual interactions, thoughts, and feelings that precede or accompany arousal, and any concerns the individual may have about sexual functioning. It is also important to assess whether these problems are specific to certain sexual partners, behaviors, or contexts or generalized to all sexual behaviors. For example,

> One married woman with a history of incest reported in marital therapy positive attitudes toward sex, including an ability to enjoy multiple orgasms with her husband. It was not until later in individual therapy that the therapist learned that oral sex was repulsive to her and a previous source of conflict with her husband. This was, not surprisingly, tied to specific childhood memories of sexual abuse that had been repressed.

This example underscores the importance of obtaining a detailed sexual history, particularly among those victim groups previously mentioned. Finally, it is important to learn the unique meanings of certain sexual behaviors for the person, as well as any connection to previous traumatization. For example, in the case described above, the therapist discovered that the client viewed oral sex, and not genital sexuality, as dirty and bad, an association that was tied to very specific childhood traumas.

> In one case of a woman with MPD, the sexual dysfunction manifested itself symbolically when she had to be hospitalized for refusing to eat. This behavior was later linked to the return of repressed memories of forced oral sex, and would never have been understood unless the therapist explored this material.

> A third client, a young man who had lost his brother tragically in childhood, complained about guilt feelings associated with masturbation. As the therapist explored this material, it became clear that the client frequently masturbated until he hurt himself physically as a punishment for unresolved survivor guilt.

Although we believe in the value of traditional sex therapy techniques (Kaplan, 1974), we have seen numerous cases where sex therapy was initiated prematurely, before the meanings of the sexual dysfunction were explored thoroughly. For example, an incest survivor had gone to her physician with complaints of sexual arousal dysfunction, without revealing her trauma history. She was offered some common sense instructions about self-pleasuring and went home to try them out. The exercises stimulated memory fragments that had been buried and she experienced a panic reaction.

Other survivors have spoken about being demoralized by attempting sex therapy techniques too early, thus precipitating feelings of failure and hopelessness. In some cases, where the memory work has only just begun, we recommend that clients postpone behavioral sex therapy until they are ready to handle the powerful emotions that often emerge. Focal couples work to help the partner understand the context of the dysfunction may also be beneficial so the survivor doesn't feel under pressure to perform and both partners feel less frustration.

Social Support

In line with our constructivist thinking, we view social support as the support that an individual perceives as available to him or her from others, a view shared by other theorists in the field (e.g., Figley & Burge, 1983). The bereaved person's perceptions of others' responses are an important determinant of recovery from stressful life events such as divorce (Pearlman, 1985) as well as trauma (Figley, 1986; Figley, 1983; Green, Wilson, & Lindy, 1985; McCubbin & Figley, 1983). Constructivist self development theory suggests that survivors will perceive as supportive those individuals and situations that meet their psychological needs and are consistent with their schemas. Thus, one accident victim with an extremely strong need for independence grew increasingly furious with a friend who came to her home daily and insisted upon doing everything for her because of her "invalid status." Over time she kept to herself more and more of her needs, eventually preferring to go without food in the house rather than letting him know that she needed help getting groceries. Those family members and friends who would be helpful and supportive must be aware of how to approach the survivor. The therapist can help the survivor be direct about his or her needs for contact or distance, as well as helping those in the social network understand how the client might experience their overtures.

THERAPEUTIC MODALITIES

Crisis Management

We do not encourage frequent or lengthy telephone contact with clients because we want to convey to the client the belief that he or she already possesses or is on the way to developing the necessary resources and capacities to manage difficult emotional times. In addition, these calls can be draining for the therapist and we try to minimize them in order to preserve our own resources. From time to time, of course, clients in crisis may telephone the therapist for various reasons. Understanding the client's self capacities and psychological needs and the meanings of the telephone contact helps the therapist understand how to manage such calls.

Some clients may call for extra support when something extraordinary has happened in their lives. Some of the more severely impaired trauma survivors may call in order to establish that the therapist is present and available. Clients with a strong need for independence may be reluctant to call even when they are in crises that are potentially dangerous. In anticipation of this problem, it is helpful to explore with these clients what it might mean to them to call and to reframe calling the therapist as a way of taking care of oneself.

In general, we tend to be somewhat more directive and supportive in these crisis contacts than in regularly scheduled therapy sessions. Our approach is to first try to understand why the client is calling now, then to help the client develop a way of soothing and calming himself or herself. We work with clients who are in distress to develop a plan that will hold them over until the next therapy session. This may include seeking support or safety with friends or family, as well as using previously developed imagery, relaxation, or other soothing or expressive techniques. In extreme cases, suggesting the client go to a hospital emergency room may be indicated.

Group Therapy

Group therapy can be very important for trauma survivors, providing them with many of the same benefits that non-trauma clients obtain from the group experience (Yalom, 1970). The value of group therapy and its applications have been described in the literature among a number of survivor groups, including survivors of Vietnam combat (e.g., Frick & Bogart, 1982; Parson, 1984b; Shatan, 1973), incest (Agosta & Loring, 1988; Cole & Barney, 1987; Courtois, 1988; Deighton & McPeek, 1985; Goodman & Nowak-Scibelli, 1985; Herman & Schatzow, 1984), and Holocaust survivors and their offspring (Danieli, 1985; Fogelman & Savran, 1980).

A therapy group can be a place where individuals normalize their reactions, and is especially useful with clients who feel they are "going crazy" because they are experiencing common post-trauma symptoms.

Group can help overcome the sense of isolation that so often accompanies posttrauma functioning. Many survivors feel no one else can understand their experience. One survivor said she felt "like I'm under water, just out of reach of other people, isolated."

Particularly for incest survivors who may never have spoken about their experiences nor heard much from other survivors, joining a therapy group can be a very powerful experience. We find that a successful incest survivor group member is most likely to be someone who is aware she was abused and has been able to talk to some extent about the memories in individual therapy. This means that some memory work will likely have to be done before the client is referred to group therapy. Because of the power of a group to elicit memories and strong affect, we prefer that incest survivors and others with severe PTSD be in individual therapy simultaneously with group. In general, group therapy works best for clients whose self capacities are not severely impaired. Thus some period of self-building work may be another necessary prelude to group therapy.

It is very helpful for the group therapist to be aware of the members' psychological needs as a way of understanding the group dynamics. Members with thwarted independence, power, or dependency/trust needs, for example, can come into conflict with one another over their different ways of responding to their situations and their own areas of disturbance. Knowing this helps the therapist intervene in a constructive way.

Family Therapy

Involvement of family members in the therapy of rape victims in crisis has been viewed as an extremely important part of the healing process (Silverman, 1976). Figley (1986) views family therapy with victim and veteran families as important to helping the family integrate ". . . the catastrophic experiences and their wake . . . into the family" (p. 51). Family therapy has two important aims. One is to attend to the needs of the family of a trauma survivor, which also endures a trauma by virtue of its loving connection with the victim (Figley, 1986). The second is to provide support for the victim in his or her own recovery.

Figley (1988) has outlined a five-phase treatment approach to posttrauma family therapy which includes the development of a "healing theory." We interpret this to mean that the family works together to become aware of and transform their schemas that have been disrupted by the trauma, and most important, to develop a shared frame of reference that helps them put the trauma into a context that is understandable and meaningful to the family as a whole. As Figley notes, themes related to blame and responsibility are often central issues, reflecting each person's need to make sense of why the traumatic event happened and his or her role in it. The potential for destructive blaming of each other must be monitored by the therapist and, if necessary, separate sessions with selected family members may be required to allow individuals to air these feelings without damaging one another.

Couples Therapy

In our work with a variety of survivor groups, we have found it useful at times to engage in short-term couples work in order to help stabilize the marital or couple relationship. This provides more external support for the client as he or she goes through the destabilizing process of psychotherapy. Bringing in the spouse is also an important way of helping him or her to understand that this work will be difficult, that the client may be more depressed or distressed than usual for awhile, and that this is part of the healing process. This helps the spouse support the person's continuing treatment and provides an opportunity for spouses to express their own concerns.

In cases where both people have been traumatized, as in cases where a burglary or rape occurred in the home or a child is killed, couples therapy can also be a valuable treatment modality. We find Figley's (1988) model for family therapy applicable to couples work as well.

In addition, certain insights derived from constructivist self development theory have guided our interventions with couples. One issue we have found to be particularly salient is the differences in central needs and disturbed schemas within couples. In our experience, these differences can contribute to interpersonal conflict as each member of the couple experiences the trauma through the unique filter of his or her own schemas. For example, in a number of cases where couples experienced a victimization in the home, we have observed that women tend to show greater disruptions in safety schemas while men show greater disruptions in power schemas. In some cases, long after the man has resolved any fears about recurrence, the woman has continued to evidence distress about recurrence. These women often show a preference for what Lazarus and Folkman (1984) call emotion-focused coping, such as talking in detail about what happened and engaging in emotional expression.

In contrast, we have observed many men who attempt to cope with the trauma by restoring power schemas; they restore a sense of mastery over the environment by taking action, such as installing an alarm system or moving to a new home. This coping style is consistent with Lazarus and Folkman's (1984) problem-focused approach. This difference in coping styles can stimulate conflicts if the husband gives the wife the message, "There's no point in rehashing the past. We have to take action and move on with our lives." This message can be experienced by the woman as an empathetic failure, and she will then experience a sense of alienation from her partner. Conversely, the woman's need to talk about her persistent fear can present a challenge to the man's need to restore a sense of power.

We have found it useful to identify and label the different schemas and coping styles in order to enhance a respect within the couple for their differences. As couples in crisis may tend to devalue one another's style, this approach can facilitate greater empathy and attunement as each struggles to restore disturbed schemas.

Pharmacological Interventions

As with all aspects of treatment, the use of medication must be considered in light of the individual's psychological needs. People who have a strong need for independence may be reluctant to consider taking medication because of fears of "not doing it on my own" or losing control. This is best managed by reframing taking medication as taking control over one's situation. In persons in whom trust/dependency needs are more salient, medication may present an opportunity to give up control and feel taken care of. This may be acceptable in some cases, but in other cases, it may pose a threat to the person continuing to struggle to understand his or her experience of the trauma.

Clinical evidence has suggested that both antianxiety and antidepressant medications can alleviate some of the symptoms of PTSD (e.g., van der Kolk, 1983). However, until recently, there were no carefully controlled studies on the differential effects of medication on PTSD symptoms. In the first double-blind clinical trial on the effects of antidepressant medication, Frank, Kosten, Giller, and Dan (1988) found that imipramine and phenelzine alleviated the intrusive symptoms of posttraumatic stress disorder among Vietnam veterans. In that study, antidepressants did not have much effect upon the symptoms of depression, a finding the authors speculated might relate to the moderate to low levels of depression among their Vietnam veteran subjects.

In cases of depression related to loss, especially where vegetative symptoms are present, we often refer clients for medication consultations. Particularly for seriously depressed people who are immobilized, psychotherapy can be quite difficult without the extra support medication can provide.

We typically do not recommend medication for the treatment of anxiety. With anxious clients, medication tends to remove the symptoms and thus, in some cases, the motivation for treatment. However, in cases involving acute distress after a trauma in which the anxiety is immobilizing, we will often support the short-term use of a benzodiazapine or nonaddictive sleep medication. We direct interested readers to an excellent article by Roth (1988), who discusses at length the clinical implications of pharmacotherapy.

The recent finding cited above by Frank et al. (1988) that intrusive symptoms are responsive to antidepressant medications raises a number of interesting questions. As trauma survivors often avoid talking about traumatic memories as a protection against intrusive symptoms, it is interesting to speculate whether pharmacological interventions might facilitate the therapeutic process of memory integration. Another interesting research question would be to examine whether certain medications impact upon a client's disturbed schemas. Clearly, the direction for future research is to investigate the efficacy of medication in other populations as well as to link these findings to benefits to the therapy process itself.

Spiritual Interventions

As part of their search for meaning, many survivors reevaluate their spiritual beliefs in light of their traumatic experiences. In religious persons, these beliefs are basic to frame of reference and are particularly vulnerable to disruption after traumatization. Questions about why God allowed such tragic or senseless events to occur have been noted among a number of survivor groups, such as accident victims (Bulman & Wortman, 1977) and Vietnam combat veterans (Williams, 1988). Some survivors may feel that God failed them or, more profoundly, express doubt about the existence of God.

Often, this disruption in religious beliefs is associated with a sense of meaninglessness and emptiness. Some survivors, feeling abandoned by God, become disillusioned and embittered. Life no longer makes any sense and there is little to believe in. Other survivors who struggle with survivor guilt may feel their sins are so great that God can never forgive them. Clearly, this shattering of frame of reference can impact other schemas, including one's sense of being protected by God (safety), one's belief in the constancy of God (trust), one's sense of spiritual worthiness (esteem), or one's sense of connection to some higher power (intimacy). The impact of this disruption and its unique meanings are important areas of exploration in post-trauma therapy.

Clients may be reluctant to share these feelings if they sense that the therapist has a different belief system or if they feel that their attributions appear irrational. It may indeed be difficult for the therapist to avoid challenging beliefs that God is punishing the survivor or that God will never be able to forgive him or her. Prematurely challenging these beliefs will be experienced as a failure in empathy and will invariably result in an avoidance of the topic.

We have found it useful to initiate the topic of religious beliefs, as survivors may feel that this is not an appropriate topic for therapy. Areas to explore may include how the client's relationship with God has changed, current sources of spiritual support, the quality of the client's prayer life, and current relationship to clergy. Survivors who have a special relationship with clergy may be encouraged to seek them out. Others may feel too ashamed to speak with someone they know personally and may need to seek spiritual counsel from someone outside of their religious community. We have found it helpful to develop relationships with clergy who are sensitive to survivor issues and who are amenable to our input about how they might be helpful with a particular individual.

In general, we remind clinicians of the tremendous support and strength that spiritual beliefs can offer as survivors confront the horror or shame of their traumatic experiences. This is powerfully expressed by Cheng (1986) as she endured suffering and torture at the hands of the Red Guards in Communist China:

> Throughout the years of my imprisonment, I had turned to God often and felt His presence. In the drab surroundings of the gray cell, I had known magic moments of transcendence that I had not experienced in the ease and comfort of my normal life. My belief in the ultimate triumph of truth and goodness had been restored and I had renewed courage to fight on. My faith had sustained me in these darkest hours of my life and brought me safely through privation, sickness, and torture. At the same time, my suffering had strengthened my faith and made me realize that God was always there. It was up to me to come to him. (p. 347)

In summary, although we are not advocating that clinicians become pastoral counselors, we are suggesting that the spiritual element is an important and often neglected area in secular therapy. Whatever the therapist's own beliefs, clients' religious beliefs can serve as an important resource. The acknowledgment of and respect for a client's religious beliefs and a willingness to struggle with difficult spiritual questions can be a very meaningful part of the healing process.

Community Outreach

A significant number of survivors fail to enter the mental health system, despite the evidence from long-term follow-up studies that many survivors report serious difficulties years after the trauma occurred. For example, recent data suggest that the majority of rape victims never seek treatment and may even reject treatment when it is offered in community-based programs, despite the evidence that between 40 and 75 percent of rape victims experience serious symptoms many years after the rape (Koss & Burkhart, 1989).

Lindy, Grace, and Green (1981) describe a community outreach program established in the aftermath of the Beverly Hills Supper Club fire. Their paper ends with an analysis of factors that may limit the success of such programs. An excellent review article by Solomon (1986) describes outreach programs to mobilize existing support networks among survivors of natural disasters. Effective community outreach is essential if victims are to receive the services they need in a nonstigmatizing context.

The primary example of a highly successful outreach program is the establishment of community-based Vietnam veterans' centers across the U.S.A. over the past 10 years (Blank, 1985b). An excellent recent review article describes models for community intervention models nationally as well as a conceptual framework for developing victim services (Downing, 1988). The National Organization for Victim Assistance (NOVA), based in Washington, D.C., is the major national organization that serves as a clearinghouse for victim assistance programs. Many states have agencies that provide information, support, and compensation for victims of crime.

At The Traumatic Stress Institute, we have a commitment to ongoing community education about psychological responses to trauma and about the resources available for those who need help. We are now in the process of designing an early intervention group therapy program for crime victims and their families. We chose to focus on time-limited psychoeducational groups in order to encourage persons who might not consider engaging in individual psychotherapy, whether because of uncertainties about therapy or because of the time commitment required for ongoing therapy (e.g., Marmar & Horowitz, 1988). Our hope is that an approach that normalizes reactions to trauma will destigmatize the process for those who are biased against mental health interventions. For those who require longer-term therapy, an initial positive experience may make them more receptive to continuing therapy.

13. Applying the Theory to Special Populations

We have presented constructivist self development theory as a framework for understanding the impact of trauma upon unique individuals, emphasizing the importance of the individual's psychological experience of the trauma rather than focusing primarily on the external nature of traumatic events. Yet we are aware that certain events have unique meanings associated with them, largely because of their historical significance and/or social or cultural consensus.

In this chapter, we focus on the special concerns that particular victim groups are likely to share, and which should therefore be of additional interest to the clinician in assessment and treatment planning. Just as the theory in its entirety rests on the notion that individuals differ from one another, here too we emphasize that, while these issues may be present for many clients in each victim group, only a thorough knowledge of the individual client will reveal that person's salient concerns.

The populations we focus on in this chapter are as follows: adult survivors of child abuse; female survivors of child sexual abuse; male survivors of child sexual abuse; persons with multiple personality disorder; adult children of alcoholics; victims of rape and sexual assault; other crime victims; family members of crime victims; survivors of homicide, battered women; survivors of natural and human-induced disasters; survivors of historical traumas, including Vietnam veterans and survivors of cultural victimization and genocide; and finally, persons exposed to life-threatening illness.

The omission of other survivor groups (e.g., POW's, army nurse veterans, Salvadoran refugees) does not in any way imply that they are not important populations for study. Rather, we have included here groups with which we have particular clinical experience and can contribute something useful to the clinician's work.

VIOLENCE AND TRAUMA IN CHILDHOOD

Adult Survivors of Child Abuse

Individuals who have experienced physical, sexual, or emotional abuse as children may evidence serious disturbances of the self, including underdeveloped capacities and resources, seriously unbalanced needs, and generalized disturbed schemas in a number of areas. Because their psychological development may have been impeded by the abuse, these individuals will very likely require supportive self work before they will be able to tolerate the affects associated with memory work. This requires a sensitive, ongoing assessment by the clinician to determine when the self is strong enough to uncover and process memories which may be deeply repressed, and to pace the interweaving of the self work and the memory work so the individual can tolerate the affect that is aroused by these memories. Krystal (1978) notes,

> What we observe in the direct aftereffects of severe childhood trauma in adults is a lifelong dread of the return of traumatic states and an expectation of it . . . there is a fear of one's emotions and an impairment of affect tolerance. (p. 98)

The therapist working with the adult survivor of child abuse must patiently help the client develop the capacities to tolerate strong affect, to be alone without being lonely, and so forth. When in crisis, usually triggered by the emergence of traumatic memory fragments, these individuals often experience affective overload and panic states. In survivors who are more deeply disturbed, suicidal impulses and self-mutilating behaviors may result from this work. These crises often necessitate brief contacts outside the session in which the soothing, empathetic therapist helps restore inner calm. The techniques described in Chapter 7 to enhance self-soothing capacities are often helpful in managing the frightening emergence of traumatic material. In our experience, these episodes usually resolve quickly if the therapist normalizes the client's reactions as resulting from emerging memories and actively helps the client find a way to soothe and calm himself or herself until the next session. Accurate and ongoing assessment of the evolving self capacities according to the paradigm presented in Chapter 7 is essential to successful work with these individuals.

Abuse and/or lack of protection by a presumed caretaker generally results in an impaired ability to trust oneself or others or to make accurate judgments. Such concerns can make therapy with these clients especially challenging, as they affect the formation of the therapeutic relationship. Often the main therapeutic work with such individuals is the development of the working alliance. While this may take months or years, once such an alliance is formed, the most difficult part of therapy may be over.

A lack of self-worth or damaged sense of self-esteem is quite common in adults who were abused as children. Working slowly to help such clients discover their assets and abilities and encouraging them to engage in activities at which they might excel or in which they may help others will eventually result in more positive self-esteem. Simply experiencing and gradually internalizing the therapist's steady regard and respect will itself be curative. It is important, however, not to challenge the client's beliefs about himself or herself too dramatically. Such challenges (e.g., "It's not your fault," "You're really a good person," and so forth) will be experienced as false and will inhibit the development of a trusting therapeutic alliance.

Adult Female Survivors of Child Sexual Abuse

Many women who were sexually abused as children are not conscious of this fact until adulthood or until therapy has been underway for some time. In our experience, it is useful to introduce this possibility very early in the therapy process, at the first suggestion that sexual abuse may have occurred. Clues to the therapist might include:

- A history of running away in childhood or adolescence;
- Severe character pathology or a previous diagnosis of borderline personality disorder;
- Large gaps in memories of childhood;
- Chronic sexual and interpersonal difficulties;
- Severe obesity or other eating disorders;
- Chronic low self-esteem;
- Immature presentation (e.g., an adult woman who dresses or speaks in a childlike way that is developmentally inappropriate);
- A history of chronic substance abuse or other self-destructive behaviors;
- A hatred of men in general or of father in particular;
- Disrupted needs and schemas related to intimacy, trust/dependency, and/or safety.

While none of these clues in itself is pathognomonic of childhood sexual abuse, they should suggest or may support such a hypothesis. The possibility of childhood sexual abuse should be introduced by the therapist in a gentle, yet direct, manner. If the client raises or in any way suggests the issue in an early interview, the therapist might simply ask, "Do you recall any early or inappropriate sexual experiences with older children or adults during your childhood?"

If the client does not appear to be aware of the possibility of abuse, during the history taking the therapist might say,

> Many women (who have difficulty enjoying sex/who have chronic low self-esteem/who are untrusting of males/or whatever clue the client has just provided) have experienced some sort of sexual abuse or inappropriate sexual contact as children. I'm wondering if this is something you've ever wondered about?

If the client does not respond or responds in the negative, the therapist may hold the sexual abuse possibility as a hypothesis to be confirmed or disconfirmed by later evidence. The therapist should not challenge the client's denial (if it exists) prematurely. Respect for clients' defenses is essential to developing a therapeutic relationship and supporting and strengthening the self. Rather, the therapist should listen closely to the themes and associations that emerge after this exploration. In cases where there are repressed memories of sexual abuse, the client may report dreams or other symbolic material that are an indirect expression of abuse memories.

In cases in which the abuser was a caretaker of the child, the client may have confusion concerning needs for trust/dependency and intimacy. Gelinas (1988) and Courtois (1988) present excellent descriptions of the family dynamics that are often present in such cases and family therapy treatment interventions with this survivor group. Empirical research on family dynamics associated with incest show that these families tend to be characterized by decreased adaptability, decreased cohesion (Harter, Alexander, & Neimeyer, 1988), and increased conflict (Finkelhor, 1984).

A female adult incest survivor, seeking support and connection, may be drawn to a man who appears strong and possessive. Alternatively, she may seek out a man similar to the abuser in an unconscious reenactment of her earlier experiences. Such a man may be insecure, easily threatened, and emotionally or physically abusive, perhaps because of his own unresolved history of emotional or physical abuse. When such a couple presents for therapy (often because of sexual difficulties, an absence of intimacy, etc.), we have the greatest success with couples therapy directed toward understanding and setting limits on any family violence, combined with individual therapy with the woman focusing on self-development and integration of memories. We have often discovered in such cases that the man is also a survivor of child abuse or emotional neglect. However, it is often more difficult to engage such a man in individual therapy. A more detailed description of therapeutic strategies with adult female survivors based upon constructivist self development theory can be found in McCann, Pearlman, Sakheim, and Abrahamson (1988).

Male Survivors of Child Sexual Abuse

Male survivors of child sexual abuse come forward for treatment in much smaller numbers than do female survivors. In a review of prevalence surveys of sexual abuse among boys, Finkelhor (1984) found that 2.5 percent to 8.7 percent of males were sexually abused as children. Whether these lower figures are due to a lesser occurrence of abuse of boys or to the greater reluctance of men to come for treatment and lesser ability of clinicians to identify male sexual abuse victims remains to be seen. While the usual estimate is that 15 percent of sexually abused children are male, Porter (1986) cites data that suggest that young boys and young girls may be at equal risk of sexual abuse. Just as the known prevalence of female child sexual abuse rose from an estimate of 1 in 1 million in 1955 (Weinberg, 1976) to 1 in 3 in the 1980s (Russell, 1986), the current estimate of 16 in 100 male survivors of childhood sexual abuse (from a 1985 Los Angeles Times telephone interview of 2,627 adults, cited by Johanek, 1988) may show dramatic increases in the future as case finding becomes more sophisticated. Clearly, continued research needs to be conducted on this often neglected population.

While male survivors are likely to have many of the same disturbances as female survivors, there is an additional component, which relates to the man's perception of "manliness." As Johanek (1988) points out, there are cultural beliefs that a "real" man would fight to the death rather than be the victim of sexual assault, and that male perpetrators of sexual assaults on male children are homosexuals who "taint" the victim.

The 1989 television mini-series, "I Know My First Name is Steven," portraying the true story of a boy who was kidnapped and sexually abused by a pedophile for seven years, powerfully expressed the types of reactions from the culture boys may have to internalize. When Steven returns home and his father initially learns of the abuse, the father angrily responds, "How could you let him. . . ." At school, Steven is taunted by the other boys and called a "fag." Later in his own healing, he must come to terms with his deep sense of guilt that he allowed the pedophile to abuse his friends in order to take the attention off himself. In a moving closing scene, filled with self-loathing, he cries to his mother, "What kind of person would do that to his friends?" Thus, the sexism and homophobia reflected in others' reactions may be internalized by the male victim as he struggles to make sense of his experience. Consequently, these men may have great difficulty acknowledging what happened to them. Finkelhor (1984) describes three factors that explain why boys never reach public attention:

> Boys grew up with the male ethic of self-reliance . . . Boys have to grapple with the stigma of homosexuality surrounding so much sexual abuse, and . . . boys may have more to lose by their victimizing experiences. (p. 157)

Whether boys have more to lose than girls is a subjective question that might easily detract attention from the more important issues, both social and clinical.

Johanek (1988) concurs that the major issue with this population is that of identification, as many male survivors either repress memories of the abuse, fail to label what happened to them as abusive, or are reluctant to share their feelings about what happened. We believe that community outreach and education programs which destigmatize the experience of male sexual abuse will ultimately be necessary for these persons to receive appropriate services.

Multiple Personality Disorder

As clinical experience and research findings on multiple personality disorder (MPD) accumulate, it is apparent that the primary identifiable antecedent of MPD is severe childhood abuse and torture (e.g., Braun, 1983; Braun & Sachs, 1985; Kluft, 1985). The disguised presentation of this condition often leads to misdiagnosis and therefore inappropriate treatment. Given the considerable overlap of the diagnosis of borderline personality disorder with MPD (Horevitz & Braun, 1984), we believe that all clients previously diagnosed with borderline personality who have a history of abuse should be evaluated for MPD. Clues to the presence of a dissociative disorder include:

- A history of severe child abuse;

- Amnesia for recent or remote memories;
- A lack of coherence in the presentation of personal history;
- Loss of time or blackouts;
- Chronic self-destructive behaviors;
- Fluctuating self-presentations, ranging from fearful, childlike states to angry, hostile states;
- Multiple hospitalizations characterized by a variety of diagnoses and therapeutic interventions with no improvement;
- A fluctuating, unstable symptom picture that may involve psychotic symptoms (such as hearing voices) and bizarre behavior (such as disappearing for periods of time);
- Unusual chronic, unresolved somatic complaints, such as chronic menstrual or other gynecological problems (Bliss, 1980; Braun, 1983).

In addition to these clinical indicators, there are some measures of dissociation available which are quite reliable in identifying MPD (Bernstein & Putnam, 1986).

In our experience, many survivors of childhood sexual abuse evidence some dissociative processes, a finding that is supported in the clinical literature (e.g., Ellenson, 1985; Gelinas, 1983). After a therapeutic alliance has developed and the survivor has the necessary affect tolerance, hypnotic exploration of the split-off memory fragments or parts of experience can be explored. Many survivors who otherwise show no overt symptoms of MPD spontaneously report the existence of a hidden self that remembers the abuse and may be continuing to protect the adult self through the dissociative process.

The technicalities of treating persons with MPD are beyond the purview of this book and have been discussed in a number of excellent articles (e.g., Braun, 1984; Kluft, 1984a, 1984b). However, in our own work, we have found constructivist self development theory to be useful in conceptualizing MPD. Although these individuals, by definition, have serious disorders of the self, we have observed a wide degree of variability in the degree of fragmentation among the various alters. For example, within one or more alters, there may be some well-developed self capacities and ego resources. One MPD client in therapy at the Institute was often plagued by severe anxiety and other distressing affective states. Over the course of therapy, we learned that one alter had strong capacities for self-soothing and affect regulation. When the main personality was in severe emotional distress, we developed ways of inviting the other alter out to restore a sense of inner calm. Ultimately, an integration of these two personalities provided the main personality with capacities that had been previously underdeveloped, thus decreasing the affective storms she had previously experienced.

Furthermore, we have observed that each alter may have its own unique set of pressing needs and schemas about self and world that must be explored, understood, and ultimately integrated. For example, some alters may have a great need for trust/dependency, relying on the therapist for nurturance and protection. Others, particularly adolescent or young adult alters, may have a strong need for independence, combined with a fighting spirit. These resources can be mobilized in the therapy process during stressful times when there is a risk of the client becoming hopeless. Not surprisingly, we have found that the therapy process is less stormy and tumultuous with persons who have at least one alter with strong ego resources and self capacities than for those in whom there are limited capacities and resources across all the alters.

Adult Children of Alcoholics

Although this population is often not mentioned in the traumatic stress literature, we believe the experience of growing up in an alcoholic family can constitute traumatic stress. Post-traumatic stress disorder among ACOAs is just beginning to be discussed in the literature (e.g., Dean, 1988). Often these children grow up in households in which there was emotional, physical, or sexual violence, as well as an environment in which there was continual uncertainty, insecurity, and a frustration of basic needs. As a result, they may have extremely disturbed schemas for trust and safety, being hyperalert to signs of uncertainty or unpredictability in the environment. They may have difficulty trusting that they can count on others, and consequently developed rigid schemas for independence, deciding that one can only count on oneself and that any deviation from this is a sign of weakness.

Furthermore, because of the potential for explosive outbursts in alcoholic families, ACOAs may be oversensitive to signs that emotions are getting out of control. Many of the ACOAs we work with are hypersensitive to signs of strong emotions, particularly anger, and interpret even mild, verbal expressions of annoyance as a threat to their sense of safety and power. Not surprisingly, this makes it difficult for many of them to form trusting, intimate relations with other adults in which there is a free exchange of feelings and resolution of conflicts.

Many ACOAs struggle with issues of personal responsibility, a pattern we associate with rigid schemas for independence and power. They may have taken on adult responsibility prematurely and have difficulty enjoying themselves. Many of these clients express a sense of having been deprived of a childhood, while simultaneously feeling they have not grown up. They may evidence disturbed schemas in the area of intimacy because of their fears about their ability to sustain a healthy relationship, because they do not believe they are worthy of being loved unconditionally, because they do not expect that they can depend on another person, or because, as noted above, they are not capable of the full range of emotions that are essential to a rich, satisfying intimate relationship. Those clients who have rigid schemas for independence have learned early that their needs would be met only through their own actions. While independence can, of course, be an asset, fierce or rigid independence can inhibit the formation of appropriately dependent or interdependent relationships, including that with the therapist and intimate relationships with others.

Finally, sense of humor is a resource that may not be readily available to persons who have been overburdened by life's demands at a young age. Helping these clients to step back and look at themselves and others with gentle affection and humor can be a slow process, but one that is healing.

SEXUAL ASSAULT IN ADULTHOOD

Rape and Other Sexual Assault

We have addressed above the special concerns of adult survivors of child sexual abuse. Here we discuss the unique aspects of adult rape and other sexual traumas.

Adult rape victims who have not been traumatized during childhood may well have more highly developed self capacities and ego resources. However, a trauma that occurs during adulthood can have serious disorganizing effects, even upon the most psychologically healthy individual (e.g., American Psychiatric Association, 1952; Freud, 1920/1953; Grinker & Spiegel, 1945; Kardiner & Spiegel, 1947; Parson, 1986). An adult trauma survivor may present as seriously impaired, especially immediately after the event, with a temporary disruption in capacities for affect regulation and self-soothing. As research has demonstrated, sexual traumas can disrupt previously positive schemas about self and world (e.g., Roth & Lebowitz, 1988).

Constructivist self development theory predicts that, among rape victims, disruptions in schemas most often occur in the areas of frame of reference, including attributions about causality; distrust of men; loss of safety in a malevolent, unpredictable world; and independence, especially with reference to one's freedom of movement and ability to take care of oneself. The sooner the disruptions in self capacities and schemas are addressed and resolved, the better the prospects for a good recovery. Unfortunately, research indicates that the majority of rape victims never present for treatment (Koss & Burkhart, 1989).

Much of the early rape literature focused on crisis intervention to alleviate the acute symptoms of PTSD (e.g., Burgess & Holmstrom, 1974, 1979). More recently, behavioral interventions have been developed for resolving persistent fear and anxiety reactions, and researchers suggest that crisis intervention may not be adequate for resolving the complex cognitive disruptions that accompany sexual trauma (e.g., Kilpatrick & Veronen, 1983; Koss & Burkhart, 1989). Interventions derived from constructivist self development theory can address the problems of long-term adaptation, because long after the acute symptoms have begun to resolve, the most enduring problem is often rigid or entrenched disrupted schemas which limit the woman's potential for intimacy and psychological growth. We will address these issues below.

In addition to the possible disruptions in schemas that may occur in the aftermath of any trauma, sexually abused persons must deal with the stigma that surrounds the victim of sexual abuse. Sexual assault is an intrusion of the most personal sort and represents the most severe violation of the self (second only to being murdered) (Bard & Sangrey, 1986). Perhaps because of the horror associated with such a violation, others may feel a need to distance themselves from the knowledge and understanding of sexual assault. Blaming the victim is one way of defending against disruptions to one's own schemas related to safety and invulnerability. This results in a peculiar paradox: The victim of sexual assault is shunned and treated as the guilty party. At a time when she needs to heal her broken spirit by being nurtured and supported within a community of people, she is separated from that which she needs most. In a moving essay about rape, Metzger (1976) writes:

> The basic experience of rape is isolation. Humanity depends upon community and the effect of rape is to destroy simultaneously the sense of community and the sense of person . . . the victim is isolated or isolates herself; she enters a psychic quarantine as if she were contaminated, diseased, scarred. (pp. 406-407)

Even women with previously positive support systems can experience a disruption in their schemas for intimacy and trust/dependency, resulting in a growing isolation from others and a fear of the malevolent power of males. If the woman is then exposed to a second injury (Symonds, 1980) in her dealings with the criminal justice system, she is likely to find her frame of reference seriously disrupted, resulting in a view of the world as no longer predictable or comprehensible.

Sexism plays a large role in the victim-blaming that can accompany rape, to the extent that others feel that the woman in some way wanted or deserved to be raped. In a random interview sample of almost 600 adults, Burt (1980) conducted ground-breaking research which demonstrated the prevalence of damaging cultural myths and supports for rape. In her research, Burt found that rape myths (e.g., any healthy woman can successfully resist rape if she wants to; many women have an unconscious wish to be raped, and may then set up a situation in which they are likely to be attacked; and so forth) were strongly associated with the following attitudes: acceptance of interpersonal violence as a legitimate means of control in intimate relationships; sex role stereotyping (e.g., there is something wrong with a woman who doesn't want to marry and raise children); and adversarial sexual beliefs, reflected in a distrust of the opposite sex. Macho personality has been described by Mosher and Sirkin (1984) as a constellation of three characteristic beliefs that may also be associated with cultural support for rape: the beliefs that danger is exciting, violence is manly, and women are contemptible. Our society apparently places positive value on this approach to life, as reflected in popular movies and television shows. To the extent that women accept these views as normative, they will internalize seriously disturbed self schemas in response to sexual trauma.

Sexual assault can clearly have profound long-term effects on the survivor's sexuality (e.g., Becker, Skinner, Abel, & Cichon, 1986). This, in turn, may be reflected in the individual's beliefs about herself as a partner and her ability to develop or sustain an intimate relationship with a man. An adult rape victim's recovery will be affected by her partner's expressed attitudes about what happened to her and why it happened. In our experience, couples therapy is often useful in rape cases in which the female victim has an intimate male partner (e.g., Silverman, 1978). Some individual sessions for the partner may also be necessary in order to help the partner explore his own feelings and beliefs about what happened, as well as possible disruptions to his own schemas related to safety and power.

In this, as well as in other areas, the woman's preexisting schemas will shape her psychological experience and the meanings she attributes to the event. Thus, a woman for whom rape activates latent, negative self schemas might be more likely to absorb the negative messages from society and from her abuser than would a woman who understood that rape is a reflection of serious pathology on the part of the perpetrator and of a culture that condones violence against women. (See the two cases of rape in Chapter 14 which describe these two types of responses.) Within the rape literature, there is some empirical evidence that pre-trauma self-esteem can moderate some of the harmful long-term effects of rape (Kilpatrick, Veronen, & Best, 1985).

Adult Male Rape Victims

Adult male rape victims constitute another special group (Groth & Burgess, 1980; Kaufman, Divasto, Jackson, Voorhees, & Christy, 1980). Few such persons present for psychotherapy directly related to the rape, but adult rape experiences may be reported in the course of therapy with men. In our experience with those men who do present for treatment, they often exhibit shame, again because of social beliefs that a man should be able to prevent sexual victimization. To the extent that these beliefs have been internalized, this can lead to the unwarranted conclusion that the man in some way colluded with the perpetrator. Consequently, these victims may have special concerns about their manliness and sexuality, and special fears with respect to their own sexual orientation if aspects of the experience were in any way sexually stimulating.

As with the survivor of childhood sexual abuse who feels a deep sense of shame about being stimulated by the sexual contact, the male survivor needs to be reassured that sexual arousal is a normal physiological response that can occur independently from one's emotional response. Furthermore, the male victim may experience disruptions in power schemas, with an adaptation that involves reasserting his power or dominance in maladaptive ways. Special populations at risk for male rape, which deserve mention, are men who are incarcerated or homosexual men raped and attacked by heterosexual men who are acting out their conflicts concerning homophobia.

OTHER CRIME VICTIMS

Victims of Violent Crimes

Victims of rape fall into this category, along with victims of other intentional violence, including muggings, burglaries, and aggravated assaults. The special concerns of other crime victims have been described in depth by Bard and Sangrey (1986) in their excellent book, *The Crime Victim's Handbook*. Central to the crime victim's experience are the loss of personal control (Burgess & Holmstrom, 1979), increased feelings of personal vulnerability and fear of recurrence (Krupnick & Horowitz, 1981), a sense that the entire self has been violated (Bard & Sangrey, 1986), and feelings of responsibility (Krupnick & Horowitz, 1981).

In an excellent review article which represents an updated report for the American Psychological Association Task Force on Victims of Crime and Violence, Frieze, Hymer, and Greenberg (1987) describe current research findings and theories regarding the experience of the crime victim. Common responses to violent crime described include a sense of violation of the self, feelings of inequity, perception of oneself as deviant, and a loss of a sense of safety or invulnerability.

As Bard and Sangrey (1986) have pointed out, the crime victim's response is influenced by characteristics the victim brings to the experience, such as expectations. This view is consistent with constructivist self development theory. In our clinical experience, individuals' responses to the stress of crime are colored by their salient, preexisting schemas. Persons for whom the need for safety is particularly salient prior to the victimization may be more likely to have difficulty restoring positive safety schemas. The disruption to this central need may produce long-term, entrenched fear responses that can be alleviated only through fully understanding and working through the cognitive and emotional meanings of this disruption.

Although it is common for victims of home burglaries to install burglar alarm systems or move to a new residence, this strategy may be particularly useful for the person with a strong need for power. For this individual, such instrumental, problem-focused coping behaviors (Lazarus & Folkman, 1984) may enhance feelings of power. However, for persons for whom disturbed safety schemas are salient, such strategies may not be as useful. We have observed many individuals with strong safety needs who, despite taking extra safeguards, persist in such obsessions as whether the alarm system might fail or whether the new neighborhood will be safe, and generalize these fears to manifold dangers in the environment. For example, one burglary victim was able to restore her sense of safety at home over the course of therapy. However, she then became preoccupied with the idea that many crimes and accidents occur outside the home, thus posing the fundamental dilemma, "Is there any safe place in the world for me?"

Other crime victims, for whom schemas related to independence or personal control are more salient, may experience disruptions related to feeling out of control and helpless, berating themselves for being weak and defenseless. Krupnick (1980), in a similar vein, wrote about persons who experience crime as a violation of unconscious expectations of personal control and omnipotence. These persons may experience self-loathing at the normal feelings of vulnerability and helplessness that inevitably accompany violent attacks. Working to develop self-soothing capacities is as important for these clients as focusing on the target symptoms that have brought them into therapy. For example, this type of individual is likely to overreact to feelings of anxiety or vulnerability, engaging in punitive self-statements that only exacerbate these feelings. Through therapy, these individuals need to be taught that the paradoxical approach of "going with" the feelings will ultimately lead to enhanced self-control.

Finally, as with other victim groups, a sense of isolation and estrangement from others may disrupt schemas related to intimacy. Because traumatic events are by definition non-normative, traumatized individuals may feel deviant. For example, some crime victims who live in the affluent suburbs experience themselves as being "freaks" relative to their neighbors, who have never experienced such a violation. The local news coverage given to such crimes in small towns can reinforce the sense of deviance and shame.

Family Members of Crime Victims

Family members of crime victims who themselves were not directly victimized are a neglected group. Yet the research suggests that family members can also suffer the effects of these traumas, an important topic that has been written about extensively by Figley (1983, 1986). Figley (1986) suggests that the empathy that families experience in relation to the suffering of loved ones is the very process that makes them susceptible to psychological distress. An injury suffered by a loved one is often experienced as an injury or loss to oneself. Yet family members do not often have the opportunity to process their own feelings because they may feel they must be strong and available to the victim.

In addition, family members may not know or fully understand what happened to the victim, yet feel unable to ask the victim for fear of reinjuring him or her. This can mean that family members may develop their own disturbed schemas, particularly related to safety and frame of reference, but not have the opportunity to explore and repair them. Many family members express the fear that they will say the wrong thing if they approach the victim to talk about what happened. Psychoeducational family groups may be helpful in teaching family members what to expect from the victim, giving them a forum for expressing their own concerns, and restoring or building positive or adaptive schemas. Through psychoeducational group or family treatment, families can also be helped to understand how to give the type of emotional support that meets the unique needs of the victim.

Survivors of Homicide

While it might be said of any trauma that the events cannot be undone, the finality of death is qualitatively different from that of any other human experience. The families and friends of homicide victims have a unique experience in that there is nothing they can do to restore their loved ones to life. The shock of discovering the violent murder of a loved one can produce a severe shattering of schemas in all areas, resulting in a state of acute psychic disequilibrium and distress that disrupts the entire self (Bard, Arnone, & Nemiroff, 1986; Masters, Friedman, & Getzel, 1988).

In many instances, the family may not know or ever fully understand what happened, why or under what circumstances the loved one was killed. This can lead to endless obsessions about what happened, with terrible anguish associated with what one imagines may have happened. For others, having the details of what happened presents another burden: they are often tormented with unbidden images of horror in which they replay scenes of the last moments of their loved one's life. The utter sense of helplessness and rage that ensues cannot be expressed adequately in words. In our experience with peer support groups for survivors of homicide, we have been deeply moved by the intensity of the grief, pain, and rage that persist years after the event, even after involvement in supportive interventions.

As a number of researchers have pointed out (e.g., Bard, Arnone, & Nemiroff, 1986; Lyon, 1988), the social and legal demands placed upon the family are immense and can be a source of great stress. This can range from being asked insensitive questions about what happened by friends and family to seemingly endless encounters with police, coroners, prosecutors, media, and others whose responses can be either helpful or hurtful. This process carries enormous potential to damage schemas related to trust in others and one's frame of reference with regard to a meaningful world. Receiving appropriate support from others that meets the unique needs of families is particularly important in ameliorating the radical disruption to schemas (Bard & Connolly, 1982).

In her intensive interview research with families of homicide victims, Lyon (1988) learned that one of their greatest sources of distress is their dealings with the criminal justice system. The lack of information and sense of powerlessness that accompany dealing with that overloaded system are often experienced as enormously frustrating. In addition, because legal proceedings are often so slow, the family's ability to feel that they can gain control over their pain and grieve the loss in their own time is greatly diminished.

The traumatic death of a child, whether through illness, accident, or homicide, is perhaps the most profound loss that any human being can experience. It is a violation of the natural order for parents to outlive their children. This shattering of one's frame of reference can lead to endless questions about why such terrible things happen to innocent people, and may include a loss of faith in one's God or humanity in general (e.g., Rinear, 1988). The disappearance or kidnapping of a child, a topic which has received much media attention since the movie *Adam*, represents another type of trauma; these parents live with uncertainty about what happened to their child and are often frozen in a state of incomplete mourning. In addition, parents may experience enormous guilt and self-loathing for being unable to protect the child's security or life, no matter how unrealistic this may be. In some instances, this may be compounded by others who in some way blame the parent as well.

In our experience, it is important to avoid challenging these self-blaming attributions prematurely, however painful it may be for the therapist to see a person in such great anguish over feelings of personal responsibility. As we have pointed out elsewhere, only through fully exploring the attendant meaning and affects will these schemas ultimately change and some degree of acceptance be possible.

The loss of a child can have an important negative effect on the parents' other relationships. For example, Rinear (1988) found that nearly one-half of parents who lost a child to homicide were fearful with regard to their ability to protect their surviving children, suggesting a radical disruption to safety and power schemas. The psychological effects on the siblings of the traumatic loss of a brother or sister are also immense and can be long-lasting. Any guilt they feel over surviving (as in the powerful movie, *Ordinary People*), the parents' grief and emotional unavailability, and the parents' potential overprotectiveness are all potential stressors that can disrupt the normal development of the surviving children. Finally, the couples relationship is most often dramatically disrupted by this tragic experience; many couples are unable to process their grief together, unable to bear being reminded of the child by each other's presence, or unable to tolerate their own sense of guilt toward the other. The different coping styles and psychological needs of the couple must be understood and respected in family or couples therapy if the family is to complete the grieving process and heal.

Battered Women

In Chapter 3, we described the extent to which women are seriously battered by their male partners. The severity of this problem is reflected in the findings that approximately 1,700 women die each year as a result of domestic violence (e.g., Steinmetz, 1978). We note here that men, too, may be battered by their wives, that unmarried couples also engage in battering, and that gay and lesbian relationships are not immune to battering. The preponderance of the literature focuses on husband-wife battering, but clinicians should not overlook the possibility of such abuse in less traditional situations. While we talk below about husbands battering wives, what we say about dynamics, adaptations, and recovery can apply equally to these other situations.

That many battered women live in constant fear for their lives and for their physical and psychological well-being, as well as for their children, is well-documented in the literature on this population (e.g., Walker, 1985). The severe disruption this poses to safety schemas is apparent: many become hypervigilant, restricting their behavior and activities in a way that they believe will reduce their risk of harm. The clinical literature describes the many ways that battered women acclimate to their disrupted safety schemas: they may be hypersensitive to any cues in the environment that signal danger and restrict their own behavior and emotions in order to attempt to keep themselves safe from harm. This accommodation to continual threat clearly has great impact on the entire personality.

Many of these victims experience a deep sense of social and psychological isolation which grows over the period of the battering (Hilberman, 1980). Opportunities for intimacy and social interaction are limited, due in part to the victim's sense of shame, fear of reprisal, and the often intense jealousy of the abusive partner. In addition, like child victims, battered women experience betrayal by a trusted, intimate other, leading to disruptions in trust schemas and dependency needs. Furthermore, some battered women incorporate the abuse into their self schemas, resulting in negative self-esteem (Mills, 1984). Not only is the woman herself in situations which over time damage her self-esteem, but she also may feel helpless to protect her children and feel that she has failed in her role as mother.

An important clinical question that arises is why battered women stay in abusive relationships and how this can be addressed therapeutically. Although there is growing societal compassion for the plight of the battered woman, cultural attitudes persist that may foster victim-blaming. In a society that values self-determination and free will, it is often difficult for the community at large, as well as for therapists, to understand why women stay in abusive relationships.

The recent controversy surrounding the Hedda Nussbaum case (Weiss & Johnson, 1989) and the bitter debates among various feminist groups reflect society's continuing ambivalence about issues of blame and responsibility for battering. Although many are sympathetic to Hedda Nussbaum's plight and understand it in terms of her extreme psychological demoralization, others take the position that she was a free agent who had many opportunities to leave but always returned home. For this reason, along with her apparent complicity or passivity with regard to the neglect and abuse of her daughter, Lisa, Ms. Nussbaum was regarded by some as a responsible party who should have been tried as an accessory to Lisa's death. Even among experienced clinicians in the field, some inner voice, however small, may ask, "But WHY didn't she leave before it was too late?"

In a superb review article on why battered women stay in abusive relationships, Strube (1988) begins by citing disturbing statistics from numerous studies that suggest that approximately 50 percent of women who sought help from social service agencies, including shelters, ultimately returned home. The fact that most women leave only when the situation becomes life-threatening suggests that large numbers of women are exposing themselves to extreme danger upon returning home.

Strube (1988) reviews the research which suggests a variety of factors that influence the decision to leave an abusive relationship, including the severity and frequency of violence, religious affiliation, the longevity of the relationship, presence of child abuse, and economic dependence. Strube goes on to summarize four models which he believes, taken together, can explain this complex phenomenon.

First is the model of psychological entrapment, in which the woman seeks to justify the time and effort expended to make the relationship work in the past and feels personally responsible for the outcome of the relationship. This model suggests that women who define their self-worth in terms of making the relationship work may have a greater psychological investment in staying.

Second is the learned helplessness theory first advanced by Seligman (1975) and later adapted by Walker (1977–1978) in relation to battered women. Findings derived from the reformulated learned helpless model (Abramson, Seligman, & Teasdale, 1978) suggest that women who are predisposed to making internal, stable, and global attributions for negative outcomes are more likely to feel chronically helpless and have low self-esteem.

The third model suggests that battered women decide whether the benefits of staying in the relationship are greater than the costs of leaving. This may occur when the woman has made a high investment in the relationship and perceives a lack of alternatives or retribution if she leaves.

The fourth model draws upon a theory by Ajzen and Fishbein (1980). This theory suggests that behavioral intentions are determined by the individual's beliefs that the action will result in desired outcomes and avoid undesired outcomes, much like social learning theory (Rotter, 1954) which postulates that behavior is determined by the expectations that it will lead to certain outcomes and the importance of those outcomes. Applying this model to women who stay in battering relationships, Strube (1988) suggests that a woman who stays may hold unrealistic or exaggerated beliefs about what will happen if she leaves (e.g., a belief that she will be unable to survive on her own, a fear of being alone). In this regard, Strube suggests

> altering unrealistic evaluations calls for interventions that educate, inform, and perhaps avail women of the direct experiences that can serve to alter the perceived desirability of the consequences of leaving. (1988, p. 247)

Taken together, we believe these models are very useful frameworks, consistent in many ways with constructivist self development theory. That is, self-esteem schemas that involve defining one's self-worth in terms of making the relationship work will be one area that is targeted for intervention. Second, modifying a client's tendency to make internal, stable, and global attributions for negative outcomes is related both to changing the frame of reference (e.g., attributions of causality) and the power schemas (her belief in her ability to exert control over the environment in a positive way.). The third issue relates to frame of reference schemas related to hope. This model would suggest possible benefits of changing a woman's perceptions about her alternatives by helping her become more hopeful about the future while gently challenging her generalized fears of negative consequences if she leaves.

We discuss in more detail the application of constructivist self development theory to treatment interventions with victims of family violence elsewhere (McCann & Pearlman, in press).

Survivors of Natural and Human-Induced Disasters

The psychological effects of disasters have been documented since the early reports of a devastating fire at the Coconut Grove night club (Adler, 1943; Lindemann, 1944). Later, systematic clinical and empirical research has been conducted on the Buffalo Creek flood, an event of devastating proportions that took the lives of many, as well as destroying an entire community (Erikson, 1976). In early clinical papers describing the effects of this disaster, researchers were impressed by the pervasive and long-lasting character changes observed in survivors (Titchener, Kapp, & Winget, 1976). Later empirical research on this population demonstrated high levels of chronic psychopathology and a strong relation between bereavement and threat to life and severity of symptoms on two-year follow-up (Gleser, Green, & Winget, 1981).

This same group of researchers, studying the long-term effects among survivors of a supper club fire, again demonstrated that threat to life, bereavement, and exposure to the grotesque were correlated with severity of response at one- and two-year follow-up (Green, Grace, & Gleser, 1985). The fine work by this group of researchers has added much to our understanding of the long-term effects of disaster and the characteristics of the stressor that are most often associated with long-term problems.

In analyzing these findings from the perspective of constructivist self development theory, one might hypothesize that those who were more deeply affected were individuals for whom central needs and schemas, most likely those related to safety, power, intimacy, and frame of reference, were greatly disrupted. When an entire community is destroyed, as in the Buffalo Creek disaster and more recently, the Armenian earthquake, the shattering of one's frame of reference and intimate bonds with loved ones and community is likely to produce a radical and, without treatment, long-lasting disruption to the entire self.

For the most part, disaster research, which we will not review extensively here, suggests that for most individuals the effects do not generally extend beyond the immediate post-impact period. There is, however, some evidence that disasters which are of human design and intentional have more serious impact than natural disasters. An interesting finding has been that chronic stress, such as living near the Three

Mile Island nuclear power plant after the nuclear accident in 1979, produces long-lasting effects.

In relation to this incident, a group of researchers (Baum, Fleming, & Singer, 1983; Davidson & Baum, 1986; Davidson, Fleming, & Baum, 1986) demonstrated a relation between exposure to chronic stress and mild, but chronic, symptoms of PTSD, including intrusive thoughts about the damaged reactor. An interesting finding is that chronic stress was associated with hyperarousal as measured by increased catechol-amine and cortisol levels. The authors interpret these findings in light of Lazarus's (1966) model of stress and coping, suggesting that the appraisal of threat combined with uncertainty about the future and helplessness to act might be responsible for the continued symptoms.

Interpreting these findings within constructivist self development theory, we would reformulate this to suggest that, for some individuals, disturbed safety, frame of reference, and power schemas were never restored. One is chronically exposed to an "invisible" threat that one can neither avoid nor control. Furthermore, the experience of being violated by an intentional human-induced disaster is likely to disrupt one's trust in and esteem of other people, leading to chronic cynicism, anger, and disillusionment.

Overall, constructivist self development theory suggests that interventions with disaster survivors focus on identifying those schemas that are most disrupted by the event and attempting to restore basic psychological needs, in part by organizing appropriate social support networks after a disaster. In line with our own thinking, Solomon (1986) makes the important point that survivors of disasters may be reluctant to seek the help of mental health professionals because such behavior may be discrepant with schemas related to self-esteem and independence or personal control. This poses an additional challenge to those who are designing interventions for disaster or emergency survivors and witnesses: to provide a context that can be viewed by potential service users as acceptable and helpful.

Lindy, Grace, and Green (1981) adopt the concept of the "trauma membrane" to describe the way in which family and friends often form a protective shield around the survivor in order to protect him or her from people or events that could potentially retraumatize. In order to break through the membrane, the helper must be judged by the support group to be helpful rather than harmful. One often successful approach is to organize the services around the needs of the children who may have been affected, as recommended by professionals engaged in such work (M. Braverman, personal communication, June 9, 1989; J. Mitchell, personal communication, August 25, 1989).

SURVIVORS OF HISTORICAL TRAUMAS

Vietnam Veterans

Much has been written since the mid-1970s about the special concerns of the Vietnam veteran, with many excellent books on the topic (e.g., Brende & Parson, 1985; Figley, 1978; Kelly, 1985; Lifton, 1973; Lindy, 1988; Wilson, 1978; Wilson, Harel, & Kahana, 1988). The perceived meaninglessness of this war to much of society and many of the individuals directly involved in it resulted in a tragic sense of betrayal by the young people who felt they were participating in a patriotic drama, only to find, upon returning home, that they were held in contempt by those for whose sake they had risked their lives (Brende & Parson, 1985; Figley & Leventman, 1980; Parson, 1986). This represented a serious narcissistic injury that manifested itself as serious posttrauma self disorders among some veterans (Parson, 1984, 1988).

The severe shattering of schemas related to trust has been written about extensively in relation to the disillusionment in military and government leaders and the experience of being abandoned by their country (Figley, 1978). Furthermore, the physical environment of Vietnam, fraught with often invisible and unpredictable perils that posed a threat to life and safety (Parson, 1984), may have shattered safety schemas, resulting in chronic hypervigilance to an environment that is still perceived as potentially lethal. These disrupted trust and safety schemas are often rigid and entrenched, and many veterans report an inability to establish trusting relationships with anyone, with the exception of some other veterans who they believe will not devalue or betray them. In order to compensate for the disrupted trust and safety schemas, the veteran may adopt rigid power schemas, being sensitive to any abuses of power in the environment, and seeking to control the environment through sometimes maladaptive means. Some veterans, for whom these schemas are extremely disturbed, may adopt a "paranoid state syndrome," described by Wilson and Zigelbaum (1986) as having the following characteristics:

Person tends to be angry, hostile, suspicious, irritable, and has explosive rage. Often feels exploited and persecuted by traumatic agent and is overly suspicious of authority and power. May main-

tain a hyperalertness state of perception of a chronic basis similar
to that employed in trauma. (p. 308)

In some, there is also a seriously impaired ability to connect with
others, representing a serious shattering of intimacy and trust/depen-
dency schemas. A deep sense of betrayal by "mother country" may
underlie the hostility toward women that is evident in some combat
veterans (Garte, 1986). Wilson and Zigelbaum (1986) described what
we believe to be manifestations of these seriously disrupted schemas
as isolation and withdrawal syndromes:

> . . .Person may live in remote, scarcely populated areas, avoid
> crowds, and prefers to live alone, away from others. Some prefer
> to live in the "woods" and maintain hyperalertness. Seeks a self-
> contained lifestyle that is under personal control. (p. 308)

They also describe a pattern they define as problems in intimacy
syndrome, as follows:

> Person has strained interpersonal relations (object relations) and
> is emotionally distant despite strong needs for intimacy. Intimate
> relations often pose a threat and raise fears of loss of love objects
> again. (p. 308)

Parson (1984, 1988) and Brende and Parson (1985) discuss, within
an object relations and self-psychology framework, the developmental
issues that arise from experiencing a trauma such as Vietnam combat
during adolescence when needs for idealization of parental figures are
very critical to the development of ideals and ambitions. The disrupted
adult development of many veterans, including an inability to find a
meaningful career path, has been documented (Garte, 1985). We find
Parson and Brende's analysis of posttrauma self disorders a useful
paradigm and agree that self work, often involving long-term therapy,
is necessary to repair the damaged self.

With regard to issues of personal responsibility, much has been written
about the veteran as agent in the war as well as victim. Laufer, Brett,
and Gallops (1985) reported a study comparing veterans who witnessed
atrocities with those who committed atrocities. They have related these
different experiences to symptoms of intrusion and denial. Calvert and
Hutchinson (1989) investigated the relation between engaging in war
combat and subsequent (civilian) violent behavior. Although differences
between groups on most items did not reach statistical significance,
they found that those who participated in heavy combat were more

likely to engage in personal violence (kicking, biting, or hitting with a fist) after the war.

The unique meanings of killing or harming others must be explored as the veteran internalizes split self-images of both victim and killer (Brende, 1983). This experience is associated with a severe fragmentation of the self and is likely associated with very damaged self-esteem schemas (Brende, 1983; Parson, 1984). This same dynamic may apply to individuals who witnessed the death of buddies or experienced a failed enactment (Blank, 1985) in which they perceived that someone died because of their own inability to act heroically. The various meanings of survivor guilt in this population have been written about extensively in the literature (e.g., Glover, 1984, 1988; Lifton, 1988) and include useful treatment strategies for resolving the various manifestations of unresolved guilt (e.g., Williams, 1988). Constructivist self development theory would add that engaging in combat or surviving one's buddies, like all other experiences, has unique meanings for each individual. The specific disrupted schemas and needs must be identified and addressed through the therapy process.

Survivors of Cultural Victimization and Genocide

This group includes survivors of the Nazi Holocaust, Southeast Asian refugees, and others who have been persecuted because of their nationality, ethnicity, or religion. There has been a great deal written about survivors of the Nazi Holocaust (e.g., Krystal, 1968; Niederland, 1968), including more recent follow-up studies on aging survivors (Kahana, Harel, & Kahana, 1988). The early clinical literature on Holocaust survivors presented a grim picture of severe affective, behavioral, and cognitive constriction. In describing the "survivor syndrome" in Holocaust survivors, Niederland (1968) originally identified pervasive depressed mood, survivor guilt, anxiety, and personality constriction. The kinds of horrors to which the survivors were subjected were believed to lead to a kind of psychological paralysis, which Krystal (1978) describes as a catatonoid reaction. Krystal writes, "In this state, a condemned person cooperates with his executioner" (p. 93).

Kahana et al.'s (1988) review of more recent empirical investigations with community samples of aging survivors found remarkable resilience and psychological well-being, a finding that stands in marked contrast to earlier clinical reports based on psychiatric populations. Within Kahana et al.'s sample, only 10 percent of the survivor population received any mental health treatment. Despite this, many were doing well socially and psychologically. Kahana et al. (1988) found that instrumental coping was positively correlated with positive morale, while emotional coping was not. Better psychological functioning was correlated with self-disclosure, altruism, internal locus of control, having a survivor spouse, and the perception that being a survivor is beneficial to adjustment to aging. The latter finding suggests that many survivors were able to draw positive meaning from their experience in later stages of adult development. Such well-designed research on nonclinical populations is an important step in learning more about those persons who became "survivors," in the true sense of the word.

These and other recent findings suggest that clinicians not view Holocaust survivors as one homogeneous group, a view that is consistent with our own thinking as well as that of others (e.g., Danieli, 1985). While the Holocaust experience was one of utter helplessness and terror, with the potential to shatter one's schemas in all areas and, most profoundly, one's frame of reference, it is important to understand how these schemas have been transformed over the 40 years postliberation. Continued understanding of individual variations in adaptation to such massive traumas is an important research area for the future.

In recent years, preliminary investigation of the Southeast Asian population reveals a high incidence of severe PTSD and major affective disorder among Cambodian refugees, associated with deprivation, physical injury or torture, sexual assault, incarceration in reeducation camps, and witnessing killing or torture (Kinzie, Fredrickson, Ben, Rleck, & Karis, 1984; Mollica, Wyshak, & Lavelle, 1987). The serious and apparently enduring psychological disruptions in this population, in contrast to the aging Holocaust survivors, may be explained by a number of factors: These groups have more recently experienced a devastation to the self and to the entire fabric of their social world, including the widespread destruction of their country, the widespread killing of their families and peers, the destruction of their cultural values during the Pol Pot regime from 1975–1979, and continued social dislocation in a culture that is radically different from their own.

Clinical reports of these refugees show a marked, chronic pattern of avoidance that lasts for many years, with intrusive symptoms worsening with exposure to new life stressors (Kinzie, 1988). The severity of long-term difficulties among this population is evident in the recent finding of psychosomatic blindness among Cambodian women who had witnessed atrocities committed against their loved ones (Smith, 1989, reporting the research of Gretchen Van Boemel).

The difference in time frame, with the Nazi Holocaust survivors 40 years away from their immediate trauma, in comparison with the

Southeast Asian survivors whose traumatic experiences are much closer to the present, may also contribute to the different clinical pictures presented by these two survivor groups. One might also speculate that the psychologically healthier Holocaust survivors are those who have survived these 40 years, while their peers who adapted less successfully may no longer be alive to serve as research subjects.

The findings from the Southeast Asian population suggest that treatment must be long-term and supportive and that helping the client to stabilize within a safe and predictable environment is an essential part of therapy. The chronic avoidant symptoms that persist in this population, in addition to being consistent with the acculturation of the Southeast Asian population's attitude toward pain, may suggest that the traumatic memories pose too great a threat to the individual's entire frame of reference, a discrepancy that is intolerable and psychologically retraumatizing. Whether these individuals will ultimately be able to reverse the malignant effects of chronic PTSD remains to be seen; the ability of survivors to find meaning in their new lives and to create a new psychological sense of "home" will be essential to ultimately restoring a sense of security and connection with other people and the world.

Persons Exposed to Life-Threatening Illness and Loss

Persons who are HIV positive are perhaps the newest group of victims of psychological trauma. Recent evidence suggests that this population is also at risk for PTSD (Martin, 1988). First, these individuals must face the prospect of premature death along with a serious decline in health, a difficult challenge common to all persons with serious illnesses. The diagnosis of any terminal illness disrupts one's schemas related to safety and invulnerability. The sense of uncertainty that accompanies exposure to the AIDS virus (e.g., will one ultimately die or remain chronically ill with the Aids Related Complex) is likely to be associated with feelings of personal vulnerability, fears about the future, and a loss of hope about the future.

Persons with HIV must also deal with the meanings of contagion and its impact on one's self schemas and relationships. The subjective experience of being contagious or having the terrible power to kill another through exposure is a profound psychological experience that may be associated with a self schema of malignancy and contagion (e.g., Gordon & Shontz, in press). In addition, HIV positive persons must cope with considerable stigma and social rejection, resulting in part from homophobia and in part from the denial of death among their healthy peers. As the individual internalizes these negative views from the general culture, negative esteem schemas develop. Furthermore, the disrupted independence schemas, resulting from the individual's decreasing ability to care for himself or herself, are likely to result in another blow to the self-esteem in persons for whom self-sufficiency is particularly important.

Social isolation and the difficulty sustaining intimate connections may disrupt schemas for intimacy, resulting in feelings of alienation and estrangement from others. Although clearly some AIDS victims have a large support system and a partner or family who remains constant until death, others are left to live out their lives in loneliness and isolation, abandoned by family and friends alike.

Furthermore, among the gay population, many of one's peers may also be HIV positive and in various stages of death and dying. Thus, the AIDS experience is compounded by the ongoing process of bereavement in which one must watch many of one's peers die prematurely. A well-done study by Martin (1988) found a strong relation between the number of bereavements experienced and the intensity of PTSD symptoms, a finding that is consistent with research on other populations (e.g., Wilson, Smith, & Johnson, 1985).

Finally, being afflicted with a terminal illness at a young age jars one's frame of reference; the expectations that death accompanies older age, while vitality and youth go hand in hand are shattered for the young AIDS victim.

SUMMARY

We have presented special issues that may accompany certain types of traumas, describing some of the findings regarding the commonalities in responses patterns among these various groups as well as our own thinking about the individual variations in adaptation that is derived from constructivist self development theory. Again, we remind the reader that the research on common responses and issues should serve as a guide to understanding the possible impact of these types of trauma; understanding the unique person who perceives and interprets these experiences in different ways will ultimately guide interventions that are respectful of the person.

Part 4

INTEGRATION

14. Integrating the Theory in Four Case Studies

In this chapter, we will apply the model systematically to specific victim cases as an illustration of how the theory can be useful for systematic assessment and treatment planning. In our case conferences, we use a semistructured format for case presentation which covers the areas of importance in the model. As the theory is complex, we recommend that therapists attempt to formulate cases using this general outline:

A. Life History and the Social and Cultural Context
B. The Self
    1. Ego resources and self capacities
    2. Central psychological needs and schemas
C. The Traumatic Experience(s)
    1. Central aspects of the traumatic experience
    2. Characteristics of the traumatic memories
    3. Psychological adaptation and its relation to the self
D. The Course of Psychotherapy

CASE #1: A FEMALE RAPE SURVIVOR WITH CENTRAL INDEPENDENCE SCHEMAS

Here we present the case of a woman who was recently raped by a stranger.

Life History and Social Context
Donna is a 35-year-old divorced woman who lives alone and has struggled all her life to, in her words, transcend a working class existence. Her pertinent history includes growing up with emotionally abusive

309

and irresponsible alcoholic parents. Early on, she learned that adults could not always be trusted and the only person she could rely on was herself. She characterized the male relatives in the family as irresponsible and unreliable, and she viewed the women as weak and helpless. Donna vowed to herself at a young age that she would never become like the women for whom she had little respect and that she would work hard to overcome the dysfunctional family/cultural patterns into which she had been born.

After high school, Donna married a man who she had believed was strong and reliable. In reality, he turned out to be an alcoholic who was as irresponsible and undependable as the adults in her early childhood. She divorced several years ago after suffering physical and emotional abuse in that relationship. Although this experience was very painful, it precipitated a period of personal growth for her in which she went back to college, found herself a better job, developed a new circle of friends, and generally began to experience a greater sense of control over her life.

The Self

Ego Resources and Self Capacities. Despite her deprived background, Donna had considerable ego resources. These included intelligence, a sense of humor, willpower, and the ability to introspect. Her self capacities were relatively strong, although she had a tendency to avoid situations in which she might feel overwhelmed by strong emotions or feel emotionally vulnerable. Overall, she is a warm, engaging woman with impressive strengths.

Central Psychological Needs and Schemas. Despite a difficult background, Donna developed a fighting spirit expressed in the context of her fierce independence, her determination to better herself personally and professionally, and her commitment to avoid being involved in a dysfunctional relationship again. She had worked very hard to overcome the devaluing and critical messages from her family who told her that she was undeserving and would never amount to anything. In response to this early environment, she developed strong needs for independence. This was expressed by the desire to be in control of her life and emotions and to avoid becoming vulnerable to people who might hurt or betray her.

Prior to being raped, Donna's development was progressing smoothly with the exception of an avoidance of intimate relationships with men, whom she distrusted. The disrupted schemas concerning intimacy and trust/dependency were not troublesome to her and she expressed a contentment with her life. This was tied in to her extremely strong need for independence. She viewed dependency as a weakness and believed that the only way one could get ahead in life was through one's own efforts.

The Traumatic Experience

Central Aspects of the Traumatic Experience. Donna was tied up at knife point and brutally raped by a stranger while she was jogging near her house in a wooded rural area. She had frequently jogged in this area and had never felt vulnerable. What was most salient for Donna about this experience was not the physical rape but rather the accompanying verbal degradation that seemed to go on for hours. The rapist continually told her that she was no good and deserved what was happening to her. He threatened to kill her if she screamed and it appeared that she dissociated during parts of the rape. She finally escaped after several hours, but the rapist was never apprehended.

Characteristics of the Traumatic Memories. Initially, Donna's experience of the memories was that they were continually intrusive and associated with a great deal of psychological distress. Early on, she experienced flashbacks in which she imagined the rapist approaching her unseen, an experience that was terrifying and disruptive to her everyday functioning. Aspects of her memory of the traumatic experience were fragmented, particularly those parts that occurred while she dissociated. Although many of the memories were within conscious awareness, she was unable to verbalize the imagery portion of memory because it was so overwhelming emotionally.

Psychological Adaptation and Its Relation to the Self. When Donna first came into therapy, she was in a deep depression, with uncontrollable crying and other symptoms of acute distress. Initially, she was fearful and anxious and her personal safety was a salient issue. She slept with a knife and experienced panic when she ventured out of the house alone. Initially, she needed supportive friends to stay with her and accompany her to work. What was more central for Donna, however, was that she was flooded by imagery involving the verbal humiliation and degradation she experienced during the rape. These painful images appeared to disrupt schemas related to self-esteem and independence or personal control. She was obsessed with the rapist's words to her and was overcome with intense suicidal feelings which were tied to her feelings of being degraded and permanently damaged.

Initially, her frame of reference was disrupted and she believed the rape happened because she was unworthy. Related to this was a disrupted belief in her sense of independence or self-control. She viewed her emotional reactions as a sign of weakness and helplessness. As a result, the capacities for self-soothing and affect regulation were temporarily disrupted and she responded to her normal emotional reactions with self-loathing. Finally, negative schemas related to distrust of men were activated and solidified. This event confirmed her underlying belief that men were, in her words, bastards, and that the only person one could really count on in this world was oneself.

Therapy

For Donna, the major treatment goals were mobilizing her considerable ego resources in the service of therapy, bolstering self capacities for self-soothing and affect regulation, and working through her damaged schemas related to self-esteem and independence. It is important to note that the initially disrupted safety schemas were resolved over a period of several weeks as Donna and the therapist developed a plan for gradual exposure to the feared situations, all of which entailed being alone.

After she had stabilized, therapy focused on understanding the esteem issues in light of her earlier experience of being verbally and physically degraded and devalued. With regard to the self-loathing about her emotional reactions, the therapist had to work with Donna to restore her own compassion for herself and to help her learn to tolerate the inevitable vulnerability she experienced. Feeling out of control, helpless, and weak was reframed as a normal reaction to an abnormal event which would resolve itself more quickly if she could learn to be more compassionate to herself and to soothe herself when she was in distress. The use of imagery to activate loving images of her dead grandmother, the one good internalized object in her early life, was an essential part of this process.

Another part of this process that was important to her was working through her resistance to reconnecting with God (a conflict she brought up in treatment) which resulted from her feelings of shame and self-hatred. Continually reminding her of her considerable resources was also very important, as she experienced her own psychological state as a regression which might be permanent.

In Donna's case, the acute symptoms resolved after about two months. She has remained in therapy because the work led into the long-standing negative trust and intimacy schemas. The therapist is now working on gently challenging Donna's beliefs that all men are untrustworthy and that she will be betrayed and revictimized if she allows herself to be vulnerable in a relationship with a man. Overall, the therapy has enabled her to continue developing psychologically and to move beyond her previous level of functioning.

At this point in her life, she is viewing the rape as a very painful yet growth-producing experience. The near-death experience enabled her to reevaluate her life and her values. She is now volunteering at a rape crisis center as a way of giving back a gift to the world and deriving some benefit from her experience.

CASE #2: A FEMALE RAPE SURVIVOR WITH CENTRAL SAFETY AND INTIMACY SCHEMAS

This case describes a woman who was raped by two men who broke into her home.

Life History and Social Context

Lee is a 34-year-old married mother of two preschool girls. She is a professional woman who lives in an affluent suburban community and is married to a successful and supportive husband. She grew up in a middle class family of four children and prided herself on being the independent eldest child who took care of and had authority over the younger children. Her parents were warm and supportive and she continues to be close to them. Her mother tends to be a worrier and conveyed to Lee concerns about personal safety and security.

Overall, Lee's childhood was free of any major losses or traumas and she enjoyed a sense of security and connection with family and friends. There is, however, one frightening experience in childhood whose memory was evoked by the rape. When she was in early adolescence, she was walking home from school when suddenly a black boy whom she had never seen before began chasing her. She was very frightened and was able to get help from a neighbor. We will return shortly to the unique meaning of this event for her as reformulated in later life.

The Self

Ego Resources and Self Capacities. Like Donna, Lee is a high-functioning, psychologically healthy adult woman whose life course had been progressing smoothly until the rape. She is a bright, mature woman who is aware of her own needs, is able to take initiative in her life, and has the ability to establish mature relationships with others. She has a supportive circle of friends and a close relationship with her husband. Her self-esteem has always been strong and she has never experienced any serious disruptions in her mood states. Lee would not have entered the mental health system had it not been for the trauma that disrupted her normal adult development.

Central Psychological Needs and Schemas. Lee's central needs have been to achieve a measure of independence through her professional achievements and to create a safe and secure home for herself and her family. Connection and intimacy with others in her social life and work have always been important and she has a close circle of friends. There is no evidence that any of the schemas in these areas were previously disrupted, although Lee did acknowledge that she's always been something of a worrier, like her mother. At times, prior to the rape, she would be more concerned about safety issues than her husband and at times she had thoughts about harm coming to her children or other loved ones. Overall, those concerns about safety were not disruptive in any way, although Lee did admit to the thought that she would become like her mother if she allowed this part of herself free reign.

The Traumatic Experience

Central Aspects of the Traumatic Experience. Lee and her husband had turned in for the evening on a sweltering summer night. Although they always locked the windows at night, they decided to leave one window open for ventilation as the house was so hot. Lee awoke in the middle of the night to strange noises downstairs. She didn't want to overinterpret the noises and listened carefully without waking her husband. By the time she figured out that there were indeed strangers in the house, it was too late to do anything. Lee lay helplessly on the bed as she heard footsteps on the stairs. Two men entered the bedroom in the dark and tied her husband to the bed. She was forced to lie down on the floor, while her husband was held at knife point. The rapists threatened to kill them and their sleeping children if they resisted. The rapists said many degrading things to her as they raped her and told her this was the last good time she would ever have. After an hour of terror, the assailants escaped. They were apprehended by the police and a year after the rape were sentenced to prison for many years.

Characteristics of the Traumatic Memories. Lee's experience of the traumatic memories was that they were vivid, unbidden, and terrifying. She had full recall of all the details of what happened and was able to discuss these details with the police and the therapist. No aspects of the rape were repressed. The details that were most salient to her, returning in the form of intrusive thoughts, were as follows: the helplessness of lying in bed as the rapist walked up the stairs, the thought that the rapist was going to kill her or her family, and the memory of his cruel words to her which implied that she would never feel safe again.

Psychological Adaptation and Its Relation to the Self. Lee initially suffered from typical symptoms of acute PTSD. However, she was not suicidal nor was her self-esteem in any way disrupted, despite the fact that the rapists also verbally degraded her. We attribute this difference from Donna to the fact that Lee's previous esteem schemas were not as vulnerable to a major disruption. Instead, the central schemas that were disrupted were those related to safety, independence, and intimacy, areas that were very salient for her in the past. Her previous vulnerable safety schemas were shattered and she was obsessed with the fear that she would never be able to feel safe again. She was tormented by intrusive thoughts about having left the window open and not interpreting the noises downstairs early enough, and she extended her obsessions to the decision to buy the house in the first place. She became preoccupied with the idea that any false move, any mistake in judgment, might result in future tragedy.

Initially, she and her family moved in with her parents because it was too terrifying to stay at home. The couple soon decided to sell their home. Although she was close to her family, this restriction of personal freedom further disrupted her independence schemas and made her feel as if she were regressing back to childhood. Furthermore, her increased need to depend on and be supported by others was discrepant with her self-image as a person who was in charge of herself and her life.

Therapy

Lee's therapy initially focused almost exclusively on restoring safety and independence schemas. Moving out of her home for a few months was essential as we worked through her terror of revictimization. Gradual exposure to her home began to take place about three months after the rape at her own initiative because living with her parents was too disruptive to her sense of independence. Her central concern has been, "How can I ever trust that I and my family will be safe again? I thought I was safe in the past and that was an illusion. How can I know that the precautions that I take, and have always taken, will protect me?" Initially, she was obsessed with the need to figure out ways that she could be absolutely safe. These obsessions bordered on magical thinking as she became preoccupied with predicting the future so that she could avoid danger.

The disruption to her frame of reference was also evident as she struggled to understand why the rape happened. The attribution that this was a random act of violence was not acceptable to her. She did not blame herself in any way for what happened. However, over the course of therapy she struggled with two attributions, both of which held different meanings for her. The first attribution was that perhaps there was something about her that had made her a target for her attacker. Although at one level, she knew that the rapist could not have singled her out, memories of the previous frightening encounter with a black male came to mind. Because she was raped by two black males, she also developed the attribution that some (but not all) black men hated white women and were seeking them out as targets. This stirred up racist feelings and a sense of fear whenever she was around blacks. The first attribution was associated with a sense of vulnerability while the second attribution was associated with feelings of rage at society as a whole and black men in particular. She eventually understood that her need to find a reason for what happened was a way of protecting herself from the painful knowledge that tragic events sometimes occur at random.

As Lee struggled with these issues, she continued to ruminate about how she could restore her previous sense of security. Six months into the therapy, the therapist very gently challenged her need to restore a belief in absolute safety. At first Lee ignored these interventions; then she became very angry with the therapist. When she finally assimilated what the therapist was saying, she was able to begin mourning the losses that inevitably accompany an accommodation or change in positive schemas. About nine months into the therapy, she was finally able to say, "I now accept that the world can be a dangerous place even though I will do everything in my power to make it safe for myself and my family. That's the best that I can do and I can live with that."

In the most recent phase of treatment, the therapy has shifted to a focus on intimacy schemas that were disrupted in the posttrauma environment. Although Lee has many supportive friends, many people have been unable to appreciate her experience and the fact that recovery takes a long time. As a result, she has struggled with a sense of alienation and estrangement from her friends and community and a desire to withdraw from others. This is compounded by a desire to protect other people from the knowledge that at times she still feels vulnerable and needy, an experience that disrupts her self-image as an independent person.

During the current phase of therapy, Lee has continued to mourn the loss of her previous self. She has stabilized to the point that she is no longer afraid every day and is able to sleep at night with the help of a mild tranquilizer. She continues to struggle with sadness about the fact that one terrible hour of her life could have such a profound impact on her entire life and sense of self. She has had to acknowledge and express sadness about the fact that she will never be the same, and she has had some hopeful glimpses of a future in which she will be able to resolve these losses and move on.

CASE #3: A VIETNAM VETERAN WITH STRONG DEPENDENCY NEEDS

This is the case of a Vietnam veteran with a history of childhood trauma.

Life History and Social Context

Ron is a 41-year-old married black man who grew up in a small industrial town. The youngest of six children, Ron was largely cared for by his older siblings as his parents were both employed full-time and did not apparently have sufficient resources to devote much time and attention to the children. Any spare resources generally were devoted to one of Ron's older sisters who had leukemia. Her death at age 10 sent the parents into a prolonged period of grief and relative neglect of the needs of the remaining children. The parents eventually separated, the older children left home prematurely, and the younger children, specifically Ron and his older brother, went to live with an aunt.

At the age of 18, Ron was drafted into the military and subsequently was sent to Vietnam where he did two tours of duty. While in Vietnam, he was wounded and left by his buddies who thought he was dead.

Upon returning to the states, Ron attended trade school and subsequently was employed on and off for several years in a variety of jobs. He was involved in many short, unsatisfying relationships with women, generally women several years his senior who were attracted by his fresh, boyish approach to life. He is an attractive man who seems younger than his years, and who is in a chronic state of mild depression.

The Self

Self Capacities and Ego Resources. Ron's self capacities are somewhat limited. He is readily thrown off course by external events; when things go wrong, he becomes depressed, angry, and distraught, demonstrating little ability to self-soothe. He spends much of his time alone, but tends to feel lonely when alone or when with others. It is only his external frame of reference, or his tendency to blame others for his problems, that prevents him from lapsing into self-loathing.

Ron's ego resources are not highly developed. He is a fairly bright man. He demonstrates little willpower and initiative. He shows limited awareness of his psychological needs, and has difficulty introspecting. His empathy for others is limited, as is his ability to form mature relations with others. He is capable of making self-protective judgments for the most part.

Central Psychological Needs and Schemas. His frame of reference includes a belief that he will eventually be recognized as an important or special person, but that his own best efforts to become productive and to be recognized are always sabotaged by others who do not respect or understand him. His orientation toward reinforcement is external, so that he does not display great initiative in his life.

Ron's most striking need is his need to depend upon others, coupled with his strong belief that others will let him down. In relations with women, this has manifested itself in his repeated attempts to form relationships by asking out someone new weekly, and his extreme sensitivity to signs of rejection. For example, if a woman responds to Ron's request for a first date by saying she has a partner and doesn't date, Ron experiences rage and feels she has injured him.

The obvious implication of his disturbed dependency/trust need is an inability to form intimate relations with others. This has resulted in a craving for intimacy, coupled with a belief that he will never be able to share his life with anyone. Other disrupted intimacy schemas include the belief that "women are only interested in losers."

Naturally, his inability to form the fulfilling relationship which he strongly desires results in negative self-esteem schemas and a recurring thought (which he dismisses quickly) that "something serious must be wrong with me." Because of his propensity to blame others for his disappointments, he also holds negative other-esteem schemas, such as the belief that most men demonstrate macho behavior because of their contempt for women and most women deserve this contempt.

The Traumatic Experiences

Central Aspects of the Traumatic Experience. Two traumas are central for Ron at this point in his treatment. The first is the traumatic loss of his beloved older sister who died of leukemia. Ron describes her as the one person in the family who took time for him, reading to him when he was young from her sick bed. Connected to this loss, of course, is the loss of his parents' time and attention, as well as their divorce several years later. This is a history of chronic loss and trauma which set the stage for Ron to feel neglected and to develop the belief that his own needs were not important.

The second central traumatic experience was his injury and abandonment in Vietnam. Ron reported that while he was lying in the bush, fearing his death through bleeding or attack and wondering which would come first, he also thought, "You can't count on people when you need them most." This negative trust schema relates quite clearly to his early childhood experience of neglect and abandonment.

Characteristics of the Traumatic Memories. Ron reports vivid images of connection with his sister, especially of those times they spent alone together reading and watching television just before she died. He recalls wanting her to take care of him and being aware that his parents expected him to be taking care of her because of her illness. This takes shape as a tangled web of memories of feeling guilty when she was reading to him and feeling angry when he was bringing her a glass of water. He has recurrent images of her pleading gaze just before she was taken to the hospital for the last time.

His second set of traumatic images revolves around the injury and abandonment in Vietnam. He recalls fantasizing both his death and his deliverance as he lay helpless in the bush. Because he lost consciousness before he was rescued, he has no images of his rescue. The images that plague him are those of his buddies moving away from him after they had concluded he was dead.

Psychological Adaptation and Its Relation to the Self. When he came to therapy, Ron reported a history of sleep difficulties, flashbacks, nightmares, difficulty concentrating, episodes of uncontrollable crying, and general feelings of despondency. He had been hospitalized for depression once, following a suicide attempt which was prompted by the breakup of a relationship with a woman whom Ron hoped to marry. That hospitalization led to the diagnosis of PTSD which resulted in his referral to the Institute for psychotherapy. Ron also had a long history of alcohol abuse. Although his level of use did not prevent him from holding a job, he did have a number of arrests for driving while under the influence of alcohol. When relationships with women did not go the way he hoped or when he was arrested for drunk driving, Ron would most often quit his job, stating that no employer would want an employee with these problems. The feelings of shame and his way of managing them relate back to his undeveloped self capacities as well as his unmet needs for esteem and dependency/trust.

Therapy

Ron used the first several therapy sessions to explain to the therapist how others thwarted his attempts to make something of himself. He also reported almost weekly some experience in which he felt "shot down" by a woman. Initially the therapy focused on building a trusting therapeutic relationship and on self work. Ron tested out in various ways whether the therapist would reject or abandon him. These included engaging in mildly seductive behavior with the therapist, then informing her that his therapist in the hospital ("a very attractive woman") had been more experienced and seemed to care more about him, then, gradually, risking talking about his rejections by other women to see how the therapist would respond.

The self work took the form of supportive interventions meant to ensure Ron's safety in future times of despair and exploring ways Ron might nurture himself. Because of his strong desire to be taken care of by someone else, the therapist framed this exploration in terms of his need for recognition rather than dependency. By saying, "Are there ways you can be good to yourself, give yourself some acknowledgment or recognition for the hard work you've committed to doing here?" rather than "Are there ways you can take care of yourself?" the therapist attempted to evoke a positive response.

Over time, Ron gradually began to internalize the therapist's soothing, accepting stance. As he came to trust the therapist, he was gradually able to present the facts surrounding his sister's death and eventually to explore the painful feelings and images. He has also talked about his terror at being abandoned in Vietnam and has begun to connect his disturbed trust schemas to both of these episodes. Perhaps the most difficult material ahead is the feeling of abandonment by his parents, material which he has yet to approach except in passing.

CASE #4: A FIERCELY INDEPENDENT ACCIDENT VICTIM WITH A HISTORY OF MULTIPLE TRAUMAS

This is the case of an incest survivor who came to therapy after a skiing accident.

Life History and Social Context

Wendy is a 43-year-old widowed white mother of two children. She grew up in an urban neighborhood, the eldest of five children living in close proximity to a large extended family. At an early age, Wendy had a great deal of responsibility for younger children, including cousins. Wendy's father left the family while Wendy was young; her mother subsequently married a man who did not express warmth to the children from the first marriage, and demanded of all of the children, "Think for yourself!" Her mother was somewhat passive and apparently felt comfortable giving Wendy the major mothering responsibilities, including meal preparation, grocery shopping, and babysitting at a young age.

After high school, Wendy put herself through college and graduate school and eventually obtained a responsible position as marketing executive in a large firm. Her estranged husband died in 1975. She had developed an active lifestyle, including traveling, skiing, and socializing with friends. She now lives alone, both of her children being in young adulthood and out of the house.

The Self

Self Capacities and Ego Resources. Overall, Wendy has reasonably well-developed self capacities. Prior to the skiing accident, she was able to tolerate strong affect, to be alone without being lonely, to calm herself when distraught, and to regulate her self-esteem. She had a positive sense of self-esteem.

Wendy's resources were also well-developed. She is a woman of enormous determination, her most striking resource. This, combined with well above average intelligence, enabled her to meet most challenges. She has a strong internal drive for personal growth. She was moderately able to perceive events without distortion, although at times she underestimated how demanding certain stressors were. When she first came to therapy, she was remarkably nonintrospective and had little understanding of her own psychological makeup. While she had the ability to view others from more than one perspective, and thus was capable of empathy, she was not able to apply this resource to herself. She appeared to have relied on her determination and intelligence to push her way through the various life problems she had encountered.

With respect to the resources that one relies upon to protect oneself from future harm, Wendy was able to foresee consequences, had confidence in her judgment, was able to establish mature relations with others (although her relationships with men were somewhat limited, as described below), was able to establish boundaries between herself and others (including a demanding family), and was able to make self-protective judgments.

Central Psychological Needs and Schemas. Wendy's early responsibility for younger siblings and cousins developed in her a comfort with taking charge, and moderate needs for power which she subsequently has been able to meet in mature ways, such as becoming a respected manager in various jobs. Her own lack of mothering combined with the early sexual abuse led her to believe she would have to take care of herself, resulting in strong needs for independence and, of course, related disruptions in trust/dependency schemas.

Another effect of the abuse and the abandonment by her husband was to disrupt intimacy schemas; she has friendships and sexual relationships with men but does not want to express love for or commit herself to a man. She has moderate needs for recognition, which, again, she has for the most part been able to meet through outstanding performance at work. Wendy's frame of reference includes an extremely strong internal locus of control and related attributional schemas (a willingness to look at her own role in anything that has happened, and an inability to accept that anyone else may have a role in her misfortune). She has historically been very hopeful about the future.

The Traumatic Experiences

Central Aspects of the Traumatic History. Wendy's childhood neighborhood was a tough one, and she often felt called upon to protect her siblings from physical harm, intervening in playground fights on many occasions. She herself was sexually abused by an uncle at a young age.

In addition, she has been involved in numerous automobile accidents, none of them apparently her own fault, many of which resulted in some physical injuries. During her marriage, she experienced the loss of a 2-year-old child who died of SIDS and another loss through an abortion. Toward the end of the marriage, her husband threatened to beat her, an incident which led to their eventual separation. About a year and a half before entering therapy, Wendy was involved in a skiing accident which left her with severe limitations upon her activity and physical pain. When she first came to therapy, she was unable to sit up or walk for more than about an hour at a time. She has been unemployed since the accident.

Characteristics of the Traumatic Memories. When Wendy first came to therapy, she talked about the effects of the skiing accident but did not describe it in detail for many weeks. Her memory of it appears complete. She revealed nothing of her traumatic history until memories began to return during therapy. Apparently she was aware of the sexual abuse although she had never talked about it; the extent to which these memories are whole is even yet unknown. She has vivid memories of the various automobile accidents and the death of her child.

Psychological Adaptation and Its Relation to the Self. This is a complex trauma case in that there is a recent trauma as well as a series of earlier traumatic events. Overall, Wendy's psychological adaptation was good until the skiing accident. Since that time, she had become increasingly depressed, being removed from her usual source of self-esteem and recognition (work) and experiencing the need to rely upon others for such fundamental aspects of survival as grocery shopping. In addition, this was the first time in her life that her activity was so limited that she could not keep the memories of the childhood abuse at bay. She stated, "I've got too much time to think." She reported sleep difficulties (never sleeping for more than a few hours at a time or more than five of every 24 hours), restlessness often to the point of agitation, an inability to concentrate enough to read or even to watch television, and a sense of hopelessness about her future.

Although she experienced a great deal of pain, she initially refused to consider taking any medication for this or for the depression, because of her strong need for independence. She had perhaps for the first time encountered a situation which could not be managed by bullheaded determination and increasing her activity level. In fact, the more she relied upon her usual means of coping with stress, the worse her physical condition became. Perhaps most important, her historical sense of hopefulness about the future had been deeply damaged by the experience of a year and a half of serious physical disability.

Therapy

Wendy came to therapy at the suggestion of her physician to help develop a better posttrauma adjustment. Wendy initially stated, "I don't believe this is all in my head." This has been a continuing issue in treatment; Wendy tends to equate "psychological" with "imaginary" and thus has had difficulty looking at psychological issues that might underlie or relate to her physical relapses.

Because Wendy was a relatively high-functioning woman with previously well-developed self capacities and ego resources, extensive self work was not necessary. Yet her self-esteem had suffered a gradual decline, and this had to be addressed through the therapy.

Because of the debilitating nature of her pain, therapy first focused on pain management, through hypnotherapy. Initially, therapy was mainly supportive in nature, working toward helping Wendy figure out how to get her physical needs met. This, of course, led into an exploration of the meanings of trust/dependency.

The therapist was initially unaware of the extensive trauma history. Early history-taking had not revealed much childhood trauma, yet Wendy's fierce independence suggested that something fundamental remained to be revealed. Discussions related to trust/dependency and independence, coupled with the use of relaxation and guided imagery, eventually (after about 12 sessions) led to the emergence of early memories of abuse.

Wendy was overwhelmed by the feelings that accompanied the memories of the sexual abuse. She grew agitated and distraught, and experienced a setback in her physical condition. She denied feeling angry with the therapist, but stated firmly that she did not want to deal with the earlier traumatic material because she felt she needed all of her emotional and psychological strength to deal with her current physical condition. The therapist respected this and worked, through hypnosis, to help Wendy seal over the traumatic memories again. (Wendy developed an image of herself putting the memories into a strong box and giving the box and the keys to the therapist.)

Despite this, and in part because of her continuing physical decline, Wendy continued to grow more deeply depressed. She eventually expressed that she was considering suicide. At this point, the therapist was able to hook Wendy's strong determination, expressing surprise that Wendy would ever give up on anything that was important to her. After a long and difficult weekend, Wendy accepted a referral to a local pain management program. Once she had made it through that very low point, Wendy was able to recommit herself to recovery. She accepted the pain management psychiatrist's recommendation for antidepressant medication.

Thereafter, therapy took a different turn. Because the pain management people took over the supportive aspects of therapy, this therapist was able to begin to focus with Wendy on finding new ways to meet her psychological needs and to maintain her self-esteem. But the traumatic material once again began to emerge, in a much less obvious way. After about two months on antidepressant medication, with a good response, Wendy suddenly began to experience wildly violent self-destructive fantasies and intense, inexplicable fear. The therapist suggested that the traumatic material was trying to get out of the box, a suggestion initially rejected by Wendy who thought that she must have something wrong with her physically. The therapist suggested Wendy check out this possibility with either the pain management psychiatrist or her own physician, but gently held to the hypothesis that it might be time to begin to look at the earlier traumatic material. This would require at least a six-month commitment to therapy, which Wendy has yet to decide upon. She had been in the course of planning a move to California when the skiing accident occurred, and her original postaccident plan was to make it to California "before the snow begins to fall again."

Wendy has stated that she realizes this is an important opportunity to do the trauma work, but that she may not be up to the task. The therapist believes and has conveyed to Wendy her belief that Wendy can do this work now because of her considerable resources and capacities, but will respect Wendy's decision. Meanwhile, Wendy has begun to talk in therapy about the loss of her son and the subsequent abortion which was prompted by her husband threatening her while she was pregnant and Wendy's belief that the marriage was no longer a safe environment for child-rearing.

SUMMARY

In this chapter we have described four cases that were conceptualized from the perspective of constructivist self development theory. We offer these more detailed case examples as a way of helping the clinician understand how the various aspects of the theory can be integrated to present a coherent and meaningful clinical picture, as well as providing guidance for understanding the therapy process. As mentioned earlier, we use a similar format for organizing formal case conferences at the Institute and encourage clinicians to discover the value of systematically conceptualizing case material in this way. Although it is a time-consuming process, we have found it to be valuable, providing new insights into the richness of clients' experiences as well as providing a useful framework for continued progress in therapy.

References

Abramson, L. Y., Seligman, M. E. P., & Teasdale, J. D. (1978). Learned helplessness in humans: Critique and reformulation, *Journal of Abnormal Psychology 87*, 49-74.

Adler, A. (1927). *The Practice and Theory of Individual Psychology.* New York: Harcourt, Brace & World.

Adler, A. (1935). The fundamental views of individual psychology. *International Journal of Individual Psychology, 1*, 5-8.

Adler, A. (1943). Neuropsychiatric complications in victims of Boston's Coconut Grove disaster. *Journal of the American Medical Association, 27*, 1098-1101.

Ansbacher, H. L., & Ansbacher, R. R. (Eds.). (1956). *The Individual Psychology of Alfred Adler.* New York: Basic Books.

Agosta, C., & Loring, M. (1988). Understanding and treating the adult retrospective victim of child sexual abuse. In S. Sgroi, (Ed.), *Vulnerable Populations: Evaluation and Treatment of Sexually Abused Children and Adult Survivors*, vol. 1 (pp. 115-135). Lexington, MA: Lexington Books, D.C. Heath & Co.

Ajzen, I., & Fishbein, M. (1977). Attitude-behavior relations: A theoretical analysis and review of empirical research. *Psychological Bulletin, 84*, 888-918.

Ajzen, I., & Fishbein, M. (1980). *Understanding Attitudes and Predicting Behavior*, Englewood Cliffs, NJ: Prentice-Hall.

Albee, G. W. (1982). Preventing psychopathology and promoting human potential. *American Psychologist, 37*, 1043-1050.

Albee, G. W. (1982). The politics of nature and nurture. *American Journal of Community Psychology, 10*, 4-36.

Allport, G. W. (1946). Personalistic psychology as a science: A reply. *Psychological Review, 53*, 132-135.

Allport, G. W. (1962). The general and unique in psychological science. *Journal of Personality, 30*, 405-422.

American Psychiatric Association. (1952). *Diagnostic and Statistical Manual of Mental Disorders* (1st ed.). Washington, DC: Author.

American Psychiatric Association. (1968). *Diagnostic and Statistical Manual of Mental Disorders* (2nd ed.). Washington, DC: Author.

American Psychiatric Association. (1980). *Diagnostic and Statistical Manual of Mental Disorders* (3rd ed.). Washington, DC: Author.

American Psychiatric Association. (1987). *Diagnostic and Statistical Manual of Mental Disorders*, (3rd ed., rev.). Washington, D.C.: Author.

Anderson, J. R., & Bower, G. H. (1980). *Human Associative Memory: A Brief Edition.* Hillsdale: Lawrence Erlbaum.

Andreasen, N. C. (1985). Post-traumatic stress disorder. In H. I. Kaplan, & B. J. Sadock (Eds.), *Comprehensive Textbook of Psychiatry* (pp. 918-923). Baltimore: Williams & Wilkins.

Appelbaum, S. A., & Katz, J. B. (1975). Self-help with diagnosis (A self-administered semi-projective device). *Journal of Personality Assessment, 39*, (4), 349-359.

Araji, S., & Finkelhor, D. (1986). Abusers: A review of the research. In D. Finkelhor (Ed.), *A Sourcebook on Child Sexual Abuse* (pp. 89-118). Beverly Hills, CA: Sage.

Atkeson, B. M., Calhoun, K. S., Resick, P. A., & Ellis, E.M., (1982). Victims of rape: Repeated assessment of depressive symptoms. *Journal of Consulting and Clinical Psychology*, 96-102.

Auster, P. (1987). *In the Country of Last Things*. New York: Viking Penguin.

Bagley, C., & Ramsey, R. (1985, February). *Disrupted childhood and vulnerability to sexual assault: Long-term sequels with implications for counseling*. Paper presented at the Conference on Counseling the Sexual Abuse Survivor, Winnepeg, Canada.

Baker, H. S., & Baker, M. N. (1987). Heinz Kohut's self psychology: An overview. *American Journal of Psychiatry, 144*, 1-9.

Bandura, A. (1977). Self-efficacy: Toward a unifying theory of behavioral change. *Psychological Review, 84*, 191-215.

Bard, M., & Connolly, H. (1982). *A Retrospective Study of Homicide Adaptation*. Rockville, MD: National Institute of Mental Health.

Bard, M., & Sangrey, D. (1986). *The Crime Victims' Book* (2nd ed.). New York: Brunner/Mazel.

Bard, M., Arnone, H. C., & Nemiroff, D. (1986). Contextual influences on the post-traumatic stress adaptation of homicide survivor-victims. In C. R. Figley (Ed.), *Trauma and its wake: The study and treatment of post-traumatic stress disorder* (vol. 2, pp. 292-304). New York: Brunner/Mazel.

Bartlett, F. C. (1932). *Remembering*. Cambridge, England: Cambridge University Press.

Bartlett, J. (1980). *Familiar Quotations* (15th ed.). Boston: Little, Brown & Company.

Baum, A., Fleming, R., & Singer, J. E. (1983). Coping with victimization by technological disaster. *Journal of Social Issues, 39*, 117-138.

Beck, A. T. (1967). *Depression: Clinical, Experimental and Theoretical Aspects*. NY: Harper & Row.

Beck, A. T. (1976). *Cognitive Therapy and the Emotional Disorders*. Connecticut: International Universities Press, Inc.

Beck, A. T., & Emery, G. (1985). *Anxiety disorders and phobias*. New York: Basic Books.

Becker, J. V., Skinner, L. J., Abel, G. G., & Cichon, J. (1986). Level of postassault sexual functioning in rape and incest victims. *Archives of Sexual Behavior, 15*, 37-49.

Bellah, R. N., Madsen, R., Sullivan, W. M., Swidler, A., & Topton, S. M. (1985). *Habits of the Heart: Individualism and Commitment in American Life*. Berkeley, CA: University of California Press.

Benedek, E. P. (1984). The silent scream: Countertransference reactions to victims. *The American Journal of Social Psychiatry, 4*(3), 49-52.

Bernstein, E. M., & Putnam, F. W. (1986). Development, reliability, and validity of a dissociation scale. *Journal of Nervous and Mental Disease, 174*, 727-735.

Black, W. J. (1928). *The Works of Henrik Ibsen*. New York: Black Readers' Service Company.

Blanchard, E. B., Kolb, L. C., Pallmeyer, T. P., & Gerardi, R. J. (1982). A psychophysiological study of post traumatic stress disorder in Vietnam veterans. *Psychiatric Quarterly, 54*, 220-228.

Blank, A. S. (1985b). The Veterans Administration's Vietnam veterans outreach and counseling centers. In S. M. Sonnenberg, A. S. Blank, & J. A. Talbott (Eds.), *The Trauma of War: Stress and Recovery in Vietnam Veterans* (pp. 227-261). Washington, D.C.: American Psychiatric Press.

Blank, A. S. (1987). Irrational reactions to post-traumatic stress disorder and Vietnam veterans. In S. M. Sonnenberg (Ed.), *The Trauma of War: Stress and Recovery in Vietnam Veterans*. Washington, D. C.: American Psychiatric Association Press.

Blank, A. (1989, June). *Principles of psychotherapeutic treatment of PTSD in war veterans*. Paper presented at Psychobiological Aspects of Catastrophic Trauma, New Haven, CT.

Blatt, S. J., & Erlich, H. S. (1982). Levels of resistance in the psychotherapeutic process. In P. L. Wachtel (Ed.), *Resistance: Psychodynamic and Behavioral Approaches* (pp. 69-91). New York: Plenum Press.

Bliss, E. (1980). Multiple personalities: A report of 14 cases with implications for schizophrenia and hysteria. *Archives of General Psychiatry, 37*, 1388-97.

Bowen, G. R., & Lambert, J. A. (1986). Systematic desensitization therapy with post-traumatic stress disorder cases. In C. R. Figley (Ed.), *Trauma and its Wake: The Study and Treatment of Post-Traumatic Stress Disorder* (Vol. 2, pp. 280-291). New York: Brunner/Mazel.

Bower, G. H. (1981). Mood and memory. *American Psychologist, 36,* 129-148.

Bowlby, J. (1969). *Attachment and Loss: Vol. I. Attachment.* London: Hogarth.

Braun, B. G., & Sachs, R. G. (1985). The development of multiple personality disorder: Predisposing, precipitating, and perpetuating factors. In R. P. Kluft (Ed.), *Childhood Antecedents of Multiple Personality* (pp. 38-64). Washington: American Psychiatric Press, Inc.

Braun, B. G. (1979, November). *Clinical aspects of multiple personality.* Presented at the Annual Meeting of the American Society for Clinical Hypnosis, San Francisco, CA.

Braun, B. G. (1983). Neurophysiologic changes in multiple personality due to integration: A preliminary report. *American Journal of Clinical Hypnosis, 26,* 84-92.

Braun, B. G. (1983). Psychophysiologic phenomena in multiple personality and hypnosis. *American Journal of Clinical Hypnosis, 26,* 124-137.

Braun, B. G. (1984). *Towards a theory of multiple personality and other dissociative phenomena.* Psychiatric Clinics of North America, 7(1), 171-193.

Braun, B. G. (1984). Uses of hypnosis with multiple personality disorder. *Psychiatric Annals, 14,* 34-40.

Brende, J. O., & Benedict, B. D. (1980). The Vietnam combat delayed stress response syndrome: Hypnotherapy of "dissociative symptoms". *The American Journal of Clinical Hypnosis, 23,* 34-40.

Brende, J. O., & McCann, I. L. (1984). Regressive experiences in Vietnam veterans: Their relationship to war, post-traumatic symptoms and recovery. *Journal of Contemporary Psychotherapy, 14,* 57-75.

Brende, J. O., & Parson, E. R. (1985). *Vietnam Veterans: The Road to Recovery.* New York: Plenum Press.

Brende, J. O. (1983). A psychodynamic view of character pathology in Vietnam combat veterans. *Bulletin of the Menninger Clinic, 47,* 193-216.

Brende, J. O. (1985). The use of hypnosis in post-traumatic conditions. In W. E. Kelly (Ed.), *Post-Traumatic Stress Disorder and the War Veteran Patient,* (pp. 193-210). New York: Brunner/Mazel.

Breslau, N., & Davis, G. C. (1989). Chronic posttraumatic stress disorder in Vietnam veterans. *The Harvard Medical School Mental Health Letter, 5,* 3-5.

Brett, E. A., & Mangine, W. (1985). Imagery and combat stress in Vietnam veterans. *The Journal of Nervous and Mental Disease, 173,* 309-311.

Brett, E. A., & Ostroff, R. (1985). Imagery and posttraumatic stress disorder: An overview. *American Journal of Psychiatry, 142,* 417-424.

Brett, E. (1988). *Coping with catastrophe.* Workshop presented at Connecticut Valley Hospital, November 8, 1988.

Brett, E. A. (in press). Recent psychoanalytic contributions to a model of traumatic stress. In J. P. Wilson & B. Raphael (Eds.), *International Handbook of Traumatic Stress Syndromes.* New York: Plenum Press.

Brett, E. A., Spitzer, R. L., Williams, J. B. W. (1988). DSM-III-R criteria for post-traumatic stress disorder. *American Journal of Psychiatry, 145,* 1232-1236.

Breuer, J., & Freud, S. (1895). Studies on hysteria. In J. Strachey (Ed.), *The standard edition of the complete psychological works of Sigmund Freud* (Vol. 2, pp. 1-19). London: The Hogarth Press (Original Work published, 1955).

Briere, J., & Runtz, M. (1985, August). *Symptomatology associated with prior sexual abuse in an non-clinical sample.* Paper presented at the annual meeting of the American Psychological Association, Los Angeles.

Briere, J. (1984, April). *The effects of childhood sexual abuse on later psychological functioning: Defining a post-sexual-abuse syndrome.* Paper presented at the Third National Conference on Sexual Victimization of Children, Washington, D.C.

Brill, N. Q. (1967). Gross stress reactions: II Traumatic war neuroses. In A. M. Freedman & H. L. Kaplan, (Eds.), *Comprehensive Textbook of Psychiatry* (pp. 1031-1035). Baltimore: Williams and Wilkins.

Brown, D. P., & Fromm, E. (1986). *Hypnotherapy and Hypnoanalysis*. Hillsdale, NJ: Lawrence Erlbaum Associates.

Brown, C. A., Feldberg, R., Fox, E. M., & Kohen, J. (1976). Divorce: Chance of a new lifetime. *Journal of Social Issues, 32,* 119-133.

Bryer, J. B., Miller, J. B., Nelson, B. A., & Krol, P. A. (1986, August). *Adult psychiatric symptoms, diagnoses, and medications as indicators of childhood abuse.* Paper presented at 94th Annual Convention of the American Psychological Association, Washington, DC.

Bulman, R., & Wortman, C. B. (1977). Attributions of blame and coping with the "real world": Severe accident victims react to their lot. *Journal of Personality and Social Psychology, 35,* 351-363.

Burgess, A. W., & Holmstrom, L. L. (1974). Rape trauma syndrome. *American Journal of Psychiatry, 131,* 981-985.

Burgess, A. W., & Holmstrom, L. L. (1974). *Rape: Victims of Crisis.* Bowie, MD: R. J. Brady.

Burgess, A. W., & Holmstrom, L. L. (1979). Rape: Sexual disruption and recovery. *American Journal of Orthopsychiatry, 49,* 648-657.

Burgess, A. W., & Holmstrom, L. L. (1979). Adaptive strategies and recovery from rape. *American Journal of Psychiatry, 136,* 1278-1282.

Burgess, A. W., Hartman, C. R., McCausland, M. P., & Powers, P. (1984). Response patterns in children and adolescents exploited through sex rings and pornography. *American Journal of Psychiatry, 141,* 656-662.

Burt, M. R., & Katz, B. L. (1987). Dimensions of recovery from rape: Focus on growth outcomes. *Journal of Interpersonal Violence, 2,* 57-82.

Burt, M. R. (1980). Cultural myths and supports for rape. *Journal of Personality and Social Psychology, 38,* 217-230.

Calhoun, K. S., Atkeson, B. M., & Resick, P. A. (1982). A longitudinal examination of fear reactions in victims of rape. *Journal of Counseling Psychology, 29,* 655-661.

Calvert, W. E., & Hutchinson, R. L. (1989, August). *Vietnam veteran levels of combat: Perceived and actual violence.* Paper presented at the annual meeting of the American Psychological Association, New Orleans, LA.

Camus, A. (1958). *Caligula and Three Other Plays.* New York: Alfred A. Knopf, Inc.

Carmen, E., Rieker, P. R., & Mills, R. (1984). Victims of violence and psychiatric illness. *American Journal of Psychiatry, 141,* 378-383.

Carroll, E. M., Rueger, D. B., Foy, D. W., & Donahoe, C. P. (1985). Vietnam combat veterans with posttraumatic stress disorder: Analysis of marital and cohabitating adjustment. *Journal of Abnormal Psychology, 94,* 329-337.

Center for Policy Research. (1979). *The adjustment of Vietnam era veterans to civilian life.* New York.

Chekhov, A. (1947). Gooseberries. In D. Angus (Ed.) (1962), *The Best Short Stories of the Modern Age* (pp. 27-37). Greenwich, CT: Fawcett Publications.

Cheng, N. (1986). *Life and Death in Shanghai.* New York: Grove Press.

Chessick, R. D. (1974). *The Technique and Practice of Intensive Psychotherapy.* New York: Jason Aronson.

Chessick, R. D. (1978). The sad soul of the psychiatrist. *Bulletin of the Menninger Clinic, 42,* 1-9.

Chessick, R. D. (1985). *Psychology of the Self and the Treatment of Narcissism.* Northvale, NJ: Jason Aronson.

Chodoff, P., Friedman, S. B., & Hamburg, D. A. (1964). Stress, defenses and coping behavior: Observations in parents of children with malignant disease. *American Journal of Psychiatry, 120,* 743-749.

Cole, C. H., & Barney, E. E. (1987). Safeguards and the therapeutic window: A group treatment strategy for adult incest survivors. *American Journal of Orthopsychiatry, 57,* 601-608.

Courtois, C. A. (1979). The incest experience and its aftermath. *Victimology: An International Journal, 4,* 337-347.

Courtois, C. A. (1979). Victims of rape and incest. *The Counseling Psychologist, 8,* 38-39.

Courtois, C. A. (1988). *Healing the Incest Wound: Adult Survivors in Therapy.* New York: W. W. Norton & Company.

Cummings, C., Gordon, J. R., & Marlatt, G. A. (1980). Relapse: Prevention and prediction. In W. R. Miller (Ed.), *The Addictive Behaviors.* Elmsford, NY: Pergamon Press.

Danieli, Y. (1981). Therapists' difficulties in treating survivors of the Nazi Holocaust and their children. *Dissertations Abstracts International, 42,* 4947-B.

Danieli, Y. (1985). The treatment and prevention of long-term effects and intergenerational transmission of victimization: A lesson from Holocaust survivors and their children. In C. R. Figley (Ed.), *Trauma and Its Wake: The Study and Treatment of Post-Traumatic Stress Disorder* (pp. 295-313). New York: Brunner/Mazel.

Danieli, Y. (1988). Confronting the unimaginable. Psychotherapists' reactions to victims of the Nazi Holocaust. In J. P. Wilson, Z. Harel, & B. Kahana (Eds.), *Human Adaptation to Extreme Stress* (pp. 219-238). New York: Plenum Publishing Corporation.

Davidson, L. M., & Baum, A. (1986). Chronic stress and post-traumatic stress disorders. *Journal of Consulting and Clinical Psychology, 54,* 303-308.

Davidson, L. M., Fleming, I., & Baum, A. (1986). Post-traumatic stress as a function of chronic stress and toxic exposure. In C. R. Figley (Ed.), *Trauma and Its Wake: The Study and Treatment of Post-Traumatic Stress Disorder* (vol. 2, pp. 57-77). New York: Brunner/Mazel.

Dean, R. K. (1988, July). Post-traumatic stress disorder in adult children of alcoholics. *The Counselor,* pp. 11-13.

DeFazio, V. J., Rustin, S., & Diamond, A. (1975). Symptom development in Vietnam era veterans. *American Journal of Orthopsychiatry, 45,* 158-163.

Deighton, J., & McPeek, P. (1985). Group treatment: Adult victims of childhood sexual abuse. *Social Casework, 66,* 403-410.

Deutsch, C. J. (1984). Self-reported sources of stress among psychotherapists. *Professional Psychology: Research and Practice, 15,* 833-845.

Dewald, P. A. (1969). *Psychotherapy: A Dynamic Approach.* New York: Basic Books.

Dewald, P. A. (1982). Psychoanalytic perspectives on resistance. In P. L. Wachtel (Ed.), *Resistance: Psychodynamic and Behavioral Approaches* (pp. 45-68). New York: Plenum Press.

Dobbs, D., & Wilson, W. (1960). Observations on persistance of war neurosis. *Diseases of the Nervous System, 21,* 686-691.

Dollinger, S. J., O'Donnell, J. P., & Staley, A. A. (1984). Lightning-strike disaster: Effects on children's fears and worries. *Journal of Consulting and Clinical Psychology, 52,* 1028-1038.

Dostoyevsky, F. (1944). *Crime and Punishment.* New York: Random House.

Downing, N. E. (1988). A conceptual model for victim services. *The Counseling Psychologist, 16*(4), 595-629.

Edelstein, G. M. (1981). *Trauma, Trance, and Transformation: A Clinical Guide to Hypnotherapy.* New York: Brunner/Mazel.

Egendorf, A., Kadushin, C., Laufer, R., Rothbart, G., & Sloan, L. (1981). *Legacies of Vietnam: Comparative Adjustment of Veterans and Their Peers.* (Publication No. V101 134 p-630). Washington, DC: U.S. Government Printing Office.

Eich, J. E. (1980). The cue-dependent nature of state-dependent retrieval. *Memory & Cognition, 8,* 157-173.

Ellenson, G. S. (1985). Detecting a history of incest: A predictive syndrome. *Social Casework: Journal of Contemporary Social Work, 66,* 525-532.

Ellis, E. M., Atkeson, B. M., & Calhoun, K. S. (1981). An assessment of long-term reaction to rape. *Journal of Abnormal Psychology, 90,* 263-266.

Ellman, R. (1976). *The New Oxford Book of American Verse.* New York: Oxford University Press.

Emerson, R. W. (1865). *Essays.* New York: Houghton Mifflin Company.

English, E. S. (1976). The emotional stress of psychotherapeutic practice. *Journal of American Academy of Psychoanalysis, 4,* 191-201.

Epstein, S., & Erskine, N. (1983). The development of personal theories of reality. In D. Magnusson & V. Allen (Eds.), *Human Development: An Interactional Perspective.* New York: Academic Press.

Epstein, S. (1985). The implications of cognitive-experiential self-theory for research in social psychology and personality. *Journal for the Theory of Social Behaviour, 15,* 283-310.

Epstein, S. (in press a). The self-concept, the traumatic neurosis, and the structure of personality. In D. Ozer, J. M. Healy, Jr., & A. J. Stewart (Eds.), *Perspectives on Personality* (Vol. 3). Greenwich, CT: JAI Press.

Epstein, S. (in press b). Cognitive experiential self-theory. In L. Pervin (Ed.), *Handbook of Personality Theory and Research.* NY: Guilford Publications, Inc.

Erikson, M. H., & Rossi, E. L. (1979). *Hypnotherapy: An Exploratory Casebook.* New York: Irvington.

Erikson, E. H. (1963). *Childhood and Society* (2nd ed.). New York: Norton.

Erikson, K. (1976). *Everything in its Path: Destruction of Community in the Buffalo Creek Flood.* New York: Simon & Schuster.

Erikson, K. T. (1976). Loss of communality at Buffalo Creek. *American Journal of Psychiatry, 133,* 302-305.

Eth, S., & Pynoos, R. (1985). Developmental perspective on psychic trauma in childhood. In C. R. Figley (Ed.), *Trauma and Its Wake: The Study and Treatment of Post-Traumatic Stress Disorder* (pp. 36-52). New York: Brunner/Mazel.

Fairbank, J. A., & Keane, T. M. (1982). Flooding for combat-related stress disorders: Assessment of anxiety reduction across traumatic memories. *Behavior Therapy, 13*(4), 499-510.

Farber, B. A. (1985). The genesis, development, and implications of psychological-mindedness among psychotherapists. *Psychotherapy, 22,* 170-177.

Feldman-Summers, S., Gordon, P. E., & Meagher, J. R. (1979). The impact of rape on sexual satisfaction. *Journal of Abnormal Psychology, 88,* 101-105.

Fenichel, O. (1945). *The psychoanalytic theory of neurosis.* New York: Norton.

Figley, C. R., & Burge, S. K. (1983). *Social support: Theory and measurement.* Presented at the Groves Conference on Marriage and the Family, Freeport, Grand Bahama Island, 1983.

Figley, C. R., & Leventman, S. (Ed.). (1980). *Strangers at Home: Vietnam Veterans Since the War.* New York: Praeger. (Reprinted 1990, Brunner/Mazel, New York)

Figley, C. R. (Ed.), (1978). *Stress Disorders Among Vietnam Veterans: Theory, Research, and Treatment.* New York: Brunner/Mazel.

Figley, C. R. (1983). Catastrophes: An overview of family reaction. In C. R. Figley & H. I. McCubbin (Eds.), *Stress and the Family: Coping with Catastrophe,* (Vol. 2, pp. 3-20). New York: Brunner/Mazel.

Figley, C. R. (Ed.). (1985). *Trauma and its Wake: The Study and Treatment of Post-Traumatic Stress Disorder.* New York: Brunner/Mazel.

Figley, C. R. (1985). From victim to survivor: Social responsibility in the wake of catastrophe. In C. R. Figley (Ed.), *Trauma and its Wake: The Study and Treatment of Post-Traumatic Stress Disorder* (pp. 398-415). New York: Brunner/Mazel.

Figley, C. R. (1986). Traumatic stress: The role of the family and social support. In C. R. Figley (Ed.), *Trauma and Its Wake: The Study and Treatment of Post-Traumatic Stress Disorder* (Vol. 2, pp. 39-56). New York: Brunner/Mazel.

Figley, C. R. (1988). Toward a field of traumatic stress. *Journal of Traumatic Stress, 1,* 3-16.

Figley, C. R. (1988). A five-phase treatment of post-traumatic stress disorder in families. *Journal of Traumatic Stress, 1,* 127-141.

Fine, C. G. (1989). The cognitive sequelae of incest. In R. P. Kluft (Ed.), *Incest Related Syndromes and Adult Psychopathologies.* Washington: American Psychiatric Association.

Finkelhor, D., & Browne, A. (1985). The traumatic impact of child sexual abuse: A conceptualization. *American Journal of Orthopsychiatry, 55,* 530-541.

Finkelhor, D. (1984). *Child Sexual Abuse: New Theory and Research.* New York: Free Press.

Finkelhor, D. (1986). Abusers: Special topics. In D. Finkelhor (Ed.), *A Sourcebook on Child Sexual Abuse* (pp. 119-142). Beverly Hills, CA: Sage.

Fogelman, E., & Savran, B. (1980). Brief group therapy with offspring of holocaust survivors: Leaders reactions. *American Journal of Orthopsychiatry, 50*(1), 96-108.

Fox, R. P. (1974). Narcissistic rage and the problem of combat aggression. *Archives of General Psychiatry, 31,* 807-811.

Foy, D. W., Donahoe, C. P., Carroll, E. M., Gallers, J., & Reno, R. (1987). Post-traumatic stress disorder. In L. Michelson & L. M. Ascher (Eds.). *Anxiety and Stress Disorders: Cognitive-Behavioral Assessment and Treatment,* (pp. 361-378). New York: Guilford Press.

Foy, D. W., Sipprelle, R. C., Rueger, D. B., & Carroll, E. M. (1984). Etiology of post-traumatic stress disorder in Vietnam veterans: Analysis of premilitary, military, combat exposure influences. *Journal of Consulting and Clinical Psychology, 52,* 79-87.

Frank, J. D. (1974). *Persuasion and Healing: A Comparative Study of Psychotherapy (rev. ed.).* New York: Schocken Books.

Frank, J. B., Kosten, T. R., Giller, E. L. Jr., & Dan, E. (1988). A randomized clinical trial of phenelzine and imipramine for posttraumatic stress disorder. *American Journal of Psychiatry, 145,* 1289-1291.

Frank, E., Turner, S. M., & Duffy, B. (1979). Depressive symptoms in rape victims. *Journal of Affective Disorders, 1,* 269-277.

Frank, E., Turner, S. M., & Stewart, B. D. (1980). Initial response to rape: The impact of factors within the rape situation. *Journal of Behavioral Assessment, 2*(1), 39-53.

Frankl, V. E. (1963). *Man's Search for Meaning.* New York: Washington Square Press.

Fraser, S. (1988). *My Father's House: A Memoir of Incest and of Healing.* New York: Ticknor & Fields.

Frederick, C. (1980). Effects of natural vs. human-induced violence. In L. Kivens (Ed.), *Evaluation and Change: Services for Survivors* (pp. 71-75). Minneapolis, MN: Minneapolis Medical Research Foundation.

Freud, S. (1953). *The Interpretation of Dreams.* Standard edition (Vol. 5). London: Hogarth Press, 1953. (Original Work published, 1900).

Freud, S. (1925). An autobiographical study. In J. Strachey (Ed.), *The Standard Edition of the Complete Psychological Works of Sigmund Freud* (Vol. 18). London: The Hogarth Press (Original Work published 1920).

Freud, S. (1953). Beyond the pleasure principle. In J. Strachey (Ed. and Trans.), *The Standard Edition of the Complete Psychological Works of Sigmund Freud* (Vol. 18). London: The Hogarth Press. (Original Work published 1920).

Freud, S. (1959). Inhibitions, symptoms, and anxiety. In J. Strachey (Ed. and Trans.), *The Standard Edition of the Complete Psychological Works of Sigmund Freud* (Vol. 20, pp. 77-175). London: The Hogarth Press. (Original Work published in 1926).

Freud, S. (1961). *Civilization and its Discontents* (J. Strachey, Trans. and Ed.). New York: W. W. Norton & Company. (Original Work published 1930).

Freud, S. (1964). Moses and monotheism. In J. Strachey (Ed. and Trans.), *The Standard Edition of the Complete Psychological Works of Sigmund Freud* (Vol. 23). London: The Hogarth Press. (Original Work published 1939).

Freud, S. (1946). *The Ego and the Mechanisms of the Defense.* New York: International Universities Press.

Freud, S. (1967). Comments on trauma. In S. S. First (Ed.), *Psychic Trauma* (pp. 235-245). New York: Basic Books.

Freudenberger, H. J., & Robbins, A. (1979). The hazards of being a psychoanalyst. *The Psychoanalytic Review, 66*(2), 274-296.

Freyberg, J. T. (1980). Difficulties in separation-individuation as experienced by offspring of Nazi Holocaust survivors. *American Journal of Orthopsychiatry, 50,* 87-95.

Frick, R., & Bogart, L. (1982). Transference and countertransference in group therapy with Vietnam veterans. *Bulletin of the Menninger Clinic, 46,* 429-444.

Frieze, I. H., Hymer, S., & Greenberg, M. S. (1987). Describing the crime victim: Psychological reactions to victimization. *Professional Psychology: Research and Practice, 18,* 299-315.

Fromm, E. (1955). *The Sane Society.* New York: Rinehart.

Garte, S. H. (1985). Still in Vietnam: Arrested career maturity in Vietnam veterans with post-traumatic stress disorder. *Psychotherapy in Private Practice, 3,* 49-53.

Garte, S. H. (1986). *Sexuality and intimacy in Vietnam veterans with post-traumatic stress disorder (PTSD).* Unpublished manuscript.

Gelinas, D. J. (1983). The persisting negative effects of incest. *Psychiatry, 46,* 312-332.

Gelinas, D. (1988). Family therapy: Critical early structuring. In S. Sgroi (Ed.), *Vulnerable Populations: Evaluation and Treatment of Sexually Abused Children and Adult Survivors* (Vol. 1, pp. 52-87). Lexington, MA: Lexington Books, D. C. Heath & Co.

Gelles, R. J., & Cornell, C. P. (1985). *Intimate Violence in Families.* Beverly Hills, CA: Sage.

Gelles, R. J. (1978). Violence toward children in the United States. *American Journal of Orthopsychiatry, 48,* 580-591.

Gergen, K. J. (1968). Personal consistency and the presentation of self. In C. Gordon & K. J. Gergen, *The Self in Social Interaction,* vol. 1, pp. 299-308. New York: Wiley.

Gil, T., Calev, A., Greenberg, D., Kugelmass, S., & Lerer, B. (1990). Cognitive functioning in post-traumatic stress disorder. *Journal of Traumatic Stress, 3*(1), 29–46.

Giller, E. L. (Ed.) (1990). *Biological assessment and treatment of posttraumatic stress disorder.* Washington, D.C.: American Psychiatric Press, Inc.

Gilligan, C. (1982). *In a Different Voice.* Cambridge, MA: Harvard University Press.

Gleser, G. C., Green, B. L., & Winget, C. N. (1981). *Prolonged Psychosocial Effects of Disaster: A Study of Buffalo Creek.* New York: Academic Press.

Glover, H. (1984). Survival guilt and the Vietnam veteran. *The Journal of Nervous and Mental Disease, 172,* 393-397.

Glover, H. (1984). Themes of mistrust and the posttraumatic stress disorder in Vietnam veterans. *American Journal of Psychotherapy, 37,* 445-452.

Glover, H. (1988). Four syndromes of post-traumatic stress disorder: Stressors and conflicts of the traumatized with special focus on the Vietnam combat veteran. *Journal of Traumatic Stress, 1,* 57-78.

Gold, E. R. (1986). Long-term effects of sexual victimization in childhood: An attributional approach. *Journal of Consulting and Clinical Psychology, 54,* 471-475.

Goldfried, M. R., & Robins, C. (1983). Self-schema, cognitive bias, and the processing of therapeutic experience. In P. C. Kendall (Ed.), *Advances in Cognitive-Behavioral Research and Therapy* (Vol. 2, pp. 33-80). New York: Guilford Press.

Goodman, B., & Nowak-Scibelli, D. (1985). Group treatment for women incestuously abused as children. *International Journal of Group Psychotherapy, 35,* 531-544.

Green, B. L., Grace, M. C., & Gleser, G. C. (1985). Identifying survivors at risk: Long-term impairment following the Beverly Hills Supper Club fire. *Journal of Consulting and Clinical Psychology, 53,* 672-678.

Green, B. L., Wilson, J. P., & Lindy, J. D. (1985). Conceptualizing post-traumatic stress disorder: A psychosocial framework. In C. R. Figley (Ed.), *Trauma and Its Wake: The*

Study and Treatment of Post-Traumatic Stress Disorder (pp. 53-69). New York: Brunner/Mazel.

Greenberg, M. S., & van der Kolk, B. A. (1987). Retrieval and integration of traumatic memories with the "painting cure". In B. A. van der Kolk (Ed.), *Psychological Trauma* (pp. 191-215). Washington, DC: American Psychiatric Press.

Greenson, R. R. (1967). *The Technique and Practice of Psychoanalysis* (vol. 1). New York: International Universities Press, Inc.

Greenwald, M. A. (1987). Programming treatment generalization. In L. Michelson & L. M. Ascher (Eds.), *Anxiety and Stress Disorders* (pp. 583-616). New York: Guilford Press.

Grinker, R., & Spiegel, J. (1945). *Men Under Stress*. Philadelphia: Blakiston.

Groth, A. N., & Burgess, A. W. (1980). Male rape: Offenders and victims. *American Journal of Psychiatry, 137,* 806-810.

Guy, J. D. (1987). *The personal life of the psychotherapist.* New York: John Wiley & Sons.

Haley, S. A. (1974). When the patient reports atrocities. *Archives of General Psychiatry, 30,* 191-196.

Haley, S. A. (1985). Some of my best friends are dead: Treatment of the PTSD patient and his family. In W. E. Kelly (Ed.), *Post-Traumatic Stress Disorder and the War Veteran Patient* (pp. 54-70). New York: Brunner/Mazel.

Hall, C. S., & Lindzey, G. (1978). *Theories of Personality* (3rd ed.). New York: John Wiley & Sons.

Harlow, H. F. (1974). *Learning to Love* (rev. ed.). New York: Aronson.

Harter, S., Alexander, P. C., & Neimeyer, R. A. (1988). Long-term effects of incestuous child abuse in college women: Social adjustment, social cognition, and family characteristics. *Journal of Consulting and Clinical Psychology, 56,* 5-8.

Head, H. (1920). *Studies in Neurology.* New York: Oxford University Press.

Hearst, N., Newman, T. B., & Hulley, S. B. (1986). Delayed effects of the military draft on mortality: A randomized natural experiment. *New England Journal of Medicine, 314,* 620-624.

Helzer, J. E., Robins, L. N., Wish, E., & Hesselbrock, M. (1979). Depression in Vietnam veterans and civilian controls. *American Journal of Psychiatry, 136,* 526-529.

Hendin, H., & Haas, A. P. (1984). *Wounds of War: The Psychological Aftermath of Combat in Vietnam.* New York: Basic Books.

Hendin, H., & Haas, A. P. (1984). Combat adaptations of Vietnam veterans without posttraumatic stress disorders. *American Journal of Psychiatry, 141,* 956-960.

Herman, J., & Schatzow, E. (1984). Time-limited group therapy for women with a history of incest. *International Journal of Group Psychotherapy, 34,* 605-616.

Herman, J. L. (1981). *Father-Daughter Incest.* Cambridge, MA: Harvard University Press.

Herman, J. (1981). Father-daughter incest. *Professional Psychology, 12,* 76-80.

Herman, J. L., Perry, C., & van der Kolk, B. A. (1989). Childhood trauma in borderline personality disorder. *American Journal of Psychiatry, 146*(4), 490-495.

Herrington, L. H. (1985). Victims of crime: Their plight, our concern. *American Psychologist, 40,* 99-103.

Hersey, J. (1963). *Hiroshima.* New York: Knopf.

Hilberman, E., & Munson, K. (1977-1978). Sixty battered women. *Victimology: An International Journal, 2*(3-4), 460-470.

Hilberman, E. (1980). Overview: The "wife-beater's wife" reconsidered. *American Journal of Psychiatry, 137,* 1336-1346.

Horevitz, R. P., & Braun, B. G. (1984). Are multiple personalities borderline: An analysis of 33 cases. *Psychiatric Clinics of North America, 7*(1), 69-87.

Horner, A. J. (1984). *Object Relations and the Developing Ego in Therapy.* New York: Jason Aronson, Inc.

Horner, A. (1986). *Being and Loving.* Northvale, NJ: Jason Arson.

Horowitz, M., & Solomon, G. F. (1975). A prediction of delayed stress response syndromes in Vietnam veterans. *Journal of Social Issues, 31*(4), 67-81.

Horowitz, M. J. (1973). Phase-oriented treatment of stress response syndromes. *American Journal of Psychotherapy, 27*, 506-515.

Horowitz, M. (1974). Stress response syndromes: Character style and dynamic psychotherapy. *Archives of General Psychiatry, 31*, 768-780.

Horowitz, M. J. (1975). Intrusive and repetitive thoughts after experimental stress. *Archives of General Psychiatry, 32*, 1457-1463.

Horowitz, M. J. (1976). *Stress Response Syndromes*. New York: Jason Aronson.

Horowitz, M. J. (1979). Psychological response to serious life events. In V. Hamilton & D. M. Warburton (Eds.), *Human Stress and Cognition: An Information-Processing Approach* (pp. 235-263). New York: Wiley.

Horowitz, M. (1986). *Stress Response Syndromes* (2nd ed.). New York: Aronson.

Horowitz, M. J., Marmar, C., Weiss, D., DeWitt, K., & Rosenbaum, R. (1984). Brief psychotherapy of bereavement reactions. *Archives of General Psychiatry, 41*, 438-448.

Hymer, S. (1984). The self in victimization: Developmental versus conflict perspectives. *Victimology: An International Journal, 9*, 142-150.

Jaffe, P., Wolfe, D., Wilson, S. K., & Zak, L. (1986). Family violence and child adjustment: A comparative analysis of girls' and boys' behavioral symptoms. *American Journal of Psychiatry, 143*, 74-77.

Jaffe, P., Wolfe, D., Wilson, S., & Zak, L. (1986). Similarities in behavioral and social maladjustment among child victims and witnesses to family violence. *American Journal of Orthopsychiatry, 56*, 142-146.

James, J., & Meyerding, J. (1977). Early Sexual Experience and Prostitution. *American Journal of Psychiatry, 134*, 1381-1384.

Janet, P. (1925). *Psychological healing: A Historical and Clinical Study* (E. Paul & C. Paul, Trans.). New York: Macmillan.

Janoff-Bulman, R., & Frieze, I. H. (1983). A theoretical perspective for understanding reactions to victimization. *Journal of Social Issues, 39*(2), 1-17.

Janoff-Bulman, R. (1979). Characterological versus behavioral self-blame: Inquiries into depression and rape. *Journal of Personality and Social Psychology, 37*, 1789-1809.

Janoff-Bulman, R. (1982). Esteem and control bases of blame: "Adaptive" strategies for victims versus observers. *Journal of Personality, 50*, 180-191.

Janoff-Bulman, R. (1985). The aftermath of victimization: Rebuilding shattered assumptions. In C. R. Figley (Ed.), *Trauma and its Wake: The Study and Treatment of Post-Traumatic Stress Disorder* (pp. 15-25). New York: Brunner/Mazel.

Janoff-Bulman, R. (1989a). Assumptive worlds and the stress of traumatic events: Applications of the schema construct. *Social Cognition, 7*(2), 113-136.

Janoff-Bulman, R. (1989b). The benefits of illusions, the threat of disillusionment, and the limitations of inaccuracy. *Journal of Social and Clinical Psychology, 8*(2), 158-175.

Johanek, M. F. (1988). Treatment of male victims of child sexual abuse in military service. In S. M. Sgroi (Ed.), *Vulnerable Populations: Evaluation and Treatment of Sexually Abused Children and Adult Survivors* (pp. 103-113). Lexington, MA: Lexington Books.

Jones, D. R. (1985). Secondary disaster victims: The emotional effects of recovering and identifying human remains. *American Journal of Psychiatry, 142*, 303-307.

Jordan, J. V. (1984). *Empathy and Self Boundaries*. (Work in Progress No. 16). Wellesley, Massachusetts: Wellesley College, Stone Center for Developmental Services and Studies.

Jowett, B. (Ed.). (1968). The dialogues of Plato (4th Ed., Vol 2). *The Republic* (pp. 1-163). London: Oxford University Press.

Jung, C. G. (1960). The structure and dynamics of the psyche. In H. Read, M. Fordham, & G. Adler (Eds.), *The Collected Works of C. G. Jung* (vol. 8), New York: Pantheon Books.

Jung, C. G. (1966). Psychology of the transference. *The Practice of Psychotherapy* (Vol. 16, Bollingen Series). Princeton, NJ: Princeton University Press.

Kafka, F. (1937). *The Trial.* New York: Vintage Books Edition, 1969.

Kafka, F. (1962). The metamorphosis (Part 1). In D. Angus (Ed.), *The Best Short Stories of the Modern Age.* New York: Premier Books.

Kahana, B., Harel, Z., & Kahana, E. (1988). Predictors of psychological well-being among survivors of the Holocaust. In J. P. Wilson, Z. Harel, & B. Kahana (Eds.), *Human Adaptation to Extreme Stress: From the Holocaust to Vietnam* (pp. 171-192). New York: Plenum Press.

Kaplan, H. S. (1974). *The New Sex Therapy: Active Treatment of Sexual Dysfunctions.* New York: Brunner/Mazel.

Kardiner, A., & Spiegel, H. (1947). *War Stress and Neurotic illness.* New York: Paul B. Hoeber.

Kardiner, A. (1959). Traumatic neurosis of war. In S. Arieti (Ed.), *American Handbook of Psychiatry* (Vol.1). New York: Basic Books.

Kaufman, A., Divasto, P., Jackson, R., Voorhees, S., & Christy, J. (1980). Male rape victims: Noninstitutionalized assault. *American Journal of Psychiatry, 137,* 221-223.

Kazdin, A. E., Moser, J., Colbus, D., & Bell, R. (1985). Depressive Symptoms among physically abused and psychiatrically disturbed children. *Journal of Abnormal Psychology, 94,* 298-307.

Keane, T. M., & Kaloupek, D. G. (1982). Imaginal flooding in the treatment of posttraumatic stress disorder. *Journal of Consulting and Clinical Psychology, 50,* 138-140.

Keane, T. M., Caddell, J. M., & Taylor, K. L. (1988). Mississippi scale for combat-related posttraumatic stress disorder: Three studies in reliability and validity. *Journal of Consulting and Clinical Psychology, 56,* 85-90.

Keane, T. M., Fairbank, J. A., Caddell, J. M., Zimering, R. T., & Bender, M. E. (1985). A behavioral approach to assessing and treating post-traumatic stress disorder in Vietnam veterans. In C. R. Figley (Ed.), *Trauma and Its Wake: The Study and Treatment of Post-Traumatic Stress Disorder* (pp. 257-294). New York: Brunner/Mazel.

Keane, T. M., Zimering, R. T., & Caddell, J. M. (1985). A behavioral formulation of posttraumatic stress disorder in Vietnam veterans. *Behavior Therapy, 8,* 9-12.

Kehle, T. J., & Parsons, J. P. (1988, April). *Psychological and social characteristics of children of Vietnam combat veterans.* Paper presented at the Annual Meeting of the National Association of School Psychologists, Chicago, IL.

Kelly, G. A. (1955). *The Psychology of Personal Constructs* (2 vols.). New York: Norton.

Kelly, W. E. (1985). *Post-Traumatic Stress Disorder and the War Veteran Patient.* New York: Brunner/Mazel.

Kilpatrick, D. G., & Veronen, L. J. (1983). Treatment for rape-related problems: Crisis intervention is not enough. In L. H. Cohen, W. Clairborn, & G. Specter (Eds.), *Crisis Intervention* (pp. 165-185). New York: Human Sciences Press.

Kilpatrick, D. G., Best, C. L., Veronen, L. J., Amick, A. E., Villeponteaux, L. A., and Ruff, G. A. (1985). Mental health correlates of criminal victimization: A random community survey. *Journal of Consulting and Clinical Psychology, 53,* 866-873.

Kilpatrick, D. G., Resick, P. A., & Veronen, L. J. (1981). Effects of a rape experience: A longitudinal study. *Journal of Social Issues, 37,* 105-121.

Kilpatrick, D. G., Veronen, L., & Best, C. L. (1985). Factors predicting psychological distress among rape victims. In C. R. Figley (Ed.), *Trauma and its Wake: The Study and Treatment of Post-Traumatic Stress Disorder* (pp. 113-141). New York: Brunner/ Mazel, Publishers.

Kilpatrick, D. G., Veronen, L. J., & Resick, P. A. (1979). The aftermath of rape: Recent empirical findings. *American Journal of Orthopsychiatry, 49(4),* 658-669.

Kilpatrick, D. G., Veronen, L. J., & Resick, P. A. (1979). Assessment of the aftermath of rape: Changing patterns of fear. *Journal of Behavioral Assessment, 1,* 133-148.

Kilpatrick, D. G., Veronen, L. J., & Resick, P. A. (1982). Psychological sequelae to rape: Assessment and treatment strategies. In D. M. Doleys, R. L. Meredith, & A. R. Ciminero (Eds.), *Behavioral Medicine: Assessment and Treatment Strategies* (pp. 473-497). New York: Plenum Press.

Kinzie, D. J. (1988). The psychiatric effects of massive trauma on Cambodian refugees. In J. P. Wilson, Z. Harel, & B. Kahana (Eds.), *Human Adaptation to Extreme Stress: From the Holocaust to Vietnam* (305-318). New York: Plenum Press.

Kinzie, D. J. (1989). Therapeutic approaches to traumatized Cambodian refugees. *Journal of Traumatic Stress*, 2(1), 75-91.

Kinzie, J. D., Fredrickson, R. H., Ben, R., Rleck, J., & Karis, W. (1984). PTSD among survivors of Cambodian concentration camps. *American Journal of Psychiatry*, 141, 645-650.

Kishur, G. R., & Figley, C. R. (1986). *The relationship between psychiatric symptoms of crime victims and their supporters: Evidence of the chiasmal effects of co-victimization.* Unpublished manuscript, Purdue University, W. Lafayette, IN.

Kluft, R. P. (1984). Aspects of the treatment of multiple personality disorder. *Psychiatric Annals*, 14, 51-55.

Kluft, R. P. (1984). Treatment of multiple personality disorder: A study of 33 cases. *Psychiatric Clinics of North America*, 7(1), 9-29.

Kluft, R. (1985). *Childhood Antecedents of Multiple Personality.* Washington, D. C.: American Psychiatric Press.

Kohut, H. (1971). *The Analysis of the Self.* New York: International Universities Press.

Kohut, H. (1977). *The Restoration of the Self.* New York: International Universities Press.

Kolb, L. C. (1983). Return of the repressed: Delayed stress reaction to war. *Journal of The American Academy of Psychoanalysis*, 11, 531-545.

Kolb, L. C. (1984). The post-traumatic stress disorders of combat: A subgroup with a conditioned emotional response. *Military Medicine*, 149, 237-243.

Kolb, L. C. (1988). A critical survey of hypotheses regarding post-traumatic stress disorder in light of recent research findings. *Journal of Traumatic Stress*, 1, 291-304.

Koss, M. P., & Burkhart, B. R. (1989). A conceptual analysis of rape victimization. *Psychology of Women Quarterly*, 13, 27-40.

Koss, M. P., Gidycz, C. A., & Wisniewski, J. (1987). The scope of rape: Incidence and prevalence of sexual aggression and victimization in a national sampling of higher education students. *Journal of Consulting and Clinical Psychology*, 55, 162-170.

Krupnick, J. L., & Horowitz, M. J. (1981). Stress response syndromes: Recurrent themes. *Archives of General Psychiatry*, 38, 428-435.

Krupnick, J. (1980). Brief psychotherapy with victims of violent crime. *Victimology: An International Journal*, 5, 347-354.

Krystal, H. (1968). The problem of the survivor. In H. Krystal (Ed.), *Massive Psychic Trauma.* New York: International Universities Press.

Krystal, H. (1968). *Massive Psychic Trauma.* New York: International Universities Press.

Krystal, H. (1978). Trauma and affects. *Psychoanalytic Study of the Child*, 33, 81-117.

Krystal, H. (1979). Alexithymia and psychotherapy. *American Journal of Psychotherapy*, 33(1), 17-31.

Krystal, H. (1984). Psychoanalytic views on human emotional damages. In B. A. van der Kolk (Ed.), *Post-Traumatic Stress Disorder: Psychological and Biological Sequelae*, (pp. 1-28). Washington, D.C.: American Psychiatric Press.

Krystal, H. (1988). *Integration and Self-healing: Affect, Trauma, Alexithymia.* Hillsdale, NJ: Lawrence Erlbaum Associates, Inc., The Analytic Press.

Langer, E. J. (1975). The illusion of control. *Journal of Personality and Social Psychology*, 32, 311-328.

Laufer, R. S. (1988). The serial self: War trauma, identity, and adult development. In J. P. Wilson, Z. Harel, & B. Kahana (Eds.), *Human Adaptation to Extreme Stress: From the Holocaust to Vietnam* (pp. 33-54). New York: Plenum Press.

Laufer, R. S., Brett, E., & Gallops, M. S. (1985). Symptom patterns associated with posttraumatic stress disorder among Vietnam veterans exposed to war trauma. *American Journal of Psychiatry, 142,* 1304-1311.

Laufer, R. S., Brett, E., & Gallops, M. S. (1985). Dimensions of posttraumatic stress disorder among Vietnam veterans. *The Journal of Nervous and Mental Disease, 173,* 538-545.

Lazarus, R. S., & Folkman, S. (1984). *Stress, Appraisal, and Coping.* New York: Springer.

Lazarus, R. S. (1966). *Psychological Stress and the Coping Process.* New York: McGraw Hill.

Lee, E., & Lu, F. (1989). Assessment and treatment of Asian-American survivors of mass violence. *Journal of Traumatic Stress, 2(1),* 93-120.

Lerer, B., Bleich, A., Kotler, M., Garb, R., Hertzberg, M., & Levin, B. (1987). Posttraumatic stress disorder in Israeli combat veterans. *Archives of General Psychiatry, 44,* 976-981.

Lerner, M. J., & Miller, D. T. (1978). Just world research and the attribution process: Looking back and ahead. *Psychological Bulletin, 85,* 1030-1051.

Lidz, T. (1946). Nightmares and the combat neuroses. *Psychiatry, 9,* 37-49.

Lifton, R. J., & Olson, E. (1976). Death imprint in Buffalo Creek. In H. J. Parad, H. L. P. Resnik, & L. G. Parad (Eds.), *Emergency and Disaster Management: A Mental Health Sourcebook* (pp. 295-308). Bowie, MD: The Charles Press Publishers, Inc.

Lifton, R. J. (1986). *Death in Life: Survivors of Hiroshima.* New York: Random House.

Lifton, R. J. (1973). *Home from the War.* New York: Simon & Schuster.

Lifton, R. J. (1976). *The Life of the Self.* New York: Simon & Schuster.

Lifton, R. J. (1979). *The Broken Connection.* New York: Simon & Schuster.

Lifton, R. J. (1988). Understanding the traumatized self: Imagery, symbolization, and transformation. In J. P. Wilson, Z. Harel, & B. Kahana (Eds.), *Human Adaptation to Extreme Stress: From the Holocaust to Vietnam* (pp. 7-31). New York: Plenum Press.

Lindemann, E. (1944). Symptomatology and management of acute grief. *American Journal of Psychiatry, 101,* 141-148.

Lindy, J. D. (1988). *Vietnam: A Casebook.* New York: Brunner/Mazel, Inc.

Lindy, J. D., Grace, M. C., & Green, B. L. (1981). Survivors: Outreach to a reluctant population. *American Journal of Orthopsychiatry, 51,* 468-478.

Lindy, J. D., Grace, M. C., & Green, B. (1984). Building a conceptual bridge between civilian trauma and war trauma: Preliminary psychological findings from a clinical sample of Vietnam veterans. In B. A. van der Kolk (Ed.), *Post-traumatic Stress Disorders: Psychological and Biological Sequelae,* (pp. 43-58). Washington, D. C.: American Psychiatric Press.

Lyon, E. (1988, April). *Services to families of homicide victims.* Paper presented at the Sixty-fifth Annual Meeting of the American Orthopsychiatric Association, San Francisco, CA.

Lyons, J. A., & Keane, T. M. (1989). Implosive therapy for the treatment of combat-related PTSD. *Journal of Traumatic Stress, 2(2),* 137-152.

Lyons, J. A., Gerardi, R. J., Wolfe, J., & Keane, T. M. (1988). Multidimensional assessment of combat-related PTSD: Phenomenological, psychometric, and psychophysiological considerations. *Journal of Traumatic Stress, 1,* 373-394.

Maguire, M. (1980). Impact of burglary on victims. *British Journal of Criminology, 20,* 261-275.

Mahler, M., Pine, F., & Bergman, A. (1975). *The Psychological Birth of the Human Infant.* New York: Basic Books.

Mahoney, M. J., & Lyddon, W. J. (1988). Recent developments in cognitive approaches to counseling and psychotherapy. *The Counseling Psychologist, 16,* 190-234.

Mahoney, M. J. (1981). Psychotherapy and human change process. In J. H. Harvey & M. M. Parks (Eds.), *Psychotherapy Research and Behavior Change* (pp. 73-122). Washington, DC: American Psychological Association.

Maida, C. A., Gordon, N. S., Steinberg, A., & Gordon, G. (1989). Psychosocial impact of disasters: Victims of the Baldwin Hills fire. *Journal of Traumatic Stress, 2*(1), 37-48.

Malcomb, J. (1983, December). Annals of scholarship: Trouble in the archives. Part 1. *The New Yorker*, pp. 159-152.

Mancuso, J. C. (1977). *Current motivational models in the elaboration of personal construct theory.* Nebraska symposium on Motivation, (Vol. 24). Lincoln: University of Nebraska Press.

Mangione, L. (1989). *The Art of Self-Creation.* (Manuscript in progress).

Mannarino, A. P., & Cohen, J. A. (1986). A clinical-demographic study of sexually abused children. *Child Abuse & Neglect, 10,* 17-23.

Margolin, Y. (1984, August). *"What I don't know can't hurt me": Therapist reactions to Vietnam veterans.* Paper presented at the Ninety-second Annual Convention of the American Psychological Association, Toronto, Ontario.

Marmar, C. R., & Freedman, M. (1988). Brief dynamic psychotherapy of post-traumatic stress disorders: Management of narcissistic regression. *Journal of Traumatic Stress, 1,* 323-337.

Marmar, C. R., & Horowitz, M. J. (1988). Diagnosis and phase-oriented treatment of post-traumatic stress disorder. In J. P. Wilson, Z. Harel, & B. Kahana (Eds.). *Human Adaptation to Extreme Stress: From the Holocaust to Vietnam* (pp. 81-104). New York: Plenum Press.

Martin, J. L. (1988). Psychological consequences of AIDS-related bereavement among gay men. *Journal of Consulting and Clinical Psychology, 56,* 856-862.

Maslow, A. H. (1970). *Motivation and Personality* (2nd ed.). New York: Harper & Row.

Maslow, A. H. (1971). *The Further Reaches of Human Nature.* New York: Viking Press.

Masson, J. (1984). *The Assault on Truth: Freud's Suppression of the Seduction Theory.* New York: Farrar, Straus, & Giroux.

Masters, R., Friedman, L. N., & Getzel, G. (1988). Helping families of homicide victims: A multidimensional approach. *Journal of Traumatic Stress, 1*(1), 109-125.

May, R. (1969). *Power and Innocence: A Search for the Sources of Violence.* New York: W. W. Norton.

McCaffrey, R., & Fairbank, J. (1984). *Broad spectrum behavioral assessment and treatment of post-traumatic stress disorder related to transportation accidents.* Unpublished manuscript.

McCahill, T. W., Meyer, L. C., & Fischman, A. M. (1979). *The Aftermath of Rape.* Lexington, MA: Lexington Books.

McCann, I. L. & Pearlman, L. A. (1990). Vicarious traumatization: A framework for understanding the psychological effects of working with victims. *Journal of Traumatic Stress, 3*(1), 131-149.

McCann, I. L., & Pearlman, L. A. (in press). Constructivist self development theory as a framework for assessing and treating victims of family violence. In S. Stith, M. B. Williams, & K. Rosen (Eds.), *Violence Hits Home.* New York: Springer Publishing Company.

McCann, I. L., Pearlman, L. A., Sakheim, D. K., & Abrahamson, D. J. (1988). Assessment and treatment of the adult survivor of childhood sexual abuse within a schema framework. In S. M. Sgroi (Ed.), *Vulnerable populations: Evaluation and Treatment of Sexually Abused Children and Adult Survivors,* vol. 1 (pp. 77-101). Lexington, MA: Lexington Books.

McCann, I. L., Sakheim, D. K., & Abrahamson, D. J. (1988). Trauma and victimization: A model of psychological adaptation. *The Counseling Psychologist, 16*(4), 531-594.

McCubbin, H. I., & Figley, C. R. (Eds.). (1983). *Stress and the Family,* Vol. I: *Coping with Normative Transitions.* New York: Brunner/Mazel.

Meiselman, K. (1978). *Incest: A Psychological Study of the Causes and Effects with Treatment Implications.* San Francisco: Jossey-Bass.

Melick, M. E., Logue, J. N., & Frederick, C. J. (1982). Stress and Disaster. In L. Goldberger & S. Breznitz (Eds.), *Handbook of Stress: Theoretical and Clinical Aspects* (pp. 613-620). New York: Free Press.

Menninger Foundation. (1984). *Test packet*. Unpublished questionnaire.

Metzger, D. (1976). It is always the woman who is raped. *American Journal of Psychiatry*, 133(4), 405-408.

Meyer, C. B., & Taylor, S. E. (1986). Adjustment to rape. *Journal of Personality and Social Psychology, 50*, 1226-1234.

Michelson, L. (1987). Cognitive-behavioral assessment and treatment of agoraphobia. In L. Michelson & L. M. Ascher (Eds.), *Anxiety and Stress Disorders: Cognitive Behavioral Assessment and Treatment* (pp. 213-279). New York: Guilford.

Milgram, N. A., Toubiana, Y. H., Klingman, A., Raviv, A., & Goldstein, I. (1988). Situational exposure and personal loss in children's acute and chronic stress reactions to a school bus disaster. *Journal of Traumatic Stress, 1*, 339-352.

Miller, D. T., & Porter, C. A. (1983). Self-blame in victims of violence. *Journal of Social Issues, 39*, 139-152.

Miller, J. B. (1976). *Toward a New Psychology of Women*. Boston: Beacon Press, 1976.

Mills, T. (1984). Victimization and self-esteem: On equating husband abuse and wife abuse. *Victimology, 9*, 254-261.

Mitchell, J. T. (1985). Healing the helper. In National Institute of Mental Health, (Ed.), *Role Stressors and Supports for Emergency Workers.* (pp. 105-118).

Modlin, H. C. (1967). The postaccident anxiety syndrome: Psychosocial aspects. *American Journal of Psychiatry, 123*, 1008-1012.

Mollica, R. F., Wyshak, G., & Lavelle, J. (1987). The psychosocial impact of war trauma and torture on Southeast Asian refugees. *American Journal of Psychiatry, 144*, 1567-1572.

Monane, M., Leichter, D., & Lewis, D. O. (1984). Physical abuse in psychiatrically hospitalized children and adolescents. *Journal of the American Academy of Child Psychiatry, 23*, 653-658.

Moses, R. (1978). Adult psychic trauma: The question of early predisposition and some detailed mechanisms. *International Journal of Psychoanalysis, 59*, 353-363.

Mosher, D. L., & Sirkin, M. (1984). Measuring a macho personality constellation. *Journal of Research in Personality, 18*, 150-163.

Murphy, G. (1947). *Personality: A Biosocial Approach to Origins and Structure*. New York: Harper Brothers.

Murphy, S. A. (1984). Stress levels and health status of victims of a natural disaster. *Research in Nursing and Health, 7*, 205-215.

Murray, H. A., & Kluckhohn, C. (1953). Outline of a conception of personality. In C. Kluckhohn & H. A. Murray (Eds.), *Personality in Nature, Society, and Culture*, (2nd ed., rev.) (pp. 3-49). New York: Alfred A. Knopf.

Murray, H. A. (1938). *Explorations in Personality*. New York: Oxford.

New York Times. (1987, September, 4), p. 1.

Niederland, W. (1968). The psychiatric evaluations of emotional problems in survivors of Nazi persecution. In H. Krystal (Ed.), *Massive Psychic Trauma* (pp. 8-22). New York: International Universities Press.

Norris, J., & Feldman-Summers, S. (1981). Factors related to the psychological impacts of rape on the victim. *Journal of Abnormal Psychology, 90*, 562-567.

O'Neil, J. M. (1981). Male sex-role conflicts, sexism, and masculinity: Implications for men, women, and the counseling psychologist. *The Counseling Psychologist, 9*, 61-80.

Ochberg, F., & Spates, R. (1981). Services integration for victims of personal violence. In S. Salasin (Ed.), *Evaluating Victim Services* (Vol.7). Beverly Hills, CA: Sage.

Ochberg, F. M. (Ed.) (1988). *Post-Traumatic Therapy and Victims of Violence*. New York: Brunner/Mazel.

Orne, M. T. (1986). The validity of memories retrieved in hypnosis. In B. Zilbergeld, M. G. Edelstein, & D. L. Araoz (Eds.), *Hypnosis: Questions & Answers*, pp. 45-46. New York: W. W. Norton & Co.

Orne, M. T., Whitehouse, W. G., Orne, E. C., Dinges, D. F., & Nadon, R. (1989). Commentary on the 1988 Home Office Circular No. 66. The home office position on forensic hypnosis: Comments based on the American Experience. *British Journal of Experimental and Clinical Hypnosis, 6*(1), 38-40.

Paivio, A. (1986). *Mental Representations. A Dual Coding Approach.* New York: Oxford University Press.

Parson, E. R. (1984). The reparation of the self: Clinical and theoretical dimensions in the treatment of Vietnam combat veterans. *Journal of Contemporary Psychotherapy, 4*, 4-56.

Parson, E. R. (1984). The role of psychodynamic group therapy in the treatment of the combat veteran. In H. J. Schwartz (Ed.), *Psychotherapy of the Combat Veteran* (pp. 153-220). Laurel, MD: Spectrum Publications.

Parson, E. R. (1985). Ethnicity and traumatic stress: The intersecting point in psychotherapy. In C. R. Figley (Ed.), *Trauma and its Wake: The Study and Treatment of Post-Traumatic Stress Disorder* (pp. 314-337). New York: Brunner/Mazel.

Parson, E. R. (1986). Transference and post-traumatic stress: Combat veterans' transference to the veterans administration medical center. *Journal of The American Academy of Psychoanalysis, 14*, 349-375.

Parson, E. R. (1988). Post-traumatic self disorders (PTsfD): Theoretical and practical considerations in psychotherapy of Vietnam war veterans. In J. P. Wilson, Z. Harel, & B. Kahana (Eds.), *Human Adaptation to Extreme Stress: From the Holocaust to Vietnam* (pp. 245-284). New York: Plenum Press.

Pearlman, L. A. (1985). *Social support, sense of rejection, and sense of failure and psychological adjustment among divorced mothers.* Unpublished master's thesis, University of Connecticut, Storrs, CT.

Pearlman, L. A., McCann, I. L., & Johnson, G. B. (1990a). *The TSI Life Event Questionnaire: A measure assessing traumatic life events and their psychological impact.* Unpublished manuscript.

Pearlman, L.A., McCann, I. L., & Johnson, G. B. (1990b). *The McPearl Belief Scale: A new measure of cognitive schemas.* Unpublished manuscript.

Pedersen, N. L., Plomin, R., McClearn, G. E., & Friberg, L. (1988). Neuroticism, extraversion, and related traits in adult twins reared apart and reared together. *Journal of Personality and Social Psychology, 55*(6), 950-957.

Penk, W. E., Robinowitz, R., Roberts, W. R., Patterson, E. T., Dolan, M. P., and Atkins, H. G. (1981). Adjustment differences among male substance abusers varying in degree of combat experience in Vietnam. *Journal of Consulting and Clinical Psychology, 49*, 426-437.

Pennebaker, J. W., Hughes, C. F., & O'Heeron, R. C. (1987). The psychophysiology of confession: Linking inhibitory and psychosomatic processes. *Journal of Personality and Social Psychology, 52*, 781-793.

Pennebaker, J. W., Kiecolt-Glaser, J. K., & Glaser, R. (1988). Disclosure of traumas and immune function: Health implications for psychotherapy. *Journal of Consulting and Clinical Psychology, 56*, 239-245.

Perloff, L. S. (1983). Perceptions of vulnerability to victimization, *Journal of Social Issues, 39*, 41-61.

Peters, S. D. (1984). *The relationship between childhood sexual victimization and adult depression among Afro-American and white women.* Unpublished doctoral dissertation, University of California, Los Angeles.

Peterson, C., & Seligman, M. E. (1983). Learned helplessness and victimization. *Journal of Social Issues, 2*, 103-116.

Philipson, I. (1985). Gender and narcissism. *Psychology of Women Quarterly, 9*, 213-228.

Piaget, J. (1926). *The Language and Thought of the Child.* New York: Harcourt, Brace.

Piaget, J. (1967). *Six Psychological Studies.* New York: Random House.

Piaget, J. (1970). *Structuralism.* New York: Harper & Row.

Piaget, J. (1971). *Psychology and Epistemology: Towards a Theory of Knowledge.* New York: The Viking Press.

Porter, E. (1986). *Treating the Young Male Victim of Sexual Assault.* Syracuse, NY: Safer Society Press.

Pruyser, P. W. (1987). Maintaining hope in adversity. *Bulletin of the Menninger Clinic, 51*(5), 463-474.

Puk, F. S. (Ed.). (1978). *Thomas Hardy's Chosen Poems* (p. 215). New York: Frederick Ungar Publishing Co.

Putnam, F. W. (1985). Dissociation as a response to extreme trauma. In R. P. Kluft (Ed.), *Childhood Antecedents of Multiple Personality.* Washington, DC: American Psychiatric Association.

Rich, R. (1983). *Providing services to victims: An empirical investigation.* Paper presented at the 7th World Congress of Psychiatry, Vienna, 1983.

Rinear, E. E. (1988). Psychosocial aspects of parental response patterns to the death of a child by homicide. *Journal of Traumatic Stress, 1,* 305-322.

Rogers, C. R. (1951). *Client-Centered Therapy.* New York: Houghton Mifflin Co.

Rogers, C. R. (1959). A theory of therapy, personality, and interpersonal relationships, as developed in the client-centered framework. In S. Koch (Ed.), *Psychology: A Study of Science, Study I. Conceptual and Systematic,* Vol. 3: Formulations of the Person and Social Context (pp. 184-256). New York: McGraw-Hill Book Co.

Rosenberg, M. (1979). *Conceiving the Self.* New York: Basic Books.

Roth, S., & Cohen, L. J. (1986). Approach, avoidance, and coping with stress. *American Psychologist, 41,* 813-819.

Roth, S., & Lebowitz, L. (1988). The experience of sexual trauma. *Journal of Traumatic Stress, 1,* 79-107.

Roth, S. (1989). *Coping with Sexual Trauma.* Unpublished manuscript.

Rotter, J. B. (1954). *Social Learning and Clinical Psychology.* Englewood Cliffs, NJ: Prentice Hall.

Rotter, J. B. (1966). Generalized expectancies for internal versus external control of reinforcement. *Psychological Monographs, 80* (1, Whole No. 609).

Rotter, J. B. (1975). Some problems and misconceptions related to the construct of internal versus external control of reinforcement. *Journal of Consulting and Clinical Psychology, 43,* 56-67.

Ruch, L. O., & Chandler, S. M. (1983). Sexual assault trauma during the acute phase: An exploratory model and multivariate analysis. *Journal of Health and Social Behavior, 24*(2), 174-185.

Russell, D. E. H. (1984). *Sexual Exploitation: Rape, Child Sexual Abuse, and Workplace Harassment.* Beverly Hills, CA: Sage.

Russell, D. E. H. (1984). The prevalence and seriousness of incestuous abuse: Stepfathers vs. biological fathers. *Child Abuse & Neglect, 8,* 15-22.

Russell, D. E. H. (1986). *The Secret Trauma: Incest in the Lives of Girls and Women.* New York: Basic Books.

Ryan, W. (1971). *Blaming the Victim.* New York: Pantheon Books.

Rychtarik, R., Silverman, W., van Landingham, W., & Prue, D. (1984). Treatment of an incest victim with implosive therapy. *Behavior Therapy, 15,* 410-420.

San Francisco Chronicle. (1985, August 26), p. 51.

Santiago, J. M., McCall-Perez, F., Gorcey, M., & Beigel, A. (1985). Long-term psychological effects of rape in 35 victims. *American Journal of Psychiatry, 142,* 1338-1340.

Scheppele, K. L., & Bart, P. B. (1983). Through women's eyes: Defining danger in the wake of sexual assault. *Journal of Social Issues, 39,* 63-81.

Schlesinger, H. J. (1982). Resistance as process. In P. L. Wachtel (Ed.), *Resistance: Psychodynamic and Behavioral Approaches* (pp. 25-44). New York: Plenum Press.

Scott, R. L. & Stone, D. A. (1986). MMPI measures of psychological disturbance in adolescent and adult victims of father-daughter incest. *Journal of Clinical Psychology, 42*, 251-259.

Scurfield, R. M. (1985). Post-trauma stress assessment and treatment: Overview and formulations. In C. R. Figley (Ed.), *Trauma and its Wake: The Study and Treatment of Post-Traumatic Stress Disorder* (pp. 219-256). New York: Brunner/Mazel, Publishers.

Sedney, M. A., & Brooks, B. (1984). Factors associated with a history of childhood sexual experience in a nonclinical female population. *Journal of the American Academy of Child Psychiatry, 23*, 215-218.

Segal, Z. V. (1988). Appraisal of the self-schema construct in cognitive models of depression. *Psychological Bulletin, 103*, 147-162.

Seligman, M. E. P. (1975). *Helplessness: On Depression, Development, and Death.* San Francisco: Freeman.

Sgroi, S. M., & Bunk, B. S. (1988). A clinical approach to adult survivors of child sexual abuse. In S. M. Sgroi (Ed.), *Vulnerable Populations: Evaluation and Treatment of Sexually Abused Children and Adult Survivors*, vol. 1 (pp. 137-186). Lexington, MA: Lexington Books.

Shatan, Chaim F. (1973, July). *The grief of soldiers: Vietnam combat veterans' self-help movement.* Paper presented at the 1972 annual meeting of the American Orthopsychiatric Association, Detroit, MI.

Shatan, C. F. (1974). Through the membrane of reality: Impacted grief and perceptual dissonance in Vietnam combat veterans. *Psychiatric Opinion, 11*, 6-15.

Shields, N. M., & Hanneke, C. R. (1985). Battered wives' reactions to marital rape. In D. Finkelhor, R. J. Gelles, G. T. Hotaling, & M. A. Strauss (Eds.), *The Dark Side of Families* (pp. 132-148). Beverly Hills, CA: Sage.

Shontz, F. C., & Rosenack, C. M. (1985). Models for clinically relevant research. *Professional Psychology: Research and Practice, 16*, 296-304.

Shontz, F. C. (1965). *Research Methods in Personality.* New York: Appleton-Century-Crofts.

Silver, S., & Kelly, W. (1985). Hypnotherapy of post-traumatic stress disorder in combat veterans from WWII and Vietnam. In W. B. Kelly (Ed.), *Post-Traumatic Stress Disorder and the War Veteran Patient* (pp. 211-233). New York: Brunner/Mazel.

Silver, R. L., Boon, C., & Stones, M. H. (1983). Searching for meaning in misfortune: Making sense of incest. *Journal of Social Issues, 39*, 81-102.

Singer, J. L., & Pope, K. S. (1978). *The Power of Human Imagination: New Methods of Psychotherapy.* New York: Plenum Press.

Smale, G., & Spickenheurer, H. (1979). Feelings of guilt and need for retaliation in victims of serious crimes against property and persons. *Victimology, 4*, 75-85.

Smith, A. (1989, September 7). Cambodian Witnesses to Horror Cannot See. *New York Times*, p. A-10.

Smyth, A. M. (Ed.). (1953). *Oxford Dictionary of Quotations* (2nd ed.). London: Oxford University Press.

Snygg, D., & Combs, A. W. (1949). *Individual Behavior.* New York: Harper & Row, 1949.

Solomon, S. D. (1986). Mobilizing social support networks in times of disaster. In C. R. Figley (Ed.), *Trauma and its Wake: The Study and Treatment of Post-Traumatic Stress Disorder* (Vol. 2, pp. 232-263). New York: Brunner/Mazel.

Spence, D. P. (1982). *Narrative Truth and Historical Truth.* New York: W. W. Norton.

Spiegel, D. (1981). Vietnam grief work using hypnosis, *American Journal of Clinical Hypnosis, 28*, 244-251.

Spiegel, D. (1988). Dissociation and hypnosis in post-traumatic stress disorder. *Journal of Traumatic Stress, 1*, 17-33.

Stampfl, T. G., & Levis, D. J. (1967). Essentials of implosive therapy: A learning-theory based psychodynamic behavioral therapy. *Journal of Abnormal Psychology, 86*, 276-284.

Stark, E., & Flitcraft, A. H. (1981). *Wife abuse in a medical setting: An introduction for health personnel* (Monograph No. 7). Washington, DC: Office of Domestic Violence.

Stark, E. (1984). *The battering syndrome: Social knowledge, social therapy, and the abuse of women.* Unpublished doctoral dissertation, State University of New York at Binghamton.

Steinmetz, S. K. (1978). Violence between family members. *Marriage and Family Review, 1,* 1-16.

Stevenson, B. (Ed.), (1964). *The Home Book of Quotations: Classical and Modern.* New York: Dodd, Mead, & Company.

Stewart, M. A., & de Blois, C. S. (1981). Wife abuse among families attending a child psychiatry clinic. *Journal of the American Academy of Child Psychiatry, 20,* 845-862.

Stewart, A. J., & Healy, J. M. Jr. (1989). Linking individual development and social change. *American Psychologist, 44,* 30-42.

Stolorow, R. (1984). Self psychology is not soul psychology: notes on the self-as-structure versus the person-as-agent. *Society for the Advancement of Self Psychology Newsletter, 2,* 3.

Straus, M. A., & Gelles, R. J. (1986). Societal change and change in family violence from 1975 to 1985 as revealed by two national surveys. *Journal of Marriage and the Family, 48,* 465-479.

Straus, M., Gelles, R., & Steinmetz, S. K. (1980). *Behind Closed Doors: A Survey of Family Violence in America.* New York: Doubleday.

Stretch, R. H., Vail, J. D., & Maloney, J. P. (1985). Posttraumatic stress disorder among army nurse corps Vietnam veterans. *Journal of Consulting and Clinical Psychology, 53,* 704-708.

Strube, M. J. (1988). The decision to leave an abusive relationship: Empirical evidence and theoretical issues. *Psychological Bulletin, 104,* 236-250.

Sudak, H. S., Martin, R. S., Corradi, R. B., & Gold, F. S. (1984). Antecedent personality factors and the post-Vietnam syndrome: Case reports. *Military Medicine, 149,* 550-554.

Sullivan, H. S. (1940). *Conceptions of Modern Psychiatry.* New York: Norton.

Symonds, M. (1975). Victims of violence: Psychological effects and aftereffects. *American Journal of Psychoanalysis, 35,* 19-26.

Symonds, M. (1976). The rape victim: Psychological patterns of response. *American Journal of Psychoanalysis, 36,* 27-34.

Symonds, M. (1980). The "second injury" to victims. In L. Kivens (Ed.), *Evaluation and Change: Services for Survivors* (pp. 36-38). Minneapolis, MN: Minneapolis Medical Research Foundation.

Tarter, R. E., Hegedus, A. M., Winsten, N. E., & Alterman, A. I. (1984). Neuropsychological, personality, and familial characteristics of physically abused delinquents. *Journal of the American Academy of Child Psychiatry, 23,* 668-674.

Taylor, S. E., & Brown, J. D. (1988). Illusion and well-being: A social psychological perspective on mental health. *Psychological Bulletin, 103,* 193-210.

Taylor, S. E., Wood, J. V., & Lichtman, R. R. (1983). It could be worse: Selective evaluation as a response to victimization. *Journal of Social Issues, 39,* 19-40.

Tellegen, A., Lykken, D. T., Bouchard, T. J., Wilcox, K. J., Segal, N. L., & Rich, S. (1988). Personality similarity in twins reared apart and together. *Journal of Personality and Social Psychology, 54*(6), 1031-1039.

Tennant, C. C., Goulston, K. J., & Dent, O. F. (1986). The psychological effects of being a POW: 40 years after release. *American Journal of Psychiatry, 143,* 618-621.

Tennen, H., & Affleck, G. (1989). *Blaming Others for Threatening Events.* Manuscript submitted for publication.

Tennen, H., Affleck, G., & Gershman, K. (1986). Self-blame among parents of infants with perinatal complications: The role of self-protective motives. *Journal of Personality and Social Psychology, 50*(4), 690-696.

Terr, L. C. (1981, October). *"Forbidden games" Post-traumatic childs play.* Paper presented at the annual meeting of American Academy of Child Psychiatry, Chicago, IL.

Terr, L. C. (1981). Psychic trauma in children: Observations following the Chowchilla school-bus kidnapping. *American Journal of Psychiatry, 138,* 14-19.

Terr, L. C. (1983). Chowchilla revisited: The effects of psychic trauma four years after a school-bus kidnapping. *American Journal of Psychiatry, 140,* 1543-1550.

Terr, L. C. (1983). Time sense following psychic trauma: A clinical study of ten adults and twenty children. *American Journal of Orthopsychiatry, 53,* 244-261.

Timko, C., & Janoff-Bulman, R. (1985). Attributions, vulnerability, and psychological adjustment: The case of breast cancer. *Health Psychology, 4(6),* 521-544.

Titchener, J. L., Kapp, F. T., & Winget, C. (1976). The Buffalo Creek syndrome: Symptoms and character change after a major disaster. In H. J. Parad, H. L. P. Rosnick, & L. G. Parad (Eds.), *Emergency and Disaster Management,* Bowie, MD: Charles Press.

Tufts New England Medical Center, Division of Child Psychiatry. (1984). *Sexually exploited children: Service and research project* (Final report for the Office of Juvenile Justice and Delinquency Prevention). Washington, DC: U. S. Department of Justice.

Tulving, E. (1983). *Elements of Episodic Memory.* Oxford: Oxford University Press.

Ulman, R. B., & Brothers, D. (1988). *The Shattered Self: A Psychoanalytic Study of Trauma.* Hillsdale, NJ: The Analytic Press.

Underwood, B. J. (1975). Individual differences as a crucible in theory construction. *American Psychologist, 30(2),* 128-134.

Untermeyer, L. (1942). *A Treasury of Great Poems: English and American.* New York: Simon & Schuster.

Ursano, R. J. (1981). The Vietnam era prisoner of war: Precaptivity personality and the development of psychiatric illness. *American Journal of Psychiatry, 138,* 315-318.

Ursano, R. J., Boystun, J. A., & Wheatley, R. D. (1981). Psychiatric illness in U.S. air force Viet Nam prisoners of war: A five-year follow-up. *American Journal of Psychiatry, 138,* 310-314.

Vale, J. R. (1973). Role of behavior genetics in psychology. *American Psychologist, 28,* 871-882.

van der Kolk, B. A., & Greenberg, M. S. (1987). The psychobiology of the trauma response: Hyperarousal, constriction, and addiction to traumatic reexposure. In B. A. van der Kolk (Ed.), *Psychological Trauma,* pp. 63-87. Washington, D.C.: American Psychiatric Press, Inc.

van der Kolk, I. (1983). Psychopharmacological issues in post-traumatic stress disorder. *Hospital and Community Psychiatry, 34,* 683-691.

van der Kolk, B. A. (1985). Adolescent vulnerability to posttraumatic stress disorder. *Psychiatry, 48,* 365-370.

van der Kolk, B. A. (1988). The trauma spectrum: The interaction of biological and social events in the genesis of the trauma response. *Journal of Traumatic Stress, 1,* 273-290.

van der Kolk, B. A., Greenberg, M. S., Boyd, H., & Krystal, J. (1985). Inescapable shock, neurotransmitters and addiction to trauma: Toward a psychobiology of post-traumatic stress. *Biological Psychiatry, 20,* 314-325.

Varela, F. J. (1979). *Principles of Biological Autonomy.* New York: Elsevier North Holland.

Veronen, L. J., & Kilpatrick, D. G. (1980). Self-reported fears of rape victims: A preliminary investigation. *Behavior Modification, 4,* 383-396.

Veronen, L. J., & Kilpatrick, D. G. (1982, November). *Stress innoculation training for victims of rape: Efficacy and differential findings.* Paper presented at the Association for Advancement of Behavior Therapy, Los Angeles.

Veronen, L. J., & Kilpatrick, D. G. (1983). Stress management for rape victims. In D. Meichenbaum, & M. E. Jaremko (Eds.), *Stress Reduction and Prevention.* New York: Plenum.

Walker, L. E. V. (1977-1978). Learned helplessness and battered women. *Victimology, 2,* 499-509.

Walker, L. E. (1985). The battered woman syndrome study. In D. Finkelhor, R. J. Gelles, G. T. Hotaling, & M. A. Strauss (Eds.), *The Dark Side of Families* (pp. 31-48). Beverly Hills, CA: Sage.

Weinberg, S. K. (1976). *Incest Behavior*. Secaucus, NJ: Citadel Press.

Weiss, N., & Johnson, B. (1989, February 13). A love betrayed, a brief life lost. *People*, pp. 82-95.

Weiss, R. J., & Payson, H. E. (1967). Personality disorders. IV: Gross stress reaction. In A. M. Freedman & H. I. Kaplan (Eds.), *Comprehensive Textbook of Psychiatry* (pps. 1027-1035). Baltimore, MD: Williams & Wilkins.

Werner, H. (1948). *The Comparative Psychology of Mental Development*. New York: Science Editions.

Westen, D. (1989). *Social Cognition and Object Relations*. Manuscript submitted for publication.

Westen, D., Ludolph, P., Misle, B., Ruffins, S., & Block, J. (1990). Physical and sexual abuse in adolescent girls with borderline personality disorder. *American Journal of Orthopsychiatry, 60*(1), 55-66.

White, M. T., & Weiner, M. B. (1986). *The Theory and Practice of Self-Psychology*. New York: Brunner/Mazel.

Wikler, N. (1980). Hidden injuries of war. In C. R. Figley & S. Leventman (Eds.), *Strangers at Home: Vietnam Veterans Since the War* (pp. 87-106). New York: Praeger.

Wilkinson, C. B. (1983). Aftermath of a disaster: The collapse of the Hyatt Regency Hotel skywalks. *American Journal of Psychiatry, 140*, 1134-1139.

Williams, T. (1988). Diagnosis and treatment of survivor guilt: The bad penny syndrome. In J. P. Wilson, Z. Harel, & B. Kahana (Eds.), *Human Adaptation to Extreme Stress: From the Holocaust to Vietnam* (pp. 319-336). New York: Plenum Press.

Wilson, J. P., & Krauss, G. (1982). *The Vietnam Era Stress Inventory*. Cleveland, OH: Cleveland State University.

Wilson, J. P., & Krauss, G. E. (1985). Predicting post-traumatic stress disorder among Vietnam veterans. In P. Kelly (Ed.), *Post-Traumatic Stress Disorder and the War Veteran Patient* (pp. 102-147). New York: Brunner/Mazel.

Wilson, J. P., & Zigelbaum, S. D. (1986). Post-traumatic stress disorder and the disposition to criminal behavior. In C. R. Figley (Ed.), *Trauma and its Wake: The Study and Treatment of Post-Traumatic Stress Disorder* (Vol. 2, pp. 305-322). New York: Brunner/Mazel.

Wilson, J. P. (1978). *Identity, Ideology, and Crisis: The Vietnam Veteran in Transition* (Vols. 1 & 2). Cincinnati, OH: Disabled American Veterans.

Wilson, J. P. (1980). Conflict stress and growth: Effects of war on psychosocial development. In C. R. Figley & S. Leventman (Eds.), *Strangers at Home: The Vietnam Veteran Since the War* (pp. 123-165). New York: Praeger.

Wilson, J. P., Harel, Z., & Kahana, B. (Eds.). (1988). *Human Adaptation to Extreme Stress*. New York: Plenum Publishing Corporation.

Wilson, J. P., Smith, W. K., & Johnson, S. K. (1985). A comparative analysis of PTSD among various survivor groups. In C. R. Figley (Ed.), *Trauma and its Wake: The Study and Treatment of Post-Traumatic Stress Disorder* (pp. 142-172). New York: Brunner/Mazel, Publishers.

Winnicott, D. W. (1958). The capacity to be alone. *International Journal of Psychiatry, 39*, 416-440.

Winnicott, D. W. (1965). *The Maturational Processes and the Facilitating Environment*. New York: International Universities Press.

Wirtz, P. W., & Harrell, A. V. (1987). Effects of postassault exposure to attack-similar stimuli on long-term recovery of victims. *Journal of Consulting and Clinical Psychology, 55*, 10-16.

Wolberg, L. R. (1977). *The technique of Psychotherapy, Part one* (3rd ed.). New York: Grune & Stratton, 1977.

Wolpe, J. (1969). *The Practice of Behavior Therapy.* New York: Pergamon Press.

Wortman, C. B. (1983). Coping with victimization: Conclusions and implications for future research. *Journal of Social Issues, 39,* 195-221.

Yager, T., Laufer, P., & Gallops, M. (1984). Some problems associated with war experience in men of the Vietnam generation. *Archives of General Psychiatry, 41,* 327-333.

Yalom, I. (1970). *Theory and Practice of Group Psychotherapy.* New York: Basic Books.

Young, M. B., & Erickson, C. A. (1989). Cultural impediments to recovery: PTSD in contemporary America. *Journal of Traumatic Stress 1(4),* 431-443.

Young-Eisendrath, P., & Wiedemann, F. L. (1987). *Female Authority: Empowering Women Through Psychotherapy.* New York: Guilford.

Name Index

349

Subject Index

355